MAESTROS
"In their own words."

Norman Garrad   Stirling Moss   Marcus Chambers

Graham Robson

ROOTES MAESTROS
"In their own words."

This book is published by:
Mercian Manuals Ltd
353 Kenilworth Road
Balsall Common
Coventry
CV7 7DL
+44(0)1676 533304
www.mercianmanuals.co.uk

Distribution worldwide by the same.

© Graham Robson

ISBN 9781903088463

All rights reserved. No part of this publication may be reproduced, stored in a retrieval system, or transmitted, in any form or by any means, electronic, mechanical, photocopying, recording, or otherwise, without the prior written permission of the publishers.

Contents

- Foreword — v
- Introduction — vii
- Acknowledgements — ix
- Norman Garrad: A life in Motoring — 1
- Norman Garrad: Memories of a life in Motorsport — 3
- Sunbeam Talbots and Sunbeam Alpines: 1947-1956 — 21
- Stirling Moss: A reminiscence of the 1952 Monte Carlo Rally — 69
- Humber Super Snipe: The Fifteen Countries in 90 Hours run — 75
- Sunbeam Alpine: Record runs in 1953 — 85
- The 'Works' Rapiers: 1956-1964 — 93
- 'Works' Alpines: Rallying, Le Mans and USA: 1959-1963 — 161
- Humbers on Safari, RAC and Liege-Sofia-Liege 1950s and 1960s — 185
- Marcus Chambers: A remarkable career — 193
- Marcus Chambers: 'With a Little Bit of Luck' — 195
- Tigers at Le Mans: 1964 — 213
- Tigers in rallying: 1964-1966 — 223
- 'Works' Imps in rallying: 1964-1968 — 251
- And by the way: Imps in the British Touring Car Championship — 289
- London-Sydney Marathon: The Hunter victory of 1968 — 297
- Andrew Cowan's memories of the London-Sydney Marathon — 315
- What followed? Chrysler, Talbot and Des O'Dell — 325
- Competition Highlights: Motorsport success 1948-1972 — 329

ROOTES MAESTROS
"In their own words."

Foreword

I am very pleased to be able to say something about the central characters in this book, and have very strong memories of all the events they were involved in, as I was myself.

My father, Norman Garrad, was born in Scarborough in 1901, the youngest of three brothers and two sisters. After a public school education in Louth (Lincolnshire), he joined the Arrol Johnston company in Scotland, becoming part of the sales and engineering staff. That is where his travelling around the UK began.

After a few years he joined Clement-Talbot as area manager for Scotland and the north of England, where he was a success, and increased sales by a satisfactory amount, especially after this company became a part of the new Rootes Group. Like a lot of young men at this time, in 1939 he then joined the Royal Ordnance Corps (shortly to become REME), served in Egypt, and later was part of the D-Day invasion force in Europe, until he was finally de-mobbed as a Colonel.

On his return to civilian life, he rejoined Rootes, again as area manager for Scotland and the north of England, then spent a year in New York, running the Rootes company depot in the USA.

On his return to the UK, he moved to Coventry, as Sales Manager for Sunbeam-Talbot, and that is when his great interest in motor sport became, shall we say, his obsession for the rest of his career. After this Norman developed his simple theory – that life should be a team effort. No one got very far alone, he concluded, so his initial task was to collect a large and dedicated group of people who could support, encourage, inspire and challenge him.

The Rootes family always supported him strongly, helping him to make a great success of the initial entry in motorsport, starting with British events, and then into Europe, entering teams in the Monte Carlo Rally, the French Alpine Rally, the Tulip Rally and of course the Acropolis Rally in Greece.

He always involved the local distributors in all these countries, and his arrangements with them all made life a lot simpler. He also got great support at home from Brian Rootes, and from the Sales Promotion Director Bill Elsey, who organised the financial side of the operation.

By this time I was working for him in the motorsport operation, and was proud to learn so much from him. Motor racing entries started with the Le Mans 24 Hour race, and one lesson learned very quickly was to become friendly with Ferrari. There was a problem with the size of the fuel pump on their cars and ours, and after many threats by Ferrari that they would leave, both teams were allowed through!

I am reminded that there was also a problem at the end of the 24 Hour race when the organisers got the fuel usage of our car quite wrong, but Ernie Bridges (who had kept a record of the fuel we had used) brought this to my attention. Another heated conversation with Club officials followed. They eventually agreed, and awarded the Index of Thermal Efficiency award to the team!

Norman certainly knew how to pick his drivers. He always used to call his 'boys and girls' the best group of people that he could gather round him. Stirling Moss, Peter

ROOTES MAESTROS
"In their own words."

Collins and Mike Hawthorn were Grand Prix drivers who were happy to drive for him, all of them being treated in the same way as Peter Harper, who could do things in a Rapier that no-one else could match. There were, of course, numerous other first-class drivers, including Paddy Hopkirk, Peter Procter, Sheila Van Damm and Rosemary Smith – all of whom he personally picked in the first place.

Because I worked with him for some years, I can summarise his time as Competition Manager as a man who achieved tremendous success, surrounded himself with the very best drivers and co-drivers, as well as having the best possible support staff. We all had some great times, and got on well.

****

Stirling Moss was, as I have mentioned, one of the key drivers in the team for a few years, and he rapidly demonstrated his ability in rallies as well as races, and could master almost any kind of car. He will describe some his adventures in this book, but he was of course one of the stars of the team that contested the Alpine Rally.

Stirling did his first Alpine for Rootes in 1952 when the team managed to get the team prize, coming 8-9-10 overall. Stirling won a Coupe des Alpes for coming through with no penalties. In 1953, with new cars now known as Sunbeam Alpines, the team again did very well and Stirling and John Cutts had another Coupe for their efforts. He topped that off by doing it again in 1954, which meant, after three Coupes, he won the Gold Cup. That was the year that I myself was co-driver to Peter Collins. We didn't finish, but as usual there was a great atmosphere in the team.

****

Marcus Chambers is of course best known for setting up the BMC Competitions Department. He always had a calm, intelligent and civilised attitude which helped create one of the most successful motorsport teams of all time.

He had very wide experience both in the sport and in life as a whole, and that helped in bringing something special to the sport. He was very much a car enthusiast and he has owned and run some remarkable cars - from a 1907 GP Renault to lots of hand-built specials. Among many other things, he has driven Bentleys in the Land's End Trial and at Brooklands, HRGs at Le Mans, and he was the first person to take a Mini on an International rally, finishing the 1959 Viking Rally in an off-the-line 850. With that background, it's perhaps not surprising that he built successful teams at BMC and Rootes.

When Marcus came back to Rootes and he was involved in the famous win in the London-Sydney Marathon, many people were very pleased for him and for Rootes. A very special atmosphere had been created in that team and the company.

LEWIS GARRAD
2008

Introduction

It is sixty years since the first official Rootes Competitions Department was set up, and forty years since that famous victory by a Hillman Hunter in the first London-Sydney Marathon. In that eventful twenty years, the operation was run by only two heroes – Norman Garrad until 1963, and Marcus Chambers thereafter – and because of the way they achieved so much, sometimes with very limited resources, they deserve the title of Rootes Maestros.

Just in time to celebrate the 60th Anniversary of that date, my publisher Peter Shimmell was lucky enough to get permission to use two invaluable autobiographical memories from the late Norman Garrad, and Marcus Chambers, while Sir Stirling Moss also agreed to have his own hitherto unpublished report on the 1952 Monte Carlo Rally added to the history. Within the limits of just how much material could be squeezed inside these covers, this has all helped to produce a comprehensive story of the birth, rise, and successful operation of a very famous Department.

It was, indeed, way back in 1948 that Norman Garrad set up the original Rootes Group Competitions Department, and soon made it, the cars – and himself – famous. Victory followed victory, and honour followed honour, as this became a formidably successful operation. That was the good news – the awful news came twenty years later - that no sooner had Marcus Chambers' team won the original London-Sydney Marathon of 1968, than the department was put into suspended animation. At the time no-one could understand why this was done – and even today, no sensible reason has ever been published.

Guided by these Maestros, and aided by some stupendous drivers like Stirling Moss, Sheila Van Damm, Peter Harper, Andrew Cowan and Rosemary Smith – they all have a story to tell - over the years, Rootes cars – not only Sunbeams, but Hillmans, Humbers and Sunbeam-Talbots – won races and rallies, classes and categories, all over the world. Whether it was a 24-hour race at Le Mans, a trans-continental rally, a gruelling event in the Alps, or a winter event in North America, their honours lists soon had Rootes names prominently displayed.

Just over twenty years after the Department was founded, the new owners of Rootes, Chrysler-USA, saw fit to close down the Competitions Department, their spokesmen making many pious noises, but producing nothing worthwhile as an alternative. Except that money was supposed to be tight, no-one knew why the axe had fallen, and closure was never justified by the new American bosses, who simply didn't seem to understand motorsport – or to care what famous heritage they were about to destroy with a stroke of a pen.

My connection with this story stretches well beyond the function of author, historian, researcher and rally enthusiast. As a co-driver, not only did I start my serious rallying alongside Colin Malkin's father, in a Sunbeam Rapier, but I later joined the Rootes team (alongside Peter Procter) for a time too. From the early 1960s I then worked in Coventry for the next decade, sometimes in close contact with the Rootes team, and later spent many happy hours in and out of

ROOTES MAESTROS
"In their own words."

Humber Road, and in the company of the rally team. Later, too late to have influence on the motorsport programme, I worked as an engineer for Rootes/Chrysler, where my immediate boss was Peter Wilson, who had been much involved in the Tiger programme.

Amazingly, however, no coherent history of the team has previously been attempted, and it is only the constant pressure from Rootes one-make clubs, and a great deal of help from the same sources, that has now made it possible.

Although much of the story happened so long ago, enough documentary evidence, and personal reminiscence, has survived, to make this into a complete story. It has been a real pleasure and privilege to assemble the narrative – and I hope that every Rootes car enthusiast will find a story to remind him or her of those glorious days.

GRAHAM ROBSON
2008

Acknowledgements

If it had not been the original urging of my publisher, Peter Shimmell, this book would never have been published. Even so, no ordinary publisher could have taken on such a task – but as Peter is not only a great enthusiast for all things Rootes, but owns one of the famous 'works' Alpines of the 1950s, he could at once understand all the complexities of the story.

Although many individuals, and clubs, contributed to the gathering of information, and of images, I would like to make special mention of:

** The late Norman Garrad who, many years ago, compiled an autobiographical note, which we have found invaluable in flushing out the story. His son Lewis also helped me with memories of the Le Mans operation too.

** Marcus Chambers, who has now produced the definitive story of his life (*With a Little Bit of Luck*), and who encouraged us to use the section which refer to his success and tenure of the Competition Manager's job at Rootes.

** Sir Stirling Moss, not only because he gave us permission to use his written comments on the 1952 Monte Carlo Rally, but because his prodigious memory (and energy !) made it possible for us to tap his recollection in later years.

** Des O'Dell, both at the time, and in later years when he had a little more time to reminisce.

Then, of course, I come to the many enthusiasts who have made the gathering, and writing, of material possible. In particular, I want to acknowledge Tim Sutton, of the Sunbeam Rapier Owners Club, who has not only written the Chapter referring to the exploits of the Sunbeam Rapier, but who also showed me over the Rootes Archive Centre at Westcott Venture Park, near Aylesbury. He also allowed me to use a large amount of photographs which mostly come from the Clayton collection. They were the company that Rootes used for many years for all their competition photographic work.

Others who made a difficult job so much easier, have been:

** Paul Burch, Imp enthusiast, and long-time Rootes, Chrysler and now Peugeot specialist.

** Clark Dawson, for his unrivalled knowledge of the Imp family

** Chris Derbyshire, who knows so much, about so many cars and events, from the Sunbeam-Talbot era.

ROOTES MAESTROS
"In their own words."

** Ian Hall, Marcus Chambers' deputy in the 1960s, 'works' co-driver in the 1950s and 1960s, who also has an encyclopaedic memory for Rootes fortunes in that period.

** Gordon Jarvis, for his enthusiastic research. And for allowing me to use photographs from the Colin Malkin Collection.

** Graham Rood, not only for allowing me to plunder his memory, but also to check my researches against those he made when writing *The Works Tigers*.

** Peter Wilson, for whom I worked in later years, for his insight into the way that the Tiger programme took shape.

** Leon Gibbs, for the use of photographs of MKV 21 and trophies.

Every attempt has been made to identify the supply of photographs used. My apologies go to anyone I have omitted.

Over the years, I also feel that I have been privileged to get to know the many important characters, so I will note that all these people connected with the team have helped me, either at the time or in later years, with stories, interviews, or with advice on sources:

Team members including Keith Ballisat, Raymond Baxter, Andrew Cowan, Maurice Gatsonides, Anne Hall, Ian Hall, Peter Harper, Paddy Hopkirk, 'Tiny' Lewis, Colin Malkin, Valerie Morley (was Valerie Domleo before she married Donald), Sir Stirling Moss, Peter Procter and Rosemary Smith.

Not forgetting the tireless team of mechanics, who perhaps do not figure as often as they should in this narrative. But I know, and they know that I know, just how vital their contribution was to the development of this story of *Rootes Maestros*.

GRAHAM ROBSON
2008

Norman Garrad: A life in Motoring

Although Norman Garrad was most famous for his time as Rootes' first, very distinguished, Competitions Manager, he had an extremely busy and lengthy career in and around Britain's motor industry.

Born in Scarborough in 1901, at the very end of the Victorian era, though both of his parents were Scottish, he started his working life as an apprentice, and eventually became a junior salesman, with Arrol-Johnston, the Scottish car-making concern which was based in Dumfries at that time. By the mid-1920s Arrol-Johnston was showing signs of decline, so Garrad then moved to work with Sunbeam (which was then based in Wolverhampton), but after a few years of what he sometimes called 'exile' in England, he became an Area Sales Manager for Clement Talbot (Sunbeam was part of the Sunbeam-Talbot-Darracq combine), based on Dundee in Scotland.

It was at Clement Talbot that Garrad first got involved with rallying, becoming one of the drivers who took part in the Alpine Rallies of 1932 and 1934, when Talbot won the team prize. Clement Talbot was taken over by the Rootes Group in 1935 (Rootes took over Sunbeam, in an entirely different commercial deal, at almost the same time). Garrad later recalled a rather nervy interview held in London in 1935, when he was vetted by William Rootes (who was set on pruning excess staff from his new empire), but clearly he impressed the Great Man, and would carry on working for him for many more years. In fact Garrad was retained by Rootes, not only to carry on selling Rootes-owned Talbots, then the new brand of Sunbeam-Talbots, and remained in Scotland until the outbreak of war in 1939.

Along the way he got more and more involved in rallying, competing in British internationals like the Scottish and the RAC, with a foray to Monte Carlo too: the fact that his co-driver was *The Autocar's* S.C.H. 'Sammy' Davis, meant that he was becoming extremely well known in the motoring press.

Hitler's armies then marched into Poland, after which Garrad joined the British Army. In a short time he was commissioned, became a valued member of REME (the Royal Electrical and Mechanical Engineers), and eventually became a Lieutenant-Colonel (REME was among the first formations to assault the Normandy beaches on D-Day, the 6th June 1944), but made haste to rejoin 'civvy street' as soon as His Majesty was willing to let him go.

Garrad then returned to Rootes, and was at one time appointed to run the new Rootes sales office in New York, USA. Shortly, however, he returned to the UK, went back to Dundee for a time, before being called down to Coventry (for the first time in his working career, incidentally), to become Sales Manager of Sunbeam. In theory at least, that should have keep him busy, but from 1948 Norman then combined that job with that of Rootes Competitions Manager (not a demanding post, with only two or three events in an annual programme, at this time).

It was a post which he held with real distinction until the end of 1963, when the tectonic plates moved under many ageing managers' feet at Rootes. Timothy Rootes then moved Garrad, aged 63, sideways out of Motorsport, and for the rest of his time at Rootes he was asked to deal with what was

1

ROOTES MAESTROS
"In their own words."

euphemistically called 'Special Projects', rather a non-job for a man with his experience. His very last motorsport task at Rootes was to start the Tiger-to-Le-Mans project – and there is no doubt that he was deeply hurt by not being allowed to complete that task as a 'Special Project'.

Having made a clean break from the business in the mid-1960s (it was not entirely of his own volition, it must be said) he then kept clear of the company and its motorsport efforts. For a time he moved to California, to live close to his son Ian, but later came back to the UK, eventually dying in early 1992, at the ripe old age of 91. His son, Lewis, of course, was an important part of the Rootes motorsport operation until Marcus Chambers arrived, but then moved back into the Rootes (later Chrysler) sales and marketing operation.

Norman Garrad: Memories of a life in Motorsport

Editor's note: Although Norman Garrad never found the time to write a complete story of his life in motoring, he compiled this memoir, which gives a unique insight into the motor sport of the period.

The words are entirely his own, for no 'ghost writing' was involved.

Having been continually asked to put a few words down on paper by many different people, this is my attempt to do so. Please understand that my memory is not what it used to be, so I will do my best.

Early Days

At the end of World War 1, I was de-mobbed from the British Army, which is when I joined the Arrol Johnston Motorcar Company in Dumfries, Scotland. Over a period of time, I spent many months in the various departments learning their different activities, eventually finishing up on what we called 'Chassis Test' and 'New Car Test. It was a very sporting company indeed, which entered events like the "Scottish Six Days Trial". I managed to wangle myself a drive in one of the 'works cars' in this event which I enjoyed very much, even though I seemed to spend most of my life driving up and down dried river beds, but that was actually the start of my interest in competition motoring. It may not sound very much in today's world, but you've got to get the door open some how? It must also be remembered that this was the 1920s, when the world was a totally different place.

So this is how I entered the world of competition motoring.

My first drive in the Monte Carlo Rally was very interesting indeed, and a tremendous lesson to me. Those days you prepared a car, picked your team – well, you picked your co-drivers - and off you went. Just to make things really interesting we decided to start from Riga in Latvia, which was one of the eastern Baltic states.

As you may imagine, it was quite something to get there in those days, for the signposting of the roads wasn't quite as good as it is today - but that was our plan. The crew consisted of Ernest Leveret who was Arrol Johnston's London distributor at this time, I was his second driver, and a chap called 'Doony' Clench was the third man. He was supposed to be the navigator, a youthful guy who we thought may be helpful in certain circumstances.

The problem of getting a car across the English Channel in those days was absolutely ridiculous, and you were looked upon with great suspicion if you said you wanted to take your car to Monte Carlo, via Riga in Latvia. Even in the 1920s, this was an awful lot for the customs people to swallow, but never mind. Eventually we got clear of the Channel crossing, and we started our drive. Needless to say, we soon found that we were way overloaded, with spares and all our luggage. So, we abandoned the spares!

After a tremendous struggle, we reached Berlin, where, as we thought that only the best was good enough, we stayed at the Avalon Hotel, where I soon became very friendly with the night porter. At this point,

ROOTES MAESTROS
"In their own words."

we didn't want to just dash through Berlin as we wanted to have the car looked over before carrying on.

One night I went to bed quite early. Then, at about 2 o'clock in the morning, my new porter friend knocked on the door, came in to our bedroom and stood by my bed. He then said, in very good English: "Kaput, get up, get on your way to wherever it is you're going – Riga, because if you don't go now, you'll be sealed in with snow. If you don't go now, you won't get out of Berlin tomorrow, because I know the climate here and I know the weather signs.".

I got hold of Leveret and Clench, and we made our exit. Whilst doing so I said to the chap on reception, "What about the bill?" "Oh," he said, "You give me card, I send you bill in England, you pay me later." I said, "Fine, off we go then," and we had one hell of a trip. It was snowing all the time and the signposts, such as they were, being more or less covered with snow, meant that Clench seemed to spend his life getting out and wiping off the snow to find out if we were on the right road. It must be remembered that in those days, they couldn't care less about the motorist really and we struggled on and on. Eventually, you wouldn't credit this, but we arrived in Riga on the night before the start. The scrutineering was very good indeed and they gave us dry clothes, they even offered us food and a bath - you wouldn't believe it, but this was 1929.

Later that evening a chap came up to me and said, "Would you care to speak on the radio to England?" I said, "Speak on the radio to England? What makes you think you can get England?" He said, "Oh, I can get England alright and I have a contract to broadcast this event." I said, "Well, I doubt if many people in England have receiving licences." "Never mind," he said, "you speak." So I spoke and that was my first ever time 'on the air'. How many people heard it, I never knew, but it was quite an experience to speak on the air in 1929 with a very friendly co-operative interviewer.

In those days, rally stewards were a complete joke – a bad joke – and the local organisers up in Riga at least decided to have it their way. They lined up all the cars in the big square and a young man very full of charm came up to me and said, "Garrad!" "Yes," I said "Norman Garrad?" he said. "Yes" I replied. "Please keep out of my way because there's only one way out of this square; and I'm in a hurry. I go very fast, so don't hold me up." I said, "And who are you?" "I am Rudi Caracciola." "Oh, fine", I said. He may as well have said he was John Smith for all I knew about him at the time. In any case I was young and I suppose a little stupid in those days and wondered why this man should tell me what I'd got to do!

The organisers of this particular event, which had about twelve cars at Riga, decided to have a mass start. Well of course it was against rally regulations, and absolutely crazy, but as I said, being young and stupid I decided to get to the exit of the square first, which I did, and I could understand after I got out of the town why that was an advantage, because it was only a single track lane, through the snow all the way.

I got going and in my mirror, sure enough he was there, about 100 yards back - my 'friend' Caracciola who had spoken to me. This went on for about an hour and a half, when suddenly I over-cooked it and got the car stuck in a ditch. At this point, I thought that I hadn't got very far towards Monte Carlo. Caracciola stopped, looked down at me and said "Alright?" But at least he then stopped the next three cars, and they all got to work and helped me back on the road, and off we went. In actual fact, I let them all go, and I ended up tailing Caracciola for the rest of the way, but that's not the end of the story.

Norman Garrad: Memories of a life in Motorsport

We got into the Polish Corridor (which was a political creation, one of the results of the talks which followed World War 1), and the rally really became absolutely impossible. The conditions were wicked, with very deep snow. Eventually we just couldn't move - and don't forget that in those days we didn't know enough about snow chains or anything to speak of, and we had no heater in the car, by the way, which wasn't funny at all.

About 11 o'clock that night, I could not get any further and, don't forget, I had quite a lot of experience of driving in bad weather in Scotland. The car came to a stop. There was little traffic to clear the road, the only thing visible being a horse-drawn sledge and that was that!

Well, the situation got so precarious, with the snow starting to come up the side of the car, like water in a bath, but in the distance I could see some lights. Leveret, Clench and I therefore decided to walk towards those lights, but before I left the car I remembered to drain the radiator, because in those days there was no such thing as anti-freeze.

After a lot of talking, we eventually got into a farmhouse, and the owner took us under his wing, led us upstairs and gave us some hot milk and various types of food, which helped to lift our spirits. It then took three days of various digging methods, and the use of horses, to get the car out, and to a local railhead. Don't forget that Caracciola and all the rest were all there, also stuck in the snow. We finally got back to Berlin, I saw my friend in the hotel again, and I paid him what was owed. Eventually got the car back to Boulogne, and finally back to Scotland.

That was my very first Monte - and I think it was the only one in which I personally didn't reach Monte Carlo itself. It was a very good experience for me, because it showed me that my car preparation had been lousy. I had learnt a lot, this was the start of what I wanted to be doing. I wanted to get in to a team and really have a go at doing this thing properly.

The number of Monte Carlo rallies I have done is quite considerable. I have started from Stavanger (that's in Norway), Paris, John O'Groats, Athens, and Monte Carlo itself. I really learnt the hard way, there's no shadow of doubt about that, but I always looked upon it as a sport.

After Arrol Johnson, I eventually joined the Talbot Motor Company (who were based in London), where again I was involved with the sporting side of things. It was at this time that I became involved with Talbot's engineering genius Georges Roesch, who gave me a tremendous amount of help in all the things I wanted to do.

The company entered three Talbot 105's in the 1932 Alpine Rally, and won the team prize. The drivers on this event being the Hon. Brian Lewis, Tim Rose-Richards, and myself. It was quite an experience indeed. I had nothing to do with the preparation of the cars, for that was left to a chap called Arthur Fox who did it all. Arthur not only did all the preparation, but was also the Team Manager. I learnt a lot from him.

The Rootes Group bought out Talbot in 1935, and eventually set up the Sunbeam-Talbot marque. I stayed with Talbot until 1939, when World War II broke out, and I joined the Army. 1945 saw me being demobbed from the Army, and after a while I managed to get a job at the Rootes Group, which was based in Coventry. After the war, Britain was hugely in debt, so it was not long before the edict from the Government went out to all manufacturing companies that they should "Export or Die".

Even so, as I still wanted to get back into motorsport, I thought it a good time to approach the company bosses, and ask them for a car in which to make a recce for the 1948 French Alpine Rally, by following the

ROOTES MAESTROS
"In their own words."

In 1932, Norman Garrad was one of the drivers in the Talbot 105 team which won the Team Prize in the 1932 Alpine Trial. Left to right, the drivers are: Hon. Brian Lewis, Tim Rose-Richards, and Norman Garrad.

1947 event, my reasoning being that if we could eventually gain some success it would help to improve sales. Amazingly, the powers-that-be, agreed to my request, and you could say that it changed my life. We completed the rally, which in effect told us how bad the car (a Sunbeam-Talbot 2 litre) really was. Even so, 1948 was the first year in which Rootes seriously entered cars in a competition event. All this eventually lead to me being promoted to be Rootes' Competition Manager, a role I was to hold for some fifteen years.

Now I must digress at this moment, for I should tell you about the 1947 'recce' on the French Alpine, for it was all very significant. I had made contact with the rally organisers who agreed they would accept me as a Press Man on the route of the event. They would give me Press plates when I arrived, providing that I could arrive at a certain time. With me, I had a very good man in Douglas Horton as co-driver, who was then service manager of Rootes. He was an excellent diagnostic mechanic as well. He really was outstanding and a very good "night watchman" driver too. The car we were given by the company was a Sunbeam-Talbot 2 litre Coupe.

After we got down to Marseilles, of course stupidly I didn't know any better in those days, so stayed in a hotel directly opposite the railway station. Well, in the heat of Marseilles and with all the noise, we hardly had any sleep. The club (Automobile Club of Marseilles and Provence) at that time were not very cooperative to the Press, they were more interested in the people who had actual entries, which I cannot blame them for. However, when we finally started it really

Norman Garrad: Memories of a life in Motorsport

was quite an event. This was my first introduction to the Mont Ventoux hillclimb, which was really quite interesting.

Mont Ventoux, being an extinct volcano, was a really severe climb and the great thing is you really had to get cracking up to the top because of the position of the control, and then descend down the other side to get to the one at the bottom. It was a little bit disconcerting, with your headlights shining out into a dark void now and again. However, we made the control at the top, and though I wasn't a competitor, I was just fooling around trying to see if I could make the time and kept a fairly accurate log with Douglas Horton.

On the way down I thought I was going to do very well at this game and, imagining I was a competitor, I started to drop down one of those long drops on a straight. By the time I was heading down towards the corner I went for the brakes, but they weren't there any more, and I had to act quickly. Well, I went from top gear to third, third to second, then from second to first, and then thought that Oh Boy, that was that. I eventually got the car to slow down and round the bend, under control again. My dear friend Douglas Horton just said, "That was a damn silly place to sort of try and use the gear box, was it not, why did you want to bother, the gear box is alright?" Little did he know how close I had come to messing things up in a big way.

We motored on, climbing the Stelvio Pass, in Italy, with all its corners. The Stelvio was quite a climb, at just over 9,000ft, but I knew the Stelvio from my earlier experiences with the Talbot 105s, and we eventually reached the finish.

I was invited with a lot of other chaps to go to the prize giving, which I thought was very interesting, I arrived at the prize giving with Tommy Wisdom, whom I sat next to, he and I being old friends. Suddenly my name was called out, and I thought, "Oh my God, what have I done now?" It appeared that Douglas and I had won a special prize for Press Men! As we had managed to drive the whole circuit and seemed to be on time, the organisers were getting used to seeing us, and the car, at various controls so they decided to give us a prize. I don't think I've ever lived it down – I received a prize driving on the French Alpine as a member of the Press.

Works team

Needless to say, the Rootes family, God bless them, were not the easiest people in the world to convince that competition motoring would be an asset to their output, and that the popularity of the cars would be enhanced if we could do well. First of all I went to work on the then Sir William Rootes, then tried his brother Reginald, and finally Brian Rootes, and this is where it finally rang a bell. Brian realised that if I could achieve some successes, it would help his export drive.

So, after various interviews I was allowed to enter the new Sunbeam Talbot 90 in an event. As a workshop, and to start with, Douglas Horton offered me a corner of the Service Department in the Humber Road factory in Coventry, to base the cars. Horton then agreed to let me have the use of six technicians, and I took advice from the technical director, Bernard Winter, on car preparation.

[Within a very short time – certainly within two years – Norman Garrad was convinced that he needed more space, and a dedicated operation, so with the very important help of Brian Rootes, he secured a complete, basically-equipped, building close by, also in Humber Road, This remained as the nerve-centre of the Rootes, later Chrysler, Competitions Department, for the next fifty years.]

Two views of the historic Rootes factory complex in Humber Road, Coventry, looking east (upper) and north (lower) respectively. From the late 1940s the 'works' team cars were always prepared in long-established buildings close to the recreation ground. These were demolished as recently as the summer of 2008.

Norman Garrad: Memories of a life in Motorsport

Well, the world now knows how that eventually worked out. The cars became a respected name in all international events and I say respected, because the French, and the Germans, didn't like it at the time, neither did the Italians, but we believed in ourselves and stuck to it.

Through a combination of preparing the cars properly, getting good drivers on board, as well as putting a factory-employed man in beside them, we were able to keep the balance of knowledge and experience going. It all worked out very well indeed, with some very well known results, as you all know. We improved the design and ultimately the manufacture of the cars, and they became more reliable, which was great. I know that they were heavy, but there was a bonus. People would say "Oh, they were heavy", but never mind, they got around and they held together, and just kept going, which was the most important thing.

Soon, of course the whole Rootes family gave in and decided that "there was something in this competition nonsense after all", they allocated me a budget and gave me an official title, "Competition Manager", but I still wanted to retain the job as a rally driver too, which I did.

I want to digress for a moment, because I am trying to establish myself in your minds as somebody who really did try - and I would like to point out that I was probably the first-ever factory driver in rallies. When I was employed by the Arrol Johnston Company' all the rest were either trade dealers or they were wealthy young men who had the money to do these things. But, I was the first factory driver being paid as a driver, which of course to me in my old age pleases me immensely. I'm quite certain, that my activities were one cause of many other companies eventually getting into the act, and that's why I must be allowed to take a certain amount of credit for the popularity of rallies, not only in England but also on the Continent.

By the time I retired motorsport was very big business but, when I bowed out, I did so with a certain amount of success and dignity. I think I really started this lark of rallying among British car makers and, as far as the rally boys were concerned, I was the first to really get to work on the suppliers to help me with my budget. They came through very nobly because they had faith. They realised this was a very good way to test their equipment. At the time Lucas, Dunlop, and Mintex were all very good friends of mine. The Shell organisation was marvellous to us, as were Champion. All these people helped tremendously but, looking back on it now, they just didn't supply money, albeit limited money, they also supplied a wealth of advice and experience and help, which of course eventually helped our job. I look back with great appreciation on all they did for the Sunbeam Talbots, Sunbeam Alpines, and of course the Sunbeam Rapiers. I really do, because without them, however kind my dear firm were, they did expect me to get (a) results and (b) some money from outside suppliers, and it was a great help to receive this type of assistance from these people.

I would like to highlight one or two instances involving Lucas and Dunlop. From Lucas, we wanted a light that would help us to go quickly in fog. I had a very good reputation in fog and I knew quite a bit about fog driving, but we wanted a penetration light which would give no throw back. Consequently, Dr Nelson of Lucas spent a lot of time with Douglas Horton developing this light for us. I tried them out, late at night, in all parts of the country - and that was the birth of the famous Lucas Flame Thrower, and these were a tremendous help to us in our competition life.

Dunlop also bent over backwards and made their Weather Master (all winter tread) tyre,

ROOTES MAESTROS
"In their own words."

which was brilliant at the time. We usually had a very friendly association with them but, I did have a bit of an "up and downer" with them once, when I found a tyre, a Pallas tyre from Switzerland, which turned out to be more reliable with regard to road holding and in bad weather. I had an awful lot of problems with getting Dunlop to let me use them, but eventually common sense won the day and we had some tremendous success with them. In fact the Pallas people sold a lot of their tyres into Canada and North America after that.

I'm also certain that we advanced the snow chain and the ice chain system tremendously, by using them on our cars for rallies. The snow chain people also came in and they did all they could to help us. I was very lucky, for I found a company in Oslo, Norway, which made a very good snow and ice chain. In those days the ice chains, (this was before we got the spiked tyre), had little studs on them that had tungsten tips, and these sharpened themselves as they drove along. They were a tremendous success. We also had a circular ring in the middle of the chain, with springs on it to keep them from breaking off and knocking off the wiring for the sidelights. All these details can go down to the credit of the rally boys; and I'm so happy to look back and see these things still around.

Also, think just how much brakes were improved because of our demands. The large companies played a major part, also the linings people helped us tremendously.

Then, of course we come to the man, woman or the boy behind the wheel. Our reputation became so good - and I say this with great modesty and respect - that it became quite an honour for anybody to drive our 'works' cars. We had soon reached a point where we could be selective, or at least I could be selective, in the choice of drivers. I'm certain the boys or men who drove for me in my teams knew it. None of them would dare to ask me for a financial retainer or a starting-money price to get behind the wheel of our cars!

Can you believe this? Stirling Moss drove for me for four years, and never demanded any money at any time. He always received first-rate expenses and I mean first-rate expenses, but he never received any real money - except of course when he flew over to the circuits in the USA - Sebring and Riverside - to drive for me in later years.

Another racing driver, Peter Collins, was an absolutely first rate driver, and he and Stirling were quite happy to sit behind an Alpine steering wheel and just get on with it. Then there was Graham Hill, Ivor Bueb, John Fitch (the American Sports Car Champion), all these racing drivers. Later there was Peter Harper, Paddy Hopkirk, and Peter Procter, just to mention a few, and of course my dear old problem boy Leslie Johnson who I always say knew more about the geometry of driving than anybody in the business. Believe me I've sat beside them all and they have scared the pants off me doing engineering test programs all over the Alps. I used to sit beside Leslie and say, "I don't give a damn who you are, you are never going to get round this one at this speed." Thank God he always did and I'm still around.

Then of course we come to the ladies, Mary Handley-Page, Tish Ozanne, and Francoise Clarke. The names might not mean much to you nowadays but, believe me, they did a very fine job indeed, not only for the Company but for our country too. There was always a certain amount of respect for girl drivers - or 'lady drivers' as they were called - and I was very proud of them. Sheila Van Damm and Anne Hall of course, were the most consistent, and stayed with us longer than anybody else, and really did a very fine job indeed. Sheila won the European

Norman Garrad: Memories of a life in Motorsport

Championship twice, which was first rate, but her driving ability was something I have not come across since.

Then there were the mechanics who must never be forgotten. Those who prepared the cars were the unsung heroes of the whole exercise. It was fortunate that we were able to mould a good team of mechanics together, as well as drivers. People like Jim Ashworth, and Jerry Spencer were part of the factory team. Old Jim, peculiar though he was, always did do a fine job. He kept the crowd of mechanics together well: incidentally, I always insisted that on events the mechanics should live as good, if not better, than the drivers. All that paid off because they were a happy gang, even though Jim embarrassed me now and again when I took him to a fine restaurant and he'd say, "I don't want any of this foreign muck, I just want sausage and egg," and that was that. Quite a boy, dear old Jim, but he ran a very good shop for us.

Then we had another chap, Ernie Beck, who built our engines. Not many people had even heard his name, but I knew that behind a lot of our successes the work of Ernie Beck helped us tremendously. There is little glamour in talking about these people but if you had my job you'd realise how very valuable all their efforts were.

However, the story is not finished yet by a long way. You had to have people who understood insurance, you had to have people who would get you the currency at the right time, and you had to have a man like Trevor Shepherd who used to book all our movement orders and so on. Then I had to advise the Press, to the best of my ability, through John Bullock, our promotion man. There were so many behind the scene activities to be attended to that there was never a dull moment.

In Italy, Count Johnny Lurani and I were friends, so when we entered the 1956 Mille

From 1948 to 1964, Norman Garrad (right) and his long-standing workshop manager Jim Ashworth were the pivots around which every Rootes motorsport activity revolved. The RAC Rally competition number of 122 dates this picture as November 1960, for the Rapier was driven by Peter Jopp and Les Leston on the 1960 RAC Rally.

ROOTES MAESTROS
"In their own words."

Miglia race in the new Sunbeam Rapier saloon, he got hold of me by the arm and said, "Norman, why do you bring a shopping car, to the Mille Miglia?" "Well you know, the drivers like to look at the scenery now and again," I said, "they won't get in anybody's way, they will be alright." So that was that, he just walked off. After the race, when we'd done very well indeed, with Peter Harper and Sheila Van Damm driving, he came up to me and said, "Norman, some shopping car!" "Yes," I said. " some shopping car."

The British and foreign special press liked our idea, and our way, of rallying because in no time at all we had all the press boys of any note wanting to know what was happening. Also, we went into the film business, with dear old Stanley Schofield, who made numerous films for us. His story was quite remarkable. He came to me one day and said, "I can make a film of one of your events?" I said, "What makes you think that?" He said, "I know I could, I've studied it. I could do it." I said, "Alright, what does that mean?" He replied, "Well I'll cover the event, make a film of it, and give you a costing that includes two copies. After that its up to you." So I said, "Give me the price then."

With his figures available, I went to my lords and masters and said, "This man can make a film in colour. It might not be any good, but if it is, it will be fun because if he can get the action and some of the incidents it will be quite a thing." So Bill Elsey, who was a great supporter, helped me. He said, "Alright Norman, I'll carry him on my budget." So dear old Bill got together with Stanley who then came up to the factory to see me and said, "Oh, its quite necessary for me to have a car the same colour, as your works cars." I said, "Yes, that sounds sense to me. Are you going to deduct that from your quotation?" "Well no," he said, "I really couldn't do that." And so, being a bit soft hearted at that time, I lent him a car and well, history has repeated itself.

He made a large number of quality films for us, but I'll never forget the first time he showed the first one to Lord Rootes, who in turn looked at me and said, "Any good?" I said "I hadn't seen it yet," so we all went into the next room and had a party, I think it was at Claridges, I'm not sure, but the Old Man laid on a big party for us, because we'd done something rather clever, and don't forget that Stanley had quoted me for two films.

So the Old Man - I say that with great respect - sat down and watched the film, which went on for about 28 minutes. At the end he said to me, "It's good." I said "Fine," and he said "Right, we'll order a hundred." He ordered a hundred, of which some had to be with French and Italian language commentaries, and that was the start of Stanley Schofield Productions Ltd as far as motoring was concerned. We got some very good commentators to do the voice-over, people like Raymond Baxter, so it all ticked over very nicely.

In the evening of my days, when I think back, I take great pleasure in thinking of what a team I built up. In the years 1952 and 1953 for instance, I had Stirling Moss, Peter Collins, Mike Hawthorn, Leslie Johnson, John Fitch, Peter Harper, George Hartwell, Sheila Van Damm and Anne Hall - how about that for a set up ? It really was tremendous, and they all had fun driving their cars. Another girl I don't want to forget to mention was Rosemary Seers, she did a very good job for us too, on what we call a 'fill in' drive now and again.

Of course, today all the rally cars are like Grand Prix cars, they have the support of so many service cars, its just not true, and yet I can think back to the days when service cars were not even allowed, nor were mechanics.

Norman Garrad: Memories of a life in Motorsport

It really is embarrassing now, to know that behind every entry in a rally there are about twenty other individuals, on the road, on the circuits, on the route. I think that much of the fun and achievement really has gone out of rallying now by allowing all these individuals to get in on the act, far more fun was to had in the old days.

Now I know perfectly well that the success of our efforts could never have been achieved if it had not been for a man called Bernard Winter, who was the Rootes Director of Engineering. Quietly he was always one of my biggest supporters, for he really backed me to the hilt. After I took the first car out and did that peculiar run on the Alpine Rally, and was awarded a Press cup, I wrote a report on the car and the related problems we had experienced. He then had his team set about, and put everything right for us. He and I did a deal, he said, "Now look Norman, any time you come back and anything has gone wrong with your cars, please come and see me and I'll put a committee together and we'll iron it out," and this is what he did. Also, although I ran the competition department, he was kind enough to send two of his top engineers over to our briefing and preparation meetings, so that there were many of his people involved in this, once it got going.

I'll just tell you one quick story about dear old Leslie Johnson. He and I were great friends and I greatly admired his driving. I decided he would be a really great character to come on the Monte with us because we wanted the Col des Leques, and all those climbs, done at high speed and he was a bit of an artist when doing this.

I arranged with him that he would do the event with John Cutts who was our 5-star navigator, and myself. It was all arranged for use to meet Leslie in Paris, but he was late. Eventually we got hold of him and took him on board. We were going to Stockholm and I said to John, "Now look all we want to do is keep this man rested and you and I will take this car down to the bottom of the Col des Leques which is a hell of a long way but we'll do that." We all got in the car and found our way to the start line in Stockholm. After this I was behind the wheel and we set off, Leslie slept hour after hour, John said to me, "We'd better wake him up now and again," which we did, but he soon went off to sleep again. Now at the time I hadn't rumbled it, but he was already a sick man, with a heart condition.

Suddenly John said to me, "We are within 20 minutes of where we want him to take over and really push it up this mountain and get down the other side just as fast as possible. Let's stop here and wait." So John woke him up, and he came to life and he was full of joie de vivre and ready to have a go.

I put him behind the wheel right away and he had a nice run for about 20 minutes or so to get to the start line at the bottom of the Col. He started very well, with me sitting beside him as John was in the back doing the timing on the clocks, as because the way the regulations were written it was important to do the same time going down the other side as we did going up. Leslie did a fine climb, and everything was going fine, so once the summit was reached he became so excited and said "What do you think of that?" I said it was, "First rate, but keep your mind on the job, because we've got to go down the other side as fast as you brought us up here."

All of a sudden I heard the engine revs dying and said, "Come on Les, don't fool around, get the thing down again, smartish," and down his foot went again, but almost in the same movement his foot pulled back again: Leslie had slumped over the wheel. I grabbed the wheel. On the particular car we were driving all the controls were in the

ROOTES MAESTROS
"In their own words."

middle, the hand brake was there, and I could also shut the engine off. It took about half a mile before we eventually came to a stop, but we were still on the road. This was a miracle because we were all over the place until we regained control. It was only later that I found out that Leslie had already suffered a heart attack earlier over Christmas.

"John, we'll put him in the front," I said. "No", he replied, "Let's go to Monte Carlo." Leslie recovered somewhat and said, "Monte Carlo, better doctors. In my briefcase are pills, those nitro glycerine ones," which were obviously the ones he used. Now we were absolutely shocked, believe me.

I got behind the wheel, and still had to be part of the game, I had to get this car to the control and not get disqualified. We eventually caught Sheila and I said, "You're due in before me, get in there and get an ambulance organised, there's a good girl." Off she went like a bomb and got into Monte Carlo and shouted for an ambulance, but of course they wanted to know for whom, and where the patient was, "He's coming," she told them and I eventually arrived with Leslie absolutely unconscious.

We managed to get him into a Nursing Home for what we hoped would allow him to rest and recoup. However, three times during that night I was sent for, to watch him die. There and then I made up my mind that I wasn't going to allow him to do so and, in one of his conscious moments said, "Look, Leslie I've no time for fooling around with this anymore, you are not going to die, I say again you are not going to die. Now you start perking up and lets get on with this game," In the end he did react to it. I went to see him next morning, when he said, "Norman, you'll have to do the Grand Prix circuit test, you know." I said, "It's alright, Leslie I've been around before." He said, " Watch the Gas Works corner, there's a boy."

He was full of it, and he came out of it alright. The number of people who came to see him when he was in hospital was quite amazing indeed, but it helped him pass the time whilst recouping. Cyril Siddeley took care of him, as he was living down there at the time. Eventually we managed to get him back to London, where I visited him in a Nursing Home. I later saw him again in Cheltenham. He had been advised not to drive, but insisted on driving around the local area.

It was on one of these occasions that a child playing with a ball ran off the pavement in front of him, and he hit the brakes and had another heart attack, but here's the strange thing, he did not die of a heart attack. He eventually died of a kidney disease, which was discovered on the operating table. So that was that, Leslie was a very fine man but I have always felt that if he hadn't come on the Monte that year I'm certain he would have been alive today. Very sad indeed.

Obviously over the years I've had many experiences some of them sad, some of them very amusing, and I think to cheer the whole thing up a bit, I'd better tell you one of the amusing ones:

At the end of the 1953 French Alpine, we had done extremely well, and had been awarded a number of trophies. We won the team prize and had the best performance in various categories. The Rootes people in Devonshire House became quite excited at this news, and Lord Rootes decided that he ought to get the cars back to England quickly along with their drivers, his reason being that the British Grand Prix was to be at Silverstone the coming Saturday. His idea was to try and get a lap of honour arranged for the cars and drivers prior to the big race.

My phone rang early that morning and a voice said, "Billy Rootes here, get your cars to Nice Airport as we are going to lay on a Silver City plane to pick you up along with

Norman Garrad: Memories of a life in Motorsport

the cars and fly you back to England. Once here you are going to do a lap of honour at Silverstone on GP day." I thought that was a terrific idea, so I said, " Right, what time do you expect the aircraft to arrive?" "Well," he said, "It should be there for about 10 o'clock in the morning your time." I said, "Fine." So I made everyone aware of the plans and managed to get them all along to the airport and await the plane's arrival. There was a great deal of excitement and anticipation in what we were about to do.

The weather was very hot (it was midsummer) which did not help. Ten a.m. came, and not a whisper, I thought I'd better not start creating a fuss just yet. Half past ten came, still not a whisper, so I thought I'd better go up to the control tower and see what information I could get. I went to the flight control people and said, "Tell me, have you any information about an aircraft coming in from London to pick up some cars?" "No," was the reply, "not a thing". "Are you sure?" they said, "we're absolutely sure. We have to know where everything is in the sky around here." I said, "Fine." He had no advice, none at all! This was very irritating because you can hold drivers down nicely when they are in a car behind the wheel, but when you leave them lying around airport lounges, they don't like it, in fact, neither do I.

Mid-day came and went, I thought I'd better ring London. So I called and said, "what about this aircraft, when is it arriving" "Well, there has been a small problem but it's on its way now." I said, "Are you sure?" "Oh yes, we've been advised it's on its way." So we waited, 3 o'clock came, 4 o'clock came, 5 o'clock came, and by this time we were all getting somewhat edgy.

As I have said, it was very hot and the airport did not have any air-conditioning at that time. Eventually at about 7 o'clock in the evening a chap came up and said, "Mr Garrad?" "Yes," I replied. "I just want to advise you that your aircraft will be here in about an hour," he continued. I said "Well, are you sure?" "Yes" he replied.

The aircraft eventually arrived, with us all watching it land and taxi-ing in. The pilot came over and spoke to me and asked, "Are you in charge of this little lot?" I said "Yes." He said, "Well, it's been an extraordinary experience, we didn't have time to arrange our refuelling credit in advance, and the French gentleman here refuses to give us any fuel unless we have any cash". He said we came away in such a hurry it was overlooked." I said, "Alright, I'll see what I can do."

I got into a car and hurried off to the Hotel Negresco in Nice. I went in to the reception and said to the man behind the desk, "I would like to see the manager." He said, "Do you have an appointment?" I said, "Of course not, but I do want to see the manager, and it's rather important." He took a good look at me, and I think he thought this man's going to be a bit difficult but I'll go and get the manager anyway.

The manager, who was a nice man, spoke perfect English and I said, "This might sound extraordinary to you but I want you to let me have at least ten thousand Francs." He said, "Now what on earth would make you think I would do that?" I said, "Because you're going to believe me when I tell you what has happened," so I told him the story. "Right," he said, "but what recommendation or credentials have you got?" I said, "The best in the world!, you just ring up Albert Ship the manager at the Hotel Metropole in Monte Carlo and ask him what he knows about Norman Garrad of Team Sunbeam." He eventually agreed, and retreated to a rear office for quite a few minutes, finally returning with a smile and said, "Mr Garrad, you can have whatever you want." I said, "Right, let's start with ten thousand to go on with."

ROOTES MAESTROS
"In their own words."

With the car waiting outside the Hotel, we quickly set off with me clutching the money and went back to find our pilot at the airport. We paid the people for the fuel and we were soon airborne. Now, no one had told us there was no heating in the back of the Bristol Freighter which was carrying the cars. Can you imagine what it was like, the number of hours we had to endure, flying back to England? Well, we even got to the cars, got their boots open to get some of our luggage out and put pyjamas, skirts (ladies present) on to try and keep warm. It wasn't a very enjoyable trip home!

We touched down at Blackbushe Airport in Surrey at about five past six in the morning and a reception committee, who had been waiting all night to give us a welcome home party, were there to greet us. They had drunk all the booze and they'd eaten all the food, but we had to rush off to Silverstone anyway with anything we could find. We arrived in time and had our own special car park. We did two laps of honour which, in front of the huge crowd, was quite an achievement.

Another story, this time about the French Alpine of 1955, was a very extraordinary one. I went over early with a car to do a recce over a certain section that I thought was going to be a bit tough. The idea was that John Touchwood would take over from me in England and would bring the crew and all cars over and meet me at a hotel in Lyon.

Well, that sounded perfect because at that time there was still a restriction on currency exchange and I had to wait between events before I could get any more currency, but it was all right, and the Bank of England were very good about it. They wouldn't let me have unlimited amounts so I said, "John, all you've got to do is pick up my traveller cheques with yours and bring them down to Lyon with you. I'll wait for you in the hotel in Lyon and I should have enough money to last me until you arrive." So he said, "Fine." At that time funnily enough, I had my wife and daughter with me on this trip, to have a look at the scenery etc, but I put them on the Lyon train to go home, a night sleeper, and I thought that was that.

So round about 7 o'clock in the evening, I went back to the hotel to meet John who was due there for 9 o'clock that night. When arrived, I went up to the desk and I said, "Do you have a message for me, my name is Norman Garrad?" He said, "Oh, yes we have, In fact we've been paging you all day." I said, "Oh." He said, "Yes, here it is," and he gave it to me. This little message read "Event cancelled, none of us are leaving England, see you when you return!" This was because of the big accident at Le Mans, in France, which caused many cancellations in the weeks which followed.

Now I had a big problem. I had just 50 Francs in my pocket (just a few pounds), the car needed fuel, I needed food and it was a long way to get back to the coast, and I thought "My God, now what do I do?" I didn't need to worry though as I knew the bloke in the Royal Hotel in Troyes, and as we did quite a lot of business with him and I'm was quite certain he would know me.. I set off for Troyes.

When I arrived there at about 8 o'clock in the evening, there was a big party going on and the man who ran the hotel was as drunk as a coot and said he didn't know me from Adam. He refused to recognise me and would have nothing to do with me. So I left the hotel and went out back to the car. I had just enough cash to get a little fuel and I set off for the next place.

Well, I thought, the only thing to do now was to go to one of Bruere's Hotels. I knew Bruere ran two or three hotels and I was very well known to him. So I went to the Euro Hotel in Valence. I got there and booked a room with a bath and all the trimmings. I

Norman Garrad: Memories of a life in Motorsport

had a wonderful dinner and then went to bed. I came down in the morning and had a continental breakfast, then went to the reception and I said to the man behind the counter, "I say, I've some news for you." He again spoke very good English and said, "Yes sir, what is it?" I said, "I cannot pay the bill. Not only can I not pay the bill but I want you to give me two thousand Francs as well." "Oh," he said, "we call the Gendarmes right away."

I said, "Yes, you must do that, but before you do, ring up my friend Monsieur Bruere." He looked at me and thought, here we go, and he said, "I'll do that. Company Business?" "Yes," I replied, "Company Business." Off he went, and called Bruere and he obviously said, "I've a gentleman here called Norman Garrad who not only cannot pay his bill but wants two thousand Francs!" Bruere said, "Just put him on to see if it's the Norman Garrad I know." So I spoke to Bruere, he laughed, he said, "Put the man back on again." So the other chap got back on the phone and in no time he was all smiles and gave me the money. He forgot the bill and kept it in the accounts until the next time I was passing.

So there you are, that was another amusing experience. When I got to Paris I obtained some money from my office there and the whole thing worked out wonderfully.

The year is now 1956, and we wanted to enter the Mille Miglia in our new Sunbeam Rapier model. I went to Italy in plenty of time for two or three practice runs to be made, which is a long way round, a thousand miles round each run. We had to spend about three weeks over there, but I did notice that every time the railway crossing keepers saw a green car coming they brought the barriers down and kept them there for quite a time. I did notice however, that whenever a red Italian car arrived, up went the barriers and off everyone went like a bomb, so I thought well, this didn't add up.

So overnight I had the cars re-sprayed red. What happened the next day whilst doing our run – no problem, every time they saw these red cars coming zoom, up goes the barrier and off we went without any hold up whatsoever. And I think the whole thing was a high class fiddle but it worked anyway. We felt a bit guilty running red cars but then what would you do? Don't forget I was paid to get results and that's how it goes.

Another one of the interesting jobs I took on, was that we wanted to popularise the new Humber Super Snipe and my masters said : 'Now come on, dream up something that will put the spotlight on that car'. So I said "Alright", went back to my office and I thought a bit. Let me see, I wonder how many countries I can cover in X number of hours in a Super Snipe? So I sat down and worked it out and I thought we could do 15 countries in X number of hours, which is a pretty terrific thing, but it meant of course knowing what time the various frontiers were open and what kind of fuel stops were needed here and there, and what kind of little umbrella I wanted to get me through towns very rapidly - a lot of planning involved, but well worth it, I thought, and my idea was to start the car in Lisbon and finish in Oslo.

So when we got it all put together and I got all the maps down and all the rest, I spent a lot of work on it and I obviously had to get a special budget for it and I also had to do a recce to see if I could really do it. I went to my master and told him my plan, he immediately said "Of course you're mad, only a fool would start in fine weather and finish in bad weather, Norman. Go away and turn the whole thing round, so that you start in Oslo and finish in Lisbon". He was right, absolutely right; I wish I had bumped into

ROOTES MAESTROS
"In their own words."

him a bit earlier because I'd put a lot of work in it and had done all the timing of the frontiers and so on, in any case we got it off the ground.

This trip [described in more detail on page 75] became quite amusing. We were in two cars, both the same colour, just one digit different in the registration numbers, Stanley Schofield came on board to do a bit of filming on the way down and David Humphrey was on board as well, and the three of us decided to have a go to see what we could do and to set a target for the thing. Well, it all worked out, but I learnt one very smart thing. At one point, to get into one country, I had to go straight ahead and after about an hour, two hours you had come back again and pass the same spot I had just left.

So I thought this is a damn good idea, I can drop off a couple of drivers here and one fella can go and do this thing as long as we've got the route book marked and stamped at the frontier, everything was above board, so that was fine and then of course the great moment arrived, I went to Lord Rootes my master in Devonshire House and said "I can do it, it's on" he said "Just a minute" he said "Let me sit down and give me some more details" so I told him the story he said "Right, right".

I said "Now, obviously I've got to have a separate budget for this" He said "Yes, you can have a separate budget". I said, "But now here's a thing, the actual car we are going to use I want it on the showroom floor in Devonshire House and I want you to give a little reception to the press, the gentlemen of the press who are all great friends of ours". I said and tell them what you're going to do. He said "Not on your life" I said "Oh yes you are" He said "why, what if it doesn't happen" I said "Good god, if an old man like me can do it, I said these youngsters can walk it, I said I've got Stirling Moss, Leslie Johnson I think yes, John Cutts and David Humphreys, I said they'll cakewalk it"

Oh no, obviously he didn't like that, but he went through the other office and spoke to his brother. On returning he said "Well, we've been thinking about it, alright, we'll do it" I said "fine," so we had a press reception the night before the car left to go up to Newcastle-upon-Tyne to take the ferry across to Norway and it all worked out very well. There's one little point that would amuse me was that I knew I had one danger with one climb in Norway, but the snow plough went over there every 6 hours and I thought if I could time it to get behind this plough just as he's finishing his round it's a piece of cake. I went over there and I talked to this man who was very helpful and he said "You are right, on a certain time, on a certain date, yes, I'll watch out for the car, fly the Union Jack, yes, I'll do it" and I gave him some Swiss francs and he did it and my God the whole thing worked like clockwork but, it was a bit of a chore I might tell you, poor old John Cutts did the trip twice, once with me and once on the actual run. And he did it all inside a month which was pretty good.

I had an amusing experience on that particular run, because I wanted to come back by air because I had something else I needed to attend to in England. Cutts and Humphrey also wanted to return early. We took off from Lisbon in this aircraft and were doing very nicely, when all of a sudden there was a hell of a bang, and we had an engine go out on us. The thing that made me laugh next was that there was a stewardess rushing past me with a tray and a bottle of brandy on it and two glasses, and I thought – well, what goes on. So she went up to the flight deck, and when she came back the bottle was half empty. As she passed me I just grabbed the bottle and said

Norman Garrad: Memories of a life in Motorsport

"Alright, what ever the panic was, *we* can use some of that also".

Well, do you know, the pilot had to turn round of course and we were well out over the Atlantic at this time, so he came back and circled round Lisbon for who knows how long? I could see the crash vehicles down below and all the asbestos dressed gentlemen, and thought this is going to be quite an event in my life, to get this thing down, for it was an old second hand aircraft that they bought from the Americans. Eventually, after visiting every spot above and around Lisbon, he had to have a go, so he put it down quite nicely and honour was served.

Now, I really think I have racked my brain for long enough. As you can imagine, there are far too many stories to for me to try to remember, but I hope what I have said makes sense, and you have enjoyed it.

ROOTES MAESTROS
"In their own words."

Sunbeam Talbots and Sunbeam Alpines: 1947-1956

No 'works' team probably had less experience of International rallying when the Rootes Competitions Department officially opened its doors in 1948. Not even in the more peaceful 1930s had the Rootes Group had a 'works' team of any type – nor did it have the sort of cars which might have been successful if it had. Because the whole of Europe was still struggling to recover after the Second World War had ended, motoring conditions were still extremely difficult. Not only were cars, spare parts, and fuel all still in short supply, but roads were still in a badly battered state. France and Germany, in particular, were in a parlous state, and there must have been thousands of bridges which, having once been blown up, were still to be repaired.

In Britain, and in Europe, it was not an easy task to try to restore life in general to pre-1939 conditions, and motorsport had to fight hard to become re-established. In Britain, strict rationing of petrol would persist until May 1950. In Europe, the first post-war rally of any historic significance was the French Alpine of 1947, the Monte Carlo was revived in January 1949, and the first major rally to be held in Britain was the *Daily Express* MCC rally of 1950: the RAC Rally did not run again until 1951.

As already noted by Norman Garrad in his autobiographical note, his first attempt to sample post-war rallying came in July 1947, when he took a Sunbeam-Talbot 2litre to follow the French Alpine Rally as a press man. Then, as later, the Alpine combined the high temperatures of a Mediterranean summer, with a route taking on some of the highest mountain passes in France, and a high and unrelenting time schedule.

Garrad, of all people, must have known that in standard form this was probably one of the least suitable of all cars to tackle the Alpine – indeed, to tackle almost any rally, but, then, at the time, there was nothing in the entire 1947 Rootes range of Hillmans, Humbers and Sunbeam-Talbots, which could be described as 'sporting'.

Rootes, with cars engineered under the control of Technical Director Bernard Winter, but under the dead, non-sporting, hand of Sir William Rootes who thought about sales, production, and lowering costs, but not about performance, had evolved a number of cars which were cheap to buy, smart to look at, but were devoid of technical merit. Some had engineering which harked back to the 1930s, which had merely been revived in 1945.

The Sunbeam-Talbot 2litre which Garrad chose as his 'chase' car for the French Alpine, had been introduced just before the outbreak of World War Two (but didn't go into series production until 1945), was a car with a 56bhp/1,944cc side-valve engine, puny drum brakes, beam axle front and rear suspension, and a top speed of no more than 70mph. As tested by the British magazines, it recorded 0 – 60mph in 22.1 seconds, which confirms that post-war standards were not up to much.

Even though he must have realised the magnitude of this problem, A.G.Douglas Clease, technical editor of *The Autocar*, entered his own Sunbeam-Talbot 2litre tourer for the same gruelling event, taking along his gallant wife as co-driver, and aiming not only to finish, but to write about his experiences afterwards. Although Clease

ROOTES MAESTROS
"In their own words."

was himself an accomplished and experienced driver (he had competed in SS-Jaguars, for instance, in the 1930s), he was no super-star, and the car was frankly outclassed. It was, at least, an achievement to make it back to the finish at Cannes, and for him to take a lowly sixth in his class. Perhaps this was the first 'result', if I might use that word, achieved by a Rootes car in post-war motorsport?

1948 – The birth of the 'works' team

When Rootes set out to build up a 'works' team, it was one of the British pioneers. No other company in the 'Big Six' (the others being Austin, Ford, Morris, Standard and Vauxhall) was interested, or at least able to get involved in the sport. Not that Rootes had any outstanding models to use – but at least Norman Garrad had the determination to succeed.

He was, after all, starting from a low point. Rootes enthusiasts who have read Michael Frostick's book *Works Team*, which was published more than forty years ago, may have seen the quote which follows, this being Norman Garrad's own memories of the original Sunbeam-Talbot 2litre. He found it:

'....exceedingly dangerous to drive fast down the mountain passes because of serious brake fade. Fuel starvation, tyre problems and inadequate shock absorbers had all proved problems, and the 2litre's gear ratios were ill-chosen for rally work …. Bernard Winter listened with some sympathy to what Garrad had to say. Brake lining manufacturers were consulted and Mintex produced the M20 lining after various different brake drums had effected only a partial cure.

'Similar experiment was carried on with the shock absorber settings, petrol pipes were moved to avoid the heat of the exhaust and the gearbox was re-designed to give better-spaced ratios.'

The old-type 2litre, therefore, was effectively a non-starter, so the first outing by a 'works' team had to be postponed until the new-generation car was ready. High hopes, no doubt, for the smart new-style Sunbeam-Talbot 90, which was officially announced in early July 1948, didn't look much more promising. Under that smart four-door saloon exterior was the same old chassis, complete with a beam front axle, and although the 1,944cc engine had now been converted to overhead valves, it still developed only 64bhp, and the transmission was now lumbered with the newly-developed 'Synchromatic' steering column gear change linkage. With a top speed of just 80mph, this was a model which would need much massaging to make it competitive.

Garrad, at least, managed to get hold of three early-production cars before the new model was officially launched, worked something of a preparation miracle (he had learned a lot in 1947), and rushed them through, to compete in the second post-war French Alpine Rally, which started from Marseilles on 13 July. The initial 'works' team – all of them experienced, though not young, competitors – were Scottish retailer George Murray-Frame, journalist Tommy Wisdom (with his wife Elsie), and Norman Garrad himself. Garrad was not driving just to save on drivers' fees – no-one got fees in those days! – but he thought himself at least the equal of any contemporary, and he still wanted to learn more about the behaviour of his new car, and his new team.

The new cars, in fact, did more than could ever be asked of them. On a rough-and-tough event whose route of four legs, totalling well over 1,000 miles, scaled all the high passes between the Mediterranean, the Swiss Alps, and back, only eight cars from the entire field of 61 starters, completed the entire route

Sunbeam Talbots and Sunbeam Alpines: 1947-1956

Shaping the original post-war Sunbeam-Talbot models was a task which took place at Humber Road in 1946 and 1947. The cars would eventually go on sale in 1948, and remain in production until 1956.

without penalty – and one of them was Murray-Frame's Sunbeam-Talbot! Not only that, but Murray-Frame won his class (for 1.5 – 2.0 litre cars), from Gautruche's *traction avant* Citroen, while Norman Garrad kept going, after some troubles, to take fourth in the same class. Tommy Wisdom's car suffered a deranged gearbox, could only use the two upper gears, and eventually ran out of time.

At a time when Britain was still in the grip of petrol rationing, and austerity in general, this was wonderful publicity for the new cars (and the new team), though Rootes could not immediately find another event on which to build the reputation. International rallies were still thin on the ground (there would be no RAC Rally until 1951). So Garrad had to wait, impatiently no doubt, to send his fleet to compete in the Monte Carlo Rally of 1949.

According to the records, the 'works' cars for this event were under-powered Sunbeam-Talbot 80s (their engines produced only 47bhp) which started from Glasgow, carrying GWD 668, HNX 81 and HNX 82 registration plates. This time they were driven by George Hartwell (a Rootes dealer from Bournemouth), Nick Haines (with Leslie Johnson also in the car) and Peter Monkhouse.

Did it make sense to send what the British press called 'plucky' 80s to compete in the

ROOTES MAESTROS
"In their own words."

Monte? If the weather stayed mild, probably not, as the road schedule to Monte Carlo was feasible, and the final mountain test was a contest of regularity rather than outright performance, but if not ….

In fact it was all to no avail, as the best of the cars could only finish 31st and 37th overall, with Peter Monkhouse down in fourth place in the 1.1 – 1.5 litre class. A special team prize, issued to the three cars, which all made it to the finish, was one consolation. It was time, surely, for a reality check, for although the publicists could always be guaranteed to squeeze much from little, the team would need to do better in future.

As in the showrooms, so on the rallies, the 80s were swiftly sidelined, and shortly forgotten (the model disappeared from the lists in mid-1950), but this was just the start of a real surge in the 90's fame as a competition car. Garrad's 'works' 90s had been retained after the 1948 Alpine – re-prepared, used on minor events, but otherwise not over-used, and for the 1949 French Alpine the entire fleet of four cars (GWD 100, 101 and 102 were allocated to George Hartwell, Norman Garrad and *The Autocar*'s A.G.Douglas Clease, and were joined by a fourth car, HUE 508, for Nick Haines) took part. Because the Sunbeam-Talbots 90s were still only at the start of their careers (and also, frankly, because they were still in extremely short supply, there was, as yet, no fleet of privately-owned cars to back up the works team.

At this point it is worth noting that two of the stalwarts of the 'works' team – Jim

The very first Rootes 'works' team started the French Alpine Rally in 1948, and the same fleet of 'works' cars started the 1949 Alpine too. Here they are, lined up before the start in Marseilles.

Sunbeam Talbots and Sunbeam Alpines: 1947-1956

Norman Garrad himself drove GWD 101 in the 1949 French Alpine Rally.

Ashworth, who became workshop foreman/manager/development man, and engine-builder Ernie Beck, were both involved from a very early stage. Their experience, which grew and grew as the years passed by, proved to be invaluable.

At the time this particular Alpine was reported as the fastest and most hectic rally to have been organised for many years: the French, determined to shake off the post-war atmosphere of austerity which still pervaded their nature, pulled out every stop to make it all as exciting, and as challenging, as possible.

Although it started from Marseilles, and finishing in Nice, just along the Cote d'Azur, along the way the demanding route trekked all the way to and from the Italian Dolomites at Bolzano. Although Gautruche's front-wheel-drive Citroen (which Murray-Frame had defeated in 1948, don't forget) won outright, on this occasion, the 'works' Sunbeam Talbots – Hartwell, Clease and Garrad – plugged away, with Hartwell/Monkhouse taking fifth overall, with the factory cars also taking the award for 'Best Non-French Team'. Along the way, George Murray-Frame used one of the unloved 80s to win his capacity class.

This performance was now beginning to cause quite a stir. Sir William Rootes, at least, was a realist. He did not actually expect it always to be so easy for his cars, but he soon began to require success every time the cars went out on events, which made Norman Garrad's job even more difficult, and demanding, than it might have been.

Not that the Rootes team had a very intensive programme at this stage. Nowadays, of course, we expect to see

ROOTES MAESTROS
"In their own words."

'works' teams put cars out on up to 18 World Championship events every year, and even in the early 1960s, when the Sunbeam Rapiers would be in their pomp, a 'works' team would tackle no more than six International events in a season.

Garrad's tiny operation, therefore, had tackled the French Alpine in mid-1948, the Monte in January 1949, and the next French Alpine in July 1949, with John Cutts borrowing a car to tackle the Circuit of Ireland at Eastertide in 1949. Nothing more would be seen of a 'works' 90 until January 1950. Just two events a year! No wonder that Garrad had no cause to build up a big fleet of cars, or to have star drivers under contract.

Those were the days, in fact, when their were no fees for driving, and no more than basic expenses, so by definition every 'works' driver tended to be a successful businessman first, and a rally driver second. George Hartwell was not only a successful Rootes main dealer from Bournemouth, but was well-connected with the Rootes family, George Murray Frame was a long-established tobacconist in Glasgow, whom Norman Garrad had known for years since his sales sojourn in Scotland during the 1930s. If Tommy Wisdom had not already become the doyen of the British press corps, he might not have been considered good enough for 'works' drives, while Norman Garrad (who was already nearly fifty years old) thought himself good enough to remain on the driving strength too.

The time had not yet come when the first 'young bloods' would force their way into the team on pure talent, and of course the thought of inviting some glamorous European driver to join the team on a regular basis was unthinkable. Peter Harper was still building up his own motor trade business in the Stevenage area, and no-one expected Sheila Van Damm to have gained a place on merit, if she had not already gained impeccable credentials in show business, where publicity machines were already prospering.

Preparing three cars for the 1950 Monte, therefore was quite a leisurely business. The usual fleet – GWD100, 101 and 102, were carefully refurbished – and were driven by Garrad himself, by George Hartwell (who, in those days, was effectively the team's 'No. 1' driver), and J.Pearman, all due to start from Glasgow. Fate, however, was always against Rootes on this occasion, for along with most of the Glasgow starters they found themselves engulfed in the blizzard which clamped down on the French Alps south of Lyons.

Only five competitors reached Monte Carlo without road penalties (four of them having started from Monte Carlo itself three days earlier), and one of them was the formidably experienced Maurice Gatsonides, who was in a Super Snipe which Garrad's team had also prepared. As I describe in a later section on Humbers, Gatsonides came agonisingly close to pulling off an outright victory. The Sunbeam-Talbot 90s, though, were overwhelmed by the weather, and could only finish in the middle of the pack.

Discouraging? For sure, but who was it who first said: When the going gets tough, the tough get going....'? Garrad knew that a much-changed 90 Mk 2 would be announced later in the year, but for the moment he would have to keep plugging on. For the third consecutive year, therefore, the same team of three 'works' 90s – GWD100, 101 and 102 – would tackle the French Alpine (to be held, as usual, in high summer in the French mountains behind the Mediterranean). It was time for another tour de force from George Murray-Frame, who kept going when all about him were having trouble, finished sixth overall, and was one of the winning team of three 90s.

Sunbeam Talbots and Sunbeam Alpines: 1947-1956

This was what Rootes, and the chauvinistic British press, were beginning to expect of Norman Garrad's team. The cars might be outclassed (by how much, we would see when the new models appeared later in the year!), but the drivers were gritty, and as determinedly professional as could be expected at this time. Even so, it is worth noting that Gatsonides, in a privately-entered 90, was leading all the team cars when his car suffered from a mangled rear axle differential, and had to retire. George Hartwell would undoubtedly have finished higher up, except that he collided with a non-competing car, and was delayed by French police for some time while the formalities were completed.

At the end of the season, the MCC (Motor Cycling Club) organised the first of its long distance events around Britain, sponsored by the *Daily Express*. There were no 'works' 90s in this event, not only because it was basically a long-drawn-out 'clubbie' where driving tests, not speed and endurance, would sort out the result, but because it was a National-status (as opposed to International-status), and therefore the team was not eligible. Even so, Norman Garrad and George Hartwell 'borrowed' a pair of cars to compete as private individuals, though neither figured strongly in the results.

It was on this event that Norman Garrad was persuaded to pull off one of the publicity coups for which he would become famous in future years. As ex-Rootes PR man John Bullock later wrote in his book about the Rootes family:

'His team of women drivers was second to none, led by the bouncy Sheila Van Damm, who was European champion on several occasions, and whose father owned London's Windmill theatre.... she had served as a WAAF in the Royal Air Force during the war, and became a qualified pilot in post-war years. Anne Hall, a Yorkshire housewife, was Sheila Van Damm's courageous co-driver when she won the Women's European Championship.'

The fact is that Garrad supplied Sheila, and her sister, with one of the old 90s, though as this was an event where the regulations were quite lax, it had a Mk II-type 2,267cc engine. Sheila, who later pointed out that this was the first serious rally she had ever done, but was lucky enough to draw starting number immediately behind George Hartwell, and immediately ahead of Norman Garrad, so an element of 'shepherding' took place.

On this, her very first event, Sheila was accompanied by her elder sister Nona, soon found that the 90- could exceed 85mph (though when her sister was driving she refused to exceed 60mph!), and as her motoring autobiography *No Excuses* tells us:

'This was a comparatively easy rally because the set average speed was low, and there were no "observed sections" or regularity controls. We could go as fast as we liked for as long as we liked, provided we observed the road traffic laws.....'

Although Sheila got desperately tired when the event finally dragged its way back from Scotland, and into Wales (she resorted to taking wakey-wakey pills – amphetamines, quite legal in those days – but hated them, and the after-effects), she showed off the stubborn streak for which she later became famous, and kept going. However:

'One thing was certain – I would never, never do a rally again. Sam Gilbey [the Windmill publicity chief] was welcome to his fun. Nona agreed heartily, and even said that if father told us to go again, she would refuse....'

Even so, after taking part in the final driving tests at the finish in Torquay, Sheila was astonished to find that she had finished third in the Ladies' competition. She was soon persuaded to do it all again – and this was the beginning of an illustrious career.

ROOTES MAESTROS
"In their own words."

Once again, in the autumn, there had been time, and to spare, for Garrad's team to set about building new cars for 1951, not merely because the old cars were worn out, but because there was now a new kid on the block – the Sunbeam-Talbot 90 Mk II, which not only had a massively solid new chassis frame, with coil spring independent front suspension (the original 90s had, of course, used the floppy old beam-front-axle layout of the old Sunbeam-Talbot 2 litre, which dated from the late 1930s), but the engine size had been increased to 2,267cc.

Surprisingly, Garrad and Jim Ashworth had not yet had much time to develop the new Mk II, so they were not yet ready to commit to an entire team of cars for the Monte Carlo Rally. Instead, just one newly-prepared Mk II was entered - that being KUE 90, for Tommy Wisdom and David Humphrey to drive - while Dutchman Maurice Gatsonides used a privately-prepared Mk II.

Garrad, on the other hand, was able to enter a complete factory team, by entering two of the dear old original 90s, which were approaching their third birthdays - GWD 101 for himself to drive (his co-driver was *Daily Express* journalist Basil Cardew, so we might assume that Garrad was not expecting too much...), and GWD 102 for George Hartwell to steer. The least said about this event the better, for the two cars finished, respectively, 51st and 195th.

Enter the Mk II

Once Rootes got their hands on the Sunbeam-Talbot 90 Mk II, prospects for the 'works' team bucked up considerably. At a glance, improvements made to the engine didn't seem sensational – 2,267cc instead of 1,944cc, 70bhp instead of 64bhp, and peak torque of 113lb.ft. – but, for sure, the package felt so much more substantial. Not only that, but the independent front suspension, and the Panhard rod which had been applied to the rear suspension, all made a real difference to the handling, there was a new and more substantial rear axle, and the intermediate gear ratios were all closer together.

Not only that, but it was the seemingly little things which all made this potentially a better rally car – the headlamps which had been raised, and improved night-time performance, along with extra air intakes in the front shroud panels, which meant that the front drum brakes had an easier time than before.

It was *The Autocar*'s Douglas Clease, who took a Mk II DHC, as a press man to follow the 1951 French Alpine, who summed up so well:

'I had driven two of its predecessors in Alpines....between the earlier models and the present version with its independent front suspension and larger (2,267cc) overhead valve engine there is no comparison. Climbs which were hard going in 1949, necessitating much second gear work because the reserve of power was too low to allow third to be regained after a hairpin, were romped up by the 1951 edition. Descents were easier and faster, too, the brakes being more adequate, the steering lighter and more decisive.

Amazingly, the 'works' team ignored Britain's first RAC International Rally, which was held in June 1951. One reason was that is was scheduled to run only a month before the French Alpine – an event which Rootes now saw as the 'core' to their on-going programme – and another was that there was every sign that the RAC would be a combination of a long-distance tour and a few driving tests to sort out a result: in fact the RAC Rally would not become a tough, demanding, event until the very end of the 1950s. Fortunately for Rootes, by that time their latest rally car, the Rapier, would be ideal for its purpose.

Sunbeam Talbots and Sunbeam Alpines: 1947-1956

Unhappily for Garrad's Alpine plans, George Murray-Frame had to pull out just before the start – he had damaged an ankle in a non-rallying accident back home, and even though he hobbled to the start in Marseilles, clearly he was not match fit, and had to withdraw. John Cutts therefore took his place. George Hartwell would normally have been 'works' team leader on the Alpine, but this year there seemed to be rather restricted entry – and he appeared in his own 'Hartwell Special', which was a much-modified 90, with two-door open coachwork. Looking back, this was certainly a car which inspired the birth of the Sunbeam Alpine which would appear two years later.

As it was, Hartwell was fast for days, but eventually had to retire with a broken rear suspension – while 'stand-in' driver John Cutts took third place in his class.

Later in the year, George Hartwell and Norman Garrad both 'borrowed' cars to compete in the second of the MCC/*Daily Express* National rallies and, even though this was not their favourite type of event, Hartwell won his class, while Norman Garrad finished fourth in the same category. Rootes also loaned a 90 Mk II to Sheila Van Damm: the event finished at Hastings, but to Sheila's frustration she could still not finish higher than third in the Ladies' category.

In 1952, the Rootes rally effort abruptly became a much higher profile operation, and the National Press, which was always looking for something fresh to write about, loved them for this. Not only did the 'works' team enter four brand-new 90 Mk IIs, but one of them was to be driven by Britain's most famous racing driver, Stirling Moss. According to Norman Garrad's son, Lewis, the miracle was that Stirling not only agreed to turn up, but did it all for a mere £50....

Yet, not only did Stirling turn up to do a good, professional, job, but actually took second place. Indeed, if it had not been for an absolutely stunning performance by South London car maker Sydney Allard, who became the only person ever to win the Monte in a car of his own manufacture, Moss might indeed have won the event at the first attempt.

This is how the 'works'; team lined up for the Monte:

KWK 397	Mrs Elsie 'Bill' Wisdom/ Sheila Van Damm/Nancy Mitchell
LHP 821	George Hartwell/'Chips' Chipperton/John Pearman
KKV 780	Norman Garrad/John Cutts
LHP 823	Stirling Moss/John Cooper/Desmond Scannell

Moss elected to start from Monte Carlo, so that while travelling down to the Mediterranean he could have a look at the critical sections of the route (nowadays, of course, we would call that a 'recce'), while the other three team members started from Glasgow.

As Stirling has made known in the report which I have been able to publish in this book (see pages 69–74), to complete his three-man crew he chose John Cooper (not the racing car constructor, but the Sports Editor of *The Autocar*, who was also an engineer and racing car designer well-known to Stirling), and Desmond Scannell, who was the General Secretary of the British Racing Drivers' Club.

What Stirling didn't spell out in that report was just how under-powered he thought the 90 Mk II really was, but from his book *Stirling Moss, My Cars, My Career*, we now know:

'I found on the ice, with chained tyres, that the best way was simply to keep on as much

Stirling Moss's Sunbeam-Talbot 90, high in the Alps in the 1952 French Alpine Rally, when he won the first of his Coupes for an un-penalised run on the road section.

power as the Sunbeam could offer. We were travelling at 70-75mph most of the time, near the car's maximum, and it paid off....'

According to the 'master plan' – and, make no mistake, Stirling always had a master plan for anything he tackled – John Cooper would be the competent second driver, though not expected to take the wheel on any of the competitive sections, while Scannell would be the master navigator, time-keeper, and overall 'car manager'. Stirling – well, Stirling would just be Stirling, ready to drive just as much as he felt like, *always* planning to drive on the difficult sections, particularly on the final Mountain Circuit where split second timing had to be combined with cat-like ability to find grip on the icy hairpins of the Col de Braus, and always ready to achieve the impossible.

As it happens, the weather was awful in 1952, not least in the section through the Massif Central which Stirling describes so vividly in his report. I note from my own account of this event in *Monte Carlo Rally – The Golden Age*, that only 167 of the 328 starters fought their way through to Monte Carlo, and that only 15 of them (one which was the Moss/Cooper/Scannell Sunbeam-Talbot 90 Mk II) were unpenalised.

After they had had a good rest, the climax of this phenomenal winter marathon was a Mountain Circuit of 46.2 miles to and from Monte Carlo (which included the Mont des Mules, the Col de Braus and the Col de

Stirling Moss's 'works' Sunbeam-Talbot 90 tackling the manoeuvring test at the end of the 1952 French Alpine Rally. Note the dent in the left front wing – every picture tells a story....

Castillon), over which cars had to main strict regularity at 28mph/45kph, passing through a number of secret checks which were just that – secret.

Once again, if I may quote my own words about this event:

'After the obligatory night's rest with the cars locked away, the 'top 50' then tackled the Col de Braus' loop, leaving at two-minute intervals, and taking about 1hr 40 minutes to complete the test. At *Moyenne Corniche* level there was rain and misery, while at altitude soft snow was falling, making accurate time-keeping almost impossible. Many a car left the road, brushed against the scenery, or spun its wheels on the most slippery sections, but none could keep exact time. No crew was absolutely regular – some were early, some were late at secret checks – with Sydney Allard losing a total of 140 seconds. If Stirling Moss had not ditched his Sunbeam-Talbot 90 for a short time, and spent too much time trying to get back on terms, he might not have lost four seconds more....'

The final thoughts on what had been a simply amazing Monte debut drive by Moss have to go to John Cooper, who naturally wrote up his own impressions of the event, in *The Autocar*, soon after his return to the UK. Describing it as a 'Very Great Adventure', before the finish he also noted that: 'Desmond and I were convinced after the previous few days that in Stirling we possessed a built-in advantage over almost every other crew under such conditions.'

Although the team-work was superb, and Moss's car control on the Mountain Circuit was superb, at one point: '...the road was a sheet of ice, and before we knew it, the nose of the car was buried in the soft snow at the side of the tunnel entrance, while the wheels spun uselessly in reverse. Many willing hands helped to push us out, although the minute or two lost seemed like as many hours: then we were away again, hurtling down the Col de Castillon at an incredible speed, with Stirling trying all he knew.

'All now depended on the location of the secret check, for if this were after our mishap

ROOTES MAESTROS
"In their own words."

there was no point – and in fact, yet more penalty – in regaining the time we had lost. We therefore decided to make up half of it, and, as far as possible, equalise the amount of error: as it turned out, the secret check was on this downhill run, and we finished 28 seconds early on the run from there to the finish. Had we slowed and lost just five seconds more, we would have won the rally….'

What a phenomenal result this was! The pessimists, of course, bemoaned yet another second place, and yet another near miss (the Rootes team had already notched up second places before this one….), but the fact that this was the Monte Carlo Rally, and that Stirling Moss had been driving the car, made all the difference. The fact that the other 'works' cars were either eliminated (Norman Garrad) or finished well down (George Hartwell and the ladies' crew) was easily forgotten.

'Norman Garrad and the Rootes brothers certainly seemed delighted,' Stirling later commented, 'I'm not surprised – my fee was a flat £50!'

Right at the start of the calendar year, though, this was to be the highlight of the entire season. The RAC International Rally, though tougher than before, was still a long-distance tour-cum-navigational exercise, which suited neither the 'works' cars, nor their drivers. In an event won by Godfrey Imhof in his Cadillac-engined Allard ('Goff' would later gain one or two 'works' drives from Garrad on the back of that success), none of the 90 Mk IIs shone at all.

Much, though, was expected of the team in the French Alpine. Not only was the 'A-Team' – all now seasoned competitors in Sunbeam-Talbot 90s - to comprise Stirling Moss, Leslie Johnson and George Murray-Frame in Mk IIs, but a rising young race driver called Mike Hawthorn had been invited to take part in another Mk II.

'Mike Hawthorn had joined us, 'Stirling quipped,' ….after I had told him what a terrific way this was of earning fifty quid….'

Nancy Mitchell had entered in one of the gallant old beam-axle 90s (GWD 102) which was therefore about to start its fourth French Alpine! George Hartwell would start the event in his own open-top two-seater 'Special' (LEL 333), the same car which had shown so much promise in the previous event.

Here was a rally which anyone would have been proud to finish for of the 85 starters, only 23 made it back to the finish. This must have made the ten individuals awarded Coupe des Alpes for un-penalised runs doubly pleased with their own, and their cars' performance. Starting from Marseilles, and finishing in Cannes four days later, the route took in the usual high passes in the French Alps and the Italian Dolomites, along with visits to Monza for a standing-start kilometre test, to an overnight halt in Cortina, to loops into Austria and Switzerland, and (after a further halt at Aix les Bains) to another break neck dash over the mountains, and back to the Mediterranean.

For anyone who has taken part in the Alpine (and the author has, on more than one occasion), merely to look down the list of high-passes to be tackled on that last day is spine-chilling. Consider – Cols d'Iseran, Glandon, Croix-de-Fer, Galibier, Izoard, Vars, Allos, all on roads open to the public, all against the clock, and at set road averages of 59kph/36.6mph – they had to be completed, on time, or that precious Coupe would be lost.

At the end of the event where Ian Appleyard distinguished himself by taking a third consecutive Coupe (and therefore a Coupe d'Or) in the famous XK120 (NUB 120), the 'works' Rootes cars

Sunbeam Talbots and Sunbeam Alpines: 1947-1956

Above: Among the line-up of Sunbeam-Talbots before the start of the 1952 French Alpine Rally was George Hartwell's personal 'Special. (LEL 333), a conversion which is always agreed to have inspired the birth of the original Alpine.

Below: George Hartwell's 'Special' lines up for a speed test at the Monza circuit in the 1953 French Alpine Rally.

ROOTES MAESTROS
"In their own words."

distinguished themselves. Not only did three of the 'works' Sunbeam-Talbots gain Coupes , but George Murray-Frame won his class, and Messrs Moss, Murray-Frame and Mike Hawthorn made up the winning team too, this being the only team to survive to the finish.

As far as we know, Mike Hawthorn really didn't enjoy the Alpine Rally – in his book *Challenge Me the Race* he dismissed the event in just one line – and he was certainly not tempted back to compete again, not even in one of the more glamorous Alpine two-seaters. We now know that he had been invited to compete in the 1953 Monte Carlo Rally (his chum Stirling Moss certainly had something to do with that – by suggesting that it might be cold, and it might be slippery, but that Monte Carlo could be a good place to be in the depths of a British winter – but this entry had to be cancelled when he was invited to join Ferrari for the 1953 season.

Along the way, however, the hard-working 90 Mk II, LHP 823, was gaining something of a supercar reputation. Not only did it complete this French Alpine, helping Stirling Moss to win his first Coupe, but had already provided his second overall in the Monte Carlo Rally at the beginning of the year. Unhappily, Nancy Mitchell was not so lucky, for she was forced to retire on the last day when her old 90 broke a front suspension stub axle.

Only an outright win could have made this performance perfect – and because of the way the regulations and the handicaps were written, this was never going to be possible. In every way, however, this was the sort of performance which not only stunned rival competitors who saw the way that the Rootes cars kept going, but made headlines all around the world.

For George Hartwell, too, this was by no means a perfect weekend, for early in the event the engine in his 'Special' broke a connecting rod on the Falzarego Pass (in the Italian Dolomites). Leslie Johnson (not only an accomplished race driver, but the current owner of ERA, and a man who would soon be involved in both Humber and Sunbeam Alpine record attempts) was also eliminated when he went off the road in the middle of an overtaking manoeuvre. Even so, it was typical of Stirling Moss's skill, driving ability and sheer guts, that although at one point he was delayed for 26 minutes when his 90's exhaust system came adrift, he managed to make every single minute to be back on time before the next time control.

Once again, when Garrad's team got back to Coventry, there were no other important rallies in the programme for the rest of 1952, though this did not mean that management and mechanics had nothing to do. As far as the road cars was concerned, the important development came in September, when Rootes launched the 90 Mk IIA. Although it still looked much like the Mk IIs which had already given good service, many of the original car's deficiencies had been eliminated.

Visually, the big change was that the rear wheel spats had been eliminated, and perforated wheels had been specified – both of these features meaning that brake cooling was likely to be much improved. Not only that, but the brake drums themselves were to be much wider than before – 2.25in. instead of 1.75in. – and new-type brake lining materials had also been specified. All this, and a welcome boost in engine performance, to 77bhp, meant that the Mk IIA was likely to be even more competitive in rallying than ever.

During the last weeks of 1952, therefore, the 'works' team concentrated on sprucing up the existing Mk II team cars, ready to sell them on, while getting started on the

Sunbeam Talbots and Sunbeam Alpines: 1947-1956

preparation of no fewer than eight brand-new Mk IIAs – which were registered MWK 11 to MWK 18 respectively. It was no wonder, therefore, that Sheila Van Damm used a much older Mk II (KWK 397 – as first seen in the 1952 Monte Carlo), to compete in the MCC National Rally, in which she won the Ladies Award. This, Sheila later commented, was one of the very first times in which she was not being shadowed, chaperoned, scrutinized, vetted – call it what you like – by Norman Garrad himself, and she realised that her long apprenticeship as a potential team member was at an end.

In the meantime, too, Rootes also built up a Super Snipe to tackle an ambitious '15-countries in 90 hours' driving stunt (see pages 75-81), before turning their attention to the forthcoming Monte Carlo Rally.

By the end of 1952, therefore, it seemed that tide had really turned for the Rootes 'works' team and its rallying efforts. In previous years, the 'works' team had been seen as competent, with capable but not super-star drivers, and with a very limited programme. The cars were seen as smart, but by no means specialised, and often achieved results because of their reliability and manifest good preparation, rather than their performance. Quite suddenly, though, the latest Mk IIs had began to punch well above their weight, and prospects for the future were bright.

Ambitious plans for 1953

For the season, it seemed, more events were to be entered, more 'star' drivers would appeared in the ranks, and of course the entire programme would became more glamorous following the arrival of the two-seater Alpine sports cars.

Somehow, somewhere, Norman Garrad had secured a much larger budget than ever before. This was never more obvious than in the line up for the Monte Carlo Rally: In 1952, the 'works' team comprised four Mk IIs, but for 1953 there were to be no fewer than eight cars, which lined up as follows :

MWK 11	Norman Garrad/George Murray-Frame/John Pearman
MWK 12	Leslie Johnson/David Humphrey/John Eason-Gibson
MWK 13	George Hartwell/Peter Cooper/F.Scott
MWK 14	John Fitch/John Cutts/Peter Collins
MWK 15	Godfrey Imhof/Raymond Baxter/Dr. I.Pearce
MWK 16	J.Skeggs/A.Teer/T.Cranfield (all from Hendon Police College)
MWK 17	Stirling Moss/John Cooper/Desmond Scannell
MWK 18	Sheila Van Damm/Francoise Clarke/Anne Hall

- note that the car allocated to Stirling Moss had a '7' in the registration number. Stirling was superstitious, and liked it that way. Much publicity was guaranteed for this effort, as BBC Motoring Correspondent Raymond Baxter was to accommodate 1952 RAC Rally victor 'Goff' Imhof in one of the cars, and would be reporting en-route.

One of the new names in the line-up was that of John Fitch, an American race driver who had been persuaded to try his hand at rallying, no doubt after a conversation with Stirling Moss, against who he had certainly raced in the recent past. One can only sympathise with Rootes' John Cutts for having to cope with two race drivers in the same car, especially as Fitch became known as a very meticulous person, whereas Peter

ROOTES MAESTROS
"In their own words."

Three brand-new 'works' Sunbeam-Talbot 90s, lined-up at Humber Road, before the start of the 1953 Monte Carlo Rally. MWK 18 was driven by Sheila Van Damm, MWK 11 by Norman Garrad himself, and MWK 14 by John Fitch.

Collins was already known as someone to whom order and method in his private life were real strangers.

Another new team 'name' – and one which would become much more familiar in future years, was Anne Hall, who joined Sheila Van Damm, and became her regular rallying partner. Anne had already made her name in British rallies – but this is not always known to latter-day rally enthusiasts, as when she was driving a Jaguar XK120, she had rallied under the name of Anne Newton, which was her maiden name.

For once, however, the weather on the Monte turned spring-like, so it was not sheer grit and high-speed snow driving which was going to deliver a result, but accurate timing on the final mountain circuit up and over the Col de Braus, the same test as in 1952. No fewer than 253 of the 404 starters made it to Monte Carlo without penalty, which meant that the choice of one hundred cars chosen to tackle the mountain circuit was of the fastest cars on the pre-arrival acceleration and braking test in Monte Carlo itself.

Fastest of all was Sydney Allard in a car of his own manufacture, who took 21.8sec, but the fastest Sunbeam-Talbot of all (fifth overall, in fact, at 23.0sec) was a private entrant called Peter Harper, from Stevenage – we would hear a lot of him in the next

Oh Dear! While competing in the French Alpine Rally of 1953, MWK 13 (driven by Bill Bennett and Peter Galliford) suffered a roll, and damaged most of the exterior panels. Bennett finished 35th Overall.

decade, but this was the very first time he came to our attention in this marque. Competition at the top was tight, so Stirling Moss's time of 23.2 seconds put him down in eleventh. George Hartwell, Leslie Johnson, Norman Garrad, J.R.Skeggs, Sheila Van Damm, and Godfrey Imhof all qualified too.

The Fitch/Collins/Cutts car, on the other hand, did not. Fitch's biographer James Grinnell later quoted that 'The "stupid little braking test" (as one navigator put it) involved accelerating a cold car some 225 yards, stopping, backing up and then proceeding forward another 55 yards. The Fitch-Collins team failed when the car would not go smoothly into reverse ['Synchromatic' gearchange? Whatever next?: AAGR], the stiff gearbox refusing to cooperate for a second or two….'

Fitch, though, was enthralled by his first Monte Carlo, and wanted another try, and 'looked forward to the Alpine in July with keen expectation...'

So, everything came to depend on the 46.2mile/74.3km regularity test in the mountains, for which all competing cars were given a front-end colour wash which allowed marshals at the 'secret' checks to spot them before they arrived at the (non-stop) control line. Perhaps it was as well that the strict target average had been set at 29.2mph/47kph, for this was perilously close to the performance limit of many cars.

In fact, as Stirling Moss's intrepid co-driver John Cooper later wrote:

'….we concentrated on getting a minute in hand – where possible – and gradually tapered it off during the kilometre or so before each control point. Should the average speed required have been fixed at 50kph (the maximum possible) it would have been difficult to achieve this speed on the third section, which included the ascent of the Col de Braus, but a trial run led us to believe that Stirling could manage it if necessary. However, the immediate subsequent discovery of oil in the rear brake drums, with the concomitant change of the rear axle oil seals by Jimmy and Jerry, the two cheerful and ever-helpful Rootes mechanics, decided us against further experiments in this direction – at least before "der Tag"….'

Even though development and improvement was continuous throughout its career, this, of course, was always the Sunbeam-Talbot 90's problem. It was sturdy,

ROOTES MAESTROS
"In their own words."

the team cars were always well-prepared, but because the cars were heavy, their performance was marginal in some conditions.

The entire event was to be settled over little more than 90 minutes of tippy-toe motoring. This year, of all years, was going to rely on absolute and utterly accurate time keeping. Everyone knows (because Ford has banged on about it ever since) that it was a 'works' Zephyr which won the event, and that the formidable Maurice Gatsonides only lost two seconds (yes, seconds, not minutes) on the ideal schedule, with Ian Appleyard's Jaguar Mk VII losing just three seconds.

Accordingly, the Moss/Cooper/Scannell performance, with just five seconds away from the ideal, could only finish sixth, though their performance was surely worthy of a podium placing at least. Never more than two seconds away from the ideal, theirs was a stunning Rootes performance, which no other 'works' car could reach.

To his un-allayed joy, Norman Garrad also saw his nominated team, of Stirling Moss, Leslie Johnson and Godfrey Imhof, win the much-coveted Manufacturers' Team Prize – one which they would win again, and again, and again in future years.

Amazingly, by taking 17th, with a mere eight seconds of penalty, Peter Harper's privately-campaigned Sunbeam-Talbot beat every works car except that of Stirling Moss For Rootes, the only big disappointment was that Sheila Van Damm did not take the Ladies' award which she so richly deserved. After starting well, on the fourth section (and just beyond the summit of the Col de Braus), Sheila's car (MWK 18) suddenly suffered a puncture on the front right tyre, and the wheel had to be changed.

Even though the intrepid female crew had spent a lot of time, pre-rally, in changing wheels – they got the entire operation down to less than three minutes – on the event, on a slippery road, where the car had to be tucked in close to a rock face, there were limits. Sheila later claimed that they broke all previous Personal Bests, and that the front-wheel change took only two minutes twenty seconds but :

'....that ended any chance we had of winning the Ladies' Prize. While we were changing wheels, we were passed first by Ian and Pat Appleyard, and then by Madeline Pochon. Unless she also met with misfortune, we had lost the Coupe des Dames. When the results and times went up, I was very surprised to see that we had done better over the first three sections, and but for that puncture we would almost certainly have won.

This completely threw out their average speed keeping, 141 seconds was lost at the next check point – and suddenly the contest was all over. Instead of winning, therefore, Sheila had to be content with second on the category (to Madam Pochon's Renault 750), though she had been performing better at every other control.

This was the sort of team performance which finally convinced every motoring enthusiast that the 90 Mk IIA was now *the* saloon car to use in rallying, and the numbers starting events soared. On the RAC Rally which followed in March, no fewer than twenty-two Sunbeam-Talbot cars would start, of which five 'works' machines were from the spruced-up Monte fleet: on this occasion, the ex-Moss Monte Carlo car was to be driven by Ronnie Adams. It was, of course, asking a lot for a Sunbeam-Talbot 90 to compete against sports cars and much faster saloons in an event which set driving tests, sprints and other performance-orientated among the long, dreary, road sections.

No matter. Norman Garrad invited his well-respected 'regulars' – George Hartwell and Sheila Van Damm – to join him, while a new

For the 1953 RAC Rally, these ex-Monte 90 Mk IIAs were driven by Ronnie Adams (MWK 17), George Hartwell (MWK 15) and Norman Garrad (MWK 11). Ronnie would take second place, overall.

name – Ronnie Adams of Northern Ireland – joined the team for the very first time. Right from the start, Adams (who had a well-founded reputation for being somewhat 'chippy' and needed to make a point) was competitive, and battled for the lead with Ian Appleyard's legendary Jaguar XK120.

By the time the cars reached Turnberry, in Scotland, they had already tackled several race circuit tests, much navigation in Wales, and in the Lake District, and were due for a rest. Amazingly, Adams led the event – narrowly, for sure – but ahead of three XK120s, Peter Morgan's Morgan Plus 4, and Len Shaw's MG Y-Type saloon. Then came the long trek down through Yorkshire, to the finish at Hastings, where the final challenge was a complex driving test on the promenade.

At last, and to Garrad's chagrin, outright performance and sports-car like manoeuvrability, paid off, so the redoubtable Ronnie Adams slipped one place – to second overall, and the 'works' team of Garrad, Hartwell and Ronnie Adams just lost out to a team of Jaguar XK120s. There was, though, some real icing on the cake, for not only did Sheila Van Damm take the Ladies' award, but finished sturdily in 23rd place overall. As *The Autocar*'s John Cooper wrote afterwards:

'….the whole thing went off very well, and proved far tougher than many had expected. If some of the passage controls included in the route had been made time controls, still more drivers would have lost marks: even so, the toll was considerable, for the frequent tests en route gave nobody much respite…. The crew of the Sunbeam-Talbot which

ROOTES MAESTROS
"In their own words."

finished second deserve high praise…. All in all, it was a very good rally…'

Because the 'works' team now had had to back the prototype Sunbeam Alpine sports car which tackled high-speed runs on the Jabbeke Road in Belgium, and the high-speed banked track at Montlhery in France (see the special section on this expedition, on pages 85 to 92), and also had to complete the preparation of no fewer than six brand-new Alpines to take part in the French Alpine, they chose to ignore the Circuit of Ireland and the Dutch Tulip Rally. On the weekend-long Circuit of Ireland, in fact, Houston's 90 Mk IIA won its class, and although there were lots of privately-entered 90s on the Tulip, just two of them achieved second and third in their class.

By July, somehow or other the mechanics at Humber Road had prepared six new Alpines, and this highly popular rally, which started as usual from Marseilles, also featured three of the ex-Monte saloons, all in private hands. This is how the Alpine teams lined up:

MKV 21	Stirling Moss/John Cutts
MKV 22	George Murray-Frame/John Pearman
MKV 23	Peter Collins/Ronnie Adams
MKV 24	John Fitch/Peter Miller
MKV 25	Sheila Van Damm/Anne Hall
MKV 26	Leslie Johnson/David Humphrey

Ready to leave for the 1953 French Alpine Rally, Norman Garrad poses in one of the six brand-new Sunbeam Alpines, and the Commer van which accompanied them carrying tyres, wheels and other spare parts, backed by the work force which had prepared the cars.

Sunbeam Talbots and Sunbeam Alpines: 1947-1956

Above: Another view of the line-up of new Alpines for the 1953 French Alpine Rally – the location, of course, being the sports field at Humber Road in Coventry, very close to the Competitions Department workshops.

Below: More than fifty years on, in 2008, two of the surviving Alpines pose in front of the same pavilion. Just days later, it was demolished....

ROOTES MAESTROS
"In their own words."

- all of them had been collected from Ryton-on-Dunsmore in March 1953, all had been being prepared to the same basic specification (which included overdrive, the first Rootes application of this piece of kit), and of course all of them having steering column gear changes. [I make this clear, because some of the surviving team cars have been converted to floor-change systems in later years].

The 1953 French Alpine Rally might not have been the toughest of all these classic French 'road races' – no fewer than 25 cars would be awarded Coupes des Alpes for un-penalised runs – but it was still a major six-day challenge, one which started from Marseilles, ended in Cannes, and visited Italy, Austria and Switzerland along the way. To finish was an achievement, to win an award was a real honour, and to do it all without losing any time was still remarkable.

For Rootes there were honours across the board – not only four Coupes des Alpes on the event itself (the other two cars retired!), but a Coupe d'Argent (Silver Cup) for the unassuming George Murray-Frame, who won this because he had now achieved three Coupes, in three non-consecutive years.

Norman Garrad, they say, acknowledged that the Alpine was really too sturdy and too heavy for this sort of rallying, so he tried to lighten the load by banning the use of extra electrical equipment. The drivers complained that this would handicap them at night, and that they would be slower, but Garrad would not bend – which explains why the 'works' Alpines all took part looking remarkably standard.

Stirling Moss – as expected – was the fastest of all the team drivers, but he, like his colleagues began to suffer because wheel nuts loosened repeatedly on his Alpine.

Time for a cooling drink at a control point in Italy - George Murray-Frame and John Pearman, with Alpine MWK 22, in which they won a Coupe des Alpes in the 1953 French Alpine.

Rubbing in just how reliable the 'works' Rootes team cars had become by this time – there are five Sunbeam Alpines and two 90 Mk IIA saloons in shot at this control point on the 1953 French Alpine Rally. The Alpine carrying competition number 507 was driven by Stirling Moss.

Later, it seems, this was blamed on the use of new wheels, with glossy paint jobs – for once some of the paint chipped away around the stud holes, the tension was automatically lost! Even without such niggles, the Alpines could not keep up with the more exotically-specified cars in their 2.0 – 2.6 litre class, which explains why even Moss and the redoubtable Murray-Frame had to give best to a trio of well-driven, V6-engined, Lancia Aurelias, and a V-12 engined Ferrari.

Only two of the new Alpines did not make it to the finish, one being race-driver Peter Collins' car (MKV 23) which had suffered a broken rear axle, and ran out of time before it could be repaired, the other being Leslie Johnson's machine (MKV 26), which had most undeserved engine trouble. The other four cars, triumphantly, made it without penalty, which was a truly heart-warming start to this smart two-seater's career, especially as one of those Coupes went to Sheila Van Damm/Anne Hall, who deservedly won the Ladies Award too. She was amazingly lucky, for at one point a side-swiping accident damaged the fuel filler cap/neck arrangement and, with organised assistance banned, had to have a bodge repair carried out by a French mechanic in Val d'Isere. In post-war years, this was the very first Coupe to be awarded to an all-female crew.

Ronnie Adams actually pulled out of the event, because his driver, Peter Collins, would not allow him behind the wheel! David Humphrey took Adams' place (which was absolutely against the regulations) but all this came to naught when the transmission of that car failed just before the Col de Briancon section in France. Is it still a world record that Humphrey (who had already been in Leslie Johnson's car) retired twice within twenty four hours?

Adams later commented that, beforehand, he thought he had been misled by Norman Garrad:

"When Garrad asked me to do the rally with Peter, I told him that I was under the

Above: Stirling Moss (Alpine MKV 21) high in the Dolomites, and close to the Austrian/Italian border, in the 1953 French Alpine Rally.

Below: Two of the six 'works' Alpines, high in the mountains, in the French Alpine Rally – an event where four of the cars won Coupes des Alpes.

Sunbeam Talbots and Sunbeam Alpines: 1947-1956

Above: Sheila Van Damm, Anne Hall look happy and relieved....

Below: Stirling Moss and John Cutts both pose happily at the end of the 1953 French Alpine Rally, when both won Coupes.

ROOTES MAESTROS
"In their own words."

impression the Alpine was really a one-man job. "Oh no," he assured me, "I want you to share the driving fifty-fifty. In view of what happened, this was bloody awful of Norman, and I blame him more than Peter...."

The fact is that Collins drove the entire distance, and Adams recalls that: 'Peter drove alright, basically, and I think he would have had a Coupe if he had finished, but he was unnecessarily hard on his car....'

After four days of not getting his share of the driving, Adams suddenly came down to breakfast after the final rest halt, dressed in normal clothing, as opposed to rally kit. Despite entreaties by all his team colleagues – but not, apparently, by Peter Collins – Adams could not be moved, and walked away there and then. It would be some years before he got another chance to drive a Rootes 'factory car'.

Many years later Peter Miller, who had joined Rootes as an admin assistant to Norman Garrad early in 1953, recounted his story of his Alpine-in-an-Alpine performance in this event, for he had been the American (ex-USAAF fighter pilot) John Fitch's co-driver. Fitch and Miller apparently did not hit it off at first – Fitch, the meticulous preparer of most aspects of his life, was not impressed by Miller's party-at-all-costs attitude, especially when the co-driver mislaid the American's passport for a time!

Reading the two men's accounts of the rally, it seems to have been another case of this Alpine pairing being a 'marriage of convenience', which would not be repeated. Nothing, however, was to put them off their ambition, which was to rub along as best they could, to shrug off problems as many and various as an epidemic of loosening wheel nuts, or of almost losing their rally plates (which were virtually 'car passports' in European rallies of this period).

In Peter's account, later published, of this event, he described the opposing Lancias as works cars, and 'much faster than the Sunbeams', which they undoubtedly were, so the scene was presumably set even before they rolled off the ramp in Marseilles, but :

'The new Sunbeam Alpine cars had already attracted much attention since leaving Coventry and, although heavy and rather ponderous, they were very forgiving and had remarkably good road-holding, which made them ideal for the Alpine terrain, despite their poor acceleration....'

It was on this event that Rootes could surely have complained about the organisers' regulation which forbade organised outside assistance because:

'Later that day Ronnie Clayton, the official Rootes photographer, spotted the three works Lancia Aurelia saloons, which were leading our class, receiving undoubted outside assistance beside the fully equipped official Lancia *Servizio Corsa* transporter. Clayton took pictures of this incident, provided Norman Garrad with crystal-clear prints, so that Norman could present them, with a flourish, to Lancia management before the prize giving. Lancia accepted the print with good grace – but retaliated by presenting Garrad with a picture of chief mechanic Jim Ashworth offering cans of oil to his cars as they rushed past! On the eye-for-an-eye principle, no more was said ....

So, what if the Alpines couldn't come home from their very first event with an across-the-board success? They had performed absolutely as well as could be expected (they could never have been expected to beat the Lancia Aurelia), and had confirmed Peter Miller's comments, that the cars handled well even though they were too heavy and too ponderous.

All six cars made it back to Coventry without serious damage, the successful Alpines were put on show for a time, but

46

After the 1953 French Alpine Rally. The three Alpines look very clean and new – those being the Stirling Moss (MKV 21), George Murray-Frame (MKV 22) and John Fitch (MKV 24) cars, all of which won Coupes des Alpes.

then soon went into store, as work had to start on completing the season. As already mentioned, Norman Garrad seemed to have tapped a really generous source of finance for this year and the next. This explains why two Sunbeam-Talbot 90s were then entered for the Lisbon (October), and why Sheila Van Damm was flown out to North America, to compete in the Great American Mountain Rally (November). As far as Lisbon was concerned, this was a qualifier for the European Ladies' Championship, which Rootes reckoned Sheila Van Damm could now win.

In those days, the Lisbon Rally was an important event, not of the same status as the Monte or the French Alpine, but a long and demanding endurance rally with multiple starts, and driving tests in Portugal to sort out a final result. Rootes entered two Sunbeam-Talbot 90 Mk IIAs, both fitted (since the regulations allowed this) with up-rated Sunbeam Alpine engines.

This was a typically thorough Rootes effort, with London jeweller 'Goff' Imhof and John Suter in one car, and Sheila Van Damm (partnered by Francoise Clarke) in the other machine, facing up to rivals as varied as a team of three 'works' Ford Zephyrs, Ian Appleyard's Jaguar, Porsches, Ferraris and other European sports cars. Long road sections, navigation sections, what we might now call special stages on mountain roads, and – finally – driving tests at Estoril, close to Lisbon, were all part of the mix.

The top three finishers – Porsche, Jaguar, Porsche – tell us what sort of event this had been, so Imhof's finish, in fourth place, and best of all the saloon car fraternity, was amazing. Two Zephyrs followed, then came Sheila Van Damm in the other Sunbeam-Talbot, which she had crumpled somewhat after inadvertently driving into the back of Imhof's sister car on a road section! As if that wasn't enough, Sheila then had a coming together with an on-coming truck on another section, and at one point had to have her exhaust system welded up after it began to break away.

ROOTES MAESTROS
"In their own words."

All of this, in fact, was in vain, for although Sheila finished seventh overall, she was behind Nancy Mitchell's Ford Zephyr in the Ladies' section, and was therefore just robbed of the overall Ladies' Championship.

Sheila Van Damm's trip to North America was for a rather less professional (though none-the-less serious) event, her Alpine being locally prepared, and her co-driver being a man, Ron Kessell: she was the only lady driver in the entire event. Sheila herself wrote of the rally, for *Autosport*, when she returned, and was typically modest about her achievements. One of her team mates was Norman Garrad's son Ian Garrad (who worked for the Rootes organisation in that vast country), the other being Sherwood Johnston, whose Alpine won its capacity class. Sheila took eighteenth overall, finished behind Johnston in the class, and was a delighted member of the winning Manufacturers' team. Rootes was making a habit of this!

1954 – another busy season

In the meantime Jim Ashworth, Gerry Spencer, Ernie Beck and a handful of dedicated technicians had begun building up three new cars for the 1954 Monte, which everyone was certain would be tougher (if not closer fought!) than the 1953 event had been.

Anxious to get back their reputation for toughness, the organisers had imposed a new format. Although the usual long, often turgid, and above all exhausting runs from multiple starting places were retained, all the cars concentrated at Valence, in southern France, and had to tackle a difficult 164 miles/264km regularity run over the mountains before getting to Monte Carlo, this including a dash over the Col des Leques, followed by a five-lap sprint around the Monaco GP circuit to end it all.

Stirling Moss, determined to win rallying's most famous long-distance event, while he

Race driver Mike Hawthorn and team boss Norman Garrad, in a Sunbeam Alpine, pose for the camera at the Earls Court Motor Show of 1953.

Sunbeam Talbots and Sunbeam Alpines: 1947-1956

could still spare the time to go rallying, was effectively the team leader, while Sheila Van Damm and Leslie Johnson/Norman Garrad were to back him. Moss, for no other reason except that it looked like a demanding thing to do, elected to start from Athens (the route through Greece and Jugoslavia could be *very* wintry, and this was the first time an Athens start had been organised in post-war years….), the others choosing to start from Munich instead. To Moss, there was the undoubted honour of carrying competition number One, though his 90 Mk IIA's registration number (ODU 699) did not carry its habitual '7'.

Once again, the weather was unseasonably mild – except from Athens, where all but a few entrants found themselves driving for hours on ice, packed snow, fresh snow or any combination of the three. Stirling Moss, need one say, shrugged this all off, and made it through to Valence without problems. He was fastest over the critical Col des Leques (not even the eventual rally winner Louis Chiron's Lancia Aurelia GT could beat him)

All three cars completed the event, Stirling Moss was best placed at 15th overall, and once again they were delighted to win the Charles Faroux Trophy for the best Manufacturers' team. That made it two wins in two years – and they had high hopes of making it three in 1955.

All this was achieved in spite of the alarming incident on the Col des Leques where ace driver Leslie Johnson suffered a heart attack while driving his 'works' 90 Mk IIA. This is described in great, not to say, harrowing, detail on pages 13-14, in Norman Garrad's narrative. It was altogether typical of Johnson that he somehow persuaded his colleagues – Garrad and John Cutts – to get to end of the event before committing him to hospital in Monaco, typical of them that they respected his wishes, and remarkable that he made a slow recovery afterwards. It was to be his last 'works' drive for the Rootes team, and he was much admired for all his achievements in the cars.

Although Johnson's condition had put a dampener on the team's celebrations in Monte Carlo, by March his health had stabilised, so the team were higher spirits when the RAC Rally was organised in March. This particular rally will, for ever, be remembered as the event in which the Triumph TR2 burst on the rally scene, but we must never forget that Peter Harper, in his first-ever 'works' drive, and partnered by David Humphrey, took a rousing fourth place overall, close behind 'Cuth' Harrison's Ford Zephyr, and also the second best performance by a saloon car. If Harper had not lost a single, solitary, minute on a road section in the Lake District, he would have finished third overall to Johnny Wallwork's TR2, and set up the best performance by a saloon car.

It was, of course, high time that the amazingly talented Harper should be swept into the factory team, especially as he was in the motor trade as a Rootes dealer, but the opportunity had never before been there. It was altogether fitting that he used the self-same car (ODU 699) as Stirling Moss had used on the Monte.

For the RAC, which started in Blackpool and Hastings, and finished in Blackpool several days later, competitors had to cope with circuit tests, sprints, hill-climbs, autotests, navigational exercise, and a great deal of main road motoring. Peter Harper's feline skills were well-developed for this eclectic mixture of tests, as were those of Sheila Van Damm, though Norman Garrad, more of the long-distance European specialist showed little liking for it all.

With the European Ladies' Championship in mind, Norman Garrad then took the big step of entering Sheila van Damm for the Dutch Tulip Rally for the very first time.

ROOTES MAESTROS
"In their own words."

Until then, Rootes had ignored the Tulip, which was traditionally held in the first few days of May. Starting and finishing in Holland, its route meandered down towards the south of France, and returned, with a mixture of stages, hill-climbs and circuit tests. It was not ideal for Sunbeam-Talbots, usually involved a complex performance/engine size handicap system, and was not thought to be value for Rootes' competition budget.

Norman Garrad came to terms with all this, and in 1954 he entered Sheila Van Damm in her ex-Monte Mk IIA, and backed her up with Peter Harper/John Cutts, and 'Goff' Imhof/Raymond Baxter. As it happened, none of this helped, for Harper's car had to retire with a deranged rear differential housing, while the Imhof/Baxter machine rather ignobly failed on a road section when a half-shaft broke, and shed a rear wheel: the message which went back to Rootes' engineering department was short, blunt and by no means sweet....

Ms. Van Damm, on the other hand, was as fast, and as safe as usual, finishing tenth overall, losing the same penalties as Dennis Scott's 'works' Zephyr, which otherwise won its capacity class.

The next big challenge was in the French Alpine, to which everyone seemed to be looking forward. Since 1953 the Alpines and 90s had been improved yet again (as in 1953, the Alpines had Laycock overdrives – which had first been seen, of course, on the Jabbeke/Montlhery cars more than a year earlier), the team was stronger and more experienced than ever, and Norman Garrad had the very same six cars to use, which had been blooded in July 1953.

By any standards, it seemed, this was a formidable line-up:

MKV 21	Stirling Moss/John Cutts
MKV 22	George Murray-Frame/John Pearman
MKV 23	Peter Collins/Lewis Garrad
MKV 24	George Hartwell/Dr Bill Deane
MKV 25	Sheila Van Damm/Anne Hall
MKV 26	Peter Harper/Peter Miller

Here was a team with a huge amount of experience, for all the drivers had previously driven 'works' Alpines or Sunbeam Talbots, all of them except F1 driver Peter Collins with a great deal of success. Collins's co-driver was Norman Garrad's son Lewis (who would later become Norman's deputy in the Competitions Department, but who was apparently only 17 years old at the time).

To quote Chris Nixon's comments about Collins on this occasion:

'It is reasonable to assume that the youngster did not expect to do much in the way of driving. He and Peter failed to finish, as the car broke its rear axle on the lower reaches of the Stelvio Pass....'

Mike Hawthorn, incidentally, was no longer available, as he now had an all-embracing Ferrari contract, while following his health crisis in Monte Carlo Leslie Johnson had retired from rallying.

Having conceded that the 1953 rally had, by their own standards, been too easy, the A.C.M.P. had vowed to make the latest edition of the French Alpine tougher than ever. Starting from Marseille, it would encompass night stops at St Moritz and Cortina, before returning to Cannes. The route would be 2,200 miles long, with four days and two overnight sessions, all run at very demanding average speeds, and would naturally take in almost every high pass in the French Alps and the Italian Dolomites.

As in previous years, cars could carry no more than two spare wheels/tyres, and

Sunbeam Talbots and Sunbeam Alpines: 1947-1956

theoretically have no access to official service/support vehicles. As we all know, it all depended on what was 'official', and what counted as 'support'….

This, of course, guaranteed that there would be no holiday atmosphere for competitors. While there would be twenty or thirty Sunbeam-Talbots entered in the Monte, some of those cars were driven by what the gnarled Old Pros called 'tourists'. On the 1954 Alpine, however, there were seven Alpines, none of them 'tourists' – for six cars were from the factory, the other being well-backed private entries from George Hartwell's Bournemouth-based operation. Only 83 cars would start the event – and when the hard motoring was over, a mere eleven were still un-penalised.

What followed was a grindingly difficult, fast and furious marathon, from which Rootes publicists gained a lot of great publicity. How to sum up such a colossally demanding event – by merely quoting Stirling Moss's success in winning a Coupe d'Or (Gold Cup) for completing his third consecutive un-penalised French Alpine, and by noting that Sheila van Damm won yet another Ladies' Award.

For George Murray-Frame, though, there was heartbreak, measured – literally – at a fifth of a second, for it was by that tiny margin that he failed to reach a speed mark on an autobahn test near Munich in Germany, while Peter Harper's rally came to a violent end when his car abruptly broke a stub axle when descending the Passo di Rolle, and hit the scenery in a big way. Sheila Van Damm's car, on the other hand, got away with it after her car hit a bridge in the Italian Dolomites.

As it happened, the critical test was a flat-out 1½ kilometre timed run over a stretch

Ready to start the 1954 French Alpine Rally, and posed at their Bandol hotel, are seven (count them….) Sunbeam Alpines, including all six of the cars which Humber Road had built originally for the 1953 Alpine.

51

ROOTES MAESTROS
"In their own words."

This line-up of Sunbeam Alpines for the 1954 French Alpine Rally, includes MKV 21, carrying Comp. No. 500, in which Stirling Moss would secure his Coupe d'Or.

of autobahn near Munich, where a two mile run in was allowed, but a target average of 87.5mph was imposed on the Alpine class. As John Gott later wrote in *Autosport*:

'The weather was appalling, and the autobahn had about half an inch of surface water on it….. I was, accordingly, not surprised to hear that only 19 of the cars still left "clean" had achieved their target, but we were disappointed to hear that George Murray-Frame, one of the Alpine regulars, had just missed his Gold Cup by a fifth of a second, although Stirling had achieved his time by the same margin…..'

Stirling, need I add, had used every ounce of race craft into getting his Alpine to go fast enough, which involved, among other details, blowing up his tyres to insanely high levels and:

'I had the normal oil drained out and replaced instead with thin spindle oil to reduce drag. Others didn't bother to this degree….'

By relying on his own reflexes to keep the car straight and narrow on the waterlogged surface, he just made the time required.

New team recruit Peter Harper (who naturally did not know that a later accident would make it all academic) was not so lucky, as co-driver Peter Miller made clear:

'When we were flagged off, the road was awash and we drove into the teeth of a howling gale. The rain lashed into the

Sunbeam Talbots and Sunbeam Alpines: 1947-1956

cockpit through the top of the hood, and although he could see nothing ahead, Peter kept his foot hard down. But it was hopeless. The engine simply wouldn't rev, and although Peter constantly flicked the switch between overdrive and normal top, and then back again, in a desperate effort to get more speed, we failed to achieve our target speed by two seconds. That was it, the end of our chances for a Coupe des Alpes, although we were still in the rally.'

By the time the 37 battered survivors reached Cannes (all but a handful with crumpled bodywork), Stirling Moss was leading the Sunbeam Alpine contingent, but was driving as if on egg shells, for his car was suffering severe transmission problems, while having to go as close to flat out in the mountains as was possible.

Once again to quote John Gott:

'All that remained was to carry out the Manoeuvring Test, which was also a test of brakes and steering. There was an allegation that Moss did not have all the gears in the box, which would have lost him his Coupe [due to penalties at technical scrutiny...], but after some attention from John Cutts, the car was passed out by the Assistant Clerk of the Course, M.Etienne Viano, as in order...'

This secret doctoring of the car was needed, Rootes knew, because someone had tipped off the organisers about the problems. The 'attention from John Cutts' ploy, it seems, was no more than a subterfuge, for in reality, by the end of the event, the Moss car could only select two gears – second and third - but by fiddling with a suitably modified

This was the awful state of the lower reaches of the Vivione Pass in Italy in the 1954 French Alpine Rally, Somehow or other, Stirling Moss and other team members got through the rubble without suffering punctures.

ROOTES MAESTROS
"In their own words."

overdrive switch (and without the scrutineer noticing....) Stirling made it seem as if all four gears were, indeed, operable!:

'The scrutineers asked me to demonstrate that the car still had all its gears. First and top had gone for ever, but with a scrutineer beside me I drew away from rest in normal second, chattering to him all the time. *'Voila, le premiere'*. He nodded. I accelerated, and changed up with much waggling of the steering column gearchange, surreptitiously flicking the overdrive button as I did so, into overdrive second...'

And so it went on, until the scrutineer was satisfied.

Except that the Alpines, now agreed, by one and all, friends and rivals, were seen as rock-solid but too heavy, and could not therefore always beat their rivals on pure performance, this was a wonderful result for Rootes. Stirling Moss had become only the second driver in history to win a Coupe d'Or (Ian Appleyard was first), Sheila Van Damm had confirmed yet again that she could beat every other lady, anywhere, on any surface, and the company had proved just how reliable their cars actually were.

But in this amazing season, there was more to come. In September Rootes entered Sheila Van Damm, in a Mk IIA, for the little-publicised Viking Rally of Norway, where she won the Coupe des Dames in spite of the fact that her engine threw a fan belt at one point, where she had no time to stop for ages to re-fit another one. Earlier in the season, before the French Alpine, Sheila had also been sent off on the Austrian Alpine, where she won yet another Ladies' cup, along with a class win. Rather half-heartedly, too, Rootes entered Sheila in her 90 Mk IIA in the Geneva Rally (held in the autumn), where it transpired that she (and Anne Hall) were the only all-women crew in the event, so another Ladies' Award was assured. Except on the French Alpine,

Sheila Van Damm/Anne Hall (MKV 25) ready to tackle the final manoeuvring test. Sheila had nibbled at the rear wing of her Alpine, on her way to winning the Coupes des Dames of the 1954 French Alpine Rally.

Sheila Van Damm (left) and Anne Hall, with MKV 25, and their trophies for winning the Coupes des Dames in the 1954 French Alpine Rally.

Sheila had used the same 90 saloon all season.

The result of all this was that Sheila was pronounced Women's Touring Car Champion of 1954, and I should also make special mention of Anne Hall, who accompanied her on some events, and Francoise Clarke (from Leicestershire) on some of them. It was no more than they all deserved, and it firmly established Rootes as the premier rallying brand in Britain.

Just for fun, though, Rootes also sent Sheila and Stirling Moss out to the USA in November to compete (in USA-prepared Alpines) in the second Great Mountain Rallye, which totalled 1,100 miles, and was routed through New England. Even though they led the event at first (it was a regularity rally, rather than an out-and-out speed event), both eventually got stuck in the deep mud and snow which covered much of the route. In the end hours, not seconds, were lost, and the Rootes team (which included Kasimir Krag in the third Alpine) had to be satisfied with the Manufacturers' team prize instead of individual glory.

Maestros and heroes

This is the right moment, I am sure, to provide more detail on some of Norman Garrad's driving stars. As already made

ROOTES MAESTROS
"In their own words."

clear, *the* undoubted star of the early 1950s team was Stirling Moss, who not only won his Coupe d'Or on the French Alpine, but also came within a whisker of winning the Monte Carlo Rally in 1952 and 1953. For a man whose life seemed to centre on single-seater and two-seater racing cars, and who seemed to spend much of his time in aeroplanes, rushing off to yet another far-flung race meeting, it was amazing that Stirling ever found time to go rallying – and that he should do it so well.

In the meantime, there were other heroes, all of whom deserve special mention:

George Hartwell

Although he was neither young, nor a professional rally driver at this time, George Hartwell was one of the stalwarts who performed so well, and so consistently, for Norman Garrad, when he set up a 'works' motorsport department at Rootes. As a young man, Hartwell had raced privately-prepared MGs at Brooklands and Donington Park in the mid-1930s, but had not taken rallying seriously.

As I have already made clear, in the early post-war years, Garrad was never able to

In July 1954 Stirling Moss (left) and John Cutts (right) received their much-coveted Coupe d'Or (Gold Cup) from a high official of the ACMP, for completing a third consecutive penalty-free run on the French Alpine rally. John Gott (on Moss's immediate left) gets his share of publicity.

Sunbeam Talbots and Sunbeam Alpines: 1947-1956

To celebrate the team's success in the 1954 French Alpine Rally, Sir William and Reginald Rootes hosted a celebratory dinner at the Savoy Hotel in London.

offer fees or retainers to his chosen 'works' team, so as far as George Hartwell was concerned, it was just as well that he was a prosperous motor trader too! Well before a Rootes motorsport effort had even been thought of, Hartwell had set up a garage business in his native Bournemouth

By the late 1940s Hartwell was not only a main Rootes group dealer – retailing Hillmans, Humbers, and Sunbeam-Talbot types – but he had become a firm friend of Sir William Rootes, and would eventually become involved with him in other business ventures. As I make clear in the section describing Sunbeam Alpine outings, it was George Hartwell's 90-based two seater 'special' of 1951/1952 which inspired the birth of Rootes' own Alpine.

By the 1960s, Hartwell's personal rallying days were behind him, but he remained an important and successful businessman for years after that, and for a time in the 1960s he even moved to Rootes headquarters in Coventry to become Rootes' home sales director.

When Chrysler completed their financial takeover of the Rootes Group, Hartwell was eased out of his job at the factory, and

ROOTES MAESTROS
"In their own words."

returned to the retail motor trade. He set up a major business expansion in the south of England, and after Chrysler sold out to Peugeot at the end of the 1970s, Hartwell rapidly followed suit and took on several Peugeot franchises. To this day, the Hartwell name is proudly displayed on a whole variety of garages along Britain's south coast.

Sheila Van Damm – First Lady

Norman Garrad was no fool. When Sheila Van Damm, whose father owned London's celebrated Windmill theatre, was introduced to the Rootes motorsport boss, Garrad could see that she would attract mountains of attention to the brand even if she was not great shakes as a rally driver. Yet he soon discovered that she was – and since her middle name might have been 'Publicity', wherever she drove a rally car, her exploits and sometimes her successes were closely reported.

In the first place it was the Windmill Theatre which attracted the newspapers to follow her, for during the Second World War this was the famous show-business outlet which had stayed open throughout the worst of the bombing (Motto: 'We Never Close'), and which featured tableaux of nude show girls, at a time when such things were still considered quite shocking.

If Sheila's father had not wangled a 'works' drive for her in a Sunbeam-Talbot 90 Mk II in the MCC *Daily Express* Rally of November 1950, she might never have taken up a demanding sport which made her (and the cars !) famous. The 'Old Man' – Vivian Van Damm – had sponsored motor cycle speedway racing in the 1920s before he took over the Windmill Theatre, his youngest daughter was already working in the business with him before she broke into rallying, so Vivian made sure that the words 'Windmill Girl' were painted down the side of her car when she eventually got started.

Make no mistake however. Sheila was no long-legged bimbo (quite the reverse, in fact, for this cheerful but dumpy woman could never have graced a stage on looks alone, and might also accurately be described as 'Not Interested In Men' – you draw your own conclusions), but was always a hard-working character.

Born in 1922, and after serving as a driver in the WAAF (Women's Auxiliary Air Force) during the Second World War, she later qualified as a pilot, then joined the RAFVR (Voluntary Reserve), before taking up motor sport, at her father's urging, in the 1950s. Those who did not take her seriously as a rally driver soon changed their minds, for she went on to win the European Ladies' Rally Championship twice (in 1954 and 1955), won herself a Coupe des Alpes for an un-penalised run, in an Alpine, in the French Alpine Rally, and won Coupe des Dames (Ladies' Prizes) in Monte Carlo, Tulip, Viking (Norway), Geneva, RAC (twice) and the French Alpine (twice). She was always proud of the fact that, in the 'works' team, she finished every rally which she started, and often beat the men whom, in theory, were her team mates.

When she died, sadly aged only 65, motoring writer Wilson McComb wrote that:

'Determination proved as good substitute for the mechanical knowledge – notably on the 1954 Austrian Alpine Rally, when she walloped the dynamo with a hammer because it had stopped charging, then noticed a loose wire, fixed it with Elastoplast [burning her wrist in the process: AAGR], yet went on to win her class.

'Sheila was the most disarmingly honest person I ever met. It was she who told the story of the inexperienced co-driver whose acid comment, after her first and last rally

Sunbeam Talbots and Sunbeam Alpines: 1947-1956

with Van Damm, was: 'That woman is so tough, if you threw a brick at her, it would bounce off.' It was true that Sheila yelled at co-drivers, but only because she got so keyed up during an event. It was true, too, that she tended to hog the wheel, which infuriated her more experienced partners. But as Number One she insisted on driving all the tricky bits – especially because, while still fairly new at the game, she had been badly frightened on a Monte when driven fast on ice by the more experienced Nancy Mitchell.

'Indeed, she admitted to getting little pleasure out of fast driving *per se*, although when she and Stirling Moss drove the prototype Sunbeam Alpine at Jabbeke in 1953, her two-way average of 120.135mph was on a par with his. The only race she ever did was, characteristically, the toughest in the calendar, she and Peter Harper winning their class with the Rapier in the appalling 1956 Mille Miglia.'

Once Sheila retired, decisively (somehow, when the Sunbeam Mk III was put out to grass, she decided that her time had come too), she got much involved in motor racing's Dog House Club, but after her father had died she ran the Windmill Theatre, until had closed down, its time well past, in the early 1960s. She died in 1987.

Peter Harper – modest genius

Peter was much admired by all his contemporaries for his driving skills, if not always for his rather withdrawn manner. According to all the official biographies, he was Peter Charles Edward Harper, but according to his team-mates and rivals (sometimes at one and the same time), he was just 'Harp....' For years – for more than a decade, in fact, in a rallying career which started with Sunbeam Talbot 90s, but ended with Sunbeam Tigers and Hillman Imps - he was the fastest, most consistent, and certainly the most successful of all the 'works' drivers.

Not that he was universally loved – admired, for sure, but not loved. Having been in the 'works' team while 'Harp' was in his pomp, the author can confirm that there was respect for his abilities, but very little co-operation. The phrase 'team spirit' was really not in his vocabulary, though he was certainly loyal to the Rootes team, as such, for many years.

Like many rally drivers of his time, Peter Harper started his business life in the motor trade, and juggled a profession (the trade) with his hobby (motor sport) for many years. Born in 1921, during the Second World War he had been a fighter pilot, but rarely liked to talk about it. After opening up a Rootes main dealership, first in Letchworth, later in Stevenage, he competed in his first rally in 1947, competed in the 1950 Monte Carlo (with his wife as co-driver), and by 1954 had been drafted into the 'works' team by Norman Garrad.

It wasn't long before he was recognised as the master of winter rally driving – for he was not only brave (the ex-fighter pilot's reflexes helped, no doubt), but seemed to have preternatural skills in coping with very low friction surfaces. For those of us who tried (and that included the author), it was one thing to follow him along a twisting tarmac road, but quite another to attempt to do the same on ice and snow.

All of them got their chance to demonstrate their un-earthly skills in 1955, when the 'works' team got its hands on the latest version of the saloon – now modified, up-graded, and re-named Sunbeam Mk III. The 'Talbot' part of the title had been dropped (it would be back in 1979, many years after the period covered in this book came to an

ROOTES MAESTROS
"In their own words."

end!), the style was little changed, but the overall package was more promising.

The Rootes competitions department was not really interested in the style changes – better brake cooling was promised, slots in the side of the front wings promised better engine-bay cooling, and there was provision for a rev-counter on the modified fascia/instrument panel – but there was significant improvement hidden away. Not only was a new separate-port cylinder head specified (80bhp instead of 77bhp – as on the Alpine), but Laycock overdrive became optional, though in standard form it worked only on top gear. When overdrive was ordered, the rear axle ratio was changed to 4.22:1, and the top speed was more than 90mph.

Norman Garrad's team liked what they saw (they would have liked a lot more power, of course, and a much lighter car, but then, wasn't every rally team like that?) and made haste to order four new Mk IIIs, which were to be registered PWK 603, PWK 604, PWK 605 and PWK 606. Naturally they all had overdrive transmission, whose control was easily and conveniently changed so that it could operated on intermediate gears as well as top. [So, what if it was against the regulations sometimes…. Who even knew?]

All four cars were entered for the Monte Carlo Rally, with Norman Garrad, Sheila Van Damm, Peter Harper and race-driver Jack Fairman as lead drivers, the entire team starting from Munich. Unhappily, Stirling Moss could no longer find the time to compete. Because the Monte organisers were sticklers for regulation-reading, and would scrutineer very strictly, the new Sunbeams were virtually standard, though the 'portholes' in the front wings were blanked off to help keep engine bay temperatures up on this wintry rally. Garrad also insisted on Swiss Pallas snow tyres being fitted, which caused mutterings from Dunlop (who usually supplied everything used by Rootes): Garrad's robust reply to Dunlop, apparently, was: 'When you provide anything better, we'll start using them again….'

Basic changes had once again been made to the route of this winter 'classic'. This time around, there was to be a Common Route from Chambery to Monte Carlo, with the most severe section (south of Gap) being kept secret until the very day that rally cars arrived in the area.

[This, presumably, cut down the amount of practice that could be carried out, but seasoned teams practiced what they *thought* the route might be, and in most cases they were proved correct!]

Although the event was once again let down by very mild weather, the route itself, and the demands on the crews, were more severe than ever. Gap to Monte Carlo (207 miles/333km) was difficult enough, but after a single night's sleep on arrival, the top hundred cars were then faced with a new, 202 mile/325km speed-plus-regularity Mountain Circuit run, and after all that there would be a series of brisk five-lap races around the Monaco Grand Prix circuit, where only the fastest lap would count.

Rootes' love affair with Monte Carlo had finally encouraged other British teams to take part – BMC, Ford, Standard, Jaguar, Daimler, Armstrong-Siddeley and Aston Martin were all out in force - the total entry was of 319 starters, and as far as Britain's national newspaper corps was concerned, the event's glamour was at its height.

Amazingly, and in spite of their ultra-professional preparation, the 'works' Sunbeam Mark IIIs did not fare at all well on the run down from Gap to Monte Carlo, where strict regularity schedules were required – and where the Col des Leques stood out as a test on its own. As ever on the Monte of this period, secret check-on-sight controls had featured on the run, and as cards

Sunbeam Talbots and Sunbeam Alpines: 1947-1956

were not stamped at the time, no-one really knew how they had fared until all was posted on arrival.

Three of the four 'works'; drivers – Van Damm, Harper and Jack Fairman - qualified for the final run round the mountains, with Van Damm and Harper well placed, but to everyone's surprise, highly placed at that moment were Messrs. Per Malling and Gunnar Fadum (from Norway) who had placed their privately-prepared Mk III in third place: never before had they performed so well on the Monte, and this was in a car which had only been delivered to Oslo three weeks before the start, for preparation to begin.

The roads on the final loop finally included as much snow as expected, and at the end of a hard day's motoring, the amazing privately-financed Norwegians had moved smoothly up to take the lead, by being completely un-penalised – one of eight crews to achieve a 'clean' run on this section. Peter Harper and Sheila Van Damm both crept up the leader board too – the result being that Malling only needed to make a competent run around the Grand Prix circuit to ensure his win.

Not that this was going to be easy, for Malling's Sunbeam had shed its fan belt on the way into Monte Carlo, and would have to start the five-lap race without it ! Both the Norwegians, and the Rootes team, however, had read the rules carefully. Since only the fastest lap time was to be counted, the car should surely be repaired out on the circuit itself?

And so it could. The unflappable Malling started the race without a belt, the car duly boiled, but he then stopped, fitted a new belt in a mere 40 seconds, tightened up the dynamo bolts, and carried on to finish. His had been an immaculate performance, and he thoroughly deserved outright victory – Rootes' first-ever on the Monte, and privately-owned too!

As *The Autocar*'s John Cooper noted in his post-event summary:

'The regulations imposed a maximum time for the first lap: thereafter the fastest lap of each contestant was to count. Malling spent all Saturday evening practising fitting a Sunbeam fan belt, finally reducing his time for the job to 40 seconds....'

This was the sort of performance which ensured Norman Garrad's place in the Rootes hall of fame. Not only had Malling won outright, but Sheila Van Damm had won the Coupes des Dames – again (and finished eleventh) – with Peter Harper ninth overall. Rootes also won a team prize – this time L'Equipe Challenge Trophy for the best performance by the top three cars of the same make.

On a brighter note, when the cars returned to the UK after the Monte Carlo Rally, *The Autocar*'s Charles Haywood borrowed Sheila Van Damm's car (PWK 604) for a brief appraisal before it went back to Humber Road for re-preparation:

'But the car, what is it like? A poor driver will wreck a good car and never get anywhere with a bad one. A good driver may finish an event with a bad car and, given a good one, will stand a good chance of honours, as has been amply demonstrated by the Van Damm-Sunbeam combination.

'The Mark III Sunbeam is a compact car and has a very good performance for a full four-seater saloon which is equipped as it stands on any showroom floor. It weighs, before rally equipment is fitted, almost 3,000 lb, and to the works team cars you can add the following: extra weight of snow tyres, in this case Pallas, chains, tow-rope, shovel, hydraulic jack, box of spares (the box itself the worse for wear after all those rally miles), jerrican for spare petrol, fog lamps, fire extinguisher and the personal gear of the

ROOTES MAESTROS
"In their own words."

In a magnificent private owner's effort, the Norwegian duo of Per Malling (left) and Gunnar Fadum won the 1955 Monte Carlo Rally in their Sunbeam Mk III.

crew. And the car took the lot from Munich – no easy route this year – to Monte Carlo without a murmur.

'Change the tyres, now with the tread showing the defect of fast miles on hard roads, remove the rally equipment, and it would be a normal Sunbeam indistinguishable from any other grey one. I drove one 24 hours after it got back home, still equipped (there was a vacuum flask half full of some muddy liquid, and amongst the litter on the floor, a leaflet for a night club in Monte Carlo.

'The only noise, apart from an odd rattle from the piece of Perspex against the inside of the windscreen, was that of the tyres, which rose to a crescendo as the speed increased. An easy 65 in third on the speedometer, into top, and then the lazy gait which the overdrive allows. The 2-1/4 litre engine is a lusty unit, and this one, still with the cylinder head sealed by the *plombeur*, would have easily repeated the journey without any attention. No oil leaks, no "tappity" tappets; the clock seems noisy in comparison. Apart from a k.p.h. speedometer, the instruments were as per the book, the oil pressure gauge needle was as steady as a rock, and the temperature gauge was normal, although after a few fast miles the engine ran on after being switched off. It was noticeably good in starting from cold.

'If it were to return to the Alps immediately it might be a good idea to inspect the brake

Sunbeam Talbots and Sunbeam Alpines: 1947-1956

linings, but they were adequate for English roads. The clutch was quite happy, and the gearbox was either exceptionally quiet or enveloped in some sound dampening material – the former, one would say. These Sunbeams have one of the nicer steering column changes: its action is like the car, taut and businesslike. All the electrics worked, and there was not a dent to be seen in the coachwork.

'I think they are entitled to do a little trumpet blowing at that factory in Coventry...'

Although they now had time in which to rebuild the cars, there was little rest for the small team of mechanics at Humber Road by the time they returned to base. The two most successful Monte Mk IIIs spent time on display in Rootes car showrooms (the Devonshire House, London display, across the road from the famous Ritz Hotel, was a favourite place), before they were then re-prepared for the British RAC Rally which, in 1955, started from Blackpool and Hastings, and finished in Hastings days later.

This was still an event which demanded much of the driver's skill in short, sharp, bursts on race circuits, hill climbs or driving tests, and of the co-driver in the navigation sections place in Wales, Yorkshire, the Lake District and even on Exmoor. Bravely – and rightly as it turned out – Norman Garrad expected David Humphrey to keep Peter Harper on the straight and narrow, with Anne Hall, as ever scheduled to look after Sheila Van Damm.

Perversely, it seemed (for this was March in the UK), there was snow in Lincolnshire and Cadwell Park, and some in Wales, but little anywhere else, but as expected it was the British night-rallying experts who had the measure of most events. In the end, cars like Jimmy Ray's Standard Ten, and Harold Rumsey's Triumph TR2, defeated all comers. For Rootes it didn't help, mind you, that Peter Harper's Mk III went off the approved route, became irretrievably stuck and lost more than 90 minutes before being restored to the road – but the ever-popular Sheila Van Damm plugged away to take second place in her capacity class, and she also won the Ladies' prize.

More speedy effort back at Humber Road led to the same two hard-working cars (whatever had happened to PWK 603 and PWK 606?) being re-prepared for the Dutch Tulip Rally in May to start at Noordwijk-an-Zee on Holland's north-sea coast, though there had been a variety of starting points, including London., with all routes coming together at Stuttgart, then trekking south to Montelimar, before returning to Holland. Hill-climb and circuit tests broke the monotony.

As ever, Peter Harper and Sheila Van Damm had to battle against two major problems – one being the Tulip Rally's own class handicapping system, the other being the weight and comparative lack of power of their Mk IIIs, but both put in the sort of gritty, consistent, performances for which they had become famous. After a fast but unobtrusive run, Peter Harper finished seventh overall (and second in class to a Mercedes-Benz 220), while Sheila took fifteenth place, and second in the Ladies' category. The marking system was so complex, and the competition so tight, that Harper might well have finished third overall: it would have needed only a minor improvement on any one test to make it so.

Wasted effort

What followed in June and July 1955 was the sort of drama which makes financial accountants toss and turn in their sleep, and which makes company directors wonder how they can explain this away to their colleagues.

Rootes prepared a team of brand-new Alpines to contest the 1955 French Alpine Rally – but this event was cancelled at short notice, before the cars could compete.

At the end of the 1954 season, the six 'works' Alpine two seaters – MKV 21 to MKV 26 inclusive – had been sold off (they were relatively 'young', had only competed in two major events, were by no means worn out, and soon found private customers), and for the proposed 1955 French Alpine Rally a new sextet was prepared. These were registered RHP 700 to RHP 705 inclusive, and by mid-June plans were well advanced for what had become a habitual mass Rootes entry in the French Alpine.

Tragically, however, the awful accident which occurred in France, at Le Mans in the 24 Hour race – where Pierre Levegh's Mercedes-Benz 300SLR ploughed into the crowd across the track from the pits and hospitality suites, exploded and burst into flames – then occurred, and cast a pall over motor racing throughout the world. Not only Levegh, but more than 80 spectators, were killed in the holocaust which followed.

Almost immediately, the French government reacted to this by banning major events – racing and rallies – on their territory for some months to come, while they considered further action, and other nations (including Switzerland) followed suit. Because the French Alpine Rally had been due to start in July, it was one of the first major events to suffer, and had to be cancelled at very short notice. Not postponed, you understand, but abruptly cancelled.

As far as the Rootes rally team was concerned, through no fault of their own, all preparation and pre-event practice had been in vain, six expensive new cars were now sitting at Humber Road, with no prospect of the rally being revived in the foreseeable future – and there seemed to be no alternative use for the cars. Garrad's team already had its up-to-date fleet of 'works' Sunbeam Mk III saloons in stock, the still-secret Rapier was just over the horizon (and clearly would be important to Rootes' plans), which meant that the new fleet of Alpines would have to be sold off.

Which, in due course, they were. As far as is known, they never competed as 'works' rally cars, and were sold off in a matter of months.

Sunbeam Talbots and Sunbeam Alpines: 1947-1956

In the meantime, three of the 'PWK....' Mk IIIs were sent to Norway to compete in the Viking rally, where Scandinavian expertise in special stage tests (about which the British knew very little at that stage) featured. Sheila Van Damm took third overall and third in her class – but this was merely a sideshow compared with the French Alpine which never was ....

Accordingly, it was at Monte Carlo in January 1956 that the cars made their final Monte appearance in Mk III form (the new Rapier was already on sale, the Rootes family wanted to see it promoted just as strongly, and soon as they could, and Norman Garrad had big ideas....), yet perhaps it was not surprising that there were three 'works' Mk IIIs in the lists, all of which were previously-used cars which had already had a hard life in previous events, and in the previous Monte ! Peter Harper and David Humphrey, Sheila Van Damm and Anne Hall, along with Jimmy Ray and John Cutts, all started from Stockholm. For business reasons Sheila, by the way, had already announced her imminent retirement from rallying, for she would now have to turn all her attention to the 'family firm' – the fortunes of the Windmill Theatre, in London.

For once, on this lengthy winter marathon, road conditions were mild, there only being seriously wintry conditions at height, in the final tests, behind Monte Carlo itself. No fewer than 231 cars would make it to the finish, with Peter Harper's Sunbeam in fourth place, Ray's car tenth, though Sheila van Damm finished well down after a troubled Mountain Circuit. Yet again, however, the 'works' Mk IIIs won the Manufacturers' Team Prize, which was absolutely as much as the team could have hoped. The Mk III might now be an ageing design, but its drivers were all resourceful, and could deliver the goods as long as the machinery kept going.

There was one moment of embarrassment at the prize giving. As Sheila Van Damm, quoted in her book *No Excuses*:

'We had won the team prize in 1953 and 1954, so now it was to be ours for keeps. We were quite sure about that – although not everyone else was, as we discovered at the prize-giving.

'When Peter [Harper] went up in his third position to receive his prize. They showed him the team prize, and then immediately whipped it back.

"It's ours", Peter protested.

"No, no," said the officials, and Peter had to drive on.

Norman was standing by, so he immediately took the matter up. The regulations said that the prize would be definitely awarded when it was won by the same manufacturer three times "consecutively or not". The officials had evidently overlooked the last two words....'

The dispute was finally settled in Rootes' favour, the trophy was handed over, came back to Coventry – after which Sir William Rootes commissioned another trophy, which he sent to Monte Carlo, as a replacement!

The last outing of all for these gallant cars came in the British RAC Rally of March 1956, when the weather was at least spring-like, but there were still so many blockages caused by incompetent competitors getting in the way of more experienced drivers on narrow lanes, that the result was almost meaningless.

Hastings or Blackpool, via the West Country, Yorkshire and the Lake District would have been difficult enough even in summery conditions. As it was, although 162 competitors reached the finish at Blackpool, some of them – including Peter Harper – had been held up, and were out of contention. Although he had often been baulked, in the end Peter Harper took second place in his class.

So that was that. An entirely new range of Rapiers – which would start life as an underpowered model, but which would eventually evolve into a formidable rally car – was in the wings.

ROOTES MAESTROS
"In their own words."

The famous Charles Faroux Trophy, so deservedly won in perpetuity by the Sunbeam-Talbot team in the 1950s.

Above: Peter Harper hurling his Mk III through the Tabac corner on the Monaco Grand Prix circuit in 1955, on his way to ninth overall in the Monte Carlo Rally.

Left: Having been retired from rallying in 1956, PWK 605 was lovingly preserved for the next half century, and is often seen these days at classic events.

ROOTES MAESTROS
"In their own words."

Above: MKV 21, the most famous of all the 1950s-type 'works' Sunbeam Alpines, poses in 2008 with an impressive line-up of Alpine rally awards, including the famous 'Coupe d'Or'.

Below: Two of the legendary Alpines (including publisher Peter Shimmell's MKV 23) which competed in the French Alpine Rallies of 1953 and 1954, join together again in 2008.

Stirling Moss: A reminiscence of the 1952 Monte Carlo Rally

This is the report which Stirling Moss penned immediately after driving his 'works' Sunbeam-Talbot 90 into second place in the 1952 Monte Carlo Rally

----

The story of the Monte Carlo Rally

The Monte Carlo Rally is unique. Its arduous 2,000 miles against the clock and the Regularity Test, produce conditions which would be difficult to emulate anywhere else in the world. Over Alpine passes, through snow, ice, fog, rain and blizzards, down treacherous descents and deeply rutted ice – it is indeed a unique testing and proving ground for the reliability of the car, and it is for this reason that the Rootes Group regularly compete and encourage private owners to do likewise in the Monte Carlo Rally and similar International Trials. The advantages of such testing being revealed in the inherent quality and performance of Humber, Hillman and Sunbeam-Talbot cars today.

Just what the Monte Carlo Rally is – the tremendous difficulties and strains imposed – is not always realised by the public outside Europe, and the following article written by one of the world's most notable exponents of motor sport, will give you an idea of the conditions and difficulties encountered in the world's toughest rally.

A WONDERFUL PERFORMANCE BY THE SUNBEAM TALBOT '90'
Through snow, ice, fog, rain, and blizzards.

Stirling Moss's own story of the 1952 event:

Although my main interest is in motor racing and I have never been particularly interested in trials and rallies, the one event which has always captured my imagination is that winter classic – the Monte Carlo Rally. The first event of its kind and the forerunner of the many rallies now featured in the International Calendar, the 'Monte' as it is familiarly known, is unique in many respects. It is organised by the International Sporting Club of Monaco in January of each year. Nowadays there are seven optional starting points scattered throughout Western Europe from which some 350 cars and their crews set forth on their 2,000 miles trek to the legendary principality on the sunny shores of the Mediterranean.

The 1951 Rally had lasted for three days and three nights, during which competitors were required to average not less than 31m.p.h. inclusive of all stops. To ensure that competitors do not make up time on the easy sections, the route is divided into stages, each of about 200 miles, at which control points are set up. Competitors may not leave these controls in advance of their schedule.

Although the initial stages of the rally are by no means easy, from the point where the routes converge, conditions become increasingly difficult. This year there were

ROOTES MAESTROS
"In their own words."

two hazardous mountain sections to traverse in the extremely adverse weather conditions of thick mist and deep snow which at many points was frozen solid.

Sunbeam Talbot '90'. Ideal!

My opportunity to run in the 1952 Monte Carlo Rally materialised rather unexpectedly, at the London Motor Show in October 1951. In the course of conversation with Norman Garrad, Sales Manager of Sunbeam Talbot Ltd., and the architect of his firm's competition programme, he offered me one of their cars for the event. Naturally I was delighted as the medium sized Sunbeam Talbot '90', with its high performance, was ideal and I knew would stand a good chance of success.

I was given a completely free hand in the choice of crew and starting control. For my crew I chose John Cooper of the 'Autocar' and Desmond Scannell of the British Racing Drivers' Club, and together we decided that to start from Monte Carlo itself offered distinct advantages. It allowed an opportunity of passing over the most difficult sections of the route and also enabled us to examine the 50 mile tortuous mountain section chosen for the regularity test, which would decide the winner of the rally from those who might arrive at the finish without incurring penalty marks on the road section.

And so, five days before the start of the rally, we set off for Monte Carlo. From Paris we followed the rally route and maintained the required schedule overnight through Bourges and Clermont-Ferrand to Le Puy, where we had arranged to spend 24 hours reconnoitring the various routes on to Valence.

After an uneventful run to Le Puy where we breakfasted, we set off on our reconnaissance. Our problem was to decide which of the several alternative routes we should ultimately take over this, the most difficult and mountainous section of the entire rally.

We set off on the first, and shortest, of the roads to Valence, that through Yssingeaux and Saint-Agreve. We then returned by another route, and so on; but on that particular day conditions were fairly easy throughout. However, we did decide that the shortest route was by no means the quickest, in view of the number of corners involved, and that the best was probably the northernmost route, through Montfaucon and Bourg-Argental, in spite of the fact that it was some 17 kilometres longer. After spending the night at Le Puy, we woke to find that it had been snowing heavily for some hours and appeared likely to continue so doing for some days, se we happily remarked, "Well, this is more like it!" and set off once more for Valence.

The next few hours, however, did much to destroy our self-confidence. When I drove into our first snow-drift at some velocity, and buried the windscreen in snow, Desmond, sitting beside me, was rash enough to open his window and try to reach round to clear it. There was still enough way on the car, however, for the rest of the drift to come in through the window and bury the rear-seat passenger – John – as deeply as any babe in the wood, so *that* procedure was by common consent ruled out for future occasions. And there were several of these, the next one resulting in our sliding blindly into the near-side ditch, from which we were eventually extracted with the assistance of one of the local inhabitants, two oxen and a length of chain. So efficient was this method, which I

Stirling Moss: A reminiscence of the 1952 Monte Carlo Rally

termed "two thousand Chateaubriand-power" that a discussion ensued as to the practicability of including two oxen among our unditching gear; but it was decided that the problem of feeding them would be insurmountable.

Anyway, we eventually reached Valence, though by no means within the time limit, and from here on conditions improved and we arrived in Monte Carlo without further incident.

The circuit of the regularity test was to be divided into four sections by the interposition of three controls of which the position of two would be known beforehand. The regulations as originally framed, required competitors to average exactly 31m.p.h. between each of these controls, and, in common with all other competitors, we found this speed impossible to maintain. Therefore we were pleased when the organisers announced that this average would be reduced to 28m.p.h., a decision reached after Louis Chiron – famous Grand Prix driver – had crashed in vainly attempting to maintain the original speed in his Alfa Romeo. 28m.p.h. may not seem a high speed, but it must be realised that the regularity test is a 46 mile ceaselessly winding, narrow course, which includes the corkscrew Col de Braus, rising to 3,500 ft. and the Col de Castillon. Snow and ice rarely seen so near the Mediterranean made the sinuous course as perilous as any Alpine Pass.

For checking our average speed, we were relying mainly on visual check points, such as kilometre and 100 metre stones, road intersections and the like, and not on the car's mileage recorder, for although the latter was extremely accurate, it was naturally affected by wheel spin and the likelihood of icy conditions would increase this error to an unreasonable degree. As it turned out, when we made the actual run so much snow had fallen during the previous night that the majority of the 100 metre stones were invisible, which made the task of maintaining our average very much more difficult.

It seemed that our few days in Monte Carlo had passed all too quickly when we found ourselves approaching the starting line shortly before 10p.m. on Tuesday, January 22nd. The floodlit Boulevard from which competitors were checked out at 1-minute intervals, was lined with thousands of enthusiastic spectators who had assembled to cheer them on their way, and it was an impressive thought that in many of the capitals of Western Europe similar scenes were being enacted.

Desmond was at the wheel when we started, and he afterwards confessed that for about the first ten miles he had never been so nervous in his life – imagining just what would happen were he unlucky enough to have an accident right at the beginning, but this feeling soon wore off and we were really under way.

I took over at Grasse, the first Control, for the tricky run to Digne. The one disadvantage of Monte Carlo as a starting point is that this mountainous section over the Alps Maritimes has to be covered twice, on the outward journey as well as the return; but fortunately, although there was a good deal of snow on the ground, none of it was recent and none of the competitors found this section difficult.

We arrived at Digne with ample time in hand for a welcome cup of coffee and then John took over and urged the willing

ROOTES MAESTROS
"In their own words."

Sunbeam Talbot on, over the Col de la Croix Haute, to Grenoble. Throughout this part of the route we were running on snow which persisted all the way through Chambery and Megeve, to shortly before Geneva. On the Franco-Swiss frontier, we naturally slowed down as we approached the Customs Post, only to be waved on by excited groups of Gendarmes and officials, and we entered Switzerland without undergoing any of the normal and routine inspection of Passports and stamping of Customs documents. From Geneva our route led to Bern and thence to Basle, where we were encouraged by Police who were stationed at every street intersection to speed through the outer suburbs, to the Frontier on the outskirts of the town. Here we were again waved on and returned non-stop to France. This unique disregard of the conventional frontier formalities by the meticulous Swiss is indicative of the importance attached to this famous event by the Governments of the countries through which the competitors are routed.

Superb Road Holding.

The ensuing run was comparatively easy; through Strasbourg, where we had ample time for a good dinner, and on to Luxembourg. By then there had been several changes of driver and at this point I again took over. From Luxembourg the route wound over the Ardennes, and almost all the way to the next control in Liege (Belgium) the road was ice bound. From time to time, Desmond, who was acting as my navigator, told me that I could slacken speed, but so well did the Sunbeam Talbot handle on the treacherous surface that I was reluctant to do so, regarding it as excellent practice for racing on wet circuits. We passed innumerable cars including many in the ditches on this part of the route, and arrived in Liege so far ahead of schedule that even after re-fuelling we had time to spare before proceeding into the Control.

Required Routine Service Only.

From Liege we went north through Belgium into Holland, to Amsterdam. Over this part of the route the driving was shared by John and Desmond, while I slept in the back which we had blacked out by a curtain behind the front seats and wrapping paper taped to the side windows. Then we turned south again, through The Hague, across the Dutch-Belgian frontier to Brussels. From here we crossed back into France and through Rheims, heart of the Champagne industry, to Paris. Incidentally, although the car never required more than the minimum of routine service attention, the enthusiasm and assistance of the Rootes Distributors in the Capital cities was wonderful and greatly appreciated.

Between Paris and Bourges, which, fortunately was one of the easiest sections on which time could be made up, we had our only real trouble; a puncture in one rear tyre. Unfortunately as we were going fairly fast at the time, the casing was ruined before the car could be stopped; but by one of the minor miracles of life, there was a tyre depot in Bourges open at midnight, where a suitable replacement was obtained and fitted.

Shortly before leaving Bourges, the weather conditions rapidly became worse. First of all we ran into driving snow which drastically cut visibility. Then too, there were patches of ice to negotiate, a hazard that was worsened by the thin coating of fresh snow which was then falling. Nevertheless, Clermont-Ferrand was reached with plenty of time in hand to carry out the customary

Stirling Moss: A reminiscence of the 1952 Monte Carlo Rally

re-fuelling and checking of oil and water before clocking in at the Control.

Treacherous Road Surface.

The next section to Le Puy, proved the most difficult of all. The road surface was absolutely treacherous and to add to our difficulties we ran into thick mist. However, the Sunbeam-Talbot had performed so magnificently that I now had confidence in its controllability and when the road straightened somewhat, by which time the mist had lifted, I had no hesitation in driving the car flat out despite the deeply rutted ice and snow-bound surface. That John and Desmond shared my confidence was evidenced by the fact that neither of them turned a hair! Thus we were one of the few teams to arrive in Le Puy with time in hand.

Many Penalised.

From there to Valence we took, as planned, the longer route; and here we had the advantage of daylight while the blizzard had abated somewhat. Consequently, after re-fuelling again, we had about a quarter of an hour in hand at this Control and the appalling road conditions and the wonderful handling qualities of the Sunbeam-Talbot '90' were again emphasised when we learned that out of 328 starters, only 20 remained unpenalised.

John drove the next section to Gap while Desmond took over from there to the Control at Digne. Between Digne and Grasse there are four notorious passes, the Col des Leques, the Col de Luens, the Col de Valferriere and the Pas de la Faye. These have proved the downfall of many Monte Carlo Rally hopes in the past, but this time, although slippery, they were negotiated easily in our versatile car.

Fifteen Competitors Unpenalised.

Now the worst was over and it remained only to get into Monte Carlo on time. After a brief and efficient stop in Nice to check over the car and re-fuel for the last time, we arrived, tired but happy, to discover that only fifteen others of the entire entry had finished on schedule.

On arrival all competing cars were put in parking enclosures, there to remain until the Regularity Test two days later.

Appalling Conditions.

During the night it snowed hard, and with the temperature below freezing the course, at best a combination of corkscrew and switchback, became so glazed that one could revolve a stationary car by gently pushing it with one hand. As a matter of fact, during the rally there were more accidents than ever before, and on consideration I feel it is remarkable that anyone finished at all.

At the first control during the Regularity Test, we were 6 seconds late and were penalised 6 marks, plus 4 marks for taking 24 seconds instead of the specified 20 seconds to cover the last 200 metres before the control. We estimated we were on time at the second control, but in point of fact the French timekeeper's watch was faulty and this control was subsequently nullified. On the narrow secondary road approaching the Col de Castillon we had our one mishap when the car slid into deep snow and we lost about 50 seconds in getting the car away again. However, the road-holding and performance of the Sunbeam Talbot allowed us to make up the time and we subsequently learnt that we were second.

ROOTES MAESTROS
"In their own words."

So the rally ended. For us it was a most satisfactory result, the more so as British cars had taken five out of the first six places, and we had been beaten only by Sidney Allard driving the 4,376c.c. car of his own design.

Our Sunbeam Talbot performed magnificently all the way. The run was completely trouble-free, no water was used, and very little oil, while the average petrol consumption was about 26mpg, on all but the most tricky sections, where the average fell to about 22mpg.

To sum up and pay my tribute to a fine car I quote *The Times* newspaper:

"A notable addition to the record of Sunbeam Talbots in International Rallies."

Stirling Moss drove this Mk IIA, MWK 17, to take sixth place overall in the 1953 Monte Carlo Rally.

Humber Super Snipe: The Fifteen Countries in 90 Hours run

It seemed like a good idea at the time. In reality it was one of those daft marketing stunts which all Competitions Departments are asked to tackle from time to time. And for why? Because a new-type, but still elephantine, Humber Super Snipe had just been launched – new chassis, new body style, new overhead-valve engine and all - and Rootes' publicists wanted the world to know more about it.

But how? Even though Maurice Gatsonides had come so close to winning the 1950 Monte Carlo Rally in the previous-generation car (he took second place, very close behind Marcel Becquart's much more suitable Hotchkiss 686 Gran Sport) , that success was all down to the wily and remarkable Dutchman, and not at all due to the car itself. No way was this Super Snipe, new-type or old-type, ever going to make a successful rally car – so Norman Garrad had to devise a stunt.

As he has already mentioned (see page 17) he soon concluded that a long distance driving stunt might do the trip. 'Let me see, I wonder how many countries I can cover in X number of hours in a Super Snipe?' In the beginning, and as we now know, Norman considered setting out from Lisbon (the capital of Portugal) and making for Oslo (the capital of Norway) – effectively linking north Europe with south Europe – but the effervescent Lord William Rootes, who never missed a trick where selling cars was concerned, thought that although he could attract the British press to observe an event which ended in wintry Norway, but he could hope to see more of them in balmy Portugal instead! In the beginning, the plan was to visit 15 countries in five days – but in the end the intrepid four man crew made it 16 countries in four!

Technically, the new Super Snipe was not exciting, but in all directions it was a great advance on its processor, whose chassis dated from 1935 (the arrival of 'Evenkeel' independent front suspension (which had a transverse leaf spring), with a side-valve engine whose design roots were even older than that, and whose basic body style had been around for twenty years. Suddenly there was a new model – a 113bhp/4.1litre overhead valve 'six', a new chassis frame with coil spring independent front suspension, and a smooth, Loewy-inspired, body style which was closely linked to the latest Humber Hawk – the two closely-related body shells both being supplied by Pressed Steel at Cowley.

Although this wasn't going to be a record attempt (if Rootes had claimed any records, Britain's stuffy RAC would have penalised them for 'racing on public roads') – it was certainly going to be as demanding as any long-distance rally of the period. For that reason, Garrad gathered no fewer than four of his existing 'works' rally team drivers to undertake the job - Stirling Moss, Leslie Johnson, John Cutts and David Humphrey. All of them would travel in the Super Snipe all of the time. Garrad himself would wave them off from Oslo, greet them at the finish in Lisbon, and perhaps drop in somewhere, some time, half way along the route!

Big Boys' Toy

Although the new-generation Super Snipe was no supercar, the team could at least

75

ROOTES MAESTROS
"In their own words."

expect it to keep going, all day and all night, cruising at 80mph wherever road conditions and speed limits allowed it. Road tests showed that standard cars could reach 90mph, and could sprint up to 60mph in about 16 seconds. The fact that all this would be achieved at nothing better than 16mpg didn't seem to be important in those days of cheap fuel. Performance? According to magazine road test figures, this new Super Snipe was currently the fastest Rootes production car on the market, for the Sunbeam-Talbot 90 Mk IIA topped out at 86mph, though in 1953 the new Alpine two-seater would reach 95mph. It meant that life in this well-equipped middle-class saloon was not going to be too turgid after all.

Garrad's department didn't have long to prepare the car – MRW 671 (I wonder how long it survived….?), for the new model had only been launched in mid-October 1952, and the run was scheduled to begin from Oslo on Tuesday, 2 December. At this time of the year, too, in 1952 it wasn't easy to get to Norway, for cross-North-Sea ferries were few and far between, and conditions north of Holland were almost bound to be icy, and probably covered in snow.

How early a car was this? Let's just note that in his signed report of the run in *The Autocar*, Stirling Moss noted that: This was the first run that the car had done, apart from preliminary tests, and I believe no cars had been delivered to the public.'

By modern standards, preparation could best be described as sketchy, for there was no question of wholesale strip-downs, nor of special engines, transmissions or tyre equipment being fitted. Norman Garrad just had to rely on the general worth of this new car, which was thoroughly checked out by the Engineering Department before it came to him. Inside the cabin, for instance, there were no extra safety features (no safety belts, for this was years before such fittings became normal). A Grundig tape recording machine was plumbed in so that the crew could record times, places, and occurrences, a windscreen washer kit (optional from Rootes dealerships by this time) was added, some rugs and pillows were also added, and apart from having to trust to the performance of the standard heater, that was that.

The team carried a set of chains in case of impossibly slippery conditions, but were most reluctant to use them, as it would take time to fix and unfix them, and would of course reduce the speed at which they could be used. A pair of extra driving lamps were fitted.

So, what was the challenge? Road conditions, for sure, but the other was the relentless schedule they set themselves. In theory, except for quick 'pit stops' for a meal, the crew would never stop for a general rest, but drive, turn-and-turn about, with off-duty members getting whatever sleep they could in the seats of the standard car.

The schedule which Norman Garrad set them to achieve was to complete the route (which is shown, graphically, in the map which accompanies this) of 3,380 miles, in less than five days. This translated into a running average of 'only' 28 mph, which may sound easy-peasy today, but was one to which none of them was looking forward. In the event, and after many hours of heroic driving, particularly from Stirling Moss and Leslie Johnson, they shaved a full thirty hours off this, and averaged 37.5mph instead.

Even so, this was a heroic challenge. Let us never forget that north of Italy (especially in Switzerland, Austria and the Scandinavian countries) a lot of snow and ice was to be expected. Let us also remember that in 1952 there were no bridges between Sweden and Denmark (these were not completed for another fifty years) – so two waits for the traditional ferry crossings on either side of

Humber Super Snipe: The Fifteen Countries in 90 Hours run

This was the route chosen by Rootes for the Humber Super Snipe's 'Fifteen Countries in Five Days' high-speed run. In fact the car started from Oslo, finished in Lisbon – and took only 90 hours to finish the job.

ROOTES MAESTROS
"In their own words."

Copenhagen would be inevitable. Let us also remember that Rootes had made few special border-crossing arrangements, and that some bureaucratic delays might be inevitable.

Game On

Working backwards from the time at which the first of those ferries – Helsingborg to Helsingor – might open for business, the gallant Super Snipe was actually flagged from the HQ of the Norwegian Automobile Club at 03.00HR, local time, on 2 December. For the next 436 miles, all the way down the coastline of the Skaggerak and the Kattegat, to reach Helsingborg, there was sheet ice, with blizzards sweeping across the road. All this, connected with the darkness, made a transit of 6hr 23min. quite remarkable.

The next few hours were at once boring, and frustrating. First a short delay for the ferry, then a twenty minute sea trip, then a dash through Copenhagen to Korsor, another delay, an eighty minute ferry crossing to Nyborg, followed by the rush to get out of Denmark into West Germany, just north of Flensburg, at the end of the first afternoon.

This was when the sheer grit, the rally-driving expertise, and the outright, unearthly, driving skills of Moss, Johnson and Cutts began to kick in. Some autobahns, now long-repaired after the battering they had received by Field-Marshal Montgomery's tanks in World War Two, were there to be enjoyed, but the Super Snipe still had to cruise through Hamburg, Hanover and Dusseldorf and Aachen, before it could turn west, to make for the nearby Dutch border. Dusseldorf was passed at 09.40HR (still in snowstorms), the car then turned sharply south at Maastricht, entered Belgium just a few miles down the road, then passed through Liege, and ended up at Luxembourg at 3.05PM on the Wednesday. Time for a quick lunch, yet another re-shuffle of drivers, and a long race through France – by way of Metz and Nancy, before crossing into Switzerland at Basel, and making for Italy.

Below: Stirling Moss examining the packed ice which had built up inside the rear wheel arches of the Super Snipe.

Below: David Humphrey, Leslie Johnson, Stirling Moss and John Cutts, adjusting ceremonial flags on the Super Snipe.

Humber Super Snipe: The Fifteen Countries in 90 Hours run

And still it snowed – in fact there was no clear road at all until the Super Snipe got well into Italy. By 10.40PM (Wednesday) they were in Zurich, and then it was time to face the challenge of the Alps. First to Sargans, then abruptly northwards to the Austrian border near Bregenz, a quick U-turn and south again, this time through Vaduz and the tiny principality of Lichtenstein before passing through the Swiss town of Chur.

It was now the middle of the night, the snow was getting deeper by the minute, and the team knew that it would have to fit chains to make the assault on the Julier pass which passed very close to St Moritz. Then, as Stirling Moss wrote in *The Autocar*:

'There had been much argument as to who was going to drive over the Julier; everyone wanted to. In the end it came to the spin of the coin, and I was lucky. The pass is about 7,300ft above sea level, and is kept open, if possible, by snowplough. But the plough had not been through for many hours. Owing to the fairly high wind on the mountainside, the road was buried in places with deep drifts of snow. Many times we had to engage bottom gear to force our way through snow up to 18in. deep. We found the chains a necessity. Anyway, we managed to keep going steadily, crossed the summit, and tried to make up a bit of time going down the other side….'

Suddenly, after that, it all started to seem easier. Having dropped below the snow line, and removed the chains, the crew re-stowed the Super Snipe, and set off to recover time, and distance. First off they made for Bergamo, then joined the autostrada, passed through Verona, Vicenza, and made for Trieste. Having been met by a Rootes agent, they then cruised swiftly through what was then still the 'International Zone', and arrived at the Yugoslavian border.

Here some bureaucracy could have been expected, but as Stirling Moss commented:

Stirling Moss and the crew, waving from the driving seat of the Super Snipe.

'We just rolled the car into Yugoslavia, decided we had seen quite enough, and backed out again smartly…' After that it was time for a return to Trieste, a very welcome lunch, and another dash down the autostrada to Milan, where there was a well-equipped Rootes agent, who had laid on what amounted to an Italian-style banquet – which they did not have time to eat.

Now it was Thursday evening, Lisbon was still four countries away, and there was time to be made up. Refreshed, though still avidly looking forward to a bed, two nights hence in Portugal, the crew then set out on a high-speed dash on wintry, but fortunately clear, roads. By Friday morning at 0.30HR, the Super Snipe had re-entered France, then passed swiftly through Monaco, after which the route led through Aix-en-Provence, Montpellier, Narbonne, and the low road north-east of the Pyrenees to cross the border into Spain between Biarritz and San Sebastian.

A diversion near Aix-en-Provence, where the road was being re-constructed, was ignored, which was unwise, as one section

ROOTES MAESTROS
"In their own words."

was almost impossible (but after storming the Julier pass on chains, it felt like a minor problem!). Then, with customs cleared in not more than 15 minutes, it was time to play racing drivers. It was full daylight, conditions were good, other traffic was sparse, so the 'real racers' – Moss and Johnson – decided to aim for the Spanish/Portuguese border, at Villar Formoso, in less than the four days they had once rather flippantly described as their 'high average'.

Could it be done? After three nights on the road? Without sleep in a bed which wasn't moving or being thrown about? With other traffic to be swept aside? They thought it could, and set about cruising at up to 90mph wherever this was possible, and hoping that General Franco's traffic police would not object. By way of Burgos, Valladolid and Salamanca, they thought it could – and in the end Leslie Johnson drove the final three hours at a running average of 64mph.

In a finish which would have done great credit to any thriller writer, they brought the Super Snipe, now travel stained, and beginning to rattle and groan after all its exertions, to the border in precisely 3days, 17 hours and 59 minutes – just one minute inside their self-imposed 90-hour schedule.

It was a magnificent achievement, made all the more praiseworthy because it was completed without giving any trouble. One punctured tyre had to be repaired but, once again to quote Stirling Moss: 'We just fed it with oil, water and petrol, and pressed on very fast. Many times we kept the speedometer over ninety for a quarter of an hour at stretch...'

This was the intrepid crew of the Super Snipe on its Oslo – Lisbon dash – left to right, David Humphrey, John Cutts, Leslie Johnson and Stirling Moss.

Humber Super Snipe: The Fifteen Countries in 90 Hours run

The anti-climax came the following day. The Super Snipe and its crew were due to be flown back to London, for a reception at Devonshire House, on the Sunday, but could not do so – every available airport in England was locked in under thick fog!

Countries visited, in order:

Norway
Sweden
Denmark
West Germany
Holland
Belgium
Luxembourg
France
Switzerland
Austria
Lichtenstein
Switzerland (again)
Italy
Jugoslavia
Italy (again)
France (again)
Monaco
Spain
Portugal

--- although the publicists did not claim 'Lichtenstein' as one of the countries visited, they did indeed traverse that tiny Principality.

Another magnificent achievement...
LONDON TO CAPE TOWN IN RECORD TIME
10,500 miles
through jungle, swamp and desert in
13 days 9 hrs 6 mins

DRIVERS: G. C. HINCHLIFFE · R. WALSHAW · C. A. LONGMAN

A new HUMBER SUPER SNIPE, straight off the production line, has slashed 8 days 10 hours 39 minutes off the previous best time for this arduous journey, covering 10,500 miles at an average speed of over 32 m.p.h. including stops. A fine performance by car and drivers.

FURTHER CONVINCING PROOF OF THE ENDURANCE, RELIABILITY AND SPEED OF

The NEW **HUMBER** SUPER SNIPE
BLAZING A TRAIL INTO A NEW ERA OF FINER MOTORING

Left: Another crew, another car, another fine endurance drive – garage owner George Hinchliffe's team reached Cape Town, from London, in less than 14 days in a Super Snipe in November/December 1952.

ROOTES MAESTROS
"In their own words."

Another marathon dash

At another time, in another car, the achievements of George Hinchliffe, a garage owner from Bradford, might also have got massive headlines. As it was, in November and December he, and two colleagues – R. Walshaw and C.A. Longman – took another new-model Super Snipe from London to Cape Town (South Africa) in just 13 days, 9hr 6min, by way of the Sahara desert and the forests of Central Africa – which shattered his previous exploit, in a Hillman Minx, which took eight days longer.

This was the route chosen by George Hinchliffe for his Humber Super Snipe dash to Cape Town in 1952, which involved a north-south crossing of the Sahara desert (from Algiers to Kano).

Above: The Hinchliffe crew ready to start the London – Cape Town dash in MRW 208, a Super Snipe presumably loaned to them by the factory.

Left: Just to prove the point – passing through the French city of Lyon on the way to the Mediterranean.....

Lower left: ....typical colonial conditions in central Africa....

Below: ....and time to change a punctured tyre in the sandy wastes of the Sahara Desert.

ROOTES MAESTROS
"In their own words."

Sunbeam Alpine: Record runs in 1953

Norman Garrad could have done without yet another diversion. In November and December 1952 he had fretted away, planning the Humber Super Snipe's '15 countries in 90 hours' escapade. Then, in January 1953, he had planned, and carried out, his team's assault on the Monte Carlo Rally. No sooner had he got back from Monte Carlo than the phone rang. It was the familiar urgent bark of his boss, Sir William Rootes, bursting with a bright idea, and wanting something done at once:

'I've got another task for you Garrad. The new Sunbeam Alpine is being launched in March. We need to make headlines. How can we match the figures set up by the Austin-Healey 100 last winter? Take a car to the Jabbeke Road, and beat their speeds!'

Garrad, with a sigh, realised that he was once again being asked to achieve the impossible. Along with his faithful workshop foreman/engineer Jim Ashworth, he was busy enough, in all truth - but his master had now spoken. There were no such words in Billy Rootes' vocabulary as 'can't be done', or 'no time' – so the job had to be done.

As ever, it would all have to be completed in a great hurry. The new Alpine would originally be intended for export only, would be unveiled at an exhibition in the USA in mid-March, and Sir William's bright idea was for Garrad to have a car set new speed marks on the Jabbeke highway *before* that date ! Who was it who originally coined the phrase: 'The impossible we do at once, but miracles take a little time!'

In the end, it was typical of Rootes' 'can-do' approach that they not only sent a prototype to Jabbeke on 17 March, where it achieved 120mph, but within days the same car was sent to lap the flat-out banked oval track at Montlhery, south-west of Paris, where it completed 111.20mph in an hour.

Horses for courses

So, where and what is/was the Jabbeke Road? You may already have driven along it, or at least crossed its much-developed path, in Belgium, without even knowing it. Any tourist making for Brussels, who has arrived on the European side of the English Channel, either at one of the ports in France, or at Ostend in Belgium, invariably cruises along the E5 motorway which links all those ports with the Belgian capital. Not far from the junction with the coastal autoroute which links Calais with Bruges, and at the junction with the E10 which leads into Ostend itself, is the sleepy little town of Jabbeke – and this is where the story really begins.

Where it *really* began, they say, is with Adolf Hitler, who wanted to make it easier for his Panzer divisions to reach those ports from the flat-lands of Belgium. Having swept all before them in the invasion of 1940, his generals discovered that the roads were by no means as straight and fast as those which had already been completed in Germany. With the object of linking the channel with Brussels, then Liege, and finally to the German border at Aachen, he then set his road builders to work to fill the gap.

As we now know, this was when Winston Churchill jutted his chin, spat out the phrase: 'We shall *never* surrender', and set about

85

ROOTES MAESTROS
"In their own words."

reversing the flood. By September 1944 Allied forces had swept through France, liberated Brussels, and began mopping up German military resistance on the Channel coast itself. Discovering that only a few kilometres of straight, but narrow, dual carriageway road had been completed near Jabbeke, they made it secure, and got on with the rest of the war. In the future, it was clear, more of that dual-carriageway highway should be completed – but not just yet.

If British car makers had not later concluded that they needed to convince the world of the speed of their new cars (but had nowhere in Great Britain to prove their point), we may never again have heard of Jabbeke, nor made that piece of highway so famous (as it was for less than a decade). Somehow, somewhere, and for whatever reason (now lost in the mists of time), it became known that the Jabbeke road might be available for record attempts. At that time, after all, it started nowhere, and finished nowhere, but was undoubtedly straight enough, and long enough, for its purpose.

Still grateful for the way that the Allies had given them back their peaceful future, the Belgian authorities let it be known that occasionally they might be persuaded to close the road to other traffic and let it be used for record attempts, usually early in the morning, so that the tracks could be re-opened later in the day to get that part of Belgium back to its normal state.

As far as we know, this highway was first used by 'Goldie' Gardner in October 1948, to set new high-speed marks in his MG-based EX135 record car. Later, in May 1949, Jaguar sent a prototype XK120 sports car to show off to the media where it achieved 132.596mph. The same company used that piece of road several more times thereafter, and it soon became *the* site for any demonstration, or true two-way speed record attempt.

Even so, it was not until 1953 that Rootes had any model which could be prepared, and modified, up to appropriate speeds at Jabbeke – for Sir William saw no point in sending a saloon (certainly not a Hillman or a Humber, and not even a Sunbeam-Talbot). However, it was Donald Healey's use of the very first prototype Healey (later Austin-Healey) 100, in a cheeky expedition to Belgium in October 1952, which set Sir William to thinking. If Healey's new car, soon to be re-named *Austin*-Healey, could achieve 110.974mph for the Flying Mile, and this was going to be a head-on competitor for sale of the still-secret Sunbeam Alpine, then he wanted Norman Garrad to do something about it.

Raising the performance

'Doing something about it' was a complete understatement for what Garrad needed to do. By aiming for a top speed of 120mph, he would have to raise the new car's top speed by 25mph – the road car, when tested, complete with all road equipment, and the windscreen in place, would reach just 95mph.

Not only that, but he would have only six weeks to work the miracle, as Sir William had made it clear that the record run would have to take place by mid-March, in other words, just before the new model was officially revealed to the public. There was only one solution – his old chum Leslie Johnson, who was also the owner of ERA Ltd., would have to undertake the work for him.

It was that doyen of motoring journalism, Raymond Baxter, who summed up the pressure of what happened next, for he, along with a group of Fleet Street journalists, was going out to watch the Jabbeke attempt:

'As we assembled on the quay at Ostend on the Monday afternoon and watched the

Sunbeam Alpine: Record runs in 1953

very pretty silver-blue car lowered from the ferry, fingers were bitten to the bone even more than usual on such occasions. Here was the crystallization of six-weeks' intensive effort. A new model designed for the overseas sports-car market had been brought up to a very high performance standard in a very short time by the Rootes engineers, working in conjunction with ERA Ltd., in the persons of Leslie Johnson and David Hodkin...'

In the end, three of the team of 'works' drivers – Sheila Van Damm and Stirling Moss at Jabbeke, and (on the following day) Leslie Johnson, then Stirling Moss at the Montlhery race circuit - would be involved, but there was only one car, and only one possible 'time window' for the attempt. Thankfully, not even the weather got in the way - a heavy morning fog in Belgium soon cleared – and the objectives were all achieved.

Garrad (and, equally as important, Sir William Rootes) was aiming for 120mph. As he once growled, after the event: 'People wouldn't have been impressed by 119mph – as far as they were concerned, that would just have meant 110-and-a-bit….'

Until it was allocated for this record run, MWK 969 had already been used as a photographic 'model' for the original launch (at least, that was what the registration plates told us, but who really knows…?), and neither Rootes nor ERA had any experience of this new two-seater. The 'works' 90 Mk IIA' rally cars, and George Hartwell's home-designed two-seater specials, both had their own stories to tell, but neither came close to the performance needed.

ERA, therefore, had three main problems. One was to reduce the aerodynamic drag of the new car, one was to raise the performance of the engine, and the other was to alter the gearing to make sure that the engine would

This was the very first Sunbeam Alpine prototype, as built up at Humber Road in 1952/1953 – later, I understand, converted for use in the 'works' high-speed demonstration runs.

ROOTES MAESTROS
"In their own words."

Above and below: The very first Sunbeam Alpine looking similar, but by no means identical, to the cars which would begin to go on sale in mid-1953.

Sunbeam Alpine: Record runs in 1953

not be over-revving at top speeds. Here is how it was done:

** The 2,267cc engine had to be super-tuned above any level previously seen by Rootes' own engineers, and made reliable enough for sustained high-rpm running. Certainly Rootes had never previously sent 'works' cars out with this sort of performance. By raising the compression ratio to 8.5:1, changing the camshaft profile, and using other forms of magic, ERA pushed up the peak power to 105bhp – which was 25% more than that of the standard power unit.

** Next they had to consider the overall gearing. That of the standard car was 19.9mph/1,000 rpm, which was fine for a car which topped out at 95mph (in fact that equated to 4,770rpm), but to reach 120mph that would mean revving the engine to 6,030rpm, which was both impractical and unachievable. This was an impasse: it was only on 18 February – a month before the runs were scheduled – that an approach was made to Laycock de Normanville, to see if one of their overdrives could be fitted, and used?

Such units were already being tested on Rootes models, for future road car use, so the team knew that the overdrive could, at least, be mated to the existing gearbox. Laycock agreed, the job was done and.... job done. It would soon become optional on Alpine road cars.

** Although the record car was clearly derived from the new road car, visually there were big changes. Not only was the standard windscreen removed, to be replaced by a

By the time MWK 969 was being fettled to run at Montlhery in France, it had already reached more than 120mph on the Jabbeke highway in Belgium. Here team boss Norman Garrad fills the car with fuel, while Stirling Moss merely observes, and awaits his time to drive around the banked track.

Raymond Baxter (kneeling) checks the BBC's sound-recording instruments at the side of the Jabbeke highway, watched carefully by Norman Garrad.

small and shapely cowl ahead of the driver's eye, but there was also a complete aluminium cover above the passenger side of the passenger compartment. Ahead and under the car, a new moulded shape replaced the front bumper, and blended into a full length undershield. As Triumph later discovered (with the TR2 which came to Jabbeke in May) this alone must have been responsible for up to 10mph in added top speed.

Once the fog had been cleared, and an initial misfire had been rectified by cleaning out the distributor points, all was ready for the two-way flat out. There was plenty of space at each end of the marked-out mile, so there was ample time for the car to settle at its new top speed. First of all it was Stirling Moss who had two double runs, his fastest speed being at 120.459mph. Then it was Sheila Van Damm's turn (she had never previously driven *any* car at more than 90mph, by the way….), and she recorded a two-way average of 120.135mph over the two-way flying kilometre.

Along the way, new Belgian national speed records for the 2litre to 3litre class had been established, which was good news all round. Nothing daunted, the car was then taken across northern France to the Montlhery track, and re-prepared for the following day's exploits.

This time it was Leslie Johnson's turn to play superstars, for once the car was warmed up, he settled down to lap the steeply-banked track flat-out, for a full hour, which he completed at 111.2mph. And finally, just to prove that the car had lost nothing on its previous day's performance in a straight line, Stirling Moss jumped back in, lapped at 116mph on a circuit whose high bankings must have scrubbed several mph off the Alpine's ultimate top speed, Sheila Van Damm achieved 114mph (it was the first time she had ever tackled a banked circuit), all of which wrapped up a highly successful couple of days….

Above: Ready to go at Montlhery for its one-hour run. Leslie Johnson is behind the wheel, Stirling Moss gives him encouragement, Norman Garrad (by the front wheel) approves, and David Humphrey (behind Johnson's helmet) finds something very funny....

Left: Johnson at speed on the steep banking of the Montlhery track.

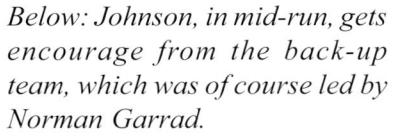

Below: Johnson, in mid-run, gets encourage from the back-up team, which was of course led by Norman Garrad.

ROOTES MAESTROS
"In their own words."

Above: Sheila Van Damm's record sheet showing her timings and speeds at Jabbeke.

Below: Well done! Norman Garrad shakes hands with Raymond Baxter of the BBC, over the head of Sheila Van Damm, who had just reached 120mph in the new Alpine on the Jabbeke highway.

The 'Works' Rapiers: 1956-1964
By Tim Sutton

When the Sunbeam Rapier was launched, the reactions of Norman Garrad and the rest of his Competition Department were not that favourable. That is the legend. The truth is more complicated.

The limitations of the Sunbeam-Talbots as rally cars, could not be ignored. The cars were heavy, and the steering and suspension showed their age. More important for Rootes was that they were increasingly expensive to make.

In the meantime, Rootes had been planning their new monocoque model range for years. The layout envisaged two-door, convertible and four-door saloon/estate versions on a common platform. The first of the new models - the Sunbeam Rapier, not its Hillman Minx and Singer Gazelle stablemates – was launched at Earls Court in October 1955. That the launch date was rushed is confirmed by the fact that dealers did not register any new cars until early 1956.

The new car caused controversy because the Sunbeam Mk III was still a successful rally car. First of all, a Sunbeam Mk III finally achieved the outright win in the Monte Carlo Rally that had so long eluded Garrad and the team, thanks to a private entry from Norwegians Per Malling and Gunnar Fadum. Then, just when the new Rapiers reached the showrooms in early 1956, the Competition Department crowned the old model's illustrious Monte record by winning the Charles Faroux trophy for the third time.

So what exactly had the Competition Department got in the new Rapier, with promise for their future?

The bodyshell was entirely new, and the 1,390cc ohv engine was only a year old, having made its debut in the last of the post-war "Mark" Minxes, the Mark VIII, in October 1954. The motoring press immediately recognised the new model's potential. In its 1955 Motor Show report, under the heading "The Rapier – a new weapon for Rally Drivers?" *Autosport* said:

"Unless we are very much mistaken, rally entry lists – and, maybe, awards lists – will soon bristle with the name 'Rapier', for the new Sunbeam two-door saloon might have been designed specifically for rallying…. With output in excess of 60 bhp… it is expected the maximum speed will be in the region of 90 mph."

It was well into 1956 before Norman Garrad and his team could properly get their hands on the car. On 10 February *The Autocar* reported that 'works' Sunbeam drivers from Stockholm on the Monte Carlo Rally were accompanied by a Rapier which "set the expert drivers of the earlier model a spanking pace which they matched only with difficulty."

Then, in March 1956 *Autosport* recorded that:

"Norman Garrad, Competition manager of Sunbeam, is at present giving a production Rapier a thorough testing on the rougher roads and mountains of France and Italy. If his report is satisfactory, the Rapier will be entered in rallies by the factory."

ROOTES MAESTROS
"In their own words."

How successful they were can be gauged by how quickly the Rapier replaced the Sunbeam Talbot as the club rallyman's mount of first choice. By the 1958 "Monte" fifty-three Series I Rapiers had taken part in serious competition, twenty-seven of them at International level alongside official 'works' team cars: in under two years Humber Road commissioned no fewer than ten official team cars.

Sporting homologation of the original Rapier was obtained in late April 1956, when it had already been announced that the Rapier's debut would be in the Mille Miglia, to be held on 28 – 29 April. Only one car was officially factory-entered, for Garrad's top drivers Peter Harper and Sheila Van Damm, but a second car had been prepared by Rootes, but privately entered and driven by a German crew, Wulf Wisnewski and Fritz Boesmiller. The first 'works' Rapier, therefore, was SHP 745.

The Competition Department made many improvements to the Rapiers, in particular by fitting an extra fuel tank in the boot with a large racing-style filler cap on the top of the rear wing. The cars had a novel air intake system and special cooling ducts for the shock absorbers, and improved breathing through twin carburettor engines. On this occasion, both the cars were prepared by Leslie Johnson's company, ERA Ltd., at Dunstable.

The Rapiers could not hope for outright victory or even high placings, given the exotic and high-powered Grand Prix-derived machinery that drivers like Fangio, Moss and Collins used for this most exciting of road races, but performed very well. The aim was to lead their class, which was achieved, for the cars took first and second in the 1,300 – 1,600 Special Series Touring class. They were in the right order, too, for Harper and Van Damm took first place with the German pair second. Harper's Rapier covered the 207 miler/333 km run to Ravenna in 2 hours, 28 minutes, an *average* speed of 83.8 mph. Overall, Harper's average speed was 66.37 mph and the Germans' 65.07 mph. Sheila Van Damm reported that on many stretches they exceeded 96 mph and the Rapier "clung to those slimy wet mountain bends like a limpet."

A story told to the author (many years later) by David Humphrey about the cars' preparation by ERA is noteworthy. For Humphrey was Norman Garrad's "man on the spot" at the ERA premises. Unhappily, the second car, as originally prepared for the Germans, was written off just four days before the cars were due to be shipped to Italy.

Driver David Hodkin was out testing, at 2.00AM, in the lanes round Dunstable when "the throttle jammed open and he hit an oak tree." Or so he said, though David always suspected that Hodkin had just dozed off at the wheel. Hodkin returned to ERA by taxi; Humphrey made him a mug of tea and asked how bad it was. "You'll have to tell the Competition Manager," said Hodkin. "Not me; you crashed the bloody thing," said David. Then he took pity on the badly-shaken Hodkin, and went out to recover the wreck. Next, and after only two hours' sleep he rang Norman Garrad at home:

"Got some bad news for you. Hodkin's written off the Germans' car."
"You are joking, aren't you?"
"No."
"How bad, then?"
"Well, the front end is pushed back three and a half inches, the suspension's wrecked…"
"Right, you'd better get back here."

On Humphrey's arrival in Coventry, Garrad asked:

The 'Works' Rapiers: 1956-1964

"Well? Where do we go from here?"
"How well do you know the folks at Thrupp and Maberly?"
"Why?"
"Well, I need a complete car, trimmed in the same colours, left hand drive, at Dunstable, today."

He got it, too: Garrad spoke to the famous coachbuilder, which was a wholly-owned Rootes subsidiary (this company painted and trimmed all Rapiers), and the new car was promised for 4.00PM that afternoon. But David Humphrey hadn't finished:

"I'll need a team of men to take it apart, put in all the extra wiring etc [for the extra lights], and rebuild it."

So a minibus was loaded with two bodyshop men, two trimmers and an electrician. Garrad even lent Humphrey his own car, saying:

"Yours will never stand all the to-ing and fro-ing. I want daily reports from you, in person."

"Surely I can phone you?" pleaded David.

"No. I want to see your face while you're telling me how it's going!"

David then organised the men into two shifts with an hour's break for beer and sandwiches at 10.00PM, and found them rooms at a pub near ERA. Garrad even gave him £100 cash to pay for the food and the petrol for his commuting, knowing that "the boy David" was permanently broke....

The replacement car was ready in two and a half days....

There was no official Rootes entry in the Tulip Rally, although a privately-entered Rapier won its class. The next 'works' outing, then, was Sweden's Midnight Sun Rally, held from 29 May – 3 June. This was the first time a British manufacturer had tackled this demanding event, which took the form of road sections linking a series of short special stages run over very rough and narrow gravel roads. Peter Harper and David Humphrey drove one of three Rapiers entered in the event, the other two being driven by Swedish crews, all being standard, Swedish-registered, cars from Rootes' Stockholm main dealer.

Harper, though only fifth in his class, was best British entry, and afterwards wrote in *"The Autocar"* that he had "never driven so hard and never been so late."

It was the 1956 French Alpine Rally, held in July, which provided the first opportunity for an outing by a full 'works' team of Rapiers. All the cars benefited from Mille Miglia tuning and ran in the Special Series Touring category. SHP 745 was of course the re-prepared Mille Miglia car. All had central gear-changes to replace the standard column shift (this was not at all popular with the 'works' drivers – not so much because of any lack of precision, but because the linkages made it more cumbersome than an almost direct change straight into the gearbox. As drivers, Garrad chose this formidable line-up:

SHP 745	Peter Harper/David Humphrey
SHP 510	Jimmy Ray/John Waddington
SWK 400	George Murray-Frame/John Pearman
SHP 323	Raymond Baxter/Leonard Miller

Unhappily, this was a disastrous outing for Garrad's men. The 2,600 mile route took in Yugoslavia for the first time, as well as all the familiar passes in the Alps and Dolomites, and was split into six stages. 79 crews left Marseilles in bright sunshine and, after twelve hours, several cols and a speed test at Monza, tackled the Italian Alps and the passes of Vivione, Tonale, Monte Giovo, Pennes, Gardena, Campolongo and

ROOTES MAESTROS
"In their own words."

Above: The German-crewed Rapier in the 1956 Mille Miglia. This car had been totally rebuilt after an accident while testing, only days before it was due to leave for the event. It finished second in class to the similar car driven by Peter Harper and Sheila Van Damm.

Below: The Sunbeam team setting off for the 1956 French Alpine Rally: (l to r) Norman Garrad, John Pearman, Peter Harper, Raymond Baxter, Leonard Miller, Jimmy Ray, John Waddington. (George Murray-Frame is not shown, nor is David Humphrey).

Above: Raymond Baxter's Series I with the full Works Team line-up in relaxed mood before the start of the 1956 "Alpine". The car was later to come to grief on the descent of the Stelvio.

Below: George Murray-Frame (with pipe in mouth) and John Pearman, making final adjustments to their new Rapier before the start of the 1956 French Alpine Rally.

ROOTES MAESTROS
"In their own words."

Falzarego, where the big problem was to pass other cars or local traffic through clouds of choking dust which masked the corners. This section caused 24 retirements, among them Murray-Frame who took a wrong turning, retraced his steps, and collided with Storez's Porsche (which survived the crash, and eventually finished second overall). Jimmy Ray also went out, when he hit a rock on the Vivione while blinded by dust.

The next three stages did not do any more damage to the 'works', though their first experience of the awful by-roads in Yugoslavia was memorable, with pot-holes and a dirt surface, and a constant cloud of white dust: at this point, Harper's Rapier remained "clean." The fifth stage to Megeve was run in heavy rain, so the passes were shrouded in cloud and the roads were extremely slippery. Baxter skidded on leaving one of the Stelvio tunnels during his descent after the timed climb while Harper failed to achieve his set time on the climb.

The final stage from Megeve to Marseilles included most of the well-known cols in the French Alps, and put paid to Harper's chances for, failing to avoid a lorry that swung in front of him, he went over the edge, landing a few feet down, on a railway line, the right way up with the engine still running. Undaunted, he bounced back onto the road, carrying on with a twisted chassis and a buckled wheel, managing to finish the rally, the only 'works' Rapier to do so. Amazingly, he was still first in the Group II (Special Series touring cars) 1,301 – 1,600 cc class. The privately-entered Rapier of Dr Bill Deane and J.M. Sparrowe won the 1,301 – 1,600 cc class in Group I (Normal Series touring cars).

1957

Normally, the 'works' team would have started their season a full entry in the Monte Carlo Rally, but the event was cancelled in

One of the publicity shots of the two Series I Rapiers being prepared for the 1957 Mille Miglia. The cars have not yet received their re-paint in Monza red.

The 'Works' Rapiers: 1956-1964

the rationing aftermath of the Suez crisis: a 'works' entry in the Tulip Rally, held in May, was also ruled out because Garrad was sending cars to the Mille Miglia.

On the Tulip, though, Jimmy Ray with Ian Hall as co-driver led a strong field of privately-entered Rapiers, in SKV 732, which carried a Coventry registration number. In an event later acknowledged to have been the easiest Tulip to date (and despite encountering very unseasonable freak wintry weather). Ray and Hall had an excellent rally, to finish seventh overall and first in the production touring cars 1,301 – 1,600 cc class. As the year turned out, this would be the Sunbeam Rapier's best showing.

For the Mille Miglia, Rootes prepared two Rapiers, the line-up being:

TWK 2	Peter Harper/Jackie Reece
TWK 1	S Van Damm/David Humphrey

In addition to already-proven modifications, the new cars had engines enlarged to 1,494 cc, larger 10 inch finned brake drums with wider Mintex M20 linings, Dunlop R3 racing tyres, oil coolers, duplicate fuel lines and SU electric fuel pumps, with twin fillers on the extra 20-gallon fuel tank fitted inside the boot, stiffened front and rear springs, Perspex side windows and racing-type bucket seats. David Humphrey confirms that the engines were again prepared by ERA. The two cars were specially painted in a non-Rootes colour, Monza Red, apparently because Norman Garrad believed that Italian level crossing keepers favoured the 'home' teams and hoped that a Rapier approaching at 100 mph might be mistaken for a Ferrari or a Maserati! The idea may have come from BMC, whose MGAs in the 1956 Alpine were reported in the motoring press as being painted red for the same reason. To tell the cars apart as they approached controls and refuelling stops, each had the driver's initial stencilled on the front grille, "P" and "S" respectively.

Sadly, there was no success to match the extensive preparations. Shortly after the start, Sheila Van Damm crashed badly near Verona after getting caught in some tram lines, while Harper/Reece had their throttle linkage break on arrival in Rome. An improvised wooden wedge failed and they

Another Mille Miglia publicity shot that shows how this year the additional fuel tanks had twin fillers.

Daniel Bailly and Rene Binet with the ex-Peter Harper Mille Miglia Series I, wearing a French registration for the 1957 Tour de France. They retired at the end of the second day.

completed the second half of the race with a hastily-improvised hand throttle rigged up with wire and a screwdriver. Nevertheless, after a good run, and cruising for long stretches at 100 mph, they were disappointed to finish only second in the Special Touring 1,301 – 1,600cc class.

With the French Alpine Rally also cancelled, the next appearance of a 'works' Rapier was in the Tour de France. Here was another example of Norman Garrad's budget-stretching expertise, and tapping the interest expressed by foreign crews who would pay their expenses: for the 'works' team was simultaneously occupied with the Viking Rally in Norway.

Daniel Bailly from Amiens and Rene Binet from Montrouge drove the Tour de France car, their Rapier (although re-registered 580 CPG) being Peter Harper's Mille Miglia car. It was not a successful first outing in this, the most demanding of French road events. A privately-entered Rapier retired after one day, and Bailly/Binet followed after Day 2. Norman Garrad would not return to the Tour de France for a number of years.

A more important, more serious, outing was in the Viking Rally, held from 20 – 23 September, where the eventual line-up was:

TKV 338	Peter Harper/Mary Handley-Page*
SKV 732	Jimmy Ray/Bill Bleakley

* Mary Handley-Page being the daughter of a famous aircraft manufacturer.

In addition, George Hartwell had entered a Rapier, co-driven by 'Tiny' Lewis.

TKV 338, it seems, was almost certainly the recce and back-up car used on the Mille Miglia, and was painted in Monza Red while Jimmy Ray, an official Rootes entry this time, had to use his own Rapier – another instance of Garrad getting the most out of other peoples' money.

The "Viking" started in Oslo and over three days and nights took in 1,200 miles including a number of special stages. Unfortunately the event was cut short after 500 miles and only five special stages, following the death of Norway's King

The 'Works' Rapiers: 1956-1964

Haakon. The results were declared, but not allowed to count towards the European Rally Championship. Not that this affected Rootes, for Harper's car retired early on with a blown engine. Jimmy Ray kept his Rapier going without damage, but the best that was achieved was Hartwell's 24th in class.

1958

Two years of intensive development by the Competition Dept had sharpened and honed the Series I, so Rootes hopes were high for the 1958 Monte. Four 'works' Rapiers were entered, all taking full advantage of the rebore tolerances allowed under the Appendix J regulations. Rally organisers chose to interpret the rules according to their event classes which were 1,001 – 1,300cc and 1,301 – 2,000cc, so the Rapiers ran in Group 2, which meant that a tighter time schedule was imposed.

The engines of all four cars were enlarged to 1,430cc by increasing their cylinder bore diameters by 0.040 in. The electrics of the Laycock de Normanville overdrive had also been modified so that it operated on all forward gears. Externally the cars featured a snow deflector on the bonnet, a full width hot air duct close to the screen and a special swivelling roof-mounted Lucas long range lamp. The cars ran on Dunlop Weathermaster tyres and carried two spares with chains already fitted.

Originally, the works entries showed just how determined Garrad was to secure an outright victory: lead drivers were to be Stirling Moss, Peter Collins and Peter Harper; with the ladies crew of Mary Handley Page, Doreen Reece and Lola Grounds. David Humphrey and Francis Scott would accompany Collins, Moss would have Peter Garnier (Sports Editor of *The Autocar*) and Doc Deane; while Harper

Garrad's girls make ready for the 1958 Monte Carlo Rally: (l to r) Lola Grounds, Mary Handley-Page and Doreen Reece.

ROOTES MAESTROS
"In their own words."

The nearly-winners of the 1958 "Monte" check their maps before the start in Oslo. The crew are (l to r) Peter Harper, Peter Elbra and Reg Phillips.

would drive with Peter Elbra (who was a Letchworth schoolmaster) and Reg Phillips from Sheffield.

Unfortunately for Rootes, at the beginning of January it became clear that Moss and Collins would have to race in the Argentine Grand Prix, which clashed, which left Garrad short of two drivers. After a hasty search, two other racing drivers of whom much more would be heard, joined the works team – with Ivor Bueb replacing Collins and Peter Jopp replaced Moss. The final line-up was therefore:

TKV 334	Jopp/Garnier/Deane
TKV 338	Harper/Elbra/Phillips
SXO 222	Handley-Page/Reece/Grounds
TRW 154	Bueb/Humphrey/Scott

The first two cars would start from Oslo while the second two were among the Paris starters.

The January weather proved the worst many competitors had known and emphasised that chance can spoil the most subtle calculations regarding starting points, and the difficulty of various routes. This year, Paris starters were among those worst affected. Early reports confirmed that it was the Paris starters who could expect the worst conditions, for further snow was forecast on top of the icy roads which made the going very tough. Not only that, but six feet of snow was reported to have blocked the Col de Quatre Pas near Mezilhac on the Mountain Circuit.

For the Paris starters, the weather was worst between Gerardmer and Villefranche and

Peter Harper and Peter Elbra on the Mountain Circuit test at the end of the 1958 "Monte". They eventually finished in 5th place after a costly navigation error.

only fourteen crews reached the latter in time, for there had been heavy snowfalls. Gerardmer to St Claude alone accounted for 41 of the Paris starters. The road was littered by vehicles immobilised by damage or by the snow, and it was on this stretch that the ladies had to abandon. The survivors pressed on into the Massif Central and more snow and re-routing around closed cols, but Bueb's Rapier eventually suffered a fuel blockage of one carb after Millau, when the engine ultimately protested and seized, so they too were out of the running.

Oslo starters fared much better, for they arrived in the Jura a day later and escaped the worst of the weather. Their equivalent misery had come on the autobahn after Hamburg, for dense swirling snow and drifts lying on the road made progress desperately slow and enormous lorries added to the difficulties. Jopp's Rapier suffered rear-end damage when rammed by a Volvo, and only just made it to St Claude in time, but Peter Harper, a master on ice and snow, was still without penalty.

A French gendarme caused an unplanned diversion after Chambery, near Tavernolles: Peter Harper who was the first to arrive had to blaze a trail along lanes that were deep in snow, which Jopp's car was able to follow. Yet they made it to Monte Carlo, and qualified for the final classification test, the Mountain Circuit of 650miles/1,077 km. Only nine remained unpenalised on the road sections, with Peter Harper's the only British crew and the sole representative from all the northern starting points. Peter Jopp's car clattered into *parc ferme* with a failed dynamo, but he was able to swap it before starting the final test.

On the Friday night, competitors had to cover the mountain circuit at average speeds of between 32mph and 43 mph. Despite the fuss subsequently made over the setting of easier target averages for Group 1 cars, this was really meaningless, for such were the conditions that average speeds could be held in only one or two places: it soon became a race to see who could be the least number of minutes late. By the second control 13 cars were eliminated because of lateness; by first light only 44 were still running, while the replacement dynamo in Jopp's car failed: he had to lose precious minutes swapping batteries to keep their lights going, but then were too late to continue.

Harper, fastest of all at the end of 16 and a half hours' continuous motoring, brought his all-red Rapier home unscathed and – as he thought - in first place. But he incurred more

ROOTES MAESTROS
"In their own words."

penalty marks than expected, partly because he believed he was running in Group 1 and completed the mountain circuit to those, slightly more generous, times. Norman Garrad's vigorous protests could only move him up from sixth to fifth place when a miscalculation was found in Maurice Gatsonides' road penalty marks.

In fact there was more to this disappointing result than met the eye. Peter Elbra later revealed what really robbed Peter Harper of what should have been an outright victory, and just why Harper may have been going faster than allowed between two of the "secret checks".

"In the 1958 Monte I was the reason why Peter and his works Rapier didn't get first place. When we got to Monte Carlo after the run from Oslo we were in about 4th or 5th place starting the Mountain Circuit. At any rate we started off in about that position on the road. Within very few miles we had overtaken all the previous starters and were first on the road. About two weeks before, we had done a recce of the Mountain Circuit and I had prepared the notes for the whole team (I suppose they would be called pace notes nowadays). Unfortunately for us, there had been very heavy snow in the previous days and a whole section was re-routed as one of the passes originally on the route had been closed and I had no large-scale maps for the new route. In the early hours of the next morning, trying to navigate from a small-scale Michelin map and with no tracks in the snow on the road to indicate our correct route, I made a navigational error at a fork in the road and two or three miles further on we found ourselves in a farmyard. The peasant farmer came out to see what this strange visitor was doing in his farm and I eventually got from him an escape route to rejoin the correct road further along. We were four minutes late at the next control! Things were very quiet in the car for a little while! I apologised to Peter, knowing I had screwed up his chances of a win but he was quite extraordinarily forgiving and said he could equally well have gone off the road to put us right out. Anyway he continued to drive even more brilliantly and we did, in fact, complete all the remaining stages without loss of time, the only competitor to do so. When we analysed our results at the end we realised that, but for my mistake, we would have won. I was not a happy bunny. To their credit, no-one in the team nor Norman Garrad ever mentioned my lapse and my sense of guilt faded. So Sunbeam would have had the outright Monte win they so much wanted – and deserved – but for me!"

So the final results showed Harper/Elbra/Phillips in 5th place in general classification and second in the Series Production Touring Class 1,301-2,000cc. The Swiss pair, Ziegler and Cots, were a worthy eighth in general classification and also second in the G.T. class.

The reason for the immense effort put in to this Monte became clear immediately afterwards, when the new Series II Sunbeam Rapier was unveiled to the press and the motoring correspondents were able to try examples, which had quietly been driven down to Monte Carlo, for themselves along carefully-chosen sunny coastal roads and some snowy mountain roads.

Press reviews of the new model were favourable, and everything boded well for its rallying future. Competition experience had led to notably larger drum brakes, the Burman "J-type" steering box and floor-change for the gearbox – though twin-carburettors and improved manifolding had already been rushed through into production with the so-called "R67" version of the Series I announced back in September 1956. The new model also had the American-

104

The 'Works' Rapiers: 1956-1964

inspired fins. Most importantly, the engine was now to be 1,494cc, with bigger valves and a higher 8.5:1 compression ratio, giving 73 bhp and a 90 mph-plus top speed.

Within weeks, the Series II was in rally action; and this time Peter Harper got the success he deserved. Britain's RAC Rally of Great Britain was held from 11 to 15 March. Rootes entered three Series IIs, and loaned one to *Autosport*. These were the crews:

VRW 471	Jopp/Humphrey
VRW 501	Handley-Page/Grounds
VRW 269	Harper/Deane

- along with the *Autosport* car:

VRW 507	Seager/Phillips

To attract the entries from the Continent, the organisers had dropped the sections of pure navigation. Instead, route card sections took competitors through Wales and then the Lake District, during the first and second nights of the rally, though this was still the "Rally of the Tests". There were 18 in 1958, covering speed, acceleration-and-braking, hill-climbing and manoeuvring, as well as time trials on race circuits.

Once again, wintry weather intervened to make the event the toughest yet – as tough as the Monte, according to some. The Arctic conditions that prevailed suited Harper's uncanny ability to maintain high average speeds on ice and snow, and he brought his Rapier home unscratched at the end of the event, to score a much-overdue outright win.

Out of the 196 starters from Hastings 135 officially completed the course – though few of them even managed to visit every control. Only 15 cars managed to climb Hardknott pass, in the Lake District, and only 82 ever reached Charterhall, the northernmost point of the route. Harper, as is to be expected, completed the 2,000 mile course, visited all 68 controls and, despite the terrible conditions during the nights in the Welsh mountains and the Lake District, kept very near to scheduled time throughout.

It was Harper's performance on the road, rather than the special tests, which told: in fact he made best performance in his class in only two tests but in the other 16 he was always among the best. Circuit tests, in particular, showed early evidence of closeness between the the Series IIs and the Riley 1.5s - a rivalry which became acute when Rapiers took to the race tracks in a serious way.

The weather worsened as competitors penetrated into Wales and the test at Eppynt gunnery range: there was solid ice downhill on the way to the hill-climb at Lydstep, near Tenby. The route turned north, and after Tregaron the cars took to mountain tracks gleaming evilly with ice or shining white with snow: Bwylch-y-Groes brought most of those who attempted the gradient to a standstill. Harper went up and over although many went round instead. The blizzard that hit Blackpool during that afternoon made the following night section north a constant struggle against wet snow with ice patches underneath. The Ulpha test in Lake District was made one of the hardest as a result. After Hardknott (which only 15 cars managed to climb), the route went over Birker Moor and down the steep hill into Ulpha where the acceleration-and-braking test started at midnight. By 10pm there was nearly five inches of snow on the hill, and it was hardly possible to stand on the steep gradient. A hasty re-think allowed re-routed competitors to to climb the hill as far as the 'in' control and return for the test and the 'out' control. But the hill was almost unclimbable and was soon chaotic with wildly sliding cars, the staccato rattle of driving chains, the smell of burning clutches and bouncing huddles

Peter Harper and Bill Deane posing with the impressive Peall Trophy awarded for their outright victory in the 1958 RAC International Rally – a good first outing for the Series II Sunbeam Rapier.

of passengers in luggage lockers, or standing on rear bumpers.

Those who survived all this struggled on to Charterhall for a half-mile sprint, then back via another test on the Otternburn ranges, where the snow had drifted badly and many cars had to be dug out of 2ft drifts. So it continued through Eastern England, for Snetterton at midnight was enlivened by another blinding snowstorm. By Mallory Park on the final morning the snow had gone, and the 'works' Sunbeams went round in team order. At Silverstone, with the rally as good as won, Harper took things gently and lost 15.5 sec against the fastest in his class. Unless anything went wrong during the final test on the promenade at Hastings, a Sunbeam victory looked likely, with Standards holding the team prize. As "Doc" Deane said to Peter Harper: 'All you have to do is not drive into the sea…'

So Peter Harper finally got the outright win he had long deserved – and it was typical of Harper, that when he and Bill Deane, crossing Bowes Moor, came upon the scene of a spectacular accident to the Nancy Mitchell/Joan Johns' Riley – which had gone end-over-end down a fifty-foot slope, they stopped to see what first aid was needed, so that 'Doc' Deane could render professional assistance.

Next stop for the 'works' cars was the Tulip Rally, where Norman Garrad fielded three cars and recalled Jimmy Ray to the team. The line up was thus:

VRW 471	Jimmy Ray/David Humphrey
VRW 501	Mary Handley-Page/Lola Grounds
VRW 269	Peter Harper/'Doc' Deane

The 'Works' Rapiers: 1956-1964

This year the organisers made the event harder, faster and more sporting than ever before. Tough "Special stages" were re-introduced – and of 196 starters fewer than half completed the road section in three days and nights of concentrated motoring: only 24 were unpenalised on the road sections.

There were six starting points - Brussels, Hamburg, London, Noordwijk-aan-Zee, Munich and Paris – which converged at the Nurburgring. The common route took competitors through the Eiffel mountains, the Vosges and Jura into the French Alps before returning through the same mountainous regions to finish as always at Noordwijk-aan-Zee. Included were ten speed tests – speed hill climbs on such places as the Ballon d'Alsace, the Col de Rousset, and the Chamrousse, ranging from 9 to 17km in length, and on the racing circuits of Francorchamps, the Nurburgring and Zandvoort. In addition ten special stages had to be covered at average speeds ranging from 62 to 75 kph.

There was heavy rain during the first night. Road works and a diversion near the Nurburgring caused many cars to arrive late, and this control was ultimately scratched, and snow on the 'Ring made the surface damp and very slippery.

It was already apparent that the Swedish Volvos were faster than anyone had expected and might well upset many calculations. Heavy hailstorms rattled the cars as they made their way through the tortuous Vosges by-roads. A detour to avoid the Col de Schlucht which was blocked by snow added 18km, then a cycle race held up the competitors!

The second night was far tougher – 317.6 miles, from Champagnole to Valence, including a timed climb of the Col de la Faucille in fog, with a little snow. Four more special stages followed, including again the Ballon d'Alsace (where there were snow banks on each side of the road at the summit). At Valence only 100 starters were still unpenalised.

On the next day, three more special stages including a timed climb of the Col du Pins, and then the Col de Rousset – 14km of twisting highspeed climbing with a terrifying drop on the outside. Coming up to the third and last night on the road, the rally moved back towards Belfort and a second climb of the Ballon d'Alsace, on the other side, where the skies turned black again, the rain poured down and the top of the climb was really foggy. The special stage which was to have followed, over the Col de la Schlucht, was cut out as such because snow made the route too difficult, but the following stage – 67 mountain miles with rain and fog prevailing – took a heavy toll: when it was over, only 26 crews were still unpenalised, including the Rapiers of Peter Harper and Mary Handley-Page. Jimmy Ray/David Humphrey struck trouble on this stage, were held up for too long when their throttle seized, and arrived two minutes late at the control.

The long run back to Holland did not significantly change things. The final speed tests at Zandvoort provided some excitement, although Mary Handley-Page could not catch Pat Moss in her Riley 1.5 in order to beat her for the Coupe des Dames. Final results showed that the rally was won by a German-crewed Volvo, while Harper/Deane were eleventh overall. Mary Handley-Page took 20th overall and third in the the Coupe des Dames, and as Ray/Humphrey also finished the team prize went to Sunbeam.

The next event in the calendar was Sweden's Rally to the Midnight Sun, where three Rapiers - two 'works' machines, and one "supported" entry – appeared. The third car was crewed by a Rootes dealer from Kent

ROOTES MAESTROS
"In their own words."

(Alan Fraser) and Robert Holmes, the full line-up being:

VRW 269	Peter Harper/'Doc' Deane
VRW 501	Mary Handley-Page/Lola Grounds
VRW 471	Alan Fraser/Robert Holmes

The Midnight Sun was shortened on this occasion, and comprised a 1,250 mile loop from Saltsjobaden to Ostersund. Three special stages were run on closed roads at very high average speeds, with eight other tests on hills or mere tracks. Only three managed the special stages unpenalised, the winners being Gunnar Andersson/N Elleman-Jakobson in a Volvo. Although Peter Harper drove his heart out, the Scandinavian conditions beat him and he only finished 30th, though highest-placed British entry.

Based on their history, though, Rootes could expect better fortune in their next International event, the French Alpine Rally. The route outlined for 1958, published well in advance, indicated that the "impossible" schedules of the past were now to become routine, and even more difficult to attain.

Rootes, among with the other British manufacturers, took the punishing event very seriously, so Norman Garrad entered five Rapiers. Raymond Baxter was recalled after an interval in which he had crewed for rival manufacturers while reporting as he usually did for the BBC (Raymond thought it unwise to stay with only one team). And there were two racing drivers of repute in the team – twice Le Mans winner Ivor "the Driver" Bueb, and Tommy Sopwith. The full line up was:

VRW 471	Mary Handley-Page/Lola Grounds
VRW 503	Raymond Baxter/David Humphrey
VRW 502	Peter Harper/Peter Jopp
VRW 507	Ivor Bueb/Jimmy Ray
WDU 303	Tommy Sopwith/Bill Deane

In order to maximise the chances of class wins, and success - and to try out further modifications - Garrad entered both modified and unmodified Rapiers. The modified cars were driven by Baxter and Bueb, while Harper and Mary Handley-Page stuck with their familiar production machines which had already served them well.

As *The Autocar* later observed, the general British reader of the motoring press found it difficult to appreciate the severity of the Alpine: for many of the passes covered territory which the normal driver never sees. The Gavia pass in Italy, 25 miles of motoring on a rutted track very little more than a car's width, to one side the irregular jagged rock face, to the other the valley floor, which could be more than a thousand feet below, was a typical example. In 1958 there were 70 listed, named cols which Alpine competitors had to cover, no fewer than 47 in the last section from Megeve.

The field was small – only 56 starters – of which only 33 cars reached the second rest halt at Megeve. Clean sheets were reduced to ten as the crews still in the running set off on the marathon last stage. Once again the timed hill-climb on the Stelvio Pass (still open to tourist bus and car traffic!) once again ended Raymond Baxter's drive, this time with engine trouble. Earlier, at the Chatelard checkpoint, Sopwith completed a phenomenally quick change of front brake shoes, while Harper cut holes in his Rapier's steel floor to get at a faulty overdrive solenoid – it only functioned when dealt shrewd blows with the jack handle. At Gap, George Hartwell and Peter Harper both squeezed time to adjust their brakes again.

Above: The full Works Team line-up for the 1958 Alpine Rally: (l to r) Peter Jopp, Peter Harper, Bill Deane, Tommy Sopwith, David Humphrey, Raymond Baxter, Mary Handley-Page, Ivor Bueb, Lola Grounds and Jimmy Ray.

Below: Peter Harper and Peter Jopp in their Series II approaching the summit of Passo di Gavia on their way to a class win and a Coupe des Alpes in the 1958 "Alpine".

ROOTES MAESTROS
"In their own words."

Above: The Series II Rapier of Sopwith and Deane receiving some attention from the Competition Department mechanics during the 1958 "Alpine". They finished second in class and missed out on a Coupe des Alpes by less than a second.

Below: Mary Handley-Page and Lola Grounds after the end of the 1958 "Alpine", both driver and car looking travel-weary. They missed out on the Coupe des Dames but finished 16th overall and 4th in class.

The 'Works' Rapiers: 1956-1964

Indeed, Harper had been making enough time to change two brake shoes at four consecutive controls. Not that it was all good news, for Bueb/Ray bounced their car off a lorry and went through a brick wall on the way down the Col de la Cayolle, on the final day's run.

In the end, just 25 cars clocked in at Marseilles on the Saturday afternoon to finish the rally within permitted lateness limits, all with penalty marks incurred in at least two places. The final speed test took place on the circuit of J-P Wimille in Marseilles where most drivers were merely intent on finishing. Tommy Sopwith, however, relished the chance of some real racing and put his Rapier round so fiercely that everyone watching doubted that it would even complete the test – but it did. Perhaps this was consolation for him missing out on a Coupe des Alpes by just four-fifths of a second.

In the end, just seven Alpine Cups were awarded, three for Britain including Harper and Jopp, and in the general classification, Harper/Jopp were 6th and Sopwith/Deane 9th. In European Championship terms, Andersson's Volvo had retired on the final night with braking problems that led to a crash, so Harper closed the gap to just two points.

The Liege-Rome-Liege followed in August, starting and finishing at Spa in Belgium, going nowhere near Rome, and deserving the reputation of being the toughest of all the International Championship events. In 1958 it was the longest and roughest post-war event, 3,340 miles/5,320 kilometres through Germany, Austria, Italy, Yugoslavia and France – all run in one continuous stage of 96 and a half hours! All the familiar Alpine and Dolomites passes were included, with some unpleasant surprises and two hundred miles of Yugoslav roads that were far worse than anything else. Only 22 of the 98 starters would eventually be classified.

Rootes had not previously entered this event, but to help his drivers' chances in the European Championship, Garrad decided to enter two Rapiers, for Harper and Handley-Page. Unhappily, Harper was unable to start, so his car was loaned to David Mackay and David Lewin of Australia. Handley-Page was accompanied by a new co-driver, Bobbie Wilton-Clark. The event began with a run through the Black Forest towards Kaiserslauten where there was a tricky junction to get onto the autobahn and where the girls, along with a number of other crews, took the wrong way. Inexplicably, they did not realise their mistake for many miles and had to make up 300 miles to reach the Munich control on time, which was impossible. Although Mackay/Lewin finished the course, they were 19th out of the 22 finishers.

Attention quickly shifted, therefore, to the next outing which was Norway's Viking Rally, where Rootes entered three Rapiers from the UK, registered VRW 269, VRW 503 and WHP 998. Peter Harper, with Jimmy Ray as his co-driver, was hoping for sufficient Championship points to beat Andersson's Volvo. Mary Handley-Page drove another car, while the third car was driven by Carsten Johansses, twice previous winner of the Viking.

The route took in some of Europe's worst roads and some of its most beautiful mountain scenery. The first night was spent in the mountains, and with the change of scenery came a severe change of temperature, which dropped to 2 deg F. On the first test, Rootes's first set-back occurred when Handley-Page's car had a puncture and lost six minutes.

The final test on the Sunday morning was a high speed slalom round oil-drums on a

111

The Team cars and some of the British drivers at the local Rootes dealership in Newcastle before leaving the Tyne by boat for Oslo, and the 1958 Viking Rally. Mary Handley-Page, Jimmy Ray and Lola Grounds pose with Minories Garage and Rootes personnel.

disused wartime German airfield outside Oslo.

72 of the 122 starters made it to the finish, but it was a disappointing event for Rootes, as the ladies were involved in an accident which put them out of the rally, while Harper/Ray, though the highest-placed British crew, could only finish tenth overall.

Norwegian crews in Volvo PV444s took first, second, fourth and fifth places in general classification, which signalled decisively that it was still impossible for British cars and crews to make much impact on the Scandinavians on their home ground.

1959

As usual, the Monte was run in January, and though one day shorter than usual, promised to be no less difficult. Stockholm replaced Oslo as the northernmost starting point, and Warsaw was added to the options. For his 'works' team, Garrad recalled Ronnie Adams while Mary Handley-Page's new co-driver was Daphne Freeman. Ivor Bueb got his second drive, while Peter Harper once again teamed up with Jimmy Ray. Works-prepared cars were again provided for *Autosport*, for Gregor Grant and Irishman Brian McCaldin, and for John Cotter of ITN. There was also some help for Courtenay Edwards, motoring correspondent of the *Daily Mail*, driving a Rapier which David Mclaren had won in a prize competition the newspaper had staged. To provide some experience David Humphrey was third-crew, no doubt to ensure that their experience provided favourable publicity. Finally, the Swiss pair, Geneva Rootes dealer Henri Ziegler and Jean Gretener, took a sixth car. This was the full line-up:

VRW 502	Peter Harper/Jimmy Ray
VRW 503	Ivor Bueb/Francis Scott
WVC 222	Ronnie Adams/Ernest McMillen
VRW 471	Mary Handley-Page/ Daphne Freeman/Joyce Howard

Peter Harper photographed in Athens before the start of the 1959 "Monte". He and Jimmy Ray failed to finish after getting stuck in a deep snowdrift south of Chambery.

WHP 998	Henri Ziegler/Jean Gretener
VRW 507	Gregor Grant/Brian McCaldin
WVC 202	Courtenay Edwards/David McLaren/David Humphrey
VRW 269	John Cotter/D Harris

Starting point choice was widespread. Peter Harper started from Athens, the *Autosport* crew chose Warsaw, the Swiss pair started from Lisbon and the rest from Stockholm.

The equipment had been improved in some respects, for co-drivers now benefited from a (Humber Super Snipe-type) Reutter-style reclining seat and a shoulder-only safety belt, while the driver's had 'bucket'-type seats to provide much better support. Externally, the Department had standardised on a single large bonnet vent to direct hot air onto the screen along with a large vertical Perspex snow deflector a bit further down the bonnet. Inside the cabin, more Perspex kept the hot air from the heating system and two Lucas electric screen demisters directed onto the screen itself. Some of the cars also had the Lucas roof-mounted swivelling spotlamp.

The organisers set a 35mph average, including all stops. Different routes came together at Chambery, for a common route to Monte Carlo. Before that came a new section from Saint Flour in a wilderness of mountains down to Altier and back to Le Puy, and the cross-country run northwards to Dole was on winding roads where passing was difficult.

The final run from Chambery was expected to decide the whole classification, for the route wound over secondary roads and passes, among the Alps of Savoy, Dauphiny and the Alpes Maritimes, with controls at frequent intervals, and "secret checks" set up at undisclosed sites. Athough the route itself was known, detail practising was impossible because no one knew the length of each section. After an overnight rest in Monte Carlo, the qualifying crews faced a Classification Test, a 270-mile mountain

ROOTES MAESTROS
"In their own words."

route with the siting of the controls known only once they reached Monte Carlo.

From Warsaw the road to Danzig and Gdynia was mostly covered by hard packed snow, though the going was easier from Gdynia to Poznan, and Poznan to Slubice, covered in daylight, was the easiest and shortest section.

From Stockholm, there was sheet ice and packed, rutted snow right through Scandinavia and across Germany. Starters from Stockholm and Warsaw joined forces at Hanover and faced a nightmare trip on the autobahn from Hamburg. To the amusement of the *Autosport* editor, Ivor Bueb had acquired a genuine Stockholm "Taxi" sign, while both he and co-driver Scott sported badges of the local hackney-drivers' association.

The ladies' Rapier fell victim to a slippery section in northern Italy, going off the road and hitting a tree. Bueb and Scott came to their aid, and got them to hospital, but still reached the Brescia control on time.

The northern starters reached France during the night, experiencing a blinding snowstorm on already frozen roads which made Mont Genevre slippery and dangerous to climb. Among those observed embedded in a 10-foot snowdrift was the Rapier of Courtenay Edwards/David Humphrey and the irrepressible winner of the Daily Mail competition. Masters of ice-dicing such as Peter Harper and Ronnie Adams were in their element, but fifteen Stockholm starters failed to reach Chambery in time.

Even so, it was the last 300 miles from Chambery, which took the greatest toll. Peter Harper's and Jimmy Ray's rally ended here, when they moved over to let Gatsonides' Triumph go through, and dropped down a steep decline.

Although 184 cars were eligible for the final classification test, which was run to strict regularity rules, the worst feature whigh followed was what looked like cheating by some teams. As Gregor Grant later wrote, calling it "the rally of the

The Series II Rapier won, along with an entry in the 1959 Monte Carlo Rally, by David McLaren in a "Daily Mail" competition. Courtenay Edwards from the newspaper and David Humphrey from the Competition Department handled the driving.

This posed pre-rally shot shows Mary Handley-Page, Daphne Freeman and Joyce Howard making cold-weather adjustments to their Series II before the 1959 Monte Carlo Rally.

Stopwatches":

"…I feel perfectly justified in stating…. that unfair methods were adopted in imparting information to certain competitors. Several cars bearing rally plates (and not in the test at all) were driven round the opposite way of the circuit and were able to spot the situation of vital controls. As the Swiss entrants Ziegler and Gretener will confirm, their Sunbeam was halted by a group of people…. but hurriedly waved on when it was discovered that they were not driving the marque which the people obviously supported. It was more than a coincidence that a passage control was situated a few kilometres further on."

Despite Harper's demise, for Rootes it had been another good Monte, for Adams and McMillen were fifth overall and Bueb/Scott 16th, and Ziegler and Gretener 23rd. Adams was also third in his capacity class.

Next came a real innovation for the 'works' team, which prepared a team of Hillman Huskies for the East African Coronation Rally, these cars being readied for Peter Harper, Peter Jopp and, in his first drive for the 'works' team, Paddy Hopkirk. Although these cars were not Rapiers, the experience would be useful in future. This year there was no success and, worse, Peter Harper overturned his Hillman Husky and broke his left arm, which put him out of action for many months.

The next Rapier entry came in the Tulip Rally which, on this occasion, started from Paris. Three Rapiers started, driven by Mary Handley-Page/Daphne Freeman, Jimmy Ray/Ian Hall and Peter Jopp/Francis Scott. This turned out to be the most difficult 'Tulip' so far held, with only five crews retaining clean sheets, a remarkably low figure for a Championship rally.

The imposed schedule was a real shock, for it entailed almost continuous motoring to hold a 60kph average, all made considerably more difficult by secret controls, and regularity checks. Special tests were arranged on Tulip 'favourites' at Clermont-Ferrand, Col du Pin, Mont Ventoux, Col Bayard, Chamrousse, Cote de

Above: Final checks and adjustments before the start of the 1959 Alpine Rally. Ronnie Adams (standing, right, with Kenneth Best in front of the Competition Department's new service "barge") was to suffer a serious accident in VRW 269 during this event, which was otherwise very successful for the Rapiers.

Below: Jack Scott looks out from the Series II Rapier he shared with Paddy Hopkirk on the 1959 "Alpine". They finished third overall and first in class.

The 'Works' Rapiers: 1956-1964

Givrins, Ballon d'Alsace, Pont de Misere and Spa-Francorchamps – and the final races at Zandvoort.

On the way south, in awful conditions, Jimmy Ray's Rapier broke its differential, while Mary Handley-Page hit the parapet of a bridge and then lost five minutes beating the wing clear of the wheel. Before that, on a steep climb towards St Julien with numerous hairpins, only Peter Jopp managed to complete the test on time. Later, for the night climb of that Tulip favourite, the Ballon d'Alsace, for the first time in many competitors' recollection, there was no cloud at the top.

Ninety-three crews made it all the way back to Noordwijk and the five-lap races at Zandvoort, including the remaining two 'works' Rapiers and a couple of privately-entered ones (one of them driven by Peter Procter). In the race for 1,600cc class cars, Gunnar Andersson's Volvo was easily in front all the way, though Peter Jopp and Peter Procter had a good scrap with another Volvo.

Once again, therefore, the Competition Department looked forward to the Alpine Rally (to be held in June) for encouragement. This time, the 'works' team would return with one of the very best results they could have anticipated. For 1959 the organisers had introduced a handicap system which favoured saloon cars and this duly provided a decisive win for small French machines.

Garrad was forced to make further changes to the team - for neither Mary Handley-Page nor Peter Harper were fit - so female interest was represented by Patricia "Tish" Ozanne, who co-drove for Ivor Bueb. Ronnie Adams inherited Peter Harper's old car VRW 269, accompanied this time by oil company competitions manager Kenneth Best; well-known racing driver Les Leston joined Peter Jopp in a new car, while Paddy Hopkirk was partnered by his usual navigator Jack Scott.

The full line-up was thus:

WHP 998	Ivor Bueb/Tish Ozanne
VRW 269	Ronnie Adams/Kenneth Best
VRW 503	Peter Jopp/Les Leston
VRW 507	Paddy Hopkirk/Jack Scott

In total, 58 cars and crews started out on an opening stage which was much easier than expected, especially as several Italian passes had now all been tarred and at an average of only 50 kph, most drivers had a comfortable margin in hand. However, if they were lulled into any sense of security, the second stage from Cortina to Merano soon dispersed it. The early section in Austria, 51.5 km from Obertilliach to Oberdrauburg, was in the true "Alpine" tradition: narrow, dirt roads, with no straights, steep, short climbs, with innumerable hairpins and no chance to unleash the cars' real power except in the 13 km run-in over tarred roads, which, however, included 14 hairpins. Although the Hopkirk/Scott and Jopp/Leston Rapiers cars were still "clean", Ronnie Adams and Ivor Bueb missed out owing to brake troubles.

With the dreaded Gavia pass blocked by snow, the third stage was easier and interest centred on the results of the timed climbs of the Stelvio and Vivione psses, the Vivione being a small car benefit: on the loose-surfaced road, under 10ft wide, and with no straights of more than about 15 yards, a large car, with power, was a handicap. The final stage, St Gervais to Cannes, covered most of the passes in the French Alps, at high average speeds. On the run in to the Col des Aravis Ronnie Adams, baulked unexpectedly by a French lorry, hit the concrete posts at a level crossing, completely demolishing the side and rear of the bodywork, reducing the famous old Rapier to scrap. Some strong rope was needed to keep it all together to the end!

ROOTES MAESTROS
"In their own words."

Above: Aftermath of Ronnie Adams' incident at a level crossing on the 1959 "Alpine". The car was subsequently re-created by the Competition Department.

Below: Paddy Hopkirk and Jack Scott pose with their Series II and their Coupe des Alpes after finishing third overall and first in class in the 1959 "Alpine".

The 'Works' Rapiers: 1956-1964

Dawn came up over the Col de la Cayolle where the remaining crews also faced a 100-mile test over the Cols de St Michel and Allos. By then, the Hopkirk/Scott Rapier, consistently the fastest team car, had crept up to third place. Final sections took everyone through the heat of Provence to the Ventoux, and 27 survivors (of which 20 were British) made it to Cannes.

Not only did Hopkirk and Scott take 3rd overall and win their class, Jopp and Leston finished 6th overall and second in class: both also won Coupes des Alpes for penalty-free runs. Sadly this was to be the last 'works' entry for Ivor "the Driver" Bueb, who died in August following an accident in a Formula 2 race.

Because Peter Harper was still not fit, after his African accident, and could not rejoin the team for Liege-Rome-Liege, while Mary Handley-Page was also still absent, Rootes entries were made for Jopp/Leston (VRW 503), Hopkirk/Cecil Vard (VRW 507) and Jimmy Ray, this time partnered by Coventry estate agent Mike Cotton in WHP 998.

As ever, this was the last of the great road-racing rallies, where any time lost had to be made up, for even a second's lateness could mean eventual exclusion; there were no handicaps or formulae and no secret checks, but a continuous 90 hours on the road: 97 cars started what was to be seen as the toughest post-war rally to date.

All three Rapiers remained unpenalised for the run into Yugoslavia. 78 crews (48 unpenalised) crossed the border; and 41 returned, but only eight were unpenalised, for appalling roads, potholes, wash-board, loose gravel and deep ruts put a great strain on the cars and crews. The organisers intended the Dolomite sections to be the worst in the event, but before then the run from Predil to Dont eliminated more crews than any other section. It was on that section that the Hopkirk/Vard Rapier was eliminated, but the Gavia was not such a challenge as usual, and the Vivione was in the middle of a long section, so there was no need to hurry over it.

Twenty-nine cars entered France still in the running, but only 14 left it – the smallest number ever on this event. The organisers had planned that the final decisive selection should be made on the Col d'Allos and the Col de l'Echarasson, but additional difficulties eliminated half the crews still running, when the police at Gap refused passage through the town on account of a fair. Final clearance for a route, 18km longer but over more difficult roads and set in the same time, was obtained under a week before the event started.

This made for an incredibly difficult final night. The section from Digne to La Morte proved murderous in nature as well as name, for the Jopp/Leston Rapier had to retire with brake troubles, yet the sole survivors, Jimmy Ray and Mike Cotton, lost only 12 minutes. The climb of Col Luitel was not "on" for any crew as it was partially hidden under low cloud. After St Jean-en-Royans came the long but easy run up through France to Spa. Only 14 crews out of 97 finished, all penalised, among them the sole surviving Rapier of Jimmy Ray/Mike Cotton, which came 4th overall in the Touring category and won a well-deserved class victory.

Fortunately for Rootes, there was a long interval before the final, major event of the year, the RAC Rally in its new November slot in the calendar. Peter Harper returned to the team, so Garrad was able to field a strong entry though, even though the new, Series III, Rapier had been launched, it was not yet ready to appear. For this event the three Rapiers were crewed by:

VRW 503   Peter Jopp/Les Leston
VRW 507   Paddy Hopkirk/Jack Scott

ROOTES MAESTROS
"In their own words."

WHP 998   Peter Harper/Peter Procter

In addition there was a strong representation of Rapiers among the private entrants, one of them being 'Codger' Malkin and Graham Robson in WWK 1.

Much about the RAC Rally was new in 1959. The controversial night navigation exercises were eliminated from a 1,900 miles route which containing sections, in the Lakelands, Scotland and Wales, designed to match anything the Europeans could have set. Organisers hoped that the rally would be won on the road, despite the number of special tests and speed events which were included as usual. It was unfortunate, therefore, that the rally had to end in real controversy, where Championship fortunes hinged on a decision - whether the snow-blocked road in the Grampians should have caused the Braemar control to be scrubbed.

As usual, the start was in Blackpool but the real challenge began in the Yorkshire Dales, where fog made conditions hazardous. Fog also abounded in the Lake District, where Hardknott claimed several victims. There was still very little ice on the roads, though a torrential downpour at Charterhall made conditions appalling for the speed test there. After a halt at Peebles, the route wound its way through Glasgow to the climb of the Rest-and-be-Thankful.

The roads to the Western Highlands were completely snow-free but covered rough terrain, and the high road to Inverness was swept by a gale which threatened to blow cars off the road. At Garvie, locals warned of heavy snow in the Cairngorms and that the road over to Braemar would be chancey – yet there were no official instructions at this juncture. Local knowledge proved spot-on, though initially the roads were bone-dry, while Tomintoul village was completely snow-free. Those cars that continued into the mountains then encountered snowdrifts, and met cars returning, who had abandoned the attempt: for the the road was completely blocked. Only 16 crews booked in at Braemar - all of them very late - and then took the very difficult road over the Devil's Elbow to Blairgowrie. These included Malkin/Robson, who were having an excellent run, as well as Jopp/Leston, though not Harper or Hopkirk.

The long main road sections into Wales were uneventful, and the really difficult road sections ended in South Wales, where fog added to the hazards. The final stages on main roads into England, enlivened by the tests at Prescott and Brands Hatch were easier for most, though the unfortunate Hopkirk broke his transmission and had to retire from the rally with only a few miles left to go.

At the end of the rally, only 53 of the original 131 starters had survived. Rootes had done well, but not well enough, for Jopp/Leston were 9th overall. Team cars had all been pipped by the private entrants, Malkin and Robson, whose excellent run brought them in 5th overall, and second in class.

Then came the aftermath, which was dominated by protests from some crews. Should the Braemar and Blairgowrie controls have been scratched from the results because the intended route via Tomintoul had been impassable? The process went on for weeks, but the protests were finally rejected, and the results stood. However, for collectors of "what might have been" stories, *Autosport* calculated the effect on the results had the protests been upheld. Not only would Jimmy Ray's Alpine have been third overall, but Harper/Procter would have been fourth, and Jopp/Leston 11th. However, because they had lost time in Yorkshire and Wales, Malkin/Robson would have slipped well down the lists!

So ended 1959, with fewer wins in aggregate for the Competition Department than in 1958. The pace of development of the rival

The 'Works' Rapiers: 1956-1964

cars in the 1,600 cc class and the increasing dominance of Volvo had also become apparent, while the front-wheel drive Saab had also begun to make its mark. With the changing attitude towards rallying of the public and the authorities, particularly in France, and the constant upgrading of the roads themselves, made commentators such as John Gott gloomily observe that:

"1959 may well mark the end of a great era in the classic rallies – an era of events which were basically nothing more than long-distance road races over Europe's best-known mountain passes. With the steady increase in traffic not only are such events becoming more dangerous, but the roads themselves are steadily being improved. Only a few years ago passes such as the Pordoi, Falzarego, Galibier and Forclaz were little better than steep, loose-surfaced tracks over which only a top driver on a good car could hold a 60kph average. Today, not only is the average speed rightly reduced in the interests of tourist traffic, but the passes are magnificently engineered main roads with impeccable surfaces…"

With the character of the sport changing, and the chances of high-profile outright victory probably reducing, how would the Competition Department respond? Racing was gradually to become almost as important as rallying for Rootes in the next few years.

1960

To start the new season, the Competition Department prepared a new fleet of entirely new Series III Rapiers, pensioning off the Series II's. The new car was still in 1.5 litre form but had the new aluminium cylinder head (originally developed for the Alpine) which increased peak power to 73bhp; front disc brakes (a great improvement, and welcomed by the drivers), and the closer-ratio gears first seen in the Alpine. Registered YWK 1 through to YWK 5, these were always hard-worked, and were to become as well-known as the consecutively-numbered Sunbeam Alpines of the Sunbeam-Talbot era had been.

Because CSI Appendix J regulations had been revised during 1959 to outlaw the Special Series Touring and Grand Touring cars from all International events, apart from the usual modifications to seating, electrics and heating/snow-clearing, the new cars were running in basically standard form. For the Monte Carlo Rally, they also ran on new-type Dunlop "Duraband" radial-ply tyres with improved steel studs.

For the Monte Carlo Rally, Norman Garrad served notice on the other works' teams that he meant business in a big way for 1960, by fielding six of the new cars. Five crews were as expected, while a sixth car was driven by Gregor Grant of *Autosport*. David Humphrey continued as a 'riding mechanic' for "novelty" crews, accompanying Philip Fotheringham-Parker and the playwright Ted Willis in one of old ex-works Series II's, while John Cotter of ITN, with ATV's production Controller Bill Ward and cameraman Jackie Howard, was again given use of VRW 269 – but thus time a re-shelled car, with the old identity of the machine which Ronnie Adams had crashed so badly on the 1959 French Alpine.

This was the full line-up:

YWK 1	Peter Jopp/Les Leston
YWK 2	Ronnie Adams/Ernest McMillen
YWK 3	Paddy Hopkirk/Jack Scott
YWK 4	Jimmy Ray/Bill Bleakley
YWK 5	Peter Harper/Raymond Baxter

ROOTES MAESTROS
"In their own words."

"Chains or studs, sir?" Crews were to need the best of both on the 1960 Monte Carlo Rally. Here, Jimmy Ray checks all is secure in the boot of his Series III Rapier, YWK 4, before the start.

YHP 288	Gregor Grant/David Dixon/Michael Durnin
VRW 503	Philip Fotheringham-Parker/David Humphrey/Ted Willis
VRW 269	John Cotter/Bill Ward/Jackie Howard

Among the large number of privately-entered Rapiers, were the Swiss pair Werner Lier and Heinrich Walter and two Jaguar apprentices, Stephens and Corbett, who chose a Rapier for their first attempt at an International rally.

To equalise the odds concerning road conditions from different starting points, Garrad sent Harper/Baxter and the *Autosport* crew to start from Frankfurt; Ray/Bleakley from Paris; Adams/McMillen and the Swiss pair from Lisbon; Hopkirk/Scott and Jopp/Leston from Oslo, while the ITN and 'playwright' crews both started from Glasgow.

This event was a severe test of crews and cars, at Chambery, where the common route commenced, only 63 competitors out of the 169 survivors were still unpenalised: by the time the event reached Monte Carlo only ten could claim clean sheets. This year, Athens starters were hard hit, for they encountered blizzards and floods in Greece and Yugoslavia. The Warsaw starters got the best

The 'Works' Rapiers: 1956-1964

of the weather (which was a help to the Mercedes-Benz team, who ultimately won).

Nothing was predictable. Oslo starters originally found that the weather was more like Monte Carlo than Scandinavia and there was no snow: then, by the time the rally was to start, a heavy fall of snow had turned Oslo into a true Monte start after all. After crossing the frontier into Sweden, crews had to change to the left-hand side of the road, the snow became much deeper, with ruts to make things more difficult.

Then, on the autobahn between Hanover and Frankfurt, where heavy lorries lay all over the place, competitors had to drive along the central reservation of the dual carriageway, then cross to the wrong side in order to get past. However the time allowance to reach the Hamburg control was generous, where the British contingent was all present and correct and none had incurred penalties. In the forest areas round Nurburgring the snow was very deep, although the weather in Northern France was much better than expected, in direct contrast to the St Claude to Chambery stage which followed, where icy roads and fog caused many delays.

For the Frankfurt starters, more heavy snowstorms were experienced. Cars were skidding and sliding about in all directions, with Gregor Grant (who was no mean driver) recording that: "It was most enlightening to be whistling along at around 120kph when my crew of David Dixon and Mike Durnin pointed out that pedestrians could not stand up on the icy roads." Fortunately the new steel-studded Dunlop Duraband tyres gave excellent grip, and were a good advertisement for the tyre company.

From the 'Ring to Liege, through the Ardennes, more snowstorms were experienced accompanied by slippery roads. On the way out of Liege, Gregor Grant slid the *Autosport* Rapier on an icy road, ending up in a field, where the car was driven out up a steep bank and a front wheel was changed.

Grant's record of the following sections, up to his eventual retirement, gives a good feel for the conditions he and Peter Harper/Raymond Baxter were encountering:

"It was easy going to Luxembourg, but care had to be taken on icy roads. More icy roads were encountered in the Moselle, and some parts of the Vosges were quite tricky, with snow-covered roads most of the way to the passage control at Colmar. This was followed by the treacherous Col de la Schlucht to Gerardmer, where Ronnie Noble and his BBC television crew gave us all quite a reception. All arrived within the time allowance, and then set off on the long haul to Cambrai where it was raining push-rods. We had the wretched luck to have a tyre burst a few kilometres from the start; much time was lost changing a wheel, as the spare had its chains in place and great difficulty was experienced in loosening the retaining clips. Black ice rather defeated an attempt to get to Boulogne on time, where we clocked in two minutes behind schedule. We now had no spare wheel so decided to go on to Blois where David Hiam of Dunlop's had the punctured tube replaced. Many parts of this route were slippery and a high wind on the road to Abbeville tended to blow the smaller cars off-course. The road to Bourges was fairly easy, but once in the Massif Central the fun really started. David [Dixon] got into a slide going down a slushy and icy hill out of La Courtine and the Rapier shot over a bank and came to rest in deep snow at an acute angle. It looked impossible to retrieve, but other competitors rapidly came to our aid. Despite the risk of lateness, these sportsmen pushed and tugged in an effort to get us back on the road, and also lent a hand when Frank Ward's MGA dived into a ditch on the opposite side. It was to no avail, and

ROOTES MAESTROS
"In their own words."

our car was later retrieved by a party of people from La Courtine, and Peter Easton/John Whitmore, whose Sunbeam Alpine had pranged at Usset, also came up to lend a hand. Considerably behind time, we diced on to Mauriac, but later had to abandon owing to wiper failure caused through some untraceable short circuit."

Glasgow starters, who had endured a Force 8 gale on their Channel crossing, found wintry conditions in the mountains after Bourges; and 27 carried penalties by the time the Figeac control was reached.

Although details of the common route from Chambery to Monaco had been published long before the rally, the situation of the controls and the average speed imposed were not made known in advance, but revealed at Chambery. The section was skilfully planned to tax crews to the uttermost: of the 63 crews which left Chambery with "clean sheets", including Hopkirk/Scott and Ray/Bleakley, only nine reached Monaco still unpenalised, none of them Rootes crews.

This had been an epic struggle against the elements, and meant that the rally would be decided on a 350-mile regularity test, where results on the run to Monaco meant little, provided that one qualified for that test: in fact, the Mercedes-Benz cars which finished first, second and third started the Mountain Circuit in 20th, 47th and 33rd place respectively). Crews well placed at Monaco included Adams/McMillen and Ray/Bleakley. Peter Harper and Raymond Baxter were also in with a chance, starting the test in 24th place, despite the loss of about nine minutes at Chambery, due to being involved in a collision with another vehicle when Raymond was driving. There was a set back for the 'works' team when the Paddy Hopkirk/Jack Scott Rapier left the road and was stuck in the snow.

The 92 highest-placed competitors took part in the final two-loop Mountain regularity Test: the most objectionable feature of the previous year's Test - secret checks whose whereabouts were not divulged until after the results were posted - was absent; this time round, crews were stopped at unannounced secret checks and could record their time of passage.

A further complication was that the times achieved on the first lap of 175 miles had to be matched on the second circuit, or further penalties were incurred. Any error, whether by driver or navigator, or any mechanical failure, would entailed so many penalty points that the crew concerned was immediately out of contention – as Jopp and Leston were to find.

There was panic before the re-start when Ronnie Adams's car broke its throttle linkage, but lightning repair work by the Rootes support crew got him to the start line on time. The weather was fine and dry when the first car left at midnight. Peter Harper had to tackle much of the navigation as well as driving, because poor Raymond Baxter was suffering from severe nausea. Courageously, though, he completed the entire mountains test while feeling like death, doing his best to help in timing and navigating Harper.

The Jaguar apprentices Stephens and Corbett lost just ten marks more than the Rootes No 1 team on the test, and were thrilled to think that they had completed the entire rally so successfully. Sadly, the Jopp/Leston Rapier broke a half-shaft at Puget-Theniers.

When the results were announced, Harper and Baxter had climbed to fourth in general classification (behind a Mercedes-Benz 1-2-3 finish), and were class winners. This success must have been some consolation for an unpleasant incident before the start, when their car was broken into in Frankfurt;

124

The 'Works' Rapiers: 1956-1964

the thieves stealing an expensive German radio Peter had bought, and also several bottles of Lucozade.

This was Harper's first serious competition after his crash in the Coronation Safari in 1959, and despite Baxter's bout of illness he had made the most of what had not had not been the best starting place. The Swiss pair Werner Lier/Heinrich Walter were 7th overall, Jimmy Ray/Bill Bleakley were 11th and Ronnie Adams/Ernie McMillen were 19th, all keeping the order in which they started the Mountain Test.

Finally, to return to the idea of a "novelty crew", the media duly reported that script writer Ted Willis had a whale of a time as third man with Philip Fotheringham-Parker and David Humphrey, busily recording his impressions even when the car was doing a spectacular waltzing act prior to coming to rest against a snow-covered bank.

The next major outing for the Competition Department was to bring a complete change of scenery, climate and weather: the East African Safari Rally, held at Eastertide. Despite the failure of the Hillman Huskies in 1959, Norman Garrad decided to enter a full team of Sunbeam Rapiers, each with a European 'works' driver, but with a local co-driver who understood the unique conditions and challenges of this event. New cars built at Humber Road were shipped out and provided with local (Kenyan) registration numbers. The line-up was:

KGM 857	Paddy Hopkirk/Kim Mandeville
KGM 858	Peter Jopp/Lee Talbot
KGM 859	Peter Harper/Emil Perros
KGM 861	Ronnie Adams/John Boyes
KGM 862	Nancy Mitchell/Ann Bush

In addition, two Canadian journalists, John O'Keefe and Heather Wilson, were to compete in another Rapier; their car being registered KGM 767. That Garrad hoped for great things is emphasised by his strategy of putting the drivers through a long period of preparation in Africa, to familiarise themselves with every possible condition.

The route involved two loops, from Nairobi south into Tanganyika to Dar-es-Salaam and then north into Uganda and back. At their best, road conditions were on a par with the worst encountered on a European Rally: at their worst, when the dust turned to liquid mud and "wash-aways" removed whole sections of what had been a driveable surface, they tested cars and crews to breaking point – often literally.

Long stretches of two-foot deep water ran across main roads, causing havoc, and many cars were to be seen with the crews wading about drying electrical parts while the insides of their cars were awash. This year the dreaded Mbulu section had to be scrubbed as a whole bridge had been washed away; a new stage from Donyo Sambu to Dutch Corner replacing it. Paddy Hopkirk, running as the last car in the rally, fortunately traversed this stage in broad daylight and was one of few competitors to do so with time in hand.

Undoubtedly this helped Paddy to complete the next special stage from Bonga to Colo with less penalty marks than anyone else, so at Dar-es-Salaam hopes were high. Paddy Hopkirk with Viscount Mandeville were leading the rally after 30 hours, closely followed by Peter Jopp with Dr Lee Talbot. Peter Harper and Ronnie Adams had lost only a few minutes more but the Rapiers were in the running for the team prize.

Even so, the terrain was to be the victor this year as well. Following the re-start, on the very rough Mzenga section, Hopkirk got bogged down in mud, lost over 100 minutes and then had his differential break. Adams also lost time clearing his engine bay of mud and was then to be seen going fast through a

125

Above: Mud and plenty of it...Peter Jopp and Dr Lee Talbot on the 1960 East African Safari Rally.

Below: Showing the locals how it isn't done...embarrassing end to a demonstration by Paddy Hopkirk at the end of the Rallye International de Gran Canaria in 1960.

The 'Works' Rapiers: 1956-1964

special stage, but in the wrong direction! The Rapiers were not the only ones to suffer on this section, and the entry had depleted considerably by daylight on the next day, when more rain made fast stages encountered the day before into greater hazards for the exhausted crews. Nancy Mitchell's Rapier developed clutch trouble and came to a stop in one of the "lakes" across the road south of Makoyuni. The Canadian journalists retired after 1,500 miles, after their engine had been swamped with mud.

This left only two cars - Harper and Jopp. After a 12 hour rest period, hopes were raised by weather reports suggesting that the 1,400 mile northern leg might be easier. Unhappily, hostile locals evened the odds, for while passing through a Kikuyu reserve some crews were stoned, among them Jopp, who received a cut on the shoulder. The tribesmen had also placed large rocks in the hardened ruts, so cars had to leave these and drive in the soft mud at the side of the road or risk a damaged wheel. The sand which drifted on the road in this region would clog under crankshaft pulleys and make a fan-belt fly off – all of these being real hazards.

Worse was to follow, for between Musake and Meru Jopp passed Peter Harper's Rapier stopped, with the crew trying to repair broken suspension but this proved impossible. This left Jopp in the only remaining team car, but his Rapier then suffered suspension failure; he had to remove a fractured shock-absorber and then travel another 200 miles to Thomson Falls to try to effect a repair. Then, on finding cracks that had appeared in the wishbone mounting brackets, the last Rapier had reluctantly to be retired. All in all, a most disappointing African adventure for the Competition Department; though at least it proved the value of testing to destruction over the most challenging terrain.

Despite Paddy Hopkirk's absence from his 'home' event, Rootes fared well on the Circuit of Ireland, where works-entered and privately-entered Rapiers achieving a 1-2-4-6 in their class. The Rapiers were crewed by, respectively, J Piele/R Bell, P McNally/J I Vickers, Brian Waddell (of *Autosport*)/ J Coventry, and J Allen/K Proudfoot; the works-supplied cars coming first and fourth.

Because Peter Harper did not make himself available for the 1960 Tulip Rally – after a long absence "on safari" he still had a dealership to run – Norman Garrad put together a team of four cars (including two ladies' crews) - Paddy Hopkirk/Jack Scott, Jimmy Ray/Bill Bleakley, Nancy Mitchell/Rosemary Seers and Mary Handley-Page/Nesta Gilmour. The Swiss pairing of Lier/Walter were also entered.

On this occasion, there were changes to the general plan of the event, for the final races at Zandvoort had been scrapped, and special speed tests were included along the route instead. The rally began deceptively easily; but with the pace tightening during the 64km St Flour-Raulhac stage, the Tulip was on with a vengeance. From then there was no let up whatsoever. Competitors were now in the Alpes Maritimes and the route went on to La Bollene at the bottom of the Col du Turini. The climb of the famous Turini (12km through successive hairpins with loose gravel and wet roads between the snow banks nearer the summit, to be covered in just under 12 to 13 minutes according to category and class) proved so tight that only 11 crews from 165 starters made it on time. Jimmy Ray, Paddy Hopkirk, Mary Handley-Page and Werner Lier all incurred a one-minute penalty.

Paddy Hopkirk/Jack Scott later broke a half-shaft on their Rapier and shed a wheel near Castellane, and in spite of speedy work by the Rootes dealer in Nice 60 miles away, he ran out of time. Later, the Mary Handley-

ROOTES MAESTROS
"In their own words."

Page/Nicky Gilmour Rapier suffered a serious petrol pump leak; a fellow-competitor stopped to lend a hand, but over-tightened the union nut and snapped the pipe. The girls lost over 25 minutes before they could get going again.

The biggest excitement of the final stages was a spectacular crash suffered by the Citroen ID19 of Verrier/Trautmann just five miles from the finish, caused when Trautmann fell asleep; they roped the door back on, wedged the roof panel in the rear seat and finished, to be declared as winners once the penalties and handicaps had been calculated. The Rapier's best was Ray's 2nd in class.

For the Acropolis Rally that followed, Peter Harper returned to the team. This event remained one of the most traditional in its format, where average target speeds in all the special stages were between 70 kph and 80 kph, much higher than was usually allowed on Continental rallies at this time. The roads were also second only to Yugoslavia in terms of ruggedness. Two YWKs, 1 and 5, were driven by Peter Harper/Peter Procter, and by Peter Jopp/Les Leston, plus a Greek-crewed Rapier driven by the Rootes dealer in Athens, Nicky Filinis.

All went well until into the second day, the Rapier team still standing a good chance, although the Jopp/Leston Rapier had been losing oil from a faulty overdrive, which meant refilling the gearbox every 50kms: this finally split, before Gravenna, forcing their retirement. At the final refuelling point just outside Athens, the drivers had time to check their car over and to change wheels in anticipation of the race at Tatoi airfield – they even had personal barbers available to give them a shave!

Harper was very fast on the final 'wiggle-woggle' test, but just clipped one of the barrels although this did not affect the marking. The next day the cars left for Tatoi airfield in convoy from *parc ferme*. The grid positions for the race were awarded on the times obtained in the five practice laps. Harper worked his way through the field from a bad grid position, to finish a very creditable third, behind the Mercedes 220SE of Schock which won the event.

The final test, a 10km hill climb of Mount Parnis, was also crucial in the marking system: if the highest placed competitor in any class did not finish in either of the tests three per cent higher than the fasest car in the engine capacity class below, then he was penalised according to the best performance of the lower class.

The results confirmed that it had been Harper's best run for some time; he and Procter finishing third overall and first in the 1,301 – 1,600 cc class, with Filinis/Mourtzopoulos fourth overall and second in class.

At the same time as the "A" team had been busy in Greece, the team had also supported another short interlude abroad, where Garrad had entered a Rapier in the Rally International de Gran Canaria: Paddy Hopkirk was chosen to drive, and was accompanied by Norman Garrad's son Lewis. The car was a 1959 team car, YVC 431. The event involved relatively easy road sections interspersed with challenging hill-climbs such as the aptly-named Teror-La Laguna, and concluded with a figure-of-eight driving test round two traffic islands in the centre of Las Palmas. Hopkirk and Garrad finished tenth overall and third in class, which was probably as good as could be expected.

Embarrassment followed. After the rally proper had concluded, Hopkirk was asked to demonstrate the forward and reverse spin turns favoured by most experienced British drivers for clipping seconds on driving tests. Unfortunately, the hot and dry tarmac in Las Palmas proved his undoing (along with

The 'Works' Rapiers: 1956-1964

Dunlop's excellent tyre adhesion, of course) and the car went over onto its side. But the crowd applauded and the oil Paddy had split helped him make a much better show on a following attempt.

Serious business then resumed in earnest for the Competition Department with preparations for the French Alpine Rally. This promised to be tough, for the course was the usual one, through the Alps and the Dolomites, but the sections were shorter, at higher average speeds, and the rally was compressed slightly in distance and considerably in time; compared with 1959.

The second of the long sections, from Chamonix to Cannes, was 1,250kms/770 miles, representing the hardest final motoring of any Alpine since the war. The penultimate stage, of 34kms set in 34 minutes to Les Quatres Chemins was that which had caused Sheila Van Damm to vow in 1954 that she never wanted to do another "Alpine" – a promise she kept! The averages set were mostly 60kph over the most difficult French sections and 51 kph over the most difficult Italian sections. An old idea reintroduced was that the fastest car in each category and class set the required average for the speed tests and any car not within a percentage of that time was penalised. Reflecting the latest Appendix J regulations, much-modified saloon cars had to run in the GT category.

Rootes approached this by running their latest Series IIIs as standard touring cars. Hopes rested particularly on Paddy Hopkirk for, if he completed a penalty-free run, he would qualify for a Coupe en Argent (Silver Coupe). Along with Harper and Jopp and the Swiss crew, these were the five cars:

YWK 2	Peter Jopp/Jimmy Ray
YWK 3	Paddy Hopkirk/Jack Scott
YWK 4	Peter Harper/Peter Procter
YHP 288	Nancy Mitchell/Rosemary Seers
GE 1188 Z	Werner Lier/Heinrich Walter

The organisers had managed to include new Cols in the old "Alpine" tradition (loose-surfaced, pot-holed and dusty) for the first leg, the Cols du Soubeyrand and de la Fromagere being in prime condition. After Mont Genevre and Monza, the cars headed east towards the Dolomites to tackle the infamous Vivione and Gavia passes, where higher target averages than ever before in an Alpine presented the real challenge. Of the 77 starters, 23 crews were "clean" at Chamonix, the close of the first half of the rally.

Although the second loop was supposed to start with the Col de Rousset and a 25 km stage behind St Jean de Royans, both were cut out after a Renault overturned and started a forest fire! In another sign of the changing times, the 20 km/20 minutes up and over climb of the Col d'Izoard was much easier than before, because of its newly engineered sweeping bends and a fine tarmac surface. The final timed test was on the Col d'Allos where Peter Harper drove his Rapier brilliantly to beat Ingier's Volvo for the first time on the tests.

Fortunately for Rootes, on the the stage from Sigale to Les Quatres Chemins the Volvo lost its way, so the final results showed that the 'works' Rapiers had finished 1-2-3 in their class, led by Peter Harper who was now right back on his best form. He and Procter finished fifth overall, Hopkirk and Scott were sixth overall and Jopp/Ray took 9th overall.

Rootes did not enter the Marathon de la Route in 1960, partly because the Competiton Department's attention was focussed on British saloon car racing during the summer and autumn, and an expedition

Another dealership getting some publicity, this time in California in November 1960. The two Rapier Series III's are the cars specially-prepared for racing; Peter Harper came third overall in car no. 74 and won his class in the International Compact Car Race at the Riverside Circuit, beating Paddy Hopkirk in the sister car.

to the Riverside circuit in California for the International Compact Car race where Harper drove brilliantly in a specially-lightened Rapier to finish third overall behind a couple of 3.8 litre Jaguars.

The full team, though, was re-united just in time for the final event of the year, the RAC International Rally which was held in November. Here was the usual strong team with only a few changes between co-drivers, and this time, Mary Handley-Page was back in a Rapier:

YWK 2	Peter Jopp/Les Leston
YWK 4	Peter Harper/Peter Procter
YHP 288	Mary Handley-Page/Ann Hooper
6824 HP	Jimmy Ray/Peter Dingley
YVC 431	Paddy Hopkirk/Jack Scott

The strong field of private entrants included a large number of Rapiers, among them Julian Easten/Graham Robson in the ex-works car YWK 1.

This rally promised to be tough, though there were last-minute route changes due to an outbreak of foot and mouth disease in the countryside. Crews departed from a brilliantly-illuminated "Mille Miglia" type ramp in Blackpool – and by the time the event was 20 miles old Peter Jopp/Les Leston had taken a wrong turning and lost eight minutes. The first 180 miles between Blackpool and Brough were decisive, for thick fog combined with the heavy rain made driving very difficult.

Only six cars reached Brough without penalty, none of them being 'works' team crews, which badly dented Garrad's hopes. Up in Scotland, the Monument Hill special stage involved a two mile dash over a very rough and stone-strewn, unsealed road, which had to be covered in three minutes: only Erik Carlsson in his Saab 96 completed this without penalty. After an overnight halt in Inverness the route took in Lochinver and another special stage, called the "Scottish Safari", after which came Gairloch, where the Peter Jopp/Les Leston Rapier left the road and overturned into a field. The steering had broken just as Leston was coming out of a fast corner. Back in England, the rally finished with a section of 42 miles leading through Reigate and Redhill to the final control, on crowded

The 'Works' Rapiers: 1956-1964

main roads and at peak traffic time on a Friday evening. The event then concluded with races at Brands Hatch on the Saturday, where Mary Handley-Page brought her Rapier home third in her heat, and Jimmy Ray likewise in the last heat of the day. The published results made it clear that Erik Carlsson/Stuart Turner (Saab 96) had won convincingly. The closest that Rootes came to major honours was Jimmy Ray's third in the 1,001 – 1,600cc touring cars class.

1961

For the new season's Monte Carlo Rally, Garrad entered all the Rapiers in Group II, so the cars officially received very little modification, though all the cars ran on studded Dunlop Duraband tyres. There were six Rapiers, some with three man crews - Peter Harper/Raymond Baxter/Peter Procter; Peter Jopp/Les Leston; Paddy Hopkirk/Jack Scott; Jimmy Ray/Mike Hughes/Bill Bleakley, and Mary Handley-Page/Pauline Mayman/Daphne Freeman. Once again, a car was provided for Autosport's Gregor Grant, who teamed up with racing driver Mike Parkes and with Rootes engineer Peter Wilson. The last-mentioned car had been prepared by George Hartwell to the order of the Rootes Group and was then given its final check-over and pre-rally preparation by the Research and Development Section at Rootes.

An innovation in the 1961 regulations was the 'handicap' formula, where special stage times were subject to a weight/capacity formula for each category. Factors varied according to the type of car but it was a controversial measure which favoured small-engined cars.

This year the common route began at Charbonnieres, and for the first time special stages were included. The road section between Charbonniers and Monaco was expected to be decisive, as many of the stages were incredibly difficult given the average speeds set. The organisers had also prepared alternative routes in case the conditions became too arctic.

A well-appointed interior in one of the 1961 Series III's, showing the extra clocks as well as the Halda and the additional switch panel between the front seats. The driver's kneepad and navigator's map pocket are also visible.

ROOTES MAESTROS
"In their own words."

In the early stages the weather was diasappointingly mild. The *Autosport* Rapier had overdrive trouble before the start, which Mike Parkes and Peter Wilson fixed after several hours' hard work. Meanwhile Peter Jopp reported that in Paris there was talk of dry roads and fine weather, but then there were icy roads and snow at Belfort and Gerardmer and heavy snowfalls in the Maritime Alps. Practically the entire Glasgow contingent came to grief in the Massif Central area which also caused havoc amongst the Paris and Monte Carlo starters. The 35 Monte starters were soon in dire straits, for Jimmy Ray/Bill Bleakley went off the road, sliced off part of a telegraph pole and dropped down a miniature ravine near Chambron-en-Ligny. Deep rutted snow slowed everyone on the way to Mauriac; fog and ice intervened to Le Puy, but few eventally had trouble reaching Bourgoin. Now came their real trouble; for the difficult new section to St Claude was covered with deep snow. Peter Jopp/Les Leston turned sharp left up what they thought was the proper road but a bump and a squelch announced their arrival in a ploughed field: they went no further.

From St Claude to Charbonnieres everyone found ice in plenty and sudden patches of dense fog which prevented time being made up. Harper/Procter/Baxter arrived clean from Warsaw, while Harper commented that:

"Generally we had plenty of time, but when our overdrive packed up we were a bit pressed. The rev counter needle spent most of its time where the maker puts his name!"

Writing in *Autosport*, Gregor Grant vividly described the difficulty of the final section: "…I handed over to Mike Parkes who handled the Rapier with delicacy and uncanny anticipation on the snow and ice-covered Col du Cucheron. It was a lesson in how to drive a car at its maximum, without over-stressing the willing engine. How we blessed that overdrive – especially in second gear. On the way to St Pierre d'Entremont we overshot the partly obscured turning in a square and lost about a couple of valuable minutes extricating the car from deep snow. As we bumped our way out, the Peter Harper/Peter Procter /Raymond Baxter Rapier passed, going like a train and tailed by the Mercedes Benz of Bohringer/Socher which Harper had obviously overtaken…

From St Pierre du Chartreuse to the finish at St Laurent du Pont was decidly dicy, with packed ice on every corner…a very difficult section with poor surfaces, rutted and icy roads over the Routes de Combe Laval and Forestiere and a modified route to La Cime du Mas and the end of the timed section…for once the descent of the Rousset was fairly dry…and we slithered our way from Col de Romeyer down to Gap.

From Gap to Dignes was a short 92 kms dash…Stage 4 took us over the Col des Lecques and on to St Auban for the 3rd special stage…Mike [Parkes] hurtled into the series of ice and snow covered tunnels on roads hardly wide enough for a car to pass. Twist followed turn with bewildering regularity and Peter [Wilson] concentrated entirely on anticipating every possible hazard. One or two crews obligingly kept over to let us through and we just managed to scrape past without touching. It was often deceptively dry, to be followed by glass-like surfaces where the sun didn't reach. Parkes was thoroughly enjoying himself, and for his first rally was driving like a past-master…

Then came the final 6kms timed section between La Grave and Peille, with its deceptive hairpins and reverse cambers. It was here that the value of recce notes were brought home, as Peter recited Peter Harper's description of the route, which was

The 'Works' Rapiers: 1956-1964

uncannily accurate and must have saved many valuable seconds – especially as the terrain was completely unknown to Mike. Then came La Turbie and the first control, where Lewis Garrad and the Rootes boys were waiting to slam some fuel in the tank and check the lights etc. We were given 10 minutes to arrive at the final control on the sea-front; not a great deal of time when the organisers had cunningly routed us through the main streets of Monte Carlo and stationed many policemen to make sure that traffic regulations were obeyed. Quite a few crews arrived with seconds to spare and one feels that such a finish was entirely unnecessary – particularly with drivers still keyed up after the special stages.

Anyway we piled out of the great little Rapier which had come through from Warsaw without so much as a tiny dent, and gratefully had a drink in the bar of the Monte Carlo Rally British Competitors Club coach."

This gave a sparkling flavour of the way serious drivers had to tackle the event. The organisers selected the top 120 qualifiers for the "round the houses" final classification test, laps of the Monaco Grand Prix circuit having replaced the Mountain Test of previous years. The first test produced some really inspired driving from Peter Harper, Paddy Hopkirk and Gunnar Andersson in his Volvo, with Harper dominating the group, his best timed lap being 2 mins 15.1 secs as against Andersson's 2 mins 17.2 secs. In his race, Mike Parkes, even though caught unawares by the starter, made a fantastic start and simply streaked away from the rest of his group. His second lap was covered in just 2 mins 14.4 secs – fastest of the day. Then came near-disaster for when coming very fast into the Ste Devote corner, the car shed a wheel and crashed into the metal safety barrier, careering across the road and finishing up practically wrecked. It was typical of the Monegasque organisers that they declined to award him the official trophy for the fastest lap on the GP course - on the basis that he did not complete the test. However, Rootes as a team did not lose out because it then went to Peter Harper, whose best time was 2 mins 15.1 secs.

The final outcome was that French Panhards took 1-2-3, essentially due to the handicap factor which fabvoured small-engined/heavy cars, very disadvantageous when applied to normal cars driven by three Rapier drivers - Harper, Hopkirk and Parkes. The first 11 places in general classification were filled by cars under 1,100cc!

The Harper/Procter/Baxter car finished twelfth overall, while 'works' Rapiers were first and second in their class. For the fourth time the Sunbeam Rapier was the best finisher of British origin, and again Harper earned the distinction of being the highest-placed Brtitish entrant: there was a good collection of silverware to take back to Coventry.

The East African Safari Rally in 1961 is not relevant to this Chapter, for Norman Garrad had taken the lesson from 1960, that the Rapiers were not suitable for this event. Although Rootes entries in 1961 were three Humber Snipes and a Hillman Minx, all crewed by locals, it is satisfying to record that a Rapier did indeed win its class in this year. It was a purely private entry, entered by a Tanganyikan garage proprietor from Morogoro, J P Valumbia, carrying registration number DSZ 950. By beating the well-fancied Peugeot 403, it redeemed the reputation of the marque in East Africa and gave the Publicity Department some good copy material for use back home. As the Sunbeam advertisement proclaimed:

"For 3,350 miles over a punishing rally route through Kenya, Tanganyika and Uganda, this privately-entered Sunbeam Rapier

ROOTES MAESTROS
"In their own words."

scored over strong French, Swedish and other British competition."

Meanwhile, with no Safari Rally duty this year, Paddy Hopkirk had returned to his home event, the Circuit of Ireland Rally, where he scored his second outright victory in the event. This was no glorified clubman's event, for the route took in 1,500 of the toughest miles to be found in Ireland, along with 21 different speed and manoeuvring tests during the whole of the Easter weekend.

Although it may appear from this that the Competition Department had been taking it easy so far in 1961, much of their time and energy was being spent in serious racing, with entries by the specially-modified Sunbeam Alpines in both the Sebring 12 hour race and the Le Mans 24 hour race – these being covered in Chapter 8.

For the Tulip Rally therefore, Garrad entered just one car, to be driven by Mary Handley-Page with Pauline Mayman – for other 'works' drivers were fully occupied preparing for Le Mans and the Acropolis. As with many of the other Continental rallies of the period, the event was suffering from having to run in France, and became little more than a high-speed tour through lovely country. To counteract this, for 1961 there were 20 special stages and tests, the simple-to-understand bonus penalty system was scrubbed and a marking method adopted in which the fastest competitors in each class penalised the remainder – something similar having been used in a number of other rallies in the last couple of years. It was a disastrous failure.

In the final analysis of the 1961 event, crews found the main-road sections which had to be covered at comparatively low average speeds rather pedestrian, and it was another disappointing result for Mary Handley-Page. First she struck trouble on the Ballon d'Alsace speed hillclimb, where she and Pauline Mayman were sportingly rescued by fellow competitors John Cotter, D R Hill and I Martin in their Rapier, who thus threw away their chances, not knowing until later that the test had been scrubbed because the timing by marshals went awry. The ladies returned to the rally without losing too much time, but the Volvos in the Touring class were just that much quicker than the Rapiers so she finished a lowly 43rd overall.

The next event in Rootes's 1961 calendar was the Greek Acropolis Rally. Because rallies in Western Europe were becoming steadily easier every year, the Acropolis was acquiring more significance as a real endurance test. With this in mind, Norman Garrad entered a stronger team than ever before, including a brand new car, 6507HP, and as usual, a Greek crew was also supported. The line-up was:

6507 HP	Jimmy Ray/Ian Hall
YWK 4	Peter Harper/Peter Procter
YWK 3	Keith Ballisat/Peter Jopp
92922	Zannos/Yannicostas

After 24 uneventful hours, the crews left the convergence point of the 2 routes at Serrai, to tackle two consecutive special stages to Thessalonika over fast but twisty roads, where the organisers made sure that target speeds for these stages were in all cases well nigh impossible to maintain consistently. On the first special stage the Harper/Procter Rapier went off the road on a hairpin bend, slid down on the steep slope to the road, landed undamaged, facing the right way and pressed on undaunted, probably having even gained a second or two.

The second group of special stages, high in the Macedonian mounitains, was run in thick fog. Peter Harper slid on loose gravel, his Rapier stopping with one wheel overhanging a six-foot drop but was soon

The 'Works' Rapiers: 1956-1964

Jimmy Ray and a slightly apprehensive-looking Ian Hall before starting the 1961 "Acropolis". They finished 6th overall and third in class, one place behind Harper and Procter.

pushed back on to the road by team-mates (and after Ewy Rosqvist's Volvo crew had sportingly offered to help.) Then between Gravena and Hani Mourghani came the roughest section, two stages of 26.5 and 56.5 kms, the latter over unmade and extremely rocky roads. The only cars to complete the latter unpenalised were the Carlsson/Karlsson Saab 96 and the Andersson/Lohmander Volvo which took first and second in the final classification. After this came Volos and a loop round Mount Pilion which ended with a hillclimb of Pilion.

At this stage Zannos and Yannicostas, the highest-placed Greek crew, retired when their Rapier gearbox packed up. The sixth group of stages led from Makrakomi high over the mountains to Agrinion, including two sections of 74 and 76 km respectively. The roads were on loose and very rough gravel and for much of the way there were tremendous drops flanking the route. Keith Ballisat and Peter Jopp changed a wheel on this section and still maintained their average. From Agrinion the route led through the tobacco fields of Akarnania to the start of the seventh and last group of stages at Eratini near the Venetian castle of Nafpaktos and thence to Delphi via two sections of 20 and 9 kms. Jimmy Ray and Ian Hall ran their Rapier into a rock on a hairpin and lost 8 mins pulling the bent wing off the wheel, while Peter Harper's Rapier throttle linkage broke, and he had to jury-rig a substitute. After another timed climb the remaining crews returned to Athens. 45 finishers from

ROOTES MAESTROS
"In their own words."

the field of 76 performed a quick driving text beneath the floodlit Acropolis before a welcome night's sleep. Next day the rally concluded as usual with two races at Tatoi airfield and a timed climb of Mount Parnis but these were of little competitive significance.

This was a signal triumph for the Sunbeam Rapier team where consistency and reliability delivered the Team prize. The final results showed that Peter Harper/Peter Procter, Keith Ballisat/Peter Jopp and Jimmy Ray/Ian Hall had taken fifth, sixth and ninth places overall, though a Volvo beat them in their class.

The French Alpine Rally followed in June, where Garrad fielded a smaller team, and used entirely different cars from the Acropolis 'fleet'. The time factor, and the battering the Acropolis cars had received was certainly a factor. This was the line up:

7932 HP	Keith Ballisat/'Tiny' Lewis
YHP 288	Peter Harper/Peter Procter
YVC 431	Paddy Hopkirk/Jack Scott

The organisers divided the entry into four categories so there would be no outright winner; and all cars (except 500cc to 1,150cc types) had to meet the same target averages. The route was 3,035kms/1,900 miles long, taking in the toughest passes in the French Alps and the Italian Dolomites: in all there were 10 speed tests and 25 Special Stages over closed roads.

The rally was split into two stages – up to, and from Chamonix: the 172kms/107 miles section from Eygalayes to Chamaloc over the Cols St Jean, Roustans and Chaudiere promised to be particularly difficult. On the second stage the most difficult seemed to be the little-known dirt-surfaced 8,000-foot Croce Domini. Finally, and only 40 miles from the finish, to be completed at night, came the Sigale-Quatre Chemins section over the Col de Bleine, which only six crews had managed to do on time the previous year.

Things started off well for the Rootes team, for Carlsson's Saab suffered engine failure, while Gunnar Andersson's Volvo also did not start. The rally got under way under a blazing sun. The first stage included a 5 mile climb over the sinuous Col de la Sainte-Baume, where Hopkirk clocked 8 mins 52.4 secs to head the standard touring cars. The next speed test was a 12½ mile climb on Mont Ventoux, where Harper beat Hopkirk to keep the Rapiers one and two in the standard touring class.

During the night there were timed climbs on the Col de Rousset and on the St Jean-en-Royans circuit; where Trautmann's Citroen and the Rapiers of Harper and Hopkirk dominated their categories. After stages over the Col d'Escoulin and Col de la Charmette, only three cars were left with chance of a coupe but none of them were in the Rootes team. Most which dropped a minute on the Escoulin did the same on the Charmette. Because the St Barthelemey stage was altered at the last moment, crews who had not made a recce were badly caught out as there were several alternative routes. Peter Harper was very late here, but a protest from another crew was subsequently upheld and the stage was scrubbed from the final results. Hence, at Chamonix, after one of the hardest "Alpine" opening nights for many years, the Hopkirk/Scott and Harper/Procter Rapiers were leading the standard touring category.

The final run back to Cannes was the longest for many years, involving no less than 43 hours on the road. Fortunately, much of the planned difficulty was removed by sudden landslides on the Italian Gavia, Croce Domini, Pennes and Monte Giovo passes, which meant that they were cut from the route at the last moment. At Monza, Hopkirk proved to be the fastest Sunbeam -

The 'Works' Rapiers: 1956-1964

indeed, the fastest saloon after the big Jaguar Mk II of Gawaine Baillie/Peter Jopp.

The return across Italy to the French Alps was long and tiring but uneventful, and the timed climb up the Col d'Izoard allowed the Rootes drivers to continue their personal duel: Hopkirk beat Harper by 0.9sec and was fastest saloon car. The infamous Quatre Chemins section followed where both cars were slightly late.

And so to the finish, where, after such a splendid run on the road, the Rapiers' results were inevitably challenged. After a long argument with the scrutineers, Norman Garrad convinced them that his Rapiers were indeed standard, and the cars took most of the team prizes (except that restricted to French cars). Hopkirk/Scott were third overall, Harper/Procter fifth and Ballisat/Lewis seventh; with a convincing-sounding 1-2-3 in class too.

For the pundits, the category and overall placings were outstanding as the two leading Rapiers, running as standard touring cars, also finished ahead of improved Citroens, Alfa Romeos, 3.8 Jaguars and Volvos. The Rapiers of Hopkirk and Harper were nearly always the fastest saloons in the tests and Hopkirk's 88mph lap at Monza was far and away the best. The list of team awards was impressive: Best team of three foreign cars; Best team irrespective of size, class or nationality; Best team of three cars of the same make recording the best times in the special stages. To crown a most successful expedition, the team made the Marque Team Prize their own property, having won it before in 1949 and 1952.

Just to ensure there was no doubt about the validity of the results, Norman Garrad made sure that the formal apology received from the A.C.M.P. about the Rapiers' categorisation dispute was widely publicised. Factory PR staff circulated this:

"At the conclusion of the Rallye des Alpes rumours were rife that the successful Sunbeam Rapiers were not quite standard. These were proved to be completely unfounded and, as a result, Mr Norman Garrad has received a full apology from the organisers. M Duclos, rally director, states: 'I would like to apologise to you for the difficulty you experienced at the end of the Coupe des Alpes, which was due to a bad interpretation of the English language on the subject of alterations that you had carried out to your cars. It was a regrettable intervention and I hope that you will not take offence, and we look forward to receiving your entries for the Coupe des Alpes in 1962, which will be the 30th anniversary of the Rally'....."

After the intervention of more saloon car racing (this programme is described separately at the end of the Chapter), the Rapiers' next outing was a novelty for the 'works' cars – in the ten-day Tour de France. On this occasion, and as a 'sighting shot' with the future in mind, two cars were entered – for Peter Harper/Peter Procter, and for Paddy Hopkirk/'Tiny' Lewis. All were accomplished drivers –for one of the regulations of the Tour insisted that so-called 'co-drivers' should also drive in some of the speed tests.

Once again there were technical novelties. Seat belts/safety harness were now standard for driver and navigator, while a "magic box" was fitted to the cars, containing switches for screen washers, fog light, "Eolite" plug and two-speed windscreen wiper: this had been installed as the drivers found the normal dashboard switches difficult to reach when wearing a safety harness.

The event was held in mid-September. Starting from Nice, the 3,300 miles Tour was a close and most rugged contemporary equivalent to a road race – for the timed road

ROOTES MAESTROS
"In their own words."

sections through France and Belgium were interlaced with six races on famous circuits and nine speed hill-climbs on tortuous mountain passes. In addition, in 1961 the cars and crews would be shipped to and from Corsica for a timed circuit of the island.

In a last-minute upset, 'Tiny' Lewis had to fly home before the start because of a 'family' bereavement, to be replaced by Jack Scott, Hopkirk's usual rally partner. Everything went wrong from the start. At the first circuit test, Clermont-Ferrand, the Rapiers were going very well until the Harper/Procter car lost a wheel when it was already 20 seconds ahead of the Rosinski Alfa Romeo TI. Hopkirk, who had been farther back on the grid due to fuel starvation experienced on earlier hill climb tests, was also catching the Alfa fast when his car also lost a wheel, and was unable to complete the race. These setbacks and delays left the Rapiers effectively out of the running for significant placings, for it was practically impossible to make up lost ground on subsequent stages. So the event concluded with neither Rapier anywhere near the honours. In 1962 and 1963 there would be big improvements.

As usual the RAC Rally was the last event in the year, and on this occasion there was an innovation which would define the event in future. The route covered about 2,000 miles but, thanks to permission from the Forestry Commission, about 200 miles were on their private roads and run in the form of high-speed special stages. The route linked Blackpool to Inverness, where there was a overnight halt, then returned to Brighton. It was not a direct route – for cars crossed the Pennines northwards through the first night, then crossed the Scottish border, tackling the "Rest-and-be-Thankful" hillclimb, and three more special stages before Inverness was reached shortly after dark.

The next day offered some of the hardest sections of the rally, the route wending its way through the Highlands before turning south again for England and a breakfast halt at Scarborough. An easy run across the Midlands to the Welsh border included five lap races at Mallory Park and a high-speed test at Oulton Park. The next night the crews faced time and navigation trials along twisting roads in Wales before crossing back into England for a timed ascent of the Prescott hillclimb. The rally then concluded with speed tests on Madeira Drive in Brighton.

As usual there was a strong Rootes entry. The line-up was:

5190 RW	Peter Harper/Ian Hall
5191 RW	Peter Procter/Graham Robson
5192 RW	Paddy Hopkirk/Jack Scott
5193 RW	'Tiny' Lewis/David Stone

All the team cars were new, being Series IIIA models, complete with 1,592 cc engines, and different gearbox ratios. With new cars and such a strong team, expectations for the RAC were particularly high.

Problems surfaced at once. On an early special stage in Kielder, 'Tiny' Lewis suffered bad luck, when the drain-plug on the radiator of his Rapier came open, let out all the coolant and causing the engine to sieze. 'Tiny' then emptied out a spare petrol jerry-can, ran back down the road for a quarter of a mile to find water, and subsequently got going again. Before the route took crews deep into Scotland there were three special stages, of 20, 4.3 and 7.1 miles respectively, in the Kielder and Redesdale Forests in the Hawick area. All were Forestry Commission stages to be covered at 43 mph, very rough, their wet, unsealed roads being very slippery and miles

The 'Works' Rapiers: 1956-1964

Above: Preparing the new Series III A Sunbeam Rapiers. Jim Ashworth and Norman Garrad (standing, right) supervise proceedings.

Below: Ian Hall and Peter Harper before the start of the 1961 RAC International Rally in which they finished third overall.

ROOTES MAESTROS
"In their own words."

at a stretch had a grassy sump-polishing hump up the middle. Early on in the first Kielder section there was a ford, followed in extremely rapid succession by a series of acute bends: here 'Tiny' Lewis and David Stone slid off but were back on very quickly. At the Peebles halt most competitors managed to have some time in hand and the Sunbeam team cars all had their radiator drain taps wired up following 'Tiny' Lewis' experience.

After the first three stages six crews were still clean, including Peter Harper. The route then went on to the Rest-and-be-Thankful hillclimb, this time over the full 2 miles, this being followed by a 2.6 mile special stage on Forestry Commisssion land at Onich, very rough and hairy, with acute hairpin bends flanked by considerable drops, a rough 7.2 mile section at Loch Lochy and then a halt at Inverness.

Surviving crews then tackled a 12.75 mile stage in Culbin Forest, eighty main-road miles to the Spittal of Glenshee Hotel and 60 miles more to the five mile Bridge of Balgie special stage. Over the Scottish border south came more stages, including the long Staindale Forest special stage which required a 50 mph average over its 21 mile, slippery, stone-strewn length. Finally the pace eased after a long trek to the breakfast halt in Scarborough. Along the way, 'Tiny' Lewis had a narrow escape when the one remaining spar from a five-bar gate (recently modified by team-mate Paddy Hopkirk) speared their windscreen on the driver's side, coming to rest on David Stone's head and the steering wheel.

Back in England there were familiar tests at racing circuits, that at Oulton Park being of four laps (11 miles) over the Grand Prix circuit, set at nine minutes for GT cars and ten minutes for touring cars. No-one was unpenalised here, for times recorded included Procter 10 mins 29 secs, Harper 10 mins 30 secs, Carlsson (Saab) 10 mins 34 secs, Gunnar Andersson (Volvo) 10 mins 39 secs and Hopkirk 10 mins 43 secs.

The route then took surviving crews into Wales via Dovey and on to a special stage at Eppynt where 11.5 miles had to be covered at 53 mph. Another 60 mile trek led to the 9.8 mile, 42 mph Radnor Forest special stage which was very rough indeed and, in places, had a thick covering of four- to six-inch rocks. Hopkirk lost second place overall through a puncture on this stage, and Peter Procter/Graham Robson had two rear-wheel punctures on their Rapier in quick succession: they changed one wheel for their spare and drove on as quickly as possible, nearly finishing the section on three wheels, but when they wore their fourth virtually to the brake-drum they had to stop and borrow a wheel from the Singer crew of Dr John Spare. On the 24th and last special stage at Staunton (Monmouth) there were direction arrows placed on top of the corners. Many drivers "wrong-slotted" including Erik Carlsson and Peter Harper - who lost sufficient time to drop him one place overall....

All that remained then was the long drag, over main roads to Brighton.

In the end, Erik Carlsson's Saab won convincingly, beating Pat Moss/Ann Wisdom in their Austin Healey 3000. The Rapiers of Harper and Hopkirk took third and fourth overall, with other Rapiers of La Trobe in 11th place, and 'Tiny' Lewis in 13th place. Thanks to the efforts of Procter and Robson in finishing the event at all, they also carried off the Lombank Cup, the Manufacturers' team prize, one of the most important trophies on offer.

Most importantly, for the future of the sport against increasingly ambivalent public opinion, all the fireworks of the competition took place on closed and private roads, well away from the anti-rally brigade. The

The 'Works' Rapiers: 1956-1964

'works' team could well feel satisfied at a fitting end to a good year's work.

1962

In readiness for the 1962 season and the Monte, Norman Garrad fielded the strongest team he could assemble: Peter Harper, Paddy Hopkirk, Peter Jopp and 'Tiny' Lewis were all regulars, as was Peter Procter (who again drove with Graham Robson – though this was to be Robson's last drive for the Competition Department as shortly afterwards he was recruited to lead Standard-Triumph's return to competitive motorsport). A newcomer to the team, but another experienced F1 racing driver, was Graham Hill, who was paired with Peter Jopp:

5190 RW	Peter Harper/Raymond Baxter
5191 RW	Peter Procter/Graham Robson
5192 RW	Paddy Hopkirk/Jack Scott
5193 RW	'Tiny' Lewis/Ian Hall
6145 RW	Peter Jopp/Graham Hill

In terms of starting-point, there was more logic this year, as Lewis and Harper started from Oslo, the others from Paris.

For 1962 although the organisers retained the controversial handicap system, it was much adjusted from 1961 and only penalised GT and Group 3 cars by about 6% compared to normal production vehicles. The Rootes entries would not be not affected as they were running as normal Group 1 touring cars.

In the Concentration runs, the weather conditions were abnormally mild, the chief danger to crews being boredom. At Chambery, apart from a few retirements, only two cars in the first 200 were penalised. Fortunately for the organisers, things changed immediately on the first Special Stage, with ice and snow on the Col de Granier and Col de Cucheron, which made the choice of tyres an important factor.

Graham Hill and Peter Jopp tackled the Col de Granier, with Dunlop SPs all round, wished that they had fitted studded covers; and calculated that they lost about five minutes. Peter Harper and Raymond Baxter

Graham Hill and Peter Jopp in Paris before the start of the 1962 Monte Carlo Rally. They finished 10th overall and were third Rapier home.

ROOTES MAESTROS
"In their own words."

'Tiny' Lewis and Ian Hall, starting from Oslo in the 1962 "Monte". They finished 17th overall and were last of the five Rapiers to finish.

made the same choice and also lost a bit of time. Peter Procter took other advice and chose studs. Unfortunately he then suffered a puncture and a burst offside front tyre, the resultant skid leaving the Rapier balanced on top of a parapet. The crew quickly changed the wheel. Without this puncture, Procter would surely have made best time of all, for he eventually recorded 44 mins 45 secs, and one must allow about five minutes for the delay. Paddy Hopkirk recorded a sensational 41 mins 56 secs, proving that handling rather than out-and-out power was what mattered in these conditions; Graham Hill did 46 mins 33 secs and Peter Harper 44 mins 43 secs, despite using non-studded tyres; though Erik Carlsson in his Saab (who eventually won the rally) was fastest of all with 40 mins 27 secs.

Mont Ventoux was cold but bone dry, with all the Rapiers under 11 minutes 30 seconds, though well behind the fastest Porsche. Peter Procter was the fastest Rapier driver on the next two sections, though one and a half minutes behind the fastest Mercedes 220SE; then, on similar roads for the 25½ kms section to Pont des Miolans, his 20m 59s was just 28 seconds slower than the fastest Austin Healey.

There was a certain amount of snow at the summit of the Col de Turini, which caught out a number of drivers, including Procter who got into a tremendous slide, and finished up against a wall, luckily without damaging the car. Even so, he was again fastest of the Rapiers, in 32m 11s, six seconds quicker than Hopkirk and comfortably ahead of Hill (32m 53s) and Harper (33m 50s).

The final eliminating test was over 4 laps of the Grand Prix circuit, which did not produce any spectacular upset, though Rapiers needed to keep their positions to retain their hold on the team prizes. In fact, not only did they do just that, but Peter Harper drove a magnificent test, catching up on Graham Hill on every lap, and finally finishing 6 seconds ahead. Race times varied from 8min 48.4sec (Peter Harper) to 9min. 3.1 sec (Hopkirk) while Graham Hill bounced off the tobacconist's kiosk past the chicane and dropped one or two seconds getting his Rapier straight again.

All in all, the final results were remarkable, with Hopkirk/Scott and Procter/Robson finishing third and fourth overall. Rapiers were first, second, fourth, fifth and sixth in the 1,301 – 1,600 cc series class and also won the Charles Faroux Challenge trophy (a nominated manufacturer's team) and the Challenge L'Equipe(the three best-placed cars of one make)

The main attention of the Competition Department then switched to racing, with the

Above: Peter Procter and Graham Robson in the 1962 "Monte" in which they finished 4th in general classification.

Below: Paddy Hopkirk and Jack Scott in the 1962 "Monte" in which they finished 3rd in general classification and were the first Rapier home.

The last 'works' Rapier with Peter Harper and Peter Procter at Strasbourg, at the start of the 1963 Tour de France.

entry of Alpines in the 12-hour race at Sebring and also in the Le Mans 24-hour race. As Garrad's entries for the East African Safari were a Humber Super Snipe and Hillman Minxes, the Rapier's next outing was the Circuit of Ireland, where Paddy Hopkirk used 5190 RW.

Paddy, determined to win his 'native' rally, put up a spirited performance, battling hard for many hours against Bobby Parkes's Austin-Healey 3000 and Adrian Boyd's Sprite. The concluding braking test in Bangor was very exciting, with Hopkirk putting in a terrific performance – for unlike Gran Canaria in 1961 he was careful not to roll the Rapier.

A delay of 36 hours then dragged on, while 5190 RW's differential was removed and examined by RAC scrutineers, for there had been a protest. This was eventually rejected, which confirmed that Paddy Hopkirk and his Rapier had won the Circuit of Ireland outright for the second year in succession. The Circuit of Ireland was not to be Hopkirk's last 'fairy-tale' rally with the Competition Department (he was to move to BMC in mid-summer), for he was next to tackle the Greek "Acropolis" Rally.

Rugged road conditions in Greece suited the skills of Garrad's top drivers especially Peter Harper and Paddy Hopkirk, so Garrad once again entered a full team for this year's event. This included Rosemary Smith in her first official drive. The four RW cars were readied for Peter Harper/Ian Hall, Paddy Hopkirk/Jack Scott, 'Tiny' Lewis/Keith Ballisat and Rosemary Smith/Rosemary Seers. There was also the usual works-prepared but Greek-crewed Rapier, this being driven by Steven Zannos, Greece's leading rally driver of the day.

After the Rapiers started from Athens, for 24 hours the going was fairly easy and over good roads. After a three-hour rest at Serrai,

The 'Works' Rapiers: 1956-1964

the route almost immediately entered the first group of special stages, on the roads to Thessalonika. Disaster then struck the 'works' team when within the space of a single kilometre all three front-line Rapiers retired with engine bearing failure. Officially, as the media was told at the time, this was a result of restricted oil flow caused by a new type of oil cooler. This was curious, for the other two Rapiers (Rosemary Smith and Zannos) were supposed to have identical engines and equipment to the team cars, and for remainder of the rally, their cars never missed a beat. Very odd, and further guesswork is fruitless.

The next challenge was the Portaria climb on Mount Pilion, said to be the most difficult of the event, where Rosemary Smith turned in 4 m 45s and Zannos 4m 38s – which shows that Norman Garrad's new recruit was well worth her salt. Even so, Rosemary Smith lost much time while struggling to regain the road after a four-foot drop off the mountain road on the second part of the loop from Volos back to Volos. All part of the learning experience.

In the final results, with the front-line team cars all eliminated, the only face-saver was that Zannos won the 1,301 – 1,600 cc touring cars class, while the two Rosemarys - Smith and Seers - were second in class.

Garrad and the team then decided that they could not enter the Alpine Rally in 1962, but had to concentrate on the entry of the Sunbeam Alpines at Le Mans, but three completely refreshed Rapiers were entered in the Tour de France in September, where Peter Harper/Peter Procter, Keith Ballisat/ 'Tiny' Lewis and Rosemary Smith/ Rosemary Seers drove the cars.

As ever, the Tour de France was a fierce eight-and-a-half day combination of seven circuit races and seven timed mountain climbs, all linked by over 3,000 miles of fast road sections. A new classification system was introduced, separating Grand Touring machines (such as Ferrari 250GTOs) from Touring cars. A general classification recorded how the cars actually fared within each category, while a classification based on handicap factors gave, in theory at least, an equal chance to cars of all capacities within their respective category.

Starting in a style showing they meant business, Peter Harper and Keith Ballisat were first and second in the 1,600cc class in the hour's race at the Rouen circuit. The Mont-Dore hill-climb was won by a Fiat in 4 minutes 11 seconds, though Harper was again the fastest Rapier in 4m 17.2 s. After the Circuit d'Auvergne at Charade, another 1-hour race over the superb mountain circuit, it was on to Le Puy. In the next one hour event at Albi, the Harper/Procter Rapier was tenth fastest, the Ballisat/Lewis car being eleventh, while Rosemary Smith/Rosemary Seers were 14th.

Next came the tortuous Toulouse-Nice road section of 1,620 kms, which included two hillclimbs in the Pyrenees and the next hour's race at Pau. On the Col d'Aspin Ballisat and Lewis turned the tables on Harper and Procter, their car having lost its overdrive, and they closed the gap further on the Tourmalet climb. At Pau, however, the order reverted to form with Harper and Procter 7th and Ballisat/Lewis 9th. But on the climb of Mont Ventoux (all the way to the top, this time), it was the latter pair who were in 11th place with 16 minutes 9.8 seconds against Harper/ Procter's 16m 21.8s (for comparison the fastest climb was a Ferrari 250 GTO in 12m 22.2s). The two Rosemarys were also still pressing on and beginning to move up the classification tables.

Next came the notorious Col de Braus (behind Monte Carlo) with its 11 hairpins and bumpy surfaces. Here the sun was

ROOTES MAESTROS
"In their own words."

shining from a cloudless blue sky and it was surprisingly hot, which did not stop a Jaguar 3.8 Mk II driven by Consten beating the class record with 6m 34.4s. Ballisat/Lewis again caught up on Harper/Procter, returning 7m 25.3s against 7m 29.7s. Rosemary Smith had a slight interlude in the scenery, which lightly damaged the front end of the Rapier, badly enough to reduce her time to 8m 22.9s.

On the next morning, the cars went north to Uriage, and the Chamrousse hillclimb, where Consten's Jaguar again recorded the best time, and Harper/Procter led the Rapiers. Next, on Mont Revard, Ballisat/Lewis narrowly beat Harper/Procter with Rosemary Smith twenty seconds adrift, though all were again slower than the big Jaguar.

With races at Spa and Rheims still to come, Harper/Procter were 8th and Ballisat/Lewis 9th in category, with Smith/Seers fourteenth. The two Rosemarys were by now the sole survivors for the Coupe des Dames. At Spa-Francorchamps the test was a two hours blind where Keith Ballisat was third fastest Touring car, completing 278.720 kms at an average speed of 86.6 mph: the Harper/Procter car, despite continued overdrive troubles, came into 6th place. At Rheims, Ballisat/Lewis were 6th, Procter 8th and Rosemary Smith 9th.

In the final classification, the team achieved, if not exceeded, all their expectations, for the three Rapiers scored a 1-2-3 in the 1,600cc Touring class, and the Coupe des Dames for Rosemary Smith/Rosemary Seers. Only 51 of the 162 starters finished the Tour, 29 of them in the Touring cars class.

The final event of the year for the 'works' cars, as usual, was RAC Rally. The recipe for the 1962 event followed the successful pattern of 1961; the 2,158-mile route including many demanding sections in Yorkshire, Scotland and Wales to satisfy the more enthusiastic rally drivers. Garrad entered a team of three Rapiers, for Harper, Procter and Lewis.

Incidentally, finding nothing new to say about the Rapiers, *Autosport* instead went overboard about one of the Rootes service "barges" as follows:

"There is, however, one particularly fascinating car at Sunbeams. This is their high-speed service vehicle which Lewis Garrad operates on rallies. It is a Hillman Estate car externally, but it is fitted with a fully works-prepared Rapier engine, Rapier racing suspension and disc brakes and overdrive on second third and top gears and is capable of well over 100mph with road-holding to match."

The 1962 rally quickly confirmed its intent for the first overnight 456 miles to Peebles included seven of the 38 special stages, which soon afflicted several Rapiers, for John La Trobe/Julian Chitty ('Fraser' Rapier) lost 17 minutes repairing a defective distributor. On this same stage, 'Tiny' Lewis/David Mabbs were about to overtake a Mini-Cooper when they hit a deep rut, smashed the Rapier's fog lamp and shorted all the lights. 'Tiny' finished the stage by following the Mini at a distance of about six feet.

Worse was to follow when Peter Harper/Ian Hall's Rapier hit a tree on a right-hander and broke its front suspension. The 20-mile Wark Forest special stage, with a target time of 24 minutes 5 seconds, was not very rough, but was so full of switchbacks that most crews seemed to spend quite a lot of their time fully airborne. Peter Procter and Barry Hughes had a fan belt jump off when their Rapier bumped over a rock. The car overheated, and continued to overheat for the rest of the rally. They also lost the use of their overdrive.

A Works Team line-up, in jovial mood, probably taken at the time of the 1962 RAC Rally. (l to r) Ian Hall, Peter Procter, Barry Hughes, Rosemary Seers, 'Tiny' Lewis, Peter Harper, Rosemary Smith, David Mabbs and Norman Garrad.

After the Peebles breakfast halt, the eighth stage, six miles of extremely rough corrugated track which had to be covered in 7 minutes 15 seconds, included a Bailey bridge, which created a step which caused the Lewis/Mabbs Rapier to leap high into the air, breaking a top wishbone on landing, but they finished the stage and drove gently along the 19 miles to the next one at Loch Ard, 'Tiny' nursing the car along without daring to use the brakes. From Loch Ard there were 150 miles of main road motoring to Inverness, which gave them time to effect a temporary repair.

Soon after Nairn came the Culbin Sands forest which the drivers tackled in gathering darkness at a target average speed of 50 mph, where a flying stone holed the radiator of the Procter/Hughes Rapier. Once again the car overheated, but after returning to Nairn the radiator was repaired and the cylinder head gasket was replaced in a local garage.

Thereafter the special stages followed thick and fast. The following day saw the cars reach Wales, where the stages were equally challenging. A long 14.7 mile stage in Dovey Forest, where the hilly terrain and rough road dictated caution, concluded with a very steep downhill section and saw the Procter/Hughes Rapier go off the road (and over the time limit). The sump of the John La Trobe/Julian Chitty 'Fraser' Rapier split on the last mile of the last stage, although they were able to reach the finish of the stage where the sump was patched up, enabling them to drive the 15 miles to the finish at Bournemouth.

In the end, Erik Carlsson and his Saab won for the third year in succession, well ahead of Hopkirk/Scott in their Austin-Healey 3000. The results were not all bad for Garrad's team, as 'Tiny' Lewis/David Mabbs were fourth overall, comfortably ahead of Andersson in the rival Volvo which was eighth. Lewis/Mabbs were also

ROOTES MAESTROS
"In their own words."

first in class, with the privately-entered Rapier of David Pollard and Tony Baines second in the 1,000 – 1,600 cc category.

1963

In many respects this was a year of transition for the Competition Department, as it was for the Rootes Group as a whole. After fifteen years during which he had taken Rootes from nowhere to the top league of British manufacturers in International rallying, Norman Garrad was eased into retirement against his wishes. His intention to step back from day-to-day management of the 'works' team was made known to the motoring press at the end of 1962. *Autosport* summed up his achievements thus:

"In the days of slap-happy amateurism, Norman's forceful methods and strict team discipline were not too popular with some drivers, but he, more perhaps than any other team manager, did the most in the early days to put Britain on the map as a really serious force in rallying."

It may have been a little premature, as Norman's son Lewis Garrad took over more of the day-to-day running of the Competition Department during 1963. Political in-fighting inside Rootes – doubtless fuelled in part by uncertainty about the whole company's future - confused and delayed the decision on who should replace Garrad as Competition manager: it was not until the very end of the year that Marcus Chambers was approached.

As far as the cars available to the Competition Department were concerned, 1963 saw the final worthwhile successes of the Sunbeam Rapier, though, to be honest, as a design it was getting long in the tooth. The Rapier had now been the Department's mainstay for seven years, and the pace of engineering development had quickened considerably during this time. Yet the long-awaited Rootes "baby" car was not formally launched until May 1963, while the Sunbeam Alpine's graduation into a really powerful Grand Touring car with the injection of V8 power was still at the stage of "promising idea" – what became the Sunbeam Tiger was not even approved by Lord Rootes until July 1963.

One significant announcement - that of much closer co-operation with Alan Fraser's privately-funded team – was important. As the motoring press reported in January:

"Alan Fraser will also once again be entering his Sunbeams in certain rallies this year. As Rootes will not be entering the "Acropolis," Fraser is entering three cars. The drivers will be Peter Harper/Ian Hall, John La Trobe/Julian Chitty and David Pollard/Paul Steiner. The Fraser team will be working in close cooperation with Rootes throughout the season. For the Circuit of Ireland, Fraser has entered one car to be driven by La Trobe/Chitty. Other events to be entered include the RAC Rally and the Tour de France. The Sunbeams will also be entered in all European Saloon Car Challenge events."

As ever, though, the 'works' team may have lacked resources, but not resolve, and made a determined onslaught on the Monte Carlo Rally. A full team of four Rapiers was entered for the 1963 Monte, three of the cars having been used hard throughout 1962. Alex Kynoch was a late replacement for Keith Ballisat alongside 'Tiny' Lewis, so the full line-up was:

5190 RW	Peter Harper/Ian Hall
5191 RW	Peter Procter/ David Mabbs
6145 RW	'Tiny' Lewis/Alex Kynoch
5439 VC	Rosemary Smith/Rosemary Seers

Peter Procter (left) and David Mabbs with the full set of equipment carried for the 1963 Monte Carlo Rally. On display are: Spare wheels fitted with spiked ice tyres, a pair of chains for deep snow, spare engine oil, spare brake fluid, spare lamp bulbs, a first aid kit, a shovel, combined fire extinguisher and tyre inflator, crash helmets, vacuum flasks, a magnifying map lamp, quick lift jacks, spare speedometer cable, nylon towrope, spare sparking plugs, two wheelbraces, inspection lamp, starting handle, spare distributor cap and coil, leads, torch, a comprehensive toolkit, maps.

ROOTES MAESTROS
"In their own words."

The choice of starting-points was again kept simple, for Harper and Lewis started from Frankfurt, while Procter and the ladies started from Paris. One of the Fraser team was the ex-Works car, 5192 RW, driven by David Pollard with Mike Kempley – an early example of that "close co-operation."

The "real Monte" was expected to begin at Chambery with the start of the special stages, though the time schedule of routes to this town had been tightened up and, as usual, separate speeds were set for the specially timed sections. The much-disliked "factor of comparison" was still applied to cars in each Group; its effect this year being that G.T. cars had a penalty of about 8% as compared to the normal production vehicles.

In sharp contrast to 1962, the rally proved a horrendously difficult event, for crews had to battle through the worst conditions experienced for many years. Snowstorms of Polar ferocity swept parts of Europe, forming deep drifts on dozens of roads and making the early stages far from a routine tour of Europe. For the first time in many years, an entire starting contingent was eliminated, as none of the 13 Athens starters even reached the first control in Jugoslavia. Only ten of the 59-strong Glasgow contingent arrived in Monaco.

The Paris starters had a hectic drive from Ghent to Boulogne over frozen roads and in occasional snowstorms. Coming out of Angers the road was like a skating rink and the Grant/Wisdom Alpine had a puncture and, when getting out to change wheels, the crew both fell flat on their backs. Peter Procter and David Mabbs turned back with their Rapier to see if they could help, and the wheel was changed. Grant described the un-welcome results in his subsequent write-up of the event:

"At the time, we had spiked tyres on the rear wheels, SPs on the front and on the spare. I might say that the experience of driving with three non-spiked and one spiked tyre was, to say the least of it, memorable. One never quite knew what the car would do, and it was a matter of being more than cautious before we could pick up a set of spikes from the excellent Dunlop service at Bourges."

Soon afterwards, Peter Procter noticed that the water temperature gauge of his Rapier was reading unusually high, the engine rapidly lost power and at Gerardmer it was found that the cylinder head gasket had blown. After they had tried radiator cement, Tommy Wisdom suggested that they stick a couple of raw eggs into the radiator. To the astonishment of Procter, this worked, and the pair carried on to Chambery with no further problems.

However the Paris crews' adventures were as nothing compared to those of the Frankfurt contingent, because of the remarkable achievement of Peter Harper/Ian Hall and 'Tiny' Lewis/Alex Kynoch in getting through at all to start on the "common route". Facing completely blocked roads on their way to the Nurburgring, the two crews did an additional 200 kms to reach their first control at Bad Driburg. Harper actually arrived four minutes before his scheduled time, but Lewis was delayed by a couple of punctures and a series of delays at level crossings.

Be cause of the severe weather, the special stages were as tough as could be expected. Over the Col du Granier Paddy Hopkirk (who was driving a Mini-Cooper for the first time) recorded 45 min 49 secs. Peter Procter, despite a delay at the start with a flat battery, returned 47 mins 47 secs; Harper did 48.05 and Lewis 47.34. The climb of the Chamrousse was the slipperiest in memory; with car after car stopped at the hairpins and having to roll back to obtain traction. In dense fog on the Col de Perty, Rosemary

The 'Works' Rapiers: 1956-1964

Smith braked hard to avoid another car and rolled over the edge, both girls being thrown out, and the car was badly damaged. Rosemary Seers was taken to hospital and received shock treatment, but Rosemary Smith was able to travel on to Monaco.

Mont Revard was almost hidden in thick fog, with the lowest temperature for years and the car windscreens became coated with ice. Peter Procter had to drive with his head out of the window - and even then visibility was almost zero. Everyone pressed on, with increasing difficulty, as Gregor Grant vividly described:

"….the field was gradually thinning out…I was so tired that I could hardly follow the route. Down came the snow again and this time it was in earnest. Often it was impossible to see where the road began – or ended – in a vast expanse of whiteness. Dawn brought relief from peering behind headlamps. The Alpine was going like a train…at Oraison we had less than 10 minutes left out of the *hors course* hour, and the snow was as thick as ever. We seemed to be all alone in the Arctic, with not a sign of another car. I took a wrong turning, and had to go back, which left us with little hope of reaching Pont Charles Albert within the time limit. Near Castellane we were overtaken by Peter Harper, so realised that it was touch and go….So at Pont Albert our rally was over."

In the fourth timed test of 7 kms on a tarmac hillclimb near Levens, Harper managed 7 min 36 secs, Lewis 8 min 7 secs and Procter 8 min 54 secs - all slower than Hopkirk's 7 min 15 secs in the Mini. It was the same story on the Col de Turini, where naturally there was snow. Harper recorded 26 min 44 secs, Procter 26 min 52 secs and Lewis 27 min 39 secs, but Hopkirk's Mini took 25 min 52 secs. There remained the 14 kms final test from Luceram on the Col St Roch, where Hopkirk turned in 7 min 16 secs, beating the Sunbeam trio (Harper, Procter and Lewis, returning 7 mins 21 secs, 7 mins 27 secs and 7 mins 32 secs respectively).

This was a severe Monte, for out of 296 starters (and the 216 who left Chambery for the special stages), only 27 crews reached Monaco without penalisation. Peter Harper and Ian Hall were the only Rapier crew to be unpenalised. The rally concluded with the now-usual series of races on the Grand Prix circuit in Monaco, this year of three laps.

At the end, it was clear that the front-wheel drive cars had made a clean sweep: Erik Carlsson won for the second successive year in his Saab, Mini-Coopers were third and sixth, the intervening places being taken by front-drive Citroens. The best-placed Rapier finished 17th (Harper/Hall), and although Harper also won his capacity class, this was not a good start to the year.

After a three-month interval, the Circuit of Ireland followed at Easter, where the team entered two Rapiers in this event. Rosemary Smith drove one of the cars in her "home" event (she was partnered by fellow-Irishwoman Sheila O'Clery); the other 'works' drive this time going to Adrian Boyd and Maurice Johnston in a new Rapier Series IIIA (7003 VC).

This was to be the toughest "Circuit" so far, won and lost on the road where there were 89 time checks, more than 14 optional checks, 7 route checks and 35 controls to be visited in a 1,300 mile route. Together with seven speed tests, 9 driving tests and 7 special sections this made for a busy Easter weekend, which quickly developed into a battle between the Boyd/Johnston Rapier and a supercharged 1,098cc Austin Healey Sprite, entered by Alexander Engineering and driven by Ian Woodside/Esler Crawford.

ROOTES MAESTROS
"In their own words."

At the end of the first leg, the Sprite was first with 8.6 marks lost, Boyd third with 10 marks lost. Overall positions then remained unchanged at the first overnight stop at Killarney in the south of Ireland.

For stage 3, the hills were shrouded in heavy cloud and flooded with incessant rain which only eased up much later in the day. At the close, overnight positions saw Boyd up in second place, and Rosemary Smith left with an uncontested run for the Ladies' prize.

The fourth leg saw real drama when the supercharged Sprite's engine caught fire after a carburettor fractured, but after a fellow competitor sacrificed his carburettor for them, Woodside and Crawford made the next control with loss of only 41 marks. Boyd was now leading; but he then lost 5 marks by hitting a pylon in one of the driving tests. At the last night stop at Sligo, Boyd looked well placed for victory, but it was not to be. After the cars crossed the border, a series of 10 time controls had to be visited in the early hours of the final morning, with no hope of making a comeback after the slightest error in navigation. Boyd and Johnston lost crucial marks from just such a navigational error while Woodside came in with a clean sheet on this section. Woodside's Sprite became the overall victor in the rally, second place went to a Group 3 Volkswagen, which just beat Boyd/Johnston into third place overall. The Rapier was first in the 1,301 – 1,600cc Touring Cars class, Rosemary Smith carried off the Ladies' Prize and, thanks to the Alan Fraser-entered Rapier also coming third in class, Sunbeams won the one-make Team Prize.

Soon afterwards, the next event for Rootes was the Tulip Rally, where the team decided to enter this event for the first time in three years, with the full current team of four Rapiers. Rosemary Smith had a new co-driver, Elma Lewsey, while Peter Procter was paired with fellow-Yorkshireman Mike Kempley; otherwise the crews were unchanged, for Peter Harper was with Ian Hall, and 'Tiny' Lewis was with Keith Ballisat.

This time around, the organisers had streamlined the rally, omitting the overnight rest halt, so it lasted just three days and two nights. There were only 70 miles of special stages (almost all hill-climbs) in a rally of 1,875 miles, and a lot of relatively straightforward road driving. The route took the cars from Noordwijk south to Chamrousse near Grenoble, over mountain roads in the Rheinland-Pfalz, Saar, Vosges, Jura and Savoy Alps, with fifteen speed tests interspersed along the way. In an attempt to even out an entrant's chances, a General Classification was abandoned, the entry being split into Touring and Grand Touring categories. A complex handicapping system then made it difficult to work out what cars might be favourite, and which not….

Things went well for Rootes until the second time control at Flughafen Enshie (480 kms after the start), when the back end of the Peter Harper/Ian Hall Rapier began to make ominous noises. Much later, after more hill-climbs and speed tests, their differential finally gave up after climbing the Col de la Faucille, near Geneva – but was replaced by the Sunbeam service crew in just 17 minutes.

On the return, by way of the Ballon d'Alsace and the Col de la Schlucht came a 4.5km climb at Breitenbach where, although the rain had stopped, the steep and narrow road was very wet. This was unpleasant for Peter Harper/Ian Hall whose Rapier had now lost its overdrive and showed a disconcerting tendency to freewheel without warning. The next special stage was 129km away at Niedeck: here Keith Ballisat drove his Rapier into a concrete post after over-doing it on a sharp bend, damaging the wing. More bad luck followed on the return into

The 'Works' Rapiers: 1956-1964

Belgium, at an early-morning hill-climb at La Roche, where the Rapier of Peter Procter/Mike Kempley had to retire with a broken distributor drive.

The results, when announced, showed one surprise. Due to the complexities of the scoring system the outright winner of the Touring Class was an ex-Monte Ford Falcon V8, which had had little competition in a thinly-supported capacity class. This car, incidentally, used the same V8 4.2litre engine which was to feature in the Sunbeam Tiger).

The best that the Competition Department had to show was Harper/Hall, seventh overall in the Touring Class, and first in the 1,600 cc class; while Rosemary Smith and Elma Lewsey came 23rd overall. As a footnote, it is nice to record that the Rapier of Andrew Cowan with co-driver Johnstone Syer was runner-up for the best private entrant award.

In 1963 the French Alpine both started and finished in Marseilles, the route covering about 2,300 miles, with ever-tighter average speed schedules. Eight speed hill-climbs of the trickiest passes were included, but there were 24 special stages too, some 480 miles in all, where the roads were open to all users, but which imposed severe penalties for every second of lateness. The weather, as ever, played its part in making this a particularly harsh event, combining intense daytime heat with severe rainstorms that sent torrents of water coursing down the hills, many of which at high altitudes were still in very rough condition after the severe winter weather.

Rootes entered a full team, which included Adrian Boyd (following his works drive in the Circuit of Ireland), and David Pollard. This was the line-up:

5190 RW	Peter Harper/Ian Hall
5191 RW	Peter Procter/Adrian Boyd
5439 VC	'Tiny' Lewis/David Pollard
6145 RW	Rosemary Smith/Elma Lewsey

In what was proving to be a frustrating year, disaster struck early, on the 8.1 km climb of the Sainte Baume test, when the Harper/Hall Rapier rolled just a few yards away from Hopkirk/Scott's Austin Healey 3000, which had slid right off the road. In spite of co-operating in a rescue, both cars were irretrievably stuck and forced to retire.

The remaining special tests of the first stage were hill-climbs of Mont Ventoux and the Col de la Cayolle, in which only one Rapier was among the fastest twenty – on Ventoux with Procter/Boyd, 13th in 15m 32.2s compared with 13m 44.8s for Rene Buchet's Porsche Carrera. The second stage, of 1,121 kms, 39 cols and another three timed climbs, saw the exit of Procter and Boyd, who crashed out. By Chamonix the field of 84 starters had dropped to just 34 – including the Rapier of Lewis/Pollard which was slowly but surely improving its position.

The third and final leg saw the remaining Rapier climbing the rankings. The Col du Grand St-Bernard proved less of a challenge than feared as the weather was fine and sunny, and the run to Monza for the track race was relatively straightforward. After Monza, twelve cols had to be tackled at night, before cars returned to the Quatre Chemins loop, which had to be traversed twice. The Col d'Allos accounted for two more timed tests on this stage, where and Lewis/Pollard turned in good times, of 17m 53s (first climb) against the best time of 16 m 47.3 s returned by a Cortina, 17m 21.1s (second climb) against 16m 23.2s by one of the Mini-Cooper Ss.

There was no General Classification, for the cars were split into Touring and Grand Touring categories. The Touring Category was won by Rauno Aaltonen's Mini-Cooper S, with Ford Cortinas second and third: all

ROOTES MAESTROS
"In their own words."

incurred no road penalties. Lewis and Pollard came in 6th with 120 road penalties (two minutes lateness). In the 1,301 – 1,600cc class, the Ford Cortina GTs were first and second, with the Lewis/Pollard Rapier third.

Once again, this was a disappointing result for Rootes, one which showed the extent to which their rivals were now faster than the ageing Rapiers.

The next event in Rootes' calendar was the Tour de France, in which the Rapiers had shone so well in 1962. The Garrads and their team were hoping for another strong performance, to lift what had so far not been a good season. Two Rapiers took the start, Peter Harper/Peter Procter and 'Tiny' Lewis/David Pollard.

The Tour started from Strasbourg and was split into five stages, finishing at Nice. Sixteen hill-climbs and circuit races were interspersed with road sections that were often very tight, taking in tough mountain roads and passes in the Pyrenees as well as the usual diet of Alps and the Auvergne.

In yet another early sign of trouble, Peter Procter's Rapier had its throttle bracket break during the two-hour race at Rheims on Day Three. But Peter had once experienced this problem before, so after a slow lap he had the throttle screwed wide open and thereafter drove on the ignition key, still managing to return some good lap times ! The problem, though, eventually put them out altogether. Back on proper rally territory after the fourth day and the race at Albi, there was a whole night of cols and hairpins in the Pyrenees, when all competitors suffered penalties; but 'Tiny' Lewis and David Pollard drove consistently to match Hopkirk's Mini-Cooper S in dropping just two minutes.

The route continued through to the Alps, with three familiar hill-climbs, of Mont Ventoux and the Cols de Rousset and Chamrousse: by now, with one day to go after the final night's rest at Lyons, the saloon car field was reduced to twelve and the G.T. cars to 25 – a searching attrition rate from the combined field of 130 starters. Hopkirk's Mini position on handicap was unassailable although the Lewis/Pollard Rapier and Rosemary Smith's Alpine were still going strong, with Rosemary looking well set for the Coupe des Dames in the G.T. category.

When the final results were confirmed, Paddy Hopkirk's Mini-Cooper S amazed everyone with third on scratch and first on handicap in the Touring category), but the Competition Department could feel really satisfied, as Lewis/Pollard had clawed their way steadily up to finish just one place behind, 4th on scratch and third on handicap: they also won the 1,001 – 1,600cc Touring class, though these were barely acknowledged in the press.

As usual, the season ended with the RAC Rally, held in November, the modern style for the event, introduced in 1961, remaining. The special stages were where the rally was to be won or lost, and on this occasion there were 54 such stages for the 1963 event, accounting for almost 400 miles of the 2,200 mile route.

As described in Chapter 9, Peter Harper forsook his customary Rapier for a Humber Super Snipe, but there was still a strong Rapier entry from the combined forces of the Competition Department and the Alan Fraser team, with four and three Rapiers respectively. 'Works' drivers were Peter Procter, 'Tiny' Lewis, David Pollard and Rosemary Smith; Robin Turvey was co-driver: he would become a regular in the Tiger and Imp ranks. Andrew Cowan's Rapier was a Fraser entry; he teamed up with another driver of whom much would be heard in future, Brian Coyle.

The first rough track chosen for the special stages was to the west of Windermere, and

The 'Works' Rapiers: 1956-1964

was typical of what was to follow– an uphill, spiralling track of only single-lane width and strewn with stones and gravel. Its 8.1 mile length had to be covered in 9min 52 sec to avoid penalisation – an average speed only fractionally under 50 mph. The second stage was 5.8 miles of the tracks in Greystoke Forest. John La Trobe/Julian Chitty (Fraser Rapier) collected a puncture but pressed on to the end on one flat tyre. The 'Tiny' Lewis/Robin Turvey Rapier grounded badly on one of the roughest parts and split its fuel tank too badly to be patched up by emergency repairs; so they were forced to retire.

The rally then settled into its familiar pattern, for after the Scottish stages and at the start of Day 3, 13 of the first 20 positions were occupied by Scandinavian entrants, the phenomenal Hopkirk/Mini Cooper S combination was third overall and no Rapiers were in the provisional listing. When the surviving crews returned to Blackpool that night at the end of the first half of the rally, Peter Procter/David Mabbs (Rapier) had risen to 19th position overall. The route went on into Wales by way of Bala to Gwydyr, and 20 miles later came an 18-mile stage among the trees in Dovey. The surface here ranged from tarmac to hard-packed earth and gravel and included quite a lot of deep mud. It was smooth, fast and very slippery – and very, very bad for the prospects of the Competition Department, as the Procter/Mabbs Rapier damaged its rear axle and had its gearbox pack up.

The closing leg of the rally took the cars down to the South Coast for special stages on the Army ranges at Lulworth Cove and Wareham, where a waterlogged plain scattered with miscellaneous tanks served the gunners as targets. Here Rosemary Smith's Rapier side-swiped a wall which frustratingly ended her rally so close to the finish at nearby Bournemouth.

The final results confirmed the extent of Scandinavian domination of the rally: they took eight of the first dozen places. Rapier honours were meagre, with Pollard/Baines 19th and Cowan/Coyle 22nd.

This was a depressing end to what had been a difficult year for the Rootes Group in general. For the Competition Department, as for the company as a whole, hopes of a turn-round rested largely on the shoulders of the little Hillman Imp. That seasoned surveyor of the rallying scene, John Gott, summed the position up succinctly in his annual review of the year for *Autosport*:

"Rootes and Triumph, with cars which were either no longer competitive or which worked in a strong class, had a lean season. Early on Peter Harper kept the Sunbeam flag flying with class wins in the Monte and Tulip and Rosemary Smith finished off the good work with a fine run in the Tour de France, but in 1963 Rootes were not the force of earlier years. However, with their traditions and experience, plus the promise of a hairy big-engined car in 1964, Rootes may once again be at the top in the coming season."

As an end-note, one can see the planned importance of the launch of the Humber Sceptre in January 1963. Until relatively late in the day, this had been intended as an entirely new-look Sunbeam Rapier. Whether it would have been competitive in rallying is doubtful, as it was heavy; the sheer ruggedness of Rootes engineering was no longer sufficient to keep its cars ahead of the field even on the toughest events.

1964

Although management was now backing the Imp, the Rapier had not quite ended its Competition Department career. For the Monte, two Rapiers joined the Imps, one of

ROOTES MAESTROS
"In their own words."

them the last 'works' Rapier, 7003 VC, in which Rosemary Smith/Margaret McKenzie started from Paris; Procter/Mabbs in 5439 VC started from Oslo.

Although one Imp retired before the end of the opening stages at Rheims, the Ballisat/Cowan Imp and the Procter/Mabbs Rapier made it in good order to the special stages on the common route from Rheims to Monaco, coping well with the icy roads. The special stage following Uriage (23 kms) saw Procter turning in 16 mins 57 secs, not good enough to catch Hopkirk's 16 min 13 secs, still less the Ford Falcon driven by Ljungfeldt which managed 15 min 54 secs. On the next special stage, 46 kms from La Madeleine to Gap, Hopkirk did 34 mins 11 secs, and Ljungfeldt 33 mins 53 secs. The third stage from Chorges and Savines was all on narrow D-roads with plenty of ice and countless twists and turns. Times were as expected by now, with Hopkirk managing 15 mins 23 secs and Procter 15 mins 49 secs: the remaining stages did not alter the eventual outcome either, and the excitement for the Competition Department centred on the Ballisat/Cowan Imp.

163 of the 299 starters reached the end of the road sections and special stages(the weather was not severe), of which 120 started the final classification test of four laps around the Grand Prix circuit. At this point, the Procter/Mabbs Rapier was 11th, so the final test was important. Unfortunately the test showed up the short-comings of the organisers, for the timing equipment went wrong, causing them to stop the race after three laps and impose a re-run, not however allowing anyone to re-fuel their cars.

Competitors who had carefully calculated the amount of fuel they were carrying were faced with running out or driving far slower than before. Peter Procter was one of those involved in this heat, and protests were lodged, but rejected. Procter and Mabbs finished 15th in general classification and third in the touring cars 1,301 – 1,600 cc class. But for the final controversy, they might have won their class, at least.

This was a deeply disappointing conclusion to the Sunbeam Rapier's major International career. In fact, the Rapier would have one final outing, in the Circuit of Ireland, when Rosemary Smith, drove 7003 VC while John La Trobe/Julian Chitty were in a Fraser-prepared private entry. More emphasis was placed on the speed tests and special stages in this Circuit – there being 18 special stages totalling 45 miles and 8 hill-climbs.

It proved very gruelling, with only 39 of the 65 starters finishing. At the end of stage 1, at Sligo, Boyd's Humber was second with the La Trobe/Chitty Rapier fourth. By the end of stage 2 Boyd and Crawford were first and La Trobe/Chitty third. Boyd continued to excel, made best time on the speed hill-climb at Moll's Gap, but shortly afterwards the Humber slid into a ditch, and was effectively out of the running. By the end of the third leg, the Fraser Rapier was proving consistently faster than the 'works' entry for Rosemary Smith but a day later she was fifth to his fourth. The fifth and final leg saw La Trobe climb to second place overall while the ladies eventually finished 8th overall.

This was a reasonably successful swansong for the marque Rapier, and they repeated it in the Scottish Rally, when Alan Fraser entered Andrew Cowan in a Series IV Rapier, 5395 KV: he finished second with the La Trobe/Chitty pair third. It was fitting that the final honours went to the credit of the "unofficial" team.

From this time, though, new management was firmly in charge, Marcus Chambers' appointment as Competition Manager having been announced back in February of 1964, and the Competition Department entries for the Tulip Rally in 1964 were of

The 'Works' Rapiers: 1956-1964

Imps and one Sunbeam Alpine. As far as the Sunbeam Rapier is concerned the 'front-line' story was over.

Rapiers in motor racing

Although the 'works' Rapiers made many headlines over the years, their exploits in saloon car racing were equally distinguished. Even so, when you look at it logically, for Rootes to go motor racing was really a case of: 'Hope springs eternal....', for the company never truly had the right product at the right time. Either the cars were too heavy, or the engines were not the right size, or were not suitably tuneable for the task – sometimes all at the same time. Because there was prestige at stake, somehow the 'works' team kept plugging on, and the cars lifted trophies in the most unlikely places, and unlikely scenarios. Although the Rapier, and later the Imps, were never outright winners, they sometimes won their classes (more so with the Imps), and usually amazed the spectators.

Consider. When Peter Harper's Rapiers contested the British Saloon Car Championship in the early 1960s, his car was competitive at first, though in later years it was usually slower in a straight line than the 'works' Cortinas and the 'works' Mini Coopers. Yet it was Harper who garnered most of the headlines and pictures, not only by clashing with Christobel Carlisle's Mini-Cooper at Silverstone, but by tipping Alan Hutcheson's Riley 1.5 into a spectacular inversion at Aintree in 1962.

Consider. When the Saloon Car Championship went to Group 5 in 1966, before it all started, the 'works'-supported Fraser Imps were widely expected to be slaughtered by Ralph Broad's Ford Anglia

A Rapier swansong: an Alan Fraser-entered Series IV in the RSAC Scottish Rally in 1964. Co-driver John Aitchison adjusts the fog-lights while Andrew Cowan looks on.

ROOTES MAESTROS
"In their own words."

105Es. But they were not: Bernard Unett, in particular, fought John Fitzpatrick every inch of the way for two years.

Consider, finally, that at the started of the 1970s, Bill McGovern's privately-prepared Imp won so many 1-litre classes that it ended up winning the Championship Trophy. Not once, not twice, but three times, in 1970, 1971 and 1972.

Rallying origins

Unlike his sporting rivals at BMC and Ford, Norman Garrad never had the chance of getting the factory to build 'homologation specials- - lightweight, limited-production machines, with exotic engines - for Rootes would never even consider building anything like the Lotus-Cortinas at this time. Garrad was therefore obliged to do the best possible job that he could, in motor racing, with Sunbeam Alpines and Rapiers. Their chassis, at least, had been well-proven in rallies, but there was really no way he could get lighten, or otherwise reduce, the sturdy construction of their unit-construction body shells.

In 1960 Garrad's problem was that he was already committed to a full rallying programme, but as the Rootes family wanted him to go racing too, he ordered his 'works' chief engineer, Jim Ashworth, to prepare five, brand new aluminium-headed Series III Rapiers (YWK 1 to YWK 5 inclusive) for the coming season. Those cars, he made clear, would be worked hard, and would not only go rallying, but might also be seconded to appear on British and European race tracks too.

Running five new cars was really more than his budget could usually afford, but as he could already identify potential clashes between European Championship rallies, and Group 2 British Saloon Car Championship races, this seemed to be the only way to be well prepared.

Even though their body shells were always far too sturdy to make lightweight racing saloons (though Garrad's mechanics, and a few helpful engineers and managers closer to the assembly lines did their best by providing some thin body panels, and with the removal of sound-deadening and trim, where the regulations allowed this), the Rapiers were surprisingly versatile. By that time, in any case, Lewis Garrad (Norman's son) had managed to homologate a surprising number of options into the Rapier for Group 1 events.

Looking back to the first time author Graham Robson drove a 'works' rally car (from which these race cars were developed), he was astonished by the way the torque was delivered, by the way they handled, and by the way that such Sunbeam Alpine features as tubular exhaust manifolds had somehow been approved for the Rapiers. For British Saloon Car racing the cars had to run in homologated condition, which unhappily meant they could not use all the exotic carburation which had been developed for use on Harrington Alpines.

Alternative camshafts, however, were available - there was a most satisfying surge of torque in the mid-ranges. The real 'works' cars also had overdrives which worked on all forward gears - this was quite illegal, but the drivers were given secret ways of switching this feature in and out, in case the scrutineers found out, and got too persistent....

Accordingly while Paddy Hopkirk and Jimmy Ray tackled the Tulip Rally in 1960, Peter Harper took YWK 1 into the *Daily Express* Production Car race, where he battled with Volvos, Borgwards and Riley 1.5s. Still with a heavyweight rally car, and with a lack of race-preparation expertise to be made up, he was out-paced - but this was just the sighting shot.

When Rootes entered Rapiers in British saloon car racing in 1960, the regulations allowed much modification – which explains why this Austin A40 could keep up with Peter Harper's YWK 4 at Brands Hatch.

Two months later, Harper *and* Paddy Hopkirk contested the saloon race which supported the British F1 GP at Silverstone. The sparks flew straight away, for this was where the 'needle' between Harper and Alan Hutcheson's Riley 1.5 was established, as the cars touched and spun away from the lead.

On that occasion it was to be Hopkirk's day, but a month later Harper took YWK 4 to a well-deserved 1.6litre class victory at Brands Hatch. This was the first of many, for Rootes was rapidly accumulating race-craft, the cars were getting lighter and more powerful, and were handling better.

At the end of the year, in November, two new and much-modified 1.6-litre Rapiers were sent out to California, to contest the International Compact Car Race which was held before the USA F1 GP at Riverside, in California. They were too heavy, maybe, but Peter Harper's car still finished third overall, behind two Jaguar 3.8 Mk IIs: the Rootes distributor was delighted.....

In 1961 there were still problems with clashing programmes to be faced, not only because of the usual rally programme, but particularly as the team was also committed to sending two brand-new Alpines to the Le Mans 24 Hours race, so once again the 'works' Rapiers could only go racing occasionally.

It all started well at the *Daily Express* meeting at Silverstone in May, where Peter Harper, still using YWK 4 - one of the 1960 team cars - easily won the 1.6litre class, finishing sixth overall, and setting a new class lap record; nevertheless, the Rapier was no less than 15.6 seconds *per lap* slower than Graham Hill's winning Jaguar, which showed just how far, and how fast, saloon car had advanced in recent years.

The cars, even so, handled well, and had particularly brave drivers. In July, at a wet British GP meeting, Harper had worked his way up to third place overall (behind two Jaguar 3.8s) before he crashed out, leaving privateer Cuff Miller to win instead.

A bigger effort was proposed for 1962, but it was already clear that smaller, more nimble, cars like the Riley 1.5 might now be a problem. Not only Harper, but Peter Jopp in a second car prepared by Alan Fraser, would fly the flag for the team.

Things worked out exactly as feared. Throughout 1962 there was a running battle between Harper's Rapier and Alan Hutcheson's Riley 1.5: if the two didn't actually hate each other, they never denied it, and the body language between the two, both outside and inside the cars, told its own story. The Rapier was fastest but didn't finish at Snetterton, the Riley prevailed at Easter

ROOTES MAESTROS
"In their own words."

Goodwood, as it did, once again, at Aintree at the end if April (by 0.4sec). Harper then won his class at Silverstone in May, after the Riley had spun out on a wet track, this being a day when Rapiers took 1-2-3-4 in the 1.6litre class, and triumphed again at Crystal Palace in June.

Then came Aintree in July, where Harper spun early in the race, spend many laps carving his way back up to the Riley's back bumper, before 'accidentally' tapping the 1.5, which rolled out of the event: Harper finished fifth overall, shattering the Aintree GP circuit lap record for the class, being beaten only by four 3.8litre Jaguars, which was quite unavoidable. Then on a wet track Jopp won the class at Brands Hatch in August (with Harper third in class).

The season ended at Oulton Park in September, with Harper once again winning his capacity class, this ensuring that he finished a very close second, overall, in the British Saloon Car Championship, behind John Love's BMC Mini-Cooper, which had won its class once more often. As a finale, in *The Motor* Six-Hour race at Brands Hatch, Harper and Peter Procter used 5193 RW to finish fourth overall behind two Jaguars and a Mini-Cooper S.

All of which was very encouraging, but in every way 1963 was set to be the 'Year of the Cortina' (as a Ford publicity film later trumpeted), and Rootes was almost bound to struggle. Norman Garrad's team had to face up to the fact that the brand-new Lotus-Cortinas, even the Willment Cortina GTs, were lighter and more powerful than the Rapier (a car which had already been on the market for seven years) - but nevertheless the remarkable Harper was sent out to fight for the team once again.

It was a vain hope. Although Harper (and, initially, Peter Procter, too) drove his heart out, he was always outpaced by the Willment Cortina GTs, one of whose drivers, Jack Sears, went on to win the Championship outright in that and other Fords, including a gargantuan 7litre Galaxie. Harper's car crashed at Silverstone in May, was well-beaten at Silverstone in July, and with the even more specialised Lotus-Cortina getting its homologation papers from September 1963, Rootes wisely decided to pull the plug on this four-year programme.

Rootes dealer Alan Fraser lent much support to the 'works' team in the early 1960s, this being one of his cars racing on the Silverstone circuit.

'Works' Alpines: Rallying, Le Mans and USA: 1959-1963

How is it that the Sunbeam Alpine of the 1960s rarely seemed to figure strongly in Rootes' motorsport plans? 'Factory-prepared Austin-Healey 3000s, MG MGBs, Triumph TR3As and TR4s and Triumph Spitfires were all prominent in racing and rallying, but the Alpines often had to take a back seat, and let Rootes saloons hog the limelight instead.

One reason, for sure, is that the Alpine usually found itself in the wrong capacity classes, where exotic machinery from Porsche or Alfa Romeo was well-established, but another is that Norman Garrad only had a finite amount of money to spend every year, and usually used this to promote his Sunbeam Rapiers instead.

Fortunately, though, the glamour of the Le Mans 24 Hour race soon elbowed its way into his attention:

Sunbeam Alpines at Le Mans

Old-timers couldn't believe it when 'works' Rootes cars finally went racing in the 1960s. Rootes, after all, had brusquely got rid of all its sporting heritage in the 1930s (surely you remember the exploits of the Roesch Talbots at that time?), for road cars had turned to Loewy-inspired styling in the 1950s, and had only gone back to rallying in the 1940s when it was thought to be good publicity.

So how could it be, that in 1961, 1962 and 1963, Rootes entered near-standard Sunbeam Alpines for the world's most famous race – the Le Mans 24-Hour sports car race – where the cars always performed with honour? But it happened.

Although Rootes already had a formidable and successful rally team at this time, they had little racing experience. Using 'works' Rapiers, Peter Harper had just started saloon car racing in the UK, but that was about the height of it. Even so, and following a fine showing at the International Compact Car Race, at the USA F1 GP meeting at Riverside in November 1960, Competition Manager Norman Garrad was encouraged to enter cars in more racing events, to gain more publicity.

In particular, he was instructed to send cars to that European showpiece - the Le Mans 24 Hour race. Lord Rootes, as usual, had already seen what benefits could be reaped by his rivals – Austin-Healey, MG and Triumph had all competed with honour – and wanted a piece of that action.

Choosing a car. Preparation - and modifications

The new Alpine road car was an obvious car to use. Launched in mid-1959, with a 1,494cc engine, it was already selling well in the USA, and by 1961 the latest 1.6litre cars looked basically suitable for long-distance circuit racing. However, unless a series of special engines (such as the twin-cam 'Sabrina' units built by Triumph) could be produced, there was little point in trying to compete with non-homologated 'prototype' cars. Instead, any cars which were prepared at Humber Road would have to comply with Appendix J Group 3 regulations. Early test sessions at Silverstone proved that such cars would not be all that fast - but that they might be reliable, and last the 24 hours.

161

ROOTES MAESTROS
"In their own words."

First of all, three new Alpine IIs were sent to Sebring in Florida, USA, to take part in the famous 12-Hour race, where the two fastest Alpines, originally driven by Peter Procter and Paddy Hopkirk, jumped straight into the class lead before being overhauled by the 'works' MGAs.

One of the cars eventually survived, that one being driven by the two Peters – Harper and Procter – who were already partners in 'works' rally cars. Eventually it suffered some braking problems, but still managed to finish, third in its 1.6litre capacity class, behind the two MGs. After averaging 74.9mph over 12 hours, this was a very good effort, from which Rootes-USA managed to gain positive publicity by pointing out that the Alpine had been fastest in its price class....

After that the same cars were rushed back to Europe, and re-prepared for the traditional test weekend, which was to be held in April on the Le Mans circuit. At this stage, except that their front and rear bumpers had been removed, the hard-top Alpines looked visually standard. It was, however, abundantly clear that they were still not nearly fast enough in a straight line: not only were they lacking in power, but their aerodynamic qualities seemed to be poor. As *Autocar*'s report on the test weekend commented:

'The Alpines, production-line cars driven by Peter Harper and Michael [Mike] Parkes, managed a best lap in 5min 16.5sec (92.93mph). This lap speed, when the car's maximum speed is little over 100mph, is surprising, but there is scarcely enough margin over the 87-odd mph which they will have to maintain in the 24-Hour race, if they are to qualify as finishers.'

At this Le Mans practice weekend, in fact, the Alpines were the slowest cars on parade - 24 seconds a lap behind a 1.0litre Abarth, and no less than 55 seconds a lap behind the 'works' 1.7litre Porsche RSK (but that was, in fairness, an out and out race car).

Because the aluminium-headed 1.6litre

9203 RW, built for the 1962 Le Mans 24 Hour race, soon after completion, pictured near the Competitions Department in Coventry. The car has yet to be decorated with the race numbers and coloured nose band to help distinguish between the different cars.

'Works' Alpines: Rallying, Le Mans and USA: 1959-1963

engines were already at their tuning limit (Harrington had offered advice on extracting more power, but they were running as 'production' sports cars, which meant that all the tune-up pieces had to be homologated where the regulations said so, or capable for lasting more than 24 racing hours where they did not ….), Rootes would have to find more speed elsewhere.

At this time I was about to join the 'works' rally team as Peter Procter's co-driver, and made occasional visits to Humber Road, so that I could see what was going on. In April, quite casually, Lewis Garrad (Norman's son) mentioned the newly-launched Jaguar E-Type to his elders and betters. Jaguar, after all, was just starting to build these sensational-looking cars on the other side of Coventry.

Lewis and his father than cooked up an enterprising solution, which the Rootes family soon approved after very little discussion. If the engine could not be made more powerful, they reasoned, then the body shells ought to have their drag reduced. It would be done in two ways for the two cars which had secured an entry.

Because the Le Mans circuit was then dominated by the four mile Mulsanne straight, newly-built Alpine race cars would have to be modified, to allow a higher top speed. To do this, they decided, one car would be modified as far as the regulations would allow, to adopt a rounded nose with recessed headlamps, and a Harrington-style fastback tail - as near-copies of the E-Type coupe - while the other car would merely run as a standard-looking hard-top, with a few details smoothed out.

At this point I should explain that Thomas Harrington of Hove, in Sussex, had just launched a special-bodied version of the Alpine – logically enough it was called the Harrington Alpine - which was to be promoted and actively marketed through Rootes dealers. The Harrington company was owned by the Robins & Day Group, and since that company was wholly owned by the Rootes family, with that seasoned old rally driver, George Hartwell, in charge, it all kept itself within the family, as it were.

'Bear in mind,' Lewis Garrad recalls, 'that not one of us had been to Le Mans apart from the April test weekend. We couldn't buy expertise, we hadn't the money. We knew nothing about the

3000 RW being prepared in the Rootes Competition Department workshop prior to the Le Mans 24 Hour race. Peter Harper stands in front of the car, with mechanics Jack Walton (wearing spectacles) and Ernie Beck working on the interior of the car.

ROOTES MAESTROS
"In their own words."

intricacies of the organisers....'

Lewis later admitted: 'The cars weren't anywhere quick enough for a class win, which wasn't really so surprising at all. We came back from the test days and said [to ourselves....] right, we're not going to win, that's for sure. But if we do our job properly, we can make some petrol economy! We had another long talk with Engineering, and thought we could compete for the Index of Thermal Efficiency.'

But, who cared? Motor racing, after all, should be about driving faster, for longer, than your rivals. Did anyone really care how much fuel they used along the way? Ordinary people, maybe not, but the French were different....

The French after all, was now organising the world's most famous sports car race, but had no French-made cars of their own which might win. Accordingly, the French (who, after all, had invented chauvinism ....) therefore set out to devise categories within the race which would favour French manufacturers.

First of all, in the 1950s, this was to make sure that what they called 'Index of Performance' rules would favour small French-engined cars, but after Porsche (and, later, Lotus) got into the swing of things, they had to start again. This time, therefore, they invented a category for what they described as the 'Thermal Efficiency Index'.

To quote from the English translation of the original French text for 1961:

'The Thermal Efficiency Index is based on the relationship between the car's engine capacity, weight and quantity of fuel used during the 24 Hours. The calculations are

A race official attaching a seal to the engine of 3000 RW, to prevent unauthorised removal or changing of components during the race.

The two Alpines lined up before the 1961 Le Mans 24 Hour race. The shape of the Harrington coupé bodywork on 3000 RW is clearly shown in this picture, in contrast to the standard shape of 3001 RW parked alongside.

as follows, the Thermal Efficiency Index being IR:

$$IR = Em/Er$$

Where Er is the actual fuel consumption of the cars in litres per 100 kilometres (62.15 miles), and Em is calculated from the following formula:

Em = P-300/100 + V/25 + (V-95)2/600 + (V-140)3/21,000

V being the average hourly speed of the car for the 24 hours, and P being the weight of the car in kilogrammes (1kg = 2.2lb).

There was absolutely no point in debating with the organisers as to why and how this formula had been finalised – not only because no-one ever knowingly won an argument with a Le Mans official, the other being that they had clearly taken advice from so-called French 'experts' on the matter. As far as Rootes was concerned, they did not know whether they could win, but they did, at least, think that their Alpines might be competitive!

Lewis Garrad later admitted that his team had quite a lot of trouble in getting the two cars through pre-event scrutineering. Because it was the team's very first visit to Le Mans, where the organisers were not only arrogant, and somehow opposed to almost every team which was not French, but also had their own way of doing things:

'We knew nothing about the intricacies of the organisers,' Lewis once told me,' who were the living end. For instance, we knew nothing about the rule that the boot had to

Above: Practice for the 1961 Le Mans 24 Hour: Peter Harper leans on the pit counter while Paddy Hopkirk appears to be describing concerns with his car's handling.

Below: 3000 RW being fuelled prior to the start of the race. Careful monitoring of fuel used was important as this was one of the factors in the formula used to calculate the Index of Thermal Efficiency.

'Works' Alpines: Rallying, Le Mans and USA: 1959-1963

have space for a "standard" wooden suitcase to be fitted inside it.

'The Ferrari people were there [at scrutineering] at the same time, and they too were having trouble with the suitcase rule. In my very limited French I heard the Ferrari men say to the organisers: "Look, that's sufficient as far as we're concerned, and you either accept it, or we go back to Modena."

'They did! I thought - Blimey - if they can do it, so can I.'

Lewis, therefore, also had a spat with the scrutineers, sided with Ferrari, got his way - and got through scrutineering.

After all this, the race cars were actually five seconds a lap *slower* than in April. Rootes, it seems, had actually done nothing to reduce the drag by fitting cowled headlamps, and a Harrington-style hard top, for the standard-shape car was actually quicker, and proved to be so, throughout the race. Rootes may have looked at the E-Type for inspiration, but had then ruined the aerodynamics by fitting extra driving lamps, along with brackets which could engage with the quick-lift jacks.

The story of the race, effectively, is no news at all, for they were almost entirely reliable for the entire 24 hours. Although they got away very briskly from the Le Mans start – pictures exist showing that the Hopkirk/Jopp car had got away in front of all the special Sabrina-engined Triumph TRSs, and the sole Austin-Healey 3000, plus at least a dozen other cars, and that the Harrington-bodied car was already away, and out of sight.

From then on, the two cars raced, called in for refuelling, circulated - and so on, until the standard-shape car was disqualified at around half distance. This, by the way, was because the Hopkirk/Jopp car was suffering from overdrive problems, and later suffered an engine bearing failure.

The reason for the disqualification? The organisers said that Rootes had added some transmission oil too soon after a pit-stop. This was an innocent mistake - but as ever the Le Mans organisers were not taking prisoners. Perhaps if this had been a French Alpine-Renault instead of a British Sunbeam-Alpine, things might have been very different. Who knows?

The two Peters, Harper and Procter, continued to lap in a fast, neat and (to them) totally boring manner - never faster than in April, so there seemed to be no doubt that the Harrington modifications had been a failure - and spent only about nine minutes in their pits during the entire 24 hours. Originally their car was down in 38th place, but it grabbed fourteen places before half distance, and finally finished 16th overall. Not only was that car looking as good as new after 24 flat-out hours, but it was still going just as well. By comparison, outright victory went to a prototype Ferrari, which had a 3litre engine, completed 2782.2 miles, and averaged 115.925 mph.

Over the 24 hours, the Alpine averaged 90.92mph (it completed 2,182 miles) - and except for the two *very* special 'works' Lotus Elites, was the fastest production-based car in the race. Quite unexpectedly, too, the Alpine also won the Index of Thermal Efficiency.

'The car was using very little petrol,' Lewis later told me, 'and causing no trouble. I remember at about nine in the morning, the chief organiser told me that if we souped our car up a little we'd beat Porsche for the fuel economy thing.

'The car just kept going round and round. Frankly we couldn't believe it! It gave us no trouble at all.'

As *Autocar*'s Harry Mundy later wrote:

'Peter Harper's and Peter Procter's Thermal Efficiency Index win in the Sunbeam Alpine was praiseworthy and unexpected - particularly in view of it

Above: On its way to winning the Index of Thermal Efficiency in the 1961 Le Mans 24 Hour race. In good company about to be overtaken by the Ferrari 250 GT of Stirling Moss/Graham Hill and the Aston Martin DBR1s of Jim Clark/Ron Flockhart and Roy Salvadori/Tony Maggs.

Below: 3000 RW pictured at the 2008 Silverstone Classic event. It was sold into private ownership in 1962 after undertaking a tour of Rootes' showrooms to celebrate its race success. After languishing in a barn for some 10 years, the car was rebuilt by a member of the Harrington family over twenty years until being completed in the late 1990s.

'Works' Alpines: Rallying, Le Mans and USA: 1959-1963

being the Alpine's first appearance at Le Mans.

'This car was the slower of the two: the Hopkirk/Jopp car [the standard-bodied machine] had the advantage of a couple of hundred extra rpm, and was several places ahead of the Harper car when it was disqualified. With a required race average of 87mph, it achieved 91mph throughout the race – including pit stops. No oil was added, nor tyres changed. It's fastest lap was 95.5mph and its fastest recorded speed down the Mulsanne Straight, 115mph – with a fuel consumption of 18mpg for the race.'

We now know that the cars were both running in Harrington Stage 3 tune, which meant that peak power was about 100bhp – not a huge increase over the standard road car (which produced 80bhp), but one which meant that it should last the 24 hours – and did.

Just how ordinary this car really was, was proved in January 1962, when it was re-prepared at Humber Road, fitted out with heaters and rally equipment, and loaned to *Autosport* Editor Gregor Grant to compete in the Monte Carlo Rally. That Gregor did not bring home any awards (he told a good story, and wrote even better stories, than he drove....) was no fault of the car.

Second expedition

For 1962 Rootes wondered if they might benefit from a repeat miracle on the race track, and built-up two sets of brand-new Alpine race cars – one for use at Le Mans in June, the other set to be campaigned in the Sebring (Florida) 12 Hour race in March, where a good result might give a welcome boost to Alpine sales in North America. Naturally the Sebring cars – there were three of them, looking absolutely standard with factory hard-tops, a fourth car being privately entered, and being an early-type Harrington-style model instead.

This time, however, there was no intention to use Harrington-shaped race cars at Le Mans, even though it was accepted that the four-mile-long Mulsanne straight could clearly have a big influence on a car's lap time, if the top speed could be raised. After the 1961 event, a sober analysis of the result seemed to show that the use of a Harrington-style fastback body style had not been any more aerodynamically efficient than the car with the standard, ex-factory-hardtop, type of shape. Accordingly, although there would have been no commercial difficulties, or especially 'political' difficulties - with the Hove-based concern, it was decided not to try again.

This time, therefore, newly-built race cars started life as normal-shape hardtop models, but with large fuel filler caps protruding through the rear windows, and with a revised rear-end style including a raised boot lid profile, and a squared-off rear panel. Although these cars were already planned in the winter of 1961/1962, such machines were not sent out to Sebring. However, and as already mentioned, buoyant USA sales, and a sporting image, were commercially vital to Rootes (the MG and Triumph importers would almost certainly be supporting cars in this event too), so even though this could be a boring 12-hour motor race on a lousy, rough-surfaced, airfield perimeter track, the factory felt honour-bound to enter.

This time round, the team was pleased to discover discovered that its 1.6litre cars were, at least, a match for BMC's MGA 1600 Mk IIs, and that they were significantly faster than the factory-built TVRs which had been built under the supervision of ex-Triumph boss Ken Richardson. Rootes, however, readily accepted that they could not hope to outpace the 1.6litre Porsches

ROOTES MAESTROS
"In their own words."

which found themselves in the same class, and could therefore only hope that the Alpines would be more reliable over a 12 hour race.

In the first lap melee, Peter Harper's car was hit hard by a rather brakeless Chevrolet Corvette, and had to carry on for the full 12 hours with a damaged front door, and with marks on both front and rear wings. Soon it was the turn of Ken Miles, in another of the Alpines, to hit an Osca driven by Denise McCluggage, but this all seemed to be normal for sports car racing in the USA, and the cars carried on.

As expected, the Alpines could not keep up with the Porsches – one was driven by F1 driver Dan Gurney and would finish sixth overall at 81.466mph – but matched the TVRs until those cars wilted, and gradually pulled away from the MGAs.

Towards the end of the race, the Payne/Sheppard car suffered a major engine blow-up, and although there was apparently a hole in the crankcase after something collapsed internally, team managed Jim Ashworth realised that nothing more could be done, and sent the car back out to keep limping on. Amazingly, it kept on going – just.

At the end of a gruelling 12-hour slog, the Alpines had given the MGA 1600 MkIIs a good beating, which was an important advance over 1961 - for the two Peters (Harper and Procter) were a full lap ahead of the Sears/Hedges MG team car - but they could not match the Porsches, so had to be happy with third place in their class, and a sturdy 15th overall: it was good to note that no 'normal' sports cars finished ahead of them – for the leader board was of course crammed with prototypes, five of them being Ferraris, and three of them Porsches.

The good news, though, was that the leading Alpine averaged 74.97mph in 1962, which was significantly faster than in 1961, so real progress was clearly being made. The race cars, incidentally, were sold off soon after the completion of the race, and as far as is known, they never came back to Europe.

Following this performance, there were high hopes for the 1962 Le Mans 24 Hour race. This time the race cars - 9201RW, 9202RW and 9203RW (their Coventry-based registrations) - looked more nearly standard than they had been in 1961, though because the regulations allowed this, their front and rear bumpers had been removed and the shells tidied up, and this time the sharply cut-off tail style (which was purely for racing, and not intended for use in future production cars) not only tidied up the aerodynamics significantly, but made the cars look extremely neat. It was a style which would never feature on any Alpine or Tiger road cars.

Lewis Garrad (like father, like son) was an avid reader of all regulations (wasn't it Stirling Moss who, on another occasion, once quipped: 'The race begins when the regulations arrive...'?), and because International FIA Appendix J Group 3 regulations allowed it, these second-generation Le Mans cars were made even more special than before, having perspex side and rear 'glass', and using many aluminium body skin panels. More work had been done on the 1.6litre engines (though, in truth, this reliable old engine design was already close to the end of its development potential), and the Garrads hoped that the cars would be even more effective than in 1961.

Just one car was taken out to the April test weekend on the Le Mans circuit, where Peter Harper lapped in 5min. 8.6sec, and clocked 123mph, which was a big advance on what had been achieved at that stage of the programme, in 1961. Rootes later stated that the body style innovations had

'Works' Alpines: Rallying, Le Mans and USA: 1959-1963

reduced drag by 8 per cent - which meant that the Harrington style, complete with the cowled headlamps, hadn't been at all efficient. Looks, it seemed, were not everything ….

In 1962, unhappily, there was no repeat of the great, and unexpected, success of 1961. Throughout the race itself, both the cars suffered from intermittently sticking throttles. The Harper-Procter car kept going, against all the odds, while the second car (which was driven by Paddy Hopkirk and Peter Jopp) retired with a blown engine, after the connecting rod bearings had failed. Even so, although the fastest of the two cars lapped in 5min. 5sec - a big advance on 1961 - and the Harper-Procter car averaged 93.24mph (compared with 90.92mph in the 1961 race), on this occasion, no awards were won. All this, incidentally, was achieved in spite of a major engine rebuild (described below) and the fact that the overdrive failed later in the race.

Although the leading Alpine had covered 56 miles more, and finished in fifteenth place, it wasn't well-placed in the Thermal Efficiency *or* Index of Performance categories. Further, neither car was completely reliable.

It isn't generally known that *both* cars suffered engine big end failures. Damage to the Hopkirk/Jopp car's engine was serious, and the bearings were changed in front of the pit counter, but the rebuilt engine finally failed again after the race had been running for 18 hours. Amazingly, the other car was brought into the pits for the same work to be done, had its oil drained, then had its big end bearings changed, and the engine re-assembled - all in well under an hour !

Try asking your race mechanic – any mechanic, in fact - to complete such a job, and make him tackle it in the same way, in the maelstrom of a pit lane, at a time when he was already exhausted, it was dusty, and working conditions could not have been worse – all this at a time when he might already have been on duty for at least 16 hours in the heat, noise and drama of an International motor race, before it was done!

With the bearings changed and the engine re-assembled (to meet the rules the old engine oil had to be re-used, though it was filtered first), the car was sent out again for a few laps to 'run in' the new shells, its oil was then topped up, and 9202RW carried on as usual.

Consider, now, that the car lost at least 80 miles, maybe 90 miles, in this drama, consider that its overdrive later stopped working, and the gearbox then started jumping out of intermediate gears - then ask yourself where it *might* have finished?

A quick look at the actual finishing order suggests that the Alpine *might* have averaged nearly 98mph, and that it could have taken 10th.

Even so, many years later Lewis Garrad was not about to make any excuses:

'We made a complete mess of it. After what had been achieved in 1961, we thought that we knew it all - but money was running out, and we didn't have enough, really. It taught me a lesson. If you are going to do something, do it well, because you can't go back to it after.'

This, in any case, was achieved at the highpoint of the Rootes Group's empire, which gradually slid into loss (the Hillman Imp project had a lot to answer for....), and spending on motorsport came under pressure. Maybe this explains why, for 1963, the team kept the old cars, which had had a busy life in the meantime, to compete once again in the Le Mans 24 Hours race.

At Sebring in 1963, two Alpines were prepared for local drivers to race, and in the face of opposition from new MG MGBs, and from three TVRs, the cars managed to finish third and fourth in their class. Once again, it

171

Above: The Paddy Hopkirk/Peter Jopp Alpine during the 1962 Le Mans 24 Hour race.

Below: The interior of one of the Alpines built for Le Mans in 1962. Note that the interior is still carpeted (and remained so for the race), the chronometric rev-counter above the steering column and the addition of a padded knee brace on the driver's door.

Above: Peter Procter and Peter Harper pose for the traditional pre-race photograph. They drove together in all three of the Alpine campaigns at Le Mans.

Below: Paddy Hopkirk and Peter Jopp alongside 9203 RW, their mount for the 1962 Le Mans 24 Hour race.

Above: The classic Le Mans start, with the drivers running across the track to their cars. Starting drivers in 1962 were Peter Procter (car 32) and Paddy Hopkirk (car 33).

Below: Peter Jopp swings 9203 RW through the Dunlop curve in 1962. This car wore a yellow nose band to distinguish it from no. 32 (the Harper/Procter car) which carried a red band.

'Works' Alpines: Rallying, Le Mans and USA: 1959-1963

was pluck and reliability which paid dividends, not pace, and once again, it was good to see that most of the cars which beat them were prototypes, or had very large engines. All of the MGBs and TVRs, incidentally, retired with blown engines.

Then, for Le Mans in 1963, two of the year-old cars (9201RW and 9202RW – for 9203RW had been sold off to Alan Fraser) which had already been active in the 1962 season, were re-prepared, though with no significant technical innovations. In fact one of those two cars had been quite busy since the 1962 race, for it had spent some time as a rally car, sometimes on the roughest roads, and sometimes coping with icy, snowy, conditions!

In 1963, the Le Mans expedition was not a happy occasion. Clearly the cars were close to the limits of their development, the lack of cash to spend on motorsport was becoming obvious, and the advance made by other teams made it obvious that the Alpines were lagging behind. One car blew an engine in practice, and both cars retired during the race with broken engines - one with head gasket failure after six hours of racing, and the other with a broken crankshaft after 18 hours.

The second car (driven by 'Tiny' Lewis and Shell's Motorsport manager Keith Ballisat) had been running without overdrive for at least 12 hours (overdrive failure was something which many British 'works' teams had to endure during this period of history), but was still averaging 97mph, and leading its 3litre GT capacity class when it finally expired. The lack of overdrive, the over-revving which surely followed, and the broken crankshaft must of course have been related. For Norman and Lewis Garrad it was no consolation to know that the cars had once again been marginally faster than before - if, that is, you can measure one second in a 5min. 4sec lap - though it was finally clear that the Alpine could no longer be considered as a credible or competitive race car.

****

Le Mans 24 Hour race - the Alpine's three year record

1961

#34	Peter Harper/Peter Procter 16th - 90.92mph
#35	Paddy Hopkirk/Peter Jopp DNF - engine failure

Car #34 won the Index of Thermal Efficiency competition

1962

#32	Peter Harper/Peter Procter 15th - 93.24mph
#33	Paddy Hopkirk/Peter Jopp DNF - engine failure

1963

#32	'Tiny' Lewis - Keith Ballisat DNF - engine failure
#33	Peter Harper - Peter Procter DNF - engine failure

****

How many Alpine race cars attended Le Mans?

In **1961** there were two new cars:

3000RW	this car carried Harrington-style bodywork
3001RW	this car had normal bodywork, allied to the factory-style hardtop

175

ROOTES MAESTROS
"In their own words."

In **1962** there were two different cars:

9202RW
9203RW   both these cars had near-normal looking bodywork and the factory hardtop, except that the tail fins had been cropped, and the rear-end somewhat re-styled.

A third race car, 9201RW was also prepared in 1962, but did not race at Le Mans

In **1963** two of the three 1962 cars were used once again:

9201RW
9202RW   as in 1962, both cars had basically normal bodywork, factory hardtops, and the cropped tails.

****

Almost as a consequence of the Alpines' fine performance at Le Mans in 1961, a car was then entered in a three-hour Grand Prix d'Endurance, which was to be held on the Riverside Raceway circuit in California, just a few miles inland from Los Angeles.

Although this was not officially a 'works'-backed entry, a certain amount of factory support was provided. Double F1 World Champion Jack Brabham (who was already marketing tuning kits for the Alpine and wanted to build up his business in North America), borrowed a car from one of his North American customers, did what could be done to make it more suitable for track racing (he fitted a long range fuel tank, for example, which Rootes had already made optional), fitted a roll hoop behind the seats, and removed the windscreen completely – then persuaded his old chum and normal race rival, Stirling Moss, to share driving duties with him.

The Bud Rose entered Alpine driven by Jack Brabham and Stirling Moss to third place overall (behind two Porsches) and first in class in the 1961 3-Hour sports car race at Riverside, California.

'Works' Alpines: Rallying, Le Mans and USA: 1959-1963

Brabham and Moss, for sure, could have found rides in faster and more competitive cars, but found the prospect of racing in California, in an Alpine, to be truly intriguing! Jack, who was not at all used to taking part in massed-start production car races, found the start to be frightening, even by his high-performance standards:

'I'll never forget the traffic jam after the starter dropped the flag…. The crush was so great that it was quite terrifying for the first few laps. There were cars everywhere - on the course, off the course, up the banks, and bumping one another like dodgems on a fairground….'

Even so, Jack kept going for a full two hours, before coming into the pits, and handing over to Stirling Moss for the last hour. Throughout the entire 180 minutes, the Alpine was reliable, and handled well – though naturally it was not stupendously fast. There was one major problem, when a rear brake seal failed, and caused a 16 minute pit stop for repairs, and the gearbox was all ready to cry 'enough' at the end of the event. Even so, at the end it had covered 225 miles at an average speed of 75mph – and was placed third overall. Norman Garrad, who was there to run the pits and the lap chart, was overwhelmed by the positive publicity which followed.

And, as Brabham himself said:

'I found it a very comfortable way to go motor racing. I enjoyed myself so much I think I'd like to have another go….'

Two of the three Sunbeam Alpines built originally for the 1962 Le Mans 24 Hour race, pictured at the Silverstone Classic event in July 2008.

ROOTES MAESTROS
"In their own words."

Peter Procter, who drove in all three of Rootes' Le Mans campaigns with the Alpines from 1961 to 1963 and then in the sole outing with the Tiger in 1964, alongside the Hopkirk/Jopp car from 1962.

Alpines in rallying

While all this high-profile motor racing was going on, a few Alpine entries were made in International rallies, often alongside the 'works' Rapiers, but sometimes quite independent of the rest of the team's activities.

Right from the start, in 1959, Norman Garrad realised that his team would always struggle to make the new-generation Alpine into a competitive rally car. Mechanically, of course, it would be easy enough to transplant all the running gear from the ever-improving 'works' Rapiers (for the Alpine was based on the same, though shortened under-pan/platform, with the same front and rear suspension), but as a two-seater sports car (which would run, by definition, in the Group 3 category), the Alpine would have to face up to fierce competition from Porsche 356, Austin-Healey 3000, Triumph TR3A (later TR4) and MGA/MGB types.

Since the original Alpine used a 78bhp/1,494cc engine, and the class limit was 1.6litres, this was also a built-in handicap which had to be overcome. It was not until the arrival of the Alpine II at the end of 1960 that it got a 1,592cc engine, and could compete on more equal terms.

Purely for interest, the original Alpine of 1959 weighed 2,135lb, which provided a

178

'Works' Alpines: Rallying, Le Mans and USA: 1959-1963

power/weight ratio of 74bhp/tonne. The Rapier Series III saloon (which was just about to be announced, had 73bhp, weighed 2,340lb, and a power/weight ratio of 70bhp/tonne.

Garrad – as always, a fiercely competitive man - was simply not prepared to accept a policy of entering Alpines merely to compete with honour, so chose only to send cars to events where they might have a chance to win something. The new Alpine, in any case, was not put on sale until the summer of 1959 and by the time it had been homologated for use in motorsport the end of the season was nigh.

However, corporate policy was not always with him, as his son Lewis once told me:

'Management were determined that the volume of the Rapier would be such that we needed that sort of push behind it. They thought the Alpine would sell on its appearance – and as a matter of fact it did. It was an attractive-looking car, and was thought of as a tarty car, which the young man was bought by his Daddy. But the Rapier needed a constant promotion. That was the main reason for concentrating on the Rapier. It was more of a workhorse....'

Accordingly, there was no rush to get the Alpine into motorsport, and the very first rally appearance of a 'works' Alpine was in the RAC Rally – the event which, as already related, would eventually be mired in controversy because of the blockage of one important section by snow, and by the inability of many crews to reach the time control at Braemar.

Two cars took the start – one being a 'works' car (XWK 418) driven by Jimmy Ray and Phil Crabtree, the second (D63 – a personal number) being prepared and entered by that hyper-active Rootes dealer Alan Fraser from Kent, whose co-driver was Lesley Shenley-Price. As already noted in the Rapier section, this was an event whose results hinged around a competitor's decision when faced with the blockage in Scotland. Those who took a long diversion, around the mountains, and made it to Braemar (even though penalised for lateness) finished at the top of the lists, while those who did not finished nowhere. A total of 31 cars (from an entry of nearly 200) reached Braemar by various routes, 15 of them within the 60 minutes lateness deadline.

Alan Fraser, who had lost a lot of time at other time controls along the way, took the diversion, and was eventually classified 12th overall, and third in class (behind a Morgan Plus Four and a TR3A), while Jimmy Ray tried to force the drifts on the Tomintoul Road, failed, took a maximum penalty at Braemar, and finished fifth in class. This was a respectable, if not very distinguished, way to start a new model's career.

Although there were no 'works' Alpines in the 1960 Monte Carlo Rally, private owners filled the gap with honour. In an event where Peter Harper/Raymond Baxter took fourth overall in their factory-supported Rapier, Swedish drivers Backlund/Falk, in a private Alpine which had started from Oslo, won their capacity class in an event where accurate time keeping on the last regularity section was all important.

It was a start, but little more than that. Later in 1960, private owners also performed well in the Circuit of Ireland at Eastertime (Charles Eyre-Maunsell finished third in his capacity class after leading it for some days), while Nicky Filinis took second in his class in the Acropolis Rally (rough, tough, hot and dusty as usual). Mary Handley-Page took third in her class in the French Alpine Rally, driving a Bournemouth-registered car which had clearly been prepared by the Hartwell/Harrington organisation.

From 1961, when the Alpine had become Series II, and could therefore be faster and more powerful because of the use of its

Above: Mary Handley Page and Pauline Mayman on the Gavia Pass in the Dolomites, competing in the 1961 Alpine Rally.

Below: The team of Swedish-entered Alpines before the 1960 Monte Carlo Rally. Car no. 111, in the middle, finished 31st overall and won its class, driven by Backlund and Falk. Neither of the other two cars completed the event.

'Works' Alpines: Rallying, Le Mans and USA: 1959-1963

1.6litre engine, things looked up a little. Once again, the Rootes factory concentrated on the use of Rapiers in the high-profile Monte Carlo Rally, and were therefore astonished (and delighted) to discover that their faithful Swedish entrant, Mr Backlund, had once again won his capacity class.

This was all the more meritorious because this particular Monte Carlo Rally was afflicted by a quite ludicrous handicapping system, and was the very first to feature flat-out special stages of any type. The handicap featured a coefficient which was used to 'adjust' the special stage times – that coefficient involving a complex formula which included the sporting group, the engine size of the car, and its catalogued weight. The fact that this favoured cars like the French Panhards surprised none of the cynics (favouritism for French cars? Surely not....?), but it immediately made most normal cars uncompetitive.

The Alpine of Backlund/Falk, therefore, won its capacity class with honour, but was absolutely nowhere in general classification.

After repeat performances in Ireland (Eyre-Maunsell) and the Greek Acropolis (Filinis), Rootes was then delighted to see that John Melvin won the Scottish Rally outright. Those were the days when the Scottish was still a semi-social event, with much main road motoring, much admiring of Highland scenery, and a few driving tests and sprints to help sort out a result, though on this occasion there were a few special stages too.

Melvin, in fact, was a Scottish-based Rootes main dealer who used his personally-prepared car (registered 2 BUS) on the event. Melvin was a competent, if not perhaps a 'works' standard of driver, and there was no doubt that his car was very well prepared. On this multi-day event, where (as the author can confirm) personal alcohol poisoning was at least as hazardous as the route itself, Melvin eventually took the lead and finally provided the Alpine with its first-ever outright victory.

Garrad was delighted, as was Rootes management – especially as Melvin was a big hitter on the Scottish Rootes dealer scene – but there was still little change to the factory's attitude to 'works' Alpines, in rallying at least, though one or two singleton entries were made.

In the 1961 French Alpine where, of course, the 'works' Rapiers finished third and fifth overall (as already described), there was a single 'works' Alpine for Mary Handley-Page/Pauline Mayman, who were aiming for the Ladies' Prize (against Pat Moss's Austin-Healey 3000 – a big task, but in the end she crashed that car....), and also a class award. On that occasion, she was driving a Hartwell/Harrington-provided car, motored steadily, but lost time on the fastest and most difficult road sections, and finished second in the Ladies category (behind Ewy Rosqvist's 'works' Volvo).

Although Garrad had all but given up on the Alpine as a rally car, he dug one of the ex-1961 race cars out of store – 3001 RW, the car which had won the Index of Thermal Efficiency – re-prepared it for winter rallying, and lent it to Gregor Grant, who was Editor of Britain's motor sport weekly magazine, *Autosport*. Although Gregor was by no means up to 'works' driving standards, he could be guaranteed to write a good story, and would bring good publicity to the company.

Starting from Paris, although he finished the event, fifth in his class, this car suffered a broken overdrive (I almost wrote 'as usual' at this juncture, for Laycock problems were endemic at this time....), an accident on a road section before Chambery, and poor tyre choice on the first special stage after Chambery. Private owner (a Scottish rally victor) John Melvin had a less scary trip

181

9202 RW was a versatile machine, here being driven in the 1963 Monte Carlo Rally by Gregor Grant and Tommy Wisdom.

'Works' Alpines: Rallying, Le Mans and USA: 1959-1963

(though he, too, went off the road on the first stage, and finished third in his class.

At the end of the season, Norman Garrad then indulged his new lady driver, Rosemary Smith (who would later become justly famous for her exploits in Imps and Tigers), by setting her to tackle the British RAC Rally, using 9202 RW, the self-same machine in which the two Peters – Harper and Procter – had finished the Le Mans 24 Hour race earlier in the summer.

This was a gallant gesture, which was never likely to pay off in terms of results, for although Rosemary was a very capable driver, the Alpine (especially one particular car which had originally been built with endurance racing in mind) could not be expected to master the rocks, mud and gravel surfaces of RAC Rally special stages.

Rosemary, as everyone expected, did her level best to overcome every handicap, but was always fighting an uphill battle: at least she made it through to the finish in Bournemouth, well down the field. It didn't help that at one point, Rosemary put the car off the road in Coed-y-Brenin Forest, and found it jammed in a small planting of apprentice Christmas trees, not easily to be extracted. The legend goes that to get enough grip under the rear wheels, Rosemary had to sacrifice her suede jacket....

For the 1963 Monte Carlo Rally, Rootes once again loaned a car to *Autosport*'s Gregor Grant, who had Tommy Wisdom as his co-driver on that occasion. On this occasion, the car chosen to end a peaceful retirement in the ice and snow of the French mountains was 9202 RW (ex-Rosemary Smith/RAC Rally *and* ex-Harper/Procter in the 1962 Le Mans race), but there was absolutely no luck for the crew at all, for this was the event where a blizzard more or less closed down the event completely, one result being that Grant and Wisdom, both of them rally veterans who would not have given up until it was forced upon them, ran out of time.

Rosemary took the same old car out on the Scottish Rally, but had to retire with a radiator which would no longer hold any water. Three months later, though, with Margaret Mackenzie as her intrepid co-driver, she tackled the ten-day Tour de France, which included several hour-long races dotted around France, driving the Le Mans type Alpine in the Grand Touring category, while all her Rootes team colleagues used Rapiers on the saloon car classes.

Considering the length, severity, and the sheer physical challenge of this event, Rosemary and the Alpine put in a great performance, eventually finishing sixth overall in the GT category, third overall in the 1.6litre capacity class (behind two very hot Alfa Romeo Giulias) – and won the Coupe des Dames into the bargain. It was *Autocar* who got the flavour of everything exactly right, by providing detailed results, and a picture of her Alpine ending the Col du Rousset hillclimb! And, as the same magazine reported, Rosemary: '....beat all but two of the 12 Alfa Romeos in the 2litre class, all eight Porsches, and all the three Simca-Abarths.'

That, though, really was the end of the Alpine's run as a 'works' competition car, and Charles Eyre-Maunsell later bought that car. Not only had it come to the peak of its development, but it was clear that it would eventually be overwhelmed by several of the new breed of 'homologation specials'. Norman Garrad, in any case, was about to be moved sideways out of his job as Competitions Manager, and the still-secret Tiger was in the wings....

183

ROOTES MAESTROS
"In their own words."

Humbers on Safari, RAC and Liege-Sofia-Liege: 1950s and 1960s

It isn't only the most glamorous cars which go rallying. Although Norman Garrad usually got his own way, and entered only Sunbeams or Sunbeam-Talbots as 'works' cars, sometimes there would be pressure from above to use alternative models.

From time to time, Rootes' top management directed him to give one or other of the Humber range an outing, if only to keep their sales force happy, or to remind the general public that the brand still existed. Publicity for a brand, particularly favourable publicity, was always welcome.

In theory, there was never a Humber which was going to win anything outright – but amazingly, there would be class successes, and near misses, all of which should be recorded. Over the years, as far as Humber was concerned, there was a sprinkling of sparkling performances in Humbers, unexpected successes and – yes, let's be honest about this – a few embarrassments too.

It was one thing to unleash Maurice Gatsonides on the Monte Carlo, where he almost won in a Super Snipe in 1950 – but was it ever a good idea to send new Humber models on the East African Safari and to expect any success? Asking Peter Harper to grapple with a Super Snipe on the RAC Rally was surely a waste of his talents, but on the other hand for BBC Motoring Correspondent Raymond Baxter to win his capacity class in the RAC in another Super Snipe was a real bonus.

The heroics of the '15-Countries-in-Five-Days' run of 1952 have already been described (on pages 75 to 81), but there were other occasions when quite startling results turned up.

Monte Carlo Rally 1950

Although the Monte was already famous, and got world-wide attention from the media, after the Second World War it took years for the event to be revived. Promises of a revival in 1947 and again in 1948 were both abandoned, either because road conditions were still war-scarred, or because fuel supplies could not be guaranteed. In fact, the first post-war Monte did not occur until January 1949 when as we know, a 'works' team of Sunbeam-Talbot 90s took part.

Then came 1950, when not only did Rootes enter their Sunbeam-Talbot 90s, but they also found time to prepare a gargantuan Humber Super Snipe for that redoubtable Dutchman, Maurice Gatsonides, to drive. Even so, although this car, which carried the Coventry registration number of JHP 329, was prepared just as well as Rootes could make it, few thought that it stood any chance.

The basic specification was not promising. With a chassis frame dating from 1935, a body style modified from a 1935 shape, and with an old-design 100bhp/4.0litre side-valve six-cylinder engine to tow it along, there was nothing, mechanically, to get excited about. A Super Snipe, after all, weighed 3,360lb, had a steering column gearchange (Rootes called it Synchromatic, and expected everyone to be impressed – they were not), and was 15ft. long.

Bad news – but the fact that Gatsonides was not only gritty and determined, had more experience of Monte than most, and practised the classification test up and over the Col de Braus in the mountains behind

ROOTES MAESTROS
"In their own words."

In the 1950 Monte Carlo Rally, Maurice Gatsonides astonished everyone with his mastery of the vast Humber Super Snipe, for he took second place, just a whisker behind the victorious Hotchkiss.

Monte Carlo until he could surely have tackled it in his sleep, made it all look more promising. His co-driver, K.S.Barendregt, was also experienced, had been with Gatsonides before, and knew that one of his most important tasks was to keep well clear of his driving partner's ego.

Although 282 cars started from six far-flung European cities, the routes came together at Rheims in northern France, after which the entire field hit blizzard conditions south of Lyons, and in the mountains between there and arrival in Monte Carlo itself. Car after car slid helplessly off the road, and in the end only five cars – four of them, including Gatsonides's Humber, having started from Monte Carlo three days earlier, had kept to the schedule, and were un-penalised on arrival.

Because of the regulations which applied (and there was nothing more rigid than a Monegasque sticking to the rules!) it was only those five cars – three Simcas, Becquart's Hotchkiss and the Super Snipe – which qualified to tackle the Mountain Circuit. With conditions suddenly much better, and the snow and ice melted away, the competition was incredibly close. At the end of the day, Becquart's Hotchkiss had lost only 45.2 seconds on the strict regularity schedule imposed over the Col de Braus, Gatsonides's Humber 46.58sec, and J.Quinlin's third-placed Simca 49.34sec. Even though the Humber was handicapped

Above: Three of the Rootes works entries in the 1954 Monte Carlo Rally in Holland having started from Munich. The Humber Super Snipe was crewed by George Murray-Frame/John Pearman. The two Sunbeam-Talbots were driven by Leslie Johnson/Norman Garrad (no. 379) and Sheila van Damm/Anne Hall (no. 361). Together with the car of Stirling Moss, these Sunbeam-Talbots were awarded the Charles Faroux Trophy for the manufacturers' team award.

Below: 'Goff' Imhof and Raymond Baxter started the 1954 "Monte" in fine style from Munich, but their rally ended in a crash.

ROOTES MAESTROS
"In their own words."

quite severely by its weight, bulk and the need to tackle so many tight hairpin bends, Gatsonides had failed to win by just 1.38 seconds.

All in all, it was a remarkable show, especially as one of Gatsonides' trophies was the Barclay's Bank Ltd. Silver Challenge trophy for the best performance by a British car. It was a great performance, one that quite obliterated the third-best British-car performance, which was by a private owner called Peter Harper, in a Hillman Minx....

It's only fair to point out that this result was more to Gatso's credit than to that of the Super Snipe, which may explain why Rootes made little effort to build a serious competition programme around the brand.

Because the Humber Hawk was always too slow to be competitive, and even the re-engined Super Snipes were too elephantine, the only event where such a car might, just might, produce a result, was in the Monte. Entries in the French Alpine would have been quite uncompetitive, and even in the Tulip Rally, where a class handicap marking system sometimes helped, there was little chance of success.

For the Monte, therefore, Garrad's team at Humber Road usually gave some attention to a Super Snipe before loaning it out to a worthy (i.e. publicity-conscious) cause. Rootes dealers, in any case, often entered Super Snipes themselves (some of them, for sure, because such a car was going to give them a more comfortable three-days-three-nights journey to the Mediterranean than a Sunbeam-Talbot 90!).

In 1951, Rootes lent a car (KDU 835) to a

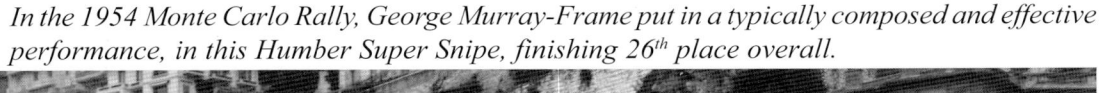

In the 1954 Monte Carlo Rally, George Murray-Frame put in a typically composed and effective performance, in this Humber Super Snipe, finishing 26th place overall.

Humbers on Safari, RAC and Liege-Sofia-Liege: 1950s and 1960s

team from London's Metropolitan Police (R.P.Minchin, Deputy Commander of the Met was the lead driver), while in 1952 Gatsonides could do no better than 42nd place. The Met also used Super Snipes in future years, performed competently, but never looked like gaining any major awards.

Clearly, Norman Garrad then took his 'Humber' responsibilities more seriously in 1954, for he originally entered not one, but three, Super Snipes, for Godfrey Imhof, George Murray-Frame and George Hartwell to drive, though Hartwell had to withdraw before the start because of a bout of ill-health. Ian McKenzie and BBC Motoring Correspondent Raymond Baxter were co-drivers in Imhof's car, which made many unexpected headlines. As Raymond wrote in his autobiography (*Tales of My Time*):

'Goff lost it in a very big way, and we hit an Alp extremely hard….Although I was wearing full harness, it was secured to the seat, rather than the floor. The seat broke away and threw me against the windscreen, which was laminated, not toughened glass, and consequently did not shatter. Crash hats were not yet worn on the Monte and although I was not knocked out, my face and forehead were a mess….'

Raymond later modestly noted that he was driven to Monte Carlo by Jaguar press officer Bob Berry, and made his scheduled broadcast from the studio about the event as it unrolled:

'….later, when I heard a recording of that broadcast, I was shocked to hear how shaky my voice was….'

Murray-Frame, 26th overall, put in a competent, rather than startling, performance, and convinced Garrad, once and for all, that a Super Snipe could not come close to winning this event, and probably not even be competitive in its class.

Super Snipe on Safari

In the meantime, Rootes was anxious to increase its sales in Africa, particularly East Africa, which perhaps explains why Norman Garrad made a trip to observe the 1957 Coronation (East African) Safari Rally. Always happy to help promote Rootes business by a successful entry in motorsport, Garrad saw that the Safari, which was strictly for 'showroom standard' cars, over long distances, on rough roads which had never been surfaced, could be quite a challenge.

Always held over the Easter weekend, at a time of year when the rainy season was just about to begin, the Safari was always held in high temperatures, sometimes in dry and dusty conditions, and sometimes in Equatorial rain, storms and floods.

Probably against his better judgement, Garrad was persuaded to enter a team of under-powered Hillman Huskies for the 1959 event, which was really the first occasion on which European 'works' teams took any interest in the event. All were driven by Rootes' 'A-team' of Peter Harper, Paddy Hopkirk and Peter Jopp, while a single new-model Humber Super Snipe was entered for Ronnie Adams, and local co-driver J.Boyes.

This particular Super Snipe had only been launched in the autumn of 1958, had a massively strong unit-construction body style, and used a 105bhp/2,651cc six-cylinder engine, which bore a startling similarity to the existing Armstrong-Siddeley Sapphire power unit. This, incidentally, was all part of a quid-pro-quo deal, whereby Armstrong-Siddeley would look after assembly of the new two-seater Sunbeam Alpine. With independent front suspension, a sturdy body shell, and with the experienced Ronnie Adams behind the wheel, it all looked promising.

ROOTES MAESTROS
"In their own words."

Unhappily, although the big Humber made it to the finish, it was never in contention for a class win, as this was a category already dominated by 'works' Zephyrs, and by Mercedes-Benz saloons. Although 63 cars started the event, only 30 reached the finish – all three of the Hillman Huskies, for instance, being eliminated.

This entry, however, had only been a one-off, and although privately-prepared Humber Super Snipes would compete in subsequent Safaris, there were no more factory-prepared cars.

Back in Britain, and as already detailed in the section concerning Rapiers, the British RAC Rally had been completely re-jigged in 1960, for the old format of driving tests plus navigation sections had then been abandoned, and from 1961 the very first special stages were included in a British event. The majority of those were held on Forestry Commission tracks, sometimes rough, always with loose surfaces – and what this meant was that cars had to be fast *and* strong.

Norman Garrad very shrewdly decided that a Super Snipe might not be agile enough to win, but it would not be embarrassing either. If a Super Snipe had survived the Safari in 1959, he reasoned, then it ought to be able to survive a 'forestry' RAC. In any case, by this time the engine had been enlarged to 121bhp/3.0litres, and front disc brakes had been standardised, which made the car altogether more competitive.

Accordingly, in November 1961 Humber Road not only prepared a quartet of 'works' Rapiers – for Peter Harper, Peter Procter, Paddy Hopkirk and 'Tiny' Lewis - but they also prepared a Humber Super Snipe (3405 RW) to be driven by BBC motoring correspondent Raymond Baxter, and Leonard Miller. Nor was this to be a gentle ride in the country, for the Over 1,600cc class also included 'works' Ford Zephyrs, Volvos and Mercedes-Benz saloons, all of which had considerable rough road rallying experience.

All in all, this was to be a remarkable rally for the Rootes Group. As already related, not only did Rapiers individually finish third and fourth overall, but they also won the Manufacturers' Team Prize. Better, even, was Baxter's feat, in keeping the Super Snipe between the trees and winning his capacity class!

As Raymond commented in his autobiography:

'Norman Garrad had assured me that the East African Safari had proved that the Humber's suspension was unbreakable. Indeed it was. Despite its size, the car designed for luxury motoring fairly flew through the forests, leaping and sliding at 80mph on surfaces which would have reduced its conventional owners to first-gear caution, were they even to attempt them.'

This was a long event, with tough stages, which soon proved to be ideal for the big Humber:

'Frankly, to my surprise, I began overtaking the opposition and when I saw the times for the first couple of stages I suddenly realised that a class win was on the cars. Five days later that judgement was proved right.'

Not that it was all easy-peasy, though it helped that the class-favourite (Eugen Bohringer and Rauno Aaltonen in a Mercedes-Benz 220SEb) crashed out in Scotland:

'Unlike today's RAC event, the road sections between the special stages were also extremely tight, particularly in Wales and the Lake District, allowing no margin for navigational error.....On one forestry stage I slid wide on a ninety right and the left corner of the rear bumper just clipped a neat pile of logs, scattering the whole across the track. Pat Moss, Stirling's sister, who was

Humbers on Safari, RAC and Liege-Sofia-Liege: 1950s and 1960s

behind us [in an Austin-Healey 3000] complained to me at the next control: "Some bastard had spread logs across the road."

Although this was an encouraging result, no-one at Rootes expected the Super Snipe to become a regular 'works' car, especially as the Mercedes-Benz 220SEb would inevitably be in the same capacity class on all events. Norman Garrad, in any case, was busy juggling with his team of super-star drivers, with the Sunbeam Rapier (which was now at its development peak) and with 'new' events in the programme like the Tour de France, to take too much interest in the Humber.

Then, in November 1963, there seemed to be time for a bit of whimsy once again. On the RAC Rally, where there was a full team of 'works' Rapiers, Garrad reflected on what Raymond Baxter had achieved in 1961, and wondered if it could perhaps be done again. This time around, though, he decided to enter a car with his most experienced driving crew – Peter Harper and Ian Hall. Although another class victory looked to be a difficult ambition – the same class included 'works' Citroens, Volvos, Ford Falcons and the Rover 3litre types, Garrad thought it worth a go.

On this occasion, however, there was no easy run for the Humber (which was registered 2362 KV). Although Peter Harper, like the seasoned pro that he undoubtedly was, tried his hardest for days, the Super Snipe could not quite keep up. Driving it just as if it was a slightly over-sized Rapier ('I pretend it's small', Harper is reputed to have told the press. 'By the way, since this car is needed by Lord Rootes to attend a function on Friday evening, I'd better not bend it…'), he somehow kept it out of the bushes for the first three days, until the transmission finally broke in the Dovey special stage in mid-Wales.

There was, however, one novelty. Co-driver Ian Hall once told me that with rally-type 'bucket' seats in the front compartment, there was enough space in the front compartment for driver and co-driver to swap places on a road section without stopping the car to do so!

Although there was still no scope for these big cars to be entered in International rallies on a regular basis, there was time for several final appearances – one on the final Spa-Sofia-Liege Marathon of August 1964, one in the RAC Rally in November. At this time, as already made clear, the Rootes Competitions Department was in transition, for Marcus Chambers had only recently become the new manager, the Rapiers had finally been retired, the Imps were still unproven, and the Tiger was the latest car to take the development attention at Humber Road. Peter Harper and Peter Procter had both been released from their contracts for the time being.

Before then, however, Rootes loaned the old car to Adrian Boyd of Northern Ireland, to compete in the Circuit of Ireland. He pedalled the big car along Ireland's narrow lanes so well at first, that he appeared towards the front of the field. Later he put it off the road, and the considerable delay involved in getting it back on the road put him right out of the running.

Even so, for the last 'classic' Liege of all time, the gallant old Super Snipe (2362 KV once again), which had been moved on to the Alan Fraser team in Kent, was pressed into service, driven by John La Trobe (a businessman from Kent) and British co-driver David Skeffington. The event, of course, was at once the toughest in the European calendar, and therefore the most suitable for the Super Snipe.

The route led from Spa in Belgium to Sofia in Bulgaria, and back to Liege in Belgium in more than 90 hours, with no night halts,

ROOTES MAESTROS
"In their own words."

and precious little time to take any rest at all. Most of the route through Jugoslavia and Bulgaria was over awful, rough, dusty and unmaintained roads and tracks, the target average speeds being quite insanely high. Even so, it was an event won in the past by big Mercedes-Benz saloons, so Rootes' hopes were high.

Although the Super Snipe was up in tenth place by the time the cars had turned for home at Sofia, and had reached the Titograd control, it was already 80 minutes off the pace. In any case, and according to *Autosport* reporter Michael Durnin, they were lucky to be still running because a diversion over a broken river bridge was badly signed and:

'John La Trobe and David Skeffington, who were driving their big Humber fast through the darkness, saw [the Citroen's] lights in the distance, but failed to see the board bearing the deviation sign until too late, and the big car demolished the board, sailed clean over the void in the middle of the Bridge, and was able to continue relatively unscathed ....'

In the end, the intrepid pair kept the big car going, finally finishing 13th overall.

The same old car, suitably re-prepared, and smartened-up, then competed in the British RAC Rally where, as usual, a long list of 61 Special Stages provided all the action in an event which started and finished in London, but took in every conceivable part of Great Britain up to special stages near Blair Atholl in central Scotland.

This time it was Bill Bengry and Barry Hughes who drove the car and, starting from No. 49, they had a tough time over stages already well cut up by earlier machines. It didn't help that the usually-reliable Bengry then spun the car in the Welsh Dovey stage, and arrived at the end of the state with a damaged car: one consequence was that they suffered a broken wishbone in the front suspension. Later, the battered old car suffered rear suspension breakages too, which required the redoubtable Bengry to use his 'Mr Fix-It' skills – and the car's emergency tow rope – to keep it going at all.

It was typical of the professionalism of this team that much of the damage was repaired before the end of the event, with the car looking almost unscathed at the finish back in London. Unhappily, it had not gone fast enough, often enough, to challenge other cars in its class, which included the 'works' Triumph 2000s, Rover 2000s, and Swedish Volvos.

That, therefore, was the point at which Rootes finally lost interest in Humbers as rally cars. The 'small Humber' – the Sceptre – was really no more than a dressed-up Hillman Super Minx with Rapier power, so was not a competitive rally car, while the Super Snipe had just been face-lifted, made larger and heavier, and would be withdrawn completely in 1967.

Marcus Chambers: A remarkable career

Born in Plymouth in 1910 (Marcus's father was a captain in the Royal Navy at that time), Marcus seems to have lived, and travelled, all over the world. After attending a range of prep schools, he eventually went up to Stowe School (near Silverstone), then to a school in France.

At the end of the 1920s, his first job, at 18 years if age, was with ICI in London, as a Junior Accountant, followed by a stint in the wool broking business, and finally moving into the retail motor trade.

Having joined the Royal; Navy Voluntary Reserve in 1935, Marcus then opened up his own London-based tuning business, became addicted to Vintage cars and racing, and got involved with HRG and their racing team, where he competed at Le Mans in 1938. After War broke out, Marcus then re-joined the Navy, where he became an officer, specialised on the smaller craft (Motor Launches in particular), and was demobilised early in 1946.

In the next few years Marcus rejoined the motor trade, sometimes ran his own tiny tuning/repair businesses, managed the HRG motor racing team, then joined the Overseas Food Corporation. Along the way he lived in East Africa, then in British Honduras.

Having joined BMC as Competitions Manager at Abingdon, in time to build up a new 'works' team in 1955, Marcus then developed it into a formidable organisation, encouraging and developing drivers like Pat Moss and Morley Twins, and cars such as the Austin-Healey 3000. Apart from managing the development and evolution of the team (this also included racing exploits as well as rallying), he also modernised the way that a rally team was supported on the events themselves.

In the summer of 1961 he then moved away from BMC (Stuart Turner then succeeded him) to become Service Manager at one of Ian Appleyard's BMC dealerships in Bradford, Yorkshire.

Returning to Coventry in 1964, he became Competitions Manager of Rootes until early 1969 (this period including the famous victory in the London-Sydney Marathon of 1968), Proving Grounds Manager in 1969/1970, after which Rootes (which had become Chrysler UK) cruelly made him redundant. For the last few years before retirement he then ran one of John Sprinzel's garage businesses, based on Brackley, near Silverstone. He finally retired in 1975, and went on to enjoy many happy years of retirement in a village close to Silverstone.

Marcus Chambers packed so much in to a long and distinguished career in motorsport. He would direct Rootes' fortunes from 1964 to 1969.

ROOTES MAESTROS
"In their own words."

Many years before he joined Rootes, Marcus Chambers had raced this HRG in the Le Mans 24 Hour race. His driving partner in the 1938 event was Peter Clark.

Marcus Chambers: 'With a Little Bit of Luck'

With Marcus Chambers' permission, we are privileged to quote from his autobiography 'With a Little Bit of Luck', notably the section which related to his colourful sojourn at the Rootes Group. Here it is:

When I left BMC at the end of September 1961 I hadn't realised how much I would miss my friends, but I made new ones in Yorkshire. Looking back over the two and a half years that we were in Yorkshire I can't say I enjoyed the work, but it could have been a lot worse if we had not had the beautiful countryside for recreation nearby.

When the new premises were opened in Bradford, where I was to be the Service Manager at one of Ian Appleyard's BMC dealerships, I had an upstairs office with a good view of the forecourt where my customers parked their cars.

Ian Appleyard rarely came to see me at Canal Road, and I was only asked to his house once in two and a half years. It was very much a case of master and man, although he did bring the first Mini Cooper over to me for appraisal.

One of the salesmen was Tony Fall, who had a demonstrator car which he used to enter in club rallies at weekends, without the permission of the management. It sometimes came back with slight damage, probably through going too near a stone wall. I had formed the opinion that Tony was worth watching and I always bribed the paint shop to cover up the blemishes, and I asked Tony how he was getting on. I went out in the snow with him on one occasion and I decided that he has worth recommending to Stuart Turner. I am glad to say that he made a name for himself in the BMC team but lost his drives later as Stuart went 100% Nordic with his crews, except for Pat Moss who was just as good as the Swedes and the Finns.

Finally at the end of 1963 Peter Wilson rang me up and asked me if I would like to take Norman Garrad's job as Competition Manager of Rootes, as Norman was retiring. I knew Peter from my early days with BMC. We had even crewed an 850cc Mini Minor together, in the Norwegian Rally (Rally Viking) in 1959. Peter asked me to come down to Coventry, to see him on January 1st 1964, and if I was interested I would be able to see one of the Rootes Directors the next day. I went down and stayed the night with Peter Wilson, and he told me how things were in Motorsport. The situation was complicated at that moment and although he tried to give me a straight answer to all my questions, I later found out that Peter was still part of a minority and his department, Engineering Development, did not have much influence when it came to policy matters.

However, he took me out in one of the development Sunbeam Tigers (this car had still not been announced) and I was impressed. He had arranged that I should see Timothy Rootes the next day, if I wanted the job. I saw Timothy Rootes the next afternoon and he told me what the agreed programme was for the next twelve months, and that I was to liaise with the Development department as much as I liked. There were

ROOTES MAESTROS
"In their own words."

to be Competition Department meetings in his office at Ryton at 9.30 am every Monday morning to report progress. I told him that I would have to give Appleyards a month's notice and that it might take some time for me to find a new home. He generously laid on a car for me to go home to Shipley at weekends until I moved south.

The deal was done. I started at the Rootes factory at Humber Road, Coventry, on February 17, and was not surprised at the sad state of affairs that I found existing in my new department. I had talked things over with Peter Procter, a Rootes racing and rally driver of considerable experience, who lived near us in Yorkshire, as soon as I knew I had got the job. He had told me a lot more about things, than I would have discovered later by myself.

There had been two other factions within the company, that felt there were individuals that should have had their names put forward as the new competition manager. One of those had been promised the job by another Director - Brian Rootes - and it was to be some time before he stopped denigrating me, although we finally became good friends. In the meantime, Norman Garrad had left the department without offering any advice as to future policy, or the merits of any of the staff or works drivers. In fact I never saw him.

There were two people that really belonged to other parts of the company, who were 'residents' in my department. One of these was John Rowe, who belonged to the Publicity department, and who had just been installed as 'Team Manager' - he was the Brian Rootes candidate. There was also a very abrasive young man called John Goff, who later stressed that he was the department's resident engineer, and was not my technical assistant. This was really a misunderstanding as he was from the Development department, and was supposed to be progressing the build of the two Sunbeam Tigers which had been entered for Le Mans.

This was a programme about which I had not been briefed, until about ten days before I arrived, which also included three production Sunbeam Tigers in the Geneva Rally. Incidentally, one of the reasons for my early trouble with Brian Rootes was that I did not allow Norman Garrad to be part of my party at Le Mans for the test days in April 1964.

As I soon discovered, there were so many faults in the Le Mans programme that it was destined to be something between a failure and farce, right from the start. The cars were being built by Brian Lister, whose Lister-Jaguars had been such a success. He would have liked to have built proper space-frame chassis jobs which would have been much lighter than the production structures which the management wanted us to use. Then he could have still produced a body which looked like a Tiger and which would accommodate the 4.7litre Ford V8 engines which Carroll Shelby used in the Le Mans Cobra, with reliability and more power than the originals. As it was we were lumbered with the 4.2litre engines, which Shelby was contracted to send us in tuned form. If the project had been started up six months earlier, we would have had the completed cars in time to do something about the various faults, all of which came to light just before the Le Mans test weekend, which was fixed for April 18th and 19th 1964.

We had some good drivers. The car which would carry No 8 was to be driven by Claude Dubois and Keith Ballisat, with car No 9 by Jimmy Blumer and Peter Procter. Early tests at the Snetterton race circuit showed that the handling was poor, and the engines had low oil pressure, and were suffering from suspected oil surge. By the time we got to Le Mans for the official trials, the engines

Marcus Chambers: 'With a Little Bit of Luck'

were still suspect. Keith Ballisat and Peter Procter were to be our test drivers at Le Mans.

Meanwhile, I was not making any progress at Timothy Rootes' Monday morning meetings; for anything of a controversial nature was being brushed aside and I had much difficulty in getting answers to matters, which needed to be settled urgently. For example, there was the matter of a replacement for John Rowe, as my assistant and team leader. I had chosen Ian Hall, who had been a works co-driver, but it took time to get him appointed. He joined us on April 1. I also needed to know if I would take the place of Norman Garrad on the Sporting Sub-Committee of the Society of Motor Manufacturers and Traders, which was a non-executive committee composed of the competition managers and trade representatives of specialist suppliers, as well as a member of the RAC Motor Sports Department. I had been the chairman of that Committee when I was the Competition manager of BMC.

We got to Le Mans in April, we found we had been booked in at a very expensive hotel, the *Hotel Ricordeau*, which Norman Garrad patronised when the Sunbeam Alpines had run so well in the 1961 Le Mans race. The presentation of the meals took no account of the fact that time might be needed for us to carry out urgent work. I had a considerable disagreement with the management concerning the size of the bill before we left for England, and made them fully aware that we could neither afford their prices, nor their old world attitude to more pressing affairs. The hotel was later sold and renamed the *Laurent*, and subsequently it was awarded a Michelin rosette.

The next day we arrived at the pits in good time and started testing with our two chosen drivers. When the car was brought in for us to hear the drivers' comments, Mike Parkes, who had left Rootes to join Ferrari, came over to the pit and very kindly offered to take the car out for a couple of laps. He came back on the third lap having timed himself on the flying lap, and through some of the sections for which he had a yardstick. He was polite, but inferred that we had a lot more to do before we could become even slightly competitive. We were no longer in the Alpine class, something that the Rootes management failed to grasp even when the race was over.

Tests showed that the only engine that we had so far received from America was running hot, with low oil pressure, caused it was thought by oil surge in the sump. We had the opinions of both Mike Parkes and Keith Ballisat to confirm that the roadholding was poor and the brakes were worse. The maestro, Mike Parkes, had lapped in 4min 26.4sec against his Ferrari time of 3min 47.1sec. We returned the next day having reduced the oil level in the sump a little, and Peter Procter did a lap of 4min 33sec and saw 6,000rpm on the straight, which was over 150mph. We were using a bigger radiator, which helped things a bit, but the real handicap was poor roadholding, even with different anti-roll bars.

There was no need to stay longer, for we knew that we could go on testing at Snetterton and at the Motor Industry Research Establishment at Nuneaton, which had a banked track. Tests went on until the end of May, the road holding and the brakes were improved, but low oil pressure was a problem on all the Shelby-built engines, of which we now had four.

On Sunday June 14 we flew the service cars and personnel from Hurn Airport, Bournemouth, for the race-cars were due to go down in a transporter, to Cherbourg, by sea. I had booked the cars into a garage at Arnage, with the mechanics in B & B nearby. The drivers, technicians, and engineering

ROOTES MAESTROS
"In their own words."

personnel were all staying at the *Hotel de Paris*, Le Mans. Scrutineering took place on the Tuesday at the track after lunch. When the car practised the next day Ballisat's car ran a big-end after only one and a half laps. This meant that the engine in No: 8 had to be changed. I was unhappy, so I rang Peter Wilson and discussed the possibility of having to withdraw both cars before the race started. I also had a long talk with John Rowe, and we decided that we had better start, even if we didn't finish.

I went back to the garage that night, and waited until the engine change was finished, then I took the car out with Jim Ashworth, the foreman, as a riding mechanic. I selected the road to La Fleche as being the best on which to do a running-in test; we went down to the end a couple of times and managed an indicated 150mph, which proved at any rate that the headlights were adequate.

Race day arrived, and the best thing that could be said of our cars was that they at least looked well turned out. Not that this helped. Car No 8 retired with piston failure after three hours, prior to which it had been timed at 161.6mph on the Mulsanne straight, although it was never better placed than 26th overall. Car No 9 ran for nine hours before it retired with a broken crankshaft, probably caused by having too much clearance in the main bearings. It had completed 123 laps at an average speed of 107mph, been timed on the Mulsanne straight at 162.2mph and had climbed to 18th position in its last hour.

Peter Procter was driving when the end came, in a dramatic fashion, and years later he recalled the episode in graphic detail:

He said "It was quite funny when it happened, funny when I got over the shock of it, that is! It was dark of course, and I was bombing past the pits; we had been doing 164 or 165mph on the Mulsanne straight and it was nearly as quick through White House and past the pits in those days – there was no barrier between the track and the pit lane. Just as I got level with the beginning of the pits the engine blew. I just remember a flash of fire coming out from under the bonnet. The steering locked absolutely solid – it was full of knuckle joints, the engine had blown up in such a big way that it jammed all these, and I just couldn't move it a fraction of an inch.

"I hit the brakes very hard and drifted over the demarcation line between the track and the pit lane. I gradually crept nearer to the pits, still going at quite a rate. Eventually I rubbed the car against the pit counter and stopped. When I got out, Marcel Becquart, I think it was, who was our pit marshal, rushed up to me and said:

'Ah, Pierre, you are in trouble, you have crossed the line, you are not allowed to do this', and so on.

I was still trying to get over the shock, so when he said:

'We must move the car', I said: 'All right, you steer, I'll push'.

So he climbed in, and after a while he said: 'It will not steer',

And I said "That's why I parked it up against the *******counter!"

Peter said to me: "It was very lucky that there was no car refuelling at that point, otherwise there would have been another disaster."

Some drivers thought the Le Mans Tiger's handling was poor, but Keith thought that it was adequate for the Le Mans circuit. Of course spoilers were in their infancy, and sportscars with fastbacks must have felt pretty light when doing 160mph. John Wyer with the Ford GT40 had already worked this out during the practice weekend at Le Mans in April as his drivers had complained about funny roadholding. When they came back they made up some spoilers and created a downforce of over 300lb at the back end, then ran their cars with spoilers during the

Marcus Chambers: 'With a Little Bit of Luck'

race. That is why the bag of sand that we tried at Snetterton seemed to make things better, but our engineers had drawn the wrong conclusion.

In the meantime, an AC Shelby Cobra finished fourth and proved that the 4.7litre Ford V8 could last for 24 hours. We were told by someone whom we could trust that he had heard that the Shelby test bed had been out of action for a fortnight at about the time when our engines were being prepared. Eventually we received a refund from Shelby and no doubt it was used to buy engines for the rally Tigers.

With the Le Mans Tigers out of the way and the first of the scheduled rallies, the Geneva, to take place at the end of October, there was still a lot to be done. The first of the production cars should have been available in July and we needed a run over rally roads to see how it would shape up. There was a delay and we had to borrow one of the Development department's cars. So it was not until 12 July, when I set out with Gerry Spencer in an estate car and Peter Riley in the Tiger to pick up 'Tiny' Lewis and John Goff in London, to drive to Dover. We felt happy at the thought of getting back on the right track. This was not to be a recce trip in the BMC and Rootes tradition; instead, it was an appraisal to see what would fall off, if the cooling system was adequate, whether the brakes would stand up to mountain driving, and if the roadholding was good enough. As to the available power and torque - we had no doubts.

We planned to take the night train ferry to Dunkirk, because one could get a cabin, and it also had the advantage of allowing a very early start in the morning. We were away by 5.00am. The Tiger was sent off, to go on ahead by an agreed route; we breakfasted at Reims and reached the *Hostellerie Val Suzon,* which is just short of Dijon, which is one of those unique establishments to which I must have been introduced either by John Gott or John Williamson in my time at BMC. The weather was perfect and lunch was served in the garden. It is still in the Guide Michelin, but one should consult the opening hours with care.

Our post-prandial contentment was marred by the failure of the Tiger's starter, but this was soon rectified and we then went by one of Tommy Wisdom's 'quiet roads' (D996) to Bourg-en Bresse, and Bourgoin to the *Parc Hotel,* Grenoble - which, I suspect, must have been one of Norman Garrad's watering holes as it was much too expensive for us. Tests started in earnest the next day, we were away at 04.15HR to attack the Col de Menée and the Col de Rousset in the French Alps. We found that the rally tyres were fouling the wings, so a bit of panel beating was needed, also the rear suspension Panhard rod retaining bracket had become unwelded, so the rod was removed temporarily. The car was sent off and the two-way radios were tested out so that the crew at the top could be warned of any descending traffic, although there was little about at that hour. Some good runs were made and we thought that the gearing seemed about right for the gradients.

We finished that section by 09.00am and we drove down to Die (close to the Rousset) for breakfast. There was not a lot to do then, except to make for our night stop, which was to be at the *Hotel Cour*, at Carpentras, which I knew as a favourite of the HRG crews and later, the BMC crews. It will not be found in the guides, if it still exists, being very unpretentious, with lace curtains hiding the view through the ground floor windows. It had a garage at the back, which was large enough to hold at least half a dozen cars, which enabled one to unpack all one's gear in comfort and re-stow it in a more accessible manner. The food was traditional French cuisine, and the welcome from the two aged

ROOTES MAESTROS
"In their own words."

proprietors made me feel that I was picking up where I had left off three years before with the BMC team.

We were lucky to find a local garage open after lunch, for July 14 was of course the *Fete Nationale*. They had a lift, so the Panhard rod bracket was soon refixed and reinforced. We turned in early, as we intended to leave at 04.30HR for cooling tests on Mont Ventoux. We had an extra electric fan fitted, we did a number of climbs, starting from the village of Bedoin, and to begin with the temperature continued to rise until the summit was reached, where the control is placed on the Alpine Rally. We took off the foglights and the bar and saw that the temperature had dropped by 8 degrees C, which was reasonable. A number of climbs were made, and the radios, when used with an observer half way up the climb, proved to be very effective. However the shock absorbers were not standing up to the work, but 'Tiny' Lewis said that they would be adequate for the tests. It is known that the exposed position of Mont Ventoux, with its summit at 1,909m, affects its climate to a marked degree, and there is nearly always a difference of 11deg C temperature between the top and the foot of the mountain.

We left the Ventoux area after lunch and reached the *Ferme Napoleon,* at Logis du Pin, on N75, by late afternoon. I think this was the hotel, incidentally, which figured in the film of *The Day of the Jackal.*

The following morning the Tiger was away at 04.30HR. Gerry Spencer and myself then made our way to Sigale, and 'Tiny' met us there as he had gone by way of the rally route from Entrevaux. We had breakfast at the tatty little café in the square by the church. Afterwards we went back via the Col de Bleine, and I thought of the last time I had driven along that road in a BMC 'Barge' with Douggie Hamblin when we had followed the Morley brothers to victory, in their Austin-Healey 3000, in the 1961 *Coupe des Alpes*. Now, here we were, a rather inefficient unit, but testing a new car with great potential; and the whole thing would have to be set up all over again. How exasperating it was to be unable to get even the most normal things done quickly and efficiently. We went back to the *Ferme Napoleon* for the night and left the next morning before 5.00HR, to climb the Col d'Allos (2,240m) by 7.00HR. On the way, the Tiger had suffered a fire in the main battery cable, which the crew had managed to insulate quite effectively. They then made a number of climbs, and decided that the axle ratio in the car was too high. After that we left for Barcelonnette, for a lunch stop and stayed at the *Vauban,* for the night and enjoyed a late start the next morning.

On that day we climbed the Col de Lautaret (2,058m), the Galibier (2,640m) and the Col du Telegraphe (1,570m), which is a great scenic drive, with plenty of snow on the side of the summits even in July. Down to St Jean-de-Maurienne, we then went past Lac d'Annecy, Francy, and Bellegarde to St Claude, which was a useful test for the Tiger. We stayed at an auberge that night and left early for Pontarlier and Belfort on the next day, to test on the Ballon d'Alsace, going by way of the Col de Bussang and the Col de Bramont, all of which were familiar, and much used on the Tulip Rally.

After that, we were back to the factory within two days, with a lot to do, before we could consider the Tiger to be a potential winner. Meanwhile by July 25 I had found somewhere to live, and we moved to the *Old Forge* at Braunston, near Rugby, which was located most conveniently opposite an old inn called *The Fox*.

At this point, I needed advice. I had known John Wyer for quite a while, since the early post-war days in fact, and I admired the way that he had brought the GT40 racing cars to

Marcus Chambers: 'With a Little Bit of Luck'

the fore, so I asked him if he knew of anyone who might join us, at Rootes, who had experience with the Ford V8 engines we were using. At the same time, Peter Wilson must also have spoken to him about our problems, and as a result it was not long before I had the services of Desmond O'Dell, who although he was working for Wyer at the time, wanted a change to a more sedentary job, for domestic reasons.

The Geneva Rally, that followed, went better than I expected and because the weather was cooler we had no overheating troubles. I now had a first class lady driver, Rosemary Smith, who had been one of Garrad's finds, she had a good co-driver and was quite capable of handling a Tiger. My other cars were manned by 'Tiny' Lewis and Barry Hughes (AHP294B) and Peter Riley and Robin Turvey (AHP295B): Rosemary Smith had ADU312B. We went to the *Hotel Moderne,* Geneva, and left the cars at the Rootes agent, who had a well equipped garage owned by Monsieur and Madame Henri Zeigler, who could not have done more if we had wanted them to. 'Tiny' took his car out the next day, and managed to get the clutch lining detached from its plate. This meant that the gearbox had to come out and the clutch was rebuilt; the fog lamp brackets were not quite right and so on, but all the cars were ready for scrutineering at 14.00HR on the Thursday. Complete with plates and numbers, our rally numbers were, 1, 2, and 3, as they were the biggest-engined cars in the GT class.

The start was at 17.00HR, and Henri Zeigler had arranged to meet them at St Claude, then at Chambery, with one of his mechanics. We went down the road to Grenoble, then Gerry Spencer went on to Recorbeau and we went to St Jean-en-Royans with SAAB service - no doubt this was Erik Carlsson's idea. The cars came through OK, but there was some fan belt trouble which I thought might affect the alternator output, so I decided to tell the crews to keep 10% of their revs in hand. The pulleys on those engines were rather far apart and the alternator pulley seemed to be too small. We should have had no problem finishing first, second, and third in the class as by this time the rest of the class were out of the rally! Rosemary Smith was annoyed with her co-driver, Margaret Mackenzie, because she had made a mistake in the route, which made them six minutes late at a control and dropped them from 16th to 20th in General Classification. On Friday morning we went round by way of Crest and Die and then on to Guillestre, where we got a snack and found the Dunlop Service truck was missing. We had to rob service cars of tyres, but we still managed to get everyone away. Then we went over the Lauteret pass to Grenoble. I finally got through to the Garage Geneve (Zeiglers) on the phone and asked them to bring some fan belts to the *Hotel Croix Blanc,* Chamonix. Dunlop were there by this time, so we could put on some fresh tyres, as well as to fuel up the cars before they went into the *parc fermé.* 'Tiny' thought he knew what was wrong with the fan belts but didn't explain what it was.

The crews had enjoyed about five and a half hours rest when I called them at 2.15am. and saw them off, then went back to bed. We were off soon after 10.00 and met Zeigler just over the Swiss frontier and went to the control there. Rosemary was 22 minutes late at the control due to another mistake by Margaret, so there was a tearful situation, which ended well, however, because the organisers cancelled the last two controls, due I think to the density of the traffic. So we had a nice looking result for the advertising people after all.

ROOTES MAESTROS
"In their own words."

Desmond was given a free hand to deal with the defects in the Tiger as I saw them at that point. He had solved the lot in time for the Monte Carlo Rally the following year.

On the 1965 Monte, the Tigers did well in the worst weather on record for that event, as purely by chance we had selected one of the more fortunate starting points. There were 276 entries that year and 237 cars started, but there were only 35 finishers in Monte Carlo. Of those, 32 came between the starting numbers between 1 and 150 and just three from 151 to 276. We had reason to be happy because we had entered two Sunbeam Tigers. Peter Harper and Ian Hall finished fourth in General Classification and first in the GT Class, with Andrew Cowan and Robin Turvey second in the GT Class and 11th overall, which must have been due to the most amazing skill, as sheer power had little to do with performance in those conditions and the Tiger was not exactly the easiest car to drive in snow.

David Pollard and Barry Hughes (running in Car No: 95) finished 15th and second in their class with a Hillman Imp, the class being for GT cars up to 1000cc. Rosemary Smith and Margaret Mackenzie, also in a 998cc Imp (Car No: 113) finished 22nd overall and fourth in their class and second in the *Coupe des Dames* to Pat Moss-Carlsson (Saab). This was the first time the Imps had used 998cc engines. John Gott then asked me if I would lend him a Sunbeam Tiger for the International Belgian Police Rally, which he had won the previous year. I obliged and he won it without losing any marks on the road and making the F.T.D on most of the speed tests.

The Alpine Rally was a debacle for Rootes, because although Peter Harper and Mike Hughes won the Grand Touring Category on the road, they were then disqualified on a scrutineering technicality The club maintained that we were running with exhaust valves that were smaller than the dimensions given in the homologation form, and therefore the engines would be more reliable. There is a clause in the homologation preamble that says that cars must be homologated in their highest state of tune. We had taken the dimensions from the engines that Carroll Shelby had sent to us after Le Mans, I think. Rootes issued a press release in which they justified our action, but the disqualification stood.

The following year the Tigers won their class in the Tulip and Acropolis Rallies, but that was the end of our programme of using Tigers in Rallies. We were now part of Chrysler, they did not like the idea that the Tiger used a Ford-USA engine, but they hadn't got an engine that would fit into a Tiger chassis. Now it was time for a new effort. It was now up to us to produce a Rallye Imp that could compete with the Cooper S with its 1071cc engine, which gave 70bhp in standard form. The Rootes production Imp engine was only 875cc and only developed 39bhp: this was due to the Board's earlier opinion that a larger engine would be unnecessarily powerful.

Leo Kuzmicki (he had once been chief engine designer with Vanwall, the F1 team) was the engineer who was given the job of designing the production engine, which was to be manufactured by Rootes and which was derived from the Coventry Climax engine, a type which had been fitted in the prototype car. Leo was very helpful about our project, and we decided that we could produce a twin carburettor engine with wet cylinder liners, instead of the cast iron cylinders that were cast in the aluminium cylinder block in the production cars.

The 1965 Monte Carlo Rally was the first event in which we expected the Imps to make a showing. We were using 998cc engines this time and running the cars in Group 3. We bored out the dry liners which had the

Marcus Chambers: 'With a Little Bit of Luck'

aluminium cylinder block cast around them in the production car, We then inserted a thin shrunk-in liner into the bored out block and increased the bore to 72.5mm. This was to be a temporary solution to the problem and later we fitted proper wet liners, but the cylinder blocks were not rigid enough to hold wet liners accurately for very long, and the dimensions had to be checked at each engine overhaul.

The Hillman Imps all started from London with the Tigers, and this rally has already been described.

At this point we had to decide which drivers we would like to retain on a permanent basis in 1966 and 1967. I had five good drivers and one brilliant private owner, all waiting for a works drive. It was unlikely that we would be able to field a team of three cars in an event.

Rosemary Smith, whose name became a byword for excellence in the two spheres, in which she chose to cultivate her talents, was an enigma when I met her in 1964. Indeed, most of the information that I had already been given about her was untrue. She was known in the motoring press as 'the dress designer from Dublin' who drove for Rootes. She had come into the International Rally scene as a novelty at the time I was still out of the sport, and working for Appleyards. Peter Procter who drove for Rootes at that time, and lived near us in Shipley, never mentioned her to me. She came from a motoring family, her father having raced a Chrysler at Brooklands before the war, and had also raced at Phoenix Park from time to time. He taught her to drive at the age of 11 and her first car was a Triumph Herald, in which she did a few club rallies and driving tests, but she did not like the car and graduated to a Mini shortly after its introduction. She progressed to more club rallies and then drove in the Circuit of Ireland Rally. Her father and her brother helped her with the upkeep of the car, and she had Frank Bigger's wife, Delcine, as co-driver. They generally did well, usually getting a class place, or the Ladies Prize. Then as Rosemary explains it, "When I was really too young to go into serious driving", she caught the eye of Norman Garrad, who offered her a works drive. This was a great opportunity as she was running out of money, having just done another Circuit of Ireland with Delcine.

So when did the dress designing come into her life? During the Mini period she had finished her course of Art at the Academy of Arts and Design in Dublin, and was now earning a living as a dress designer, which she continued to do until she became a full-time rally driver and motoring journalist.

She is the only lady rally driver I have ever known who could arrive at the end of a very tough rally section and step out of the car looking neat and tidy and well dressed.

But one should not be lulled into feeling that here was a pliant young lady who would take orders without questioning them. Her Irish sense of humour and charm, sprinkled with a great deal of common sense, could banish further argument with a withering riposte. She stood no nonsense from predatory males and sent them packing quite promptly if she felt it was necessary.

Rosemary drove for me for nearly four and a half years and during that time she drove Imps in 24 Internationals, finished in 21 of them, with one outright win (the Tulip of 1965), collected 12 *Coupe des Dames,* nine class wins, and was placed in her class at least six times. Through no fault of her own, she was unlucky to get caught up in the notorious lighting dispute and to be disqualified in the 1966 Monte Carlo Rally along with four works Mini Coopers, when she was the moral winner of the *Coupe des Dames* with Val Domleo.

ROOTES MAESTROS
"In their own words."

We eventually signed on Rosemary Smith and Andrew Cowan as retained drivers and kept four others who would be paid as needed for any event.

It is impossible to deal with the politics and interdepartmental in fighting that plagued us during that period. We had a budget but it was raided by outside teams who persuaded the management that they should be helped with their Saloon Car racing programmes. There was even another gentleman who wanted a 998cc engine to put in his hydroplane in order to break records.

In March 1968 I had to go to a meeting at Geneva for one of the International Committees, this was at the same time as the Salon d'Automobile, and I happened to meet Erik Carlsson in the foyer. He told me that he had a message for me from one of the organisers of the Liege-Sofia-Rally, who we both knew and liked. He was Michael Borislovjevic. He said that he could help us with the use of the workshops at the Engineering Faculty of the University of Belgrade, where there would be a short night stop, on the London-Sydney Marathon, about which I knew very little and was still not certain if we would be able to enter.

After the Monte Carlo Rally, we had been visited by two of the Chrysler managers, who said that they felt we should find out about the Marathon and let them know if I thought it was a suitable event for Rootes. I had discussed it with Desmond O'Dell and Ian Hall, but we thought that it was likely to be beyond our budget even if we left out some of the other events to tackle it. Of course nobody could give us the OK, due to the usual inter-departmental skirmishes, so February went by and valuable time was lost in the typical Rootes/Chrysler manner.

When I got back from Geneva, I was asked to the offices of the *Daily Express* to meet Jack Sears, one of my eminent BMC drivers, who was now on the organising committee of the Marathon, as was Tommy Sopwith, whom I knew well. He told me that the route would start in London and go across Europe to Istanbul, and then cross Turkey to Iran, by way of Teheran. Then on through Afghanistan, to Kabul, from there to Delhi via the Khyber Pass, and the survivors would then take a ship from Bombay to Fremantle (the port for Perth), in Western Australia, and go right across Australia to finish at Sydney, 10,000 miles later. The organisers emphasised that we really must enter as all the manufacturers in Europe were putting in teams.

So I rushed off to the Map Shop in Long Acre, to see what they had available between Istanbul and Bombay, but failed to find what I needed, and warned the sales person that they might soon be having a rush for Turkish, Iranian, and Afghan maps. When I got home I soon found that I already had quite a good set of maps in store, that I had collected over the years as a subscriber to the *National Geographical Magazine.* I think my drivers were surprised when they saw what I had on the office wall a few days later.

We had plenty of problems to solve, so I called a meeting of everyone who was going to be involved. We had been given a budget to prepare a car for the event, we knew that the Hillman Hunter would be the only suitable model in our range which might be suitable. We would actually have to prepare two cars, before we built the actual rally car itself. We would build the first one for testing, to see what were the weak points of the Hunter, using rally experience to strengthen the body and suspension. It would then be taken to the Army rough testing track at Chobham, Surrey and driven until something failed. From the experience gained at Chobham, we would build a recce car, and the crew that we chose would drive it to Bombay, where it would be left behind,

Marcus Chambers: 'With a Little Bit of Luck'

to be used as spare parts for the rally car itself.

Our management was in a dither as usual, as to how they were to dispense with Rosemary's services, who I had not chosen to do the event, or to provide a contract for the season. Gilbert Hunt, our Chairman, refused to see her or to tell her, as did Larry Rice, the Chrysler member on our Board. I was landed with the job because the executives were frightened of her. So, in the end, she went back to Dublin without a contract, as I had to tell her that we couldn't afford to keep her any longer. But she was lucky, as she soon got a drive in the Marathon in a Ford Lotus Cortina entered by the Irish Ford factory, and was supported during the event by the English 'works' team.

By now we knew that we could get a budget which allowed us between £18,000 and £20,000 – but it meant leaving out the Tulip, the Acropolis, the Alpine, and the RAC Rallies from our programme: we could still do the Circuit of Ireland and the Scottish Rallies. By June this arrangement was confirmed by John Panks, who was my boss at that time and the Sales Director, with whom I was always on good terms, as he supported us as well as he was able under the circumstances. Although we were already testing and preparing cars at this time, we had not officially entered the Marathon, because nobody was willing to give me the cheque to take to the organisers. Eventually Tommy Sopwith persuaded Gilbert Hunt that we had to enter, as all the other European manufacturers had already entered. I got the cheque to Sopwith the day before the entry list closed.

By now it was September and we had just two months to finish building the cars, test them and do the recce as far as Bombay, and then send the navigator to Australia where we hoped he would get help with transport from Chrysler-Australia (who were based in Adelaide), for him to have a look at the Western Australian part of the Marathon.

A few days later we had a crisis, and destroyed a set of Dunlop alloy wheels on the test track at Chobham, with the result that we realised that we would have to run on Techdel Minilite alloys like everyone else, but we would have to pay for them – whereas Dunlop's offerings had been free. The TechDel people were not certain if they could let us have the quantity of wheels we wanted, but said they would do their best. At this time we had also agreed to build a second rally car, for the RAF Motor Sport Team to use, and we were beginning to wonder if there would be enough time to do so, but Desmond seemed fairly confident that it could be done. As it happened, there were to be some unexpected benefits in so doing, which came in the way of invaluable help and advice from the RAF Transport and Medical departments. I now knew that my driver and navigator were to be Andrew Cowan and Brian Coyle, and we arranged for them and Desmond O'Dell to go to see the experts, who gave them advice on tropical medicine, dehydration problems if stranded in the desert, diet, and other things.

I had complete confidence in the workshops and I knew that Desmond would build a strong car which would be powerful enough to finish high up. I also knew that Andrew Cowan was an excellent judge of the manner in which a car handled and Desmond would give him a car in which he would have confidence.

Andrew and Brian went to Bombay in the recce car, and Brian went on to Australia as planned, while Andrew came back with his list of things needed to improve the car.

Looking back to that time, one cannot help comparing the state of communications, world wide, with the present times. The telephone systems varied so much between

ROOTES MAESTROS
"In their own words."

each country that one could waste a lot of time waiting to be transferred to an adjacent system. Nowadays, we have mobile phones, E-mail and laptop computers; a recce crew can send a report of the previous day's work from any part of the world, and the technical departments at the factory can find it on their desk when they come to work in the morning.

When they got back to England, we decided that they should take a third person and we chose Colin Malkin, who was a very fine rally driver, and a good mixer. We also heard that the Australian section was not as rough as we had thought, and it would be very important to make up as much time as possible in Asia, so as to get a good starting position at Perth and thus have fewer cars to overtake in the very dusty conditions.

For this reason we allowed Andrew and Brian to do another recce in central Turkey where there were two long alternate sections, one seemingly being much quicker than the other except under rainy conditions. They did this bit after flying out to Ankara and hiring a car for a couple of days, during which its tyres were worn smooth.

All the tests and recces were now over and the mountains of paperwork necessary to cross frontiers were completed; also consignments of spare parts and wheels and tyres had to be shipped to a number of points between London and Bombay. We had just enough time to build the RAF car to the best specification when there was a works strike and we were locked out of our department on November 8th, and not allowed back until 16th, but no overtime was permitted by the shop-stewards. By a miracle both cars were ready by 22nd.

I left with one of our best mechanics, Derek Hughes, in a Singer Vogue Estate car which was grossly overloaded, to catch the night ferry from Dover to Dunkirk. We got away at 05.30HR and lunched at Frankfurt International Airport, thence to Munich and the Austrian frontier at Kufstein, where the customs would not let us through because they said our car was overloaded. I had a solution to this problem and I unloaded half the wheels that were on our roof and drove the van through the frontier and parked it out of sight. I came back and borrowed a porter's trolley, loaded the rest of the wheels onto it and pushed them through the frontier. I then returned the trolley and we were soon away. After this delay we stopped at a lovely old inn, in the country, called the *Andreas Hofer* where we had a meal and a good night's rest. I got through to Desmond and told him that we had done 645 miles and were in Austria. He told me that all was well and they were ready for the start on Sunday 24th.

The next morning we went by way of Kitzbuhl and through the Tauern Tunnel to Villach, lunching at the Hotel Post, one of my old Liege-Sofia-Liege haunts. There was no trouble at the Yugoslav frontier and we stayed at the International at Zagreb. Monday saw us on the Autoput bound for the Hotel Metropole, Belgrade, without incident. We contacted the Engineering Professor and found that his beautiful workshops furnished with two hoists, were just round the corner, so we could leave everything safely locked up for the night.

The next morning we had everything ready early and our first car No: 45 with the RAF crew of Fl/Lt D.Carringon, Squadron/Leader A. King and Fl/ Lt J. Jones arrived at 04.45HR, with Andrew Cowan's No: 75 arriving soon afterwards. The crews had time for a meal and three hours in bed, while Derek checked over the cars.

The rally went on towards Bulgaria to our next service point in Turkey, at Istanbul, where Des and Gerry were waiting at the local agents. We were due

Marcus Chambers: 'With a Little Bit of Luck'

to leave for Athens to catch a plane going to Teheran the next evening. We left all our surplus spares with the Hillman agents, Unicomerc, who no doubt found them useful and gave us an escort out of the city on the road to Nis and Skopje. There was no need for us to see the cars off from Belgrade. We reached the Greek frontier at midnight and were outside the EFTA agents in Athens when they opened. I was tired because I had not calculated the mileage from Belgrade beforehand and the odometer now read 744 miles. We had stopped only once, at Skopje, for a meal.

As we were to catch an evening plane to Teheran, we thought we had plenty of time for a rest, but I didn't know that the car had to be put in a bonded warehouse and its documents and its passport had to be endorsed. This took longer than expected; however we got to the airport on time, only to find that the plane was late! It was about midnight by the time we reached Teheran, there was no food and there was no hot water. We were called at 04.00HR, and caught the 5.00HR plane to Kabul in Afghanistan. Desmond and Gerry had flown in from Istanbul and were to stay in Teheran until the rally arrived, where they had been promised the services of the Peykan factory where the local Hillmans were assembled, and were given every assistance, including two service cars to follow them across the desert for some distance on the morrow.

The British Leyland mechanics were on the same aircraft, and amongst them was Den Green, who had been my co-driver in a couple of International rallies at BMC, events which we had originally entered as a travelling baggage/service car. The weather was superb, and I was able to photograph the great peaks of the Hindu Kush, where one can see some of the highest mountains in the world.

On arrival we were met by Mr Irwin of Afghan Insurance, a contact that Andrew had made on his recce trip and who handled the problems we had with the importation of the spare parts, which we had flown in, most efficiently. He introduced us to Abdul Amami, a student who was to be our guide and interpreter for the next three days. Mr Irwin had also hired two Russian-built Jeeps, with their drivers, who were to be on standby for the next three days.

Desmond and his service crew arrived at lunch-time on the next day and had time to unload their packing cases and sort out spares to take to the official service point which was on the road eight miles outside the city, before the time control. I went to the time control itself, which was at the *parc fermé* close to the government buildings. I found Stuart Turner, who was a rally official this time, and waiting for the first cars to check in. There was also a crowd of fierce, fully armed Afghans who had come to watch the fun. They were looking rather aggressive and beginning to crowd us up to the Control in spite of the efforts of the police who used their belts as flails, to push them back. Stuart and myself discussed whether we should get under the nearest official limousine or climb onto its roof. The day was saved by the wife of one of the government officials, a fine Afghan lady dressed in an impressive embroidered shaggy coat which stretched down to her embroidered leather boots, her head crowned by a fur hat. She strode forward and began to lash the unruly peasants with her tongue. This seemed to be something that even the wildest tribesmen resented, and they retreated to a safe distance and stayed there.

The King of Afghanistan then drove up in a limousine, and the first rally car arrived in the floodlights at 8.49pm on November 29. All was well, and the drivers were ferried to their hotels to be fed and bedded down.

ROOTES MAESTROS
"In their own words."

Some crews were wandering around looking for someone to mend something, or find bits. The RAF crew had lost or broken their jack, one of our lads was sent out into the strange city in the dark to find one, he soon returned with a suitable jack, having bribed a local taxi driver to part with his.

I had tried to get one of our Jeeps over the Special Stage the day beforehand. But the road was in such a bad state that I decided that it would take me over two hours to cover the 47 miles, and then return by the main road. The service point was to be at Sarobi, going there by way of the Lataban Pass. I decided to stay in Kabul until the service crews returned, as I felt that being on the end of a telephone would be better than just watching Des run a service point. It was on the Lataban that F/Lt. David Carrington's car lost a wheel and wrecked a hub, but was rescued from exclusion by Derek Hughes's taking the necessary tools and parts on the back of a police motorcycle, to the stricken car. The failure was not due to the state of the road as the authorities had decided to regrade it the day before, it was due to a mistake by one of the RAF crew who had changed a wheel but omitted to put the spacer back on the hub.

After that they had to go over the famous Khyber Pass, and after braving the suicidal crowds in India, both the Hunters reached Bombay without any need for attention. We flew to Delhi where we changed planes and arrived at Bombay the day before the rally was due in. A period was allowed in a service point, and repairs were made before the cars were put in the *parc fermé* by the dockside. Everything was to be done to a prepared schedule, as Desmond had stressed that the cars had to be pre-prepared at Bombay, because we still had a tough 3,000 mile rally to do in Australia and the cars had to be 100%. All the unnecessary tools and spares were removed to lighten the cars. The next day the cars were steam cleaned before being loaded onto the old *Chusan*. The *Daily Express* and *Sydney Telegraph* had organised things well and it seemed as if the whole world now knew about the Marathon. Our car had climbed from 75th to 6th, so it meant that we would only have five cars ahead of us when starting from Perth.

Two of our mechanics flew back to Athens and to Paris to collect the service cars that they had left there. So our service crew, apart from myself, was Des O'Dell, Gerry Spencer, Dick Guy and Jack Walton.

As it transpired, Australia was where the winner of the rally was to be decided. The distances between service points were enormous, so that reliability was vital. The rally left Perth on December 16th at 16.00HR, with 350 miles to be covered in seven hours to get to a place called Youanmi, which was just a name at a cross roads to the north east – no more than that - and from there, the route went south east to Marvel Loch for 243 miles and then on to Lake King for 119 miles on Sunday morning, to arrive at 05.02HR. Des and his lads got there in time. From there our rally car had a service car scheduled to follow them for 892 miles across the Nullarbor desert to Ceduna. This is one of the most exhausting sections, as it gets very hot, and the dust is like fine powder and makes breathing difficult. They got to Ceduna all right, and were away up to the Flinders Mountains and had no trouble at all for the rest of the rally, except for a couple of involuntary excursions into the bush and one brake nipple coming loose.

When we arrived at Perth, after the old *Chusan* (which was almost ready to be pensioned off) had sailed away from Fremantle, I flew on the next day to Adelaide, where Chrysler had a big assembly plant, and was building Chrysler Valiants and Hillman Hunters. I was to be lent a Valiant, and I supervised the loading

Marcus Chambers: 'With a Little Bit of Luck'

of a Valiant Estate, which was to be loaded with a few standard Hunter parts. The Adelaide staff was very helpful and had been in touch with the New South Wales Motor Club, who produced a volunteer in the shape of Andrew Chapman, who was to accompany me when we joined the rally, and tried to chase our cars through the Flinders mountains and for the rest of the rally.

I drove all the time and Andrew told me where to go and how far it was to the next place on the map. Incidentally, we often found that names on the map were no indication as to the importance of a place, which might be anything between a name on a post, two farms and a windmill, or a village. We left for Fort Augusta on the 15th December and were lucky find Des there as they had hitched a flight with Dunlop service from Norseman. I gave them the Valiant Estate and they were away. We only saw Des once more before the finish and after we had spent the night in the car we followed the rally route most of the way to Sydney but left out the Snowy Mountains section, as did Des, because it was now a road race to the finish and there would be no time for service. Andrew Cowan titled his book about his great drive, *Why Finish Last?* and I can now understand why he did so.

We met Des and the others at Braidwood, on the Hindmarsh to Nowra section. I had been getting worried about Des, as I had not seen him since the Flinders Mountains, two days before. All was well and Des said that he would stay to see the RAF car through if we would follow Andrew to the finish. We followed, knowing that by this point our car was in second place.

It was only a few miles down the road when we came round a bend in a forest and found Lucien Bianchi's Citroen blocking half the road, with the wreckage of a Mini, which had been coming the other way. Jean-Claude Ogier, who had been driving the Citroen at the time of the accident, said that the Mini seemed to be out of control, or perhaps the driver had fallen asleep. There were plenty

As Andrew Cowan titled his book: Why Finish Last? this was the sweet moment at the end of the London-Sydney Marathon of 1968, where Marcus Chambers could savour the victory of his team's Hillman Hunter. Left to right: Brian Coyle, Colin Malkin, Marcus, and Andrew Cowan.

ROOTES MAESTROS
"In their own words."

of people helping as Paddy Hopkirk (he was driving a BMC 1800) had already raised the alarm, and help came from nearby. The radio soon announced that the Citroen had crashed, and we now knew that Andrew had only to keep going carefully, to be the winner.

At Warwick Farm, the motor racing track where the event was to finish, there were thousands of spectators, but as we had rally service plates and Chrysler Decals stuck on to the doors, we managed to get right up close to the *parc fermé*, which was enclosed by a high wire fence to keep out the public.

There were plenty of my old friends there and it was good to have a beer and watch our crews sitting on the top of their cars and enjoying the limelight. The official time for arrival at Warwick Farm was 13.19HR on December 17. 1968 and it took me a long time to realise that we had just won the longest rally that had ever been staged up to then, And I felt it was……….. *With a Little Bit of Luck*.

We managed to get our Hunters flown home on the same plane as the BMC cars as soon as the prize giving was over. And I didn't care where the £500 for the freight was coming from. Purely 'by 'chance' there was a Hercules waiting to take the RAF car and its crew back to the UK They had done well to finish 32nd, for ninety eight cars had started and fifty six had finished. We set out for home three days later, suffering from every sort of fatigue, and it took 24 hours to get to Heathrow, where we went through the VIP lounge and on to the press conference at a local hotel. It was nearly Christmas Day by the time it was all over and I have never enjoyed getting home so much. Although Rootes gained a lot from the Marathon in terms of sales and publicity, from winning the Marathon, they failed to capitalise on it as much as they should have done. By contrast, Chrysler - Adelaide had a new model Hunter with a de luxe finish all ready to be announced just as soon as the event was over. While I was in Adelaide, and the rally crews were still at sea from Bombay, I was lent a prototype to test, and having had experience in Africa with driving on corrugated dirt roads, I was able to offer some suggestions, which they carried out immediately.

By February 1969, Rootes decided that the Competition programme should be terminated, and the department should be reduced to building engines and preparing cars for private entrants, in Hillman Imps.

I was given the job of Proving Grounds Manager, and was part of the Road Proving Department, alongside Graham Robson, who is now a well-known motoring writer, and the editor of this book. My job was to investigate surplus Air Ministry aerodromes, which might be suitable for us to convert to test tracks. It was thought that Bruntingthorpe, in Leicestershire might be suitable, as it had a two-mile long main runway, and large buildings. I spent nine months looking at aerodromes and investigating design of proving grounds throughout the world, and I produced a comprehensive document on the subject. It was not a job I enjoyed, and I missed having young and energetic people around me, who were always striving to be the best at whatever they were doing.

Towards the end of the year one of Chrysler's Vice Presidents came over to look at Bruntingthorpe, and asked to see the person who had planned the conversion. He was informed that that person no longer held the post of Proving Grounds Manager, as he had recently been made redundant. That was me!

"Well, get him back!" the great man said.. I was offered a good fee to return temporarily, and I enjoyed giving Chrysler

Marcus Chambers: 'With a Little Bit of Luck'

an impolite refusal, although financially I could ill afford to turn it down

When one is out of a job at the age of sixty, it is of course not easy to find a job, as I soon found out, and one soon finds out who are one's real friends. My old friend John Sprinzel, who I had first met after the RAC Rally in which he had driven his mother's Austin A35, about fifteen years before, had by now become a well known rally driver, who usually entered Austin Healey Sprites, in which he performed brilliantly, so that I helped him whenever I could. He also became involved with the production of the Sebring Sprite, and had good relations with the Healey brothers at Warwick. He was usually partnered by Willy Cave, who is still in demand as a top class navigator in Classic Rallies to this day.

By the end of 1969 John had a large garage business with show rooms at Lancaster Gate in London, and two or three more in the provinces. He was a BMC Main Dealer and he had a good turnover. He told me that he thought he had a job for me, but it needed premises.

Our two children were boarders at two of the schools in Brackley and doing quite well there. It would be necessary for us to leave Braunston and find a house in the Brackley catchment area, so that they could become day-pupils. Early in 1971 we found a rundown property in a village near Brackley, after a lot of searching. We were lucky and found a good builder in Brackley who made it habitable in a few weeks. I can't say that the children were enthusiastic when they first saw the house, but I had been brought up to see what could be done with that sort of place from an early age.

We had bought a house of which about one third was Elizabethan, one third 18th C and the rest was late Victorian, with a butcher's shop window on the street. The sale included a slaughter-house, which we demolished, six acres of pastures, a granary, some pigsties and a large stone barn. After nearly two years we sold the house on the street and converted the granary and barn into a Cotswold stone house with extensive views over the Cherwell Valley.

In 1970 John had bought an old-established garage business in Main Street, Brackley and he also rented the derelict railway station and its yards, which was on the disused Great Central line, at the top end of Brackley. It is always known as Top Station by the locals because there used to be another station on a branch line at the bottom of the town. It was there that the new cars for John's business were delivered from the factories. I was to become manager of this place where we carried out the service, pre-delivery checks and dewaxing before the cars were sent to the showrooms in London by transporter. I did this until I retired in 1975 and enjoyed it as I had some good chaps working for me.

I soon found out that I had plenty to do at home, as our cars tended to be elderly and in need of minor work, and there were the children's cars as well. I enjoyed having more time for my hobbies such as painting in watercolours and photography, and pottering around in my workshop. I also took up writing for travel and camping magazines, and had some articles published in Classic magazines.

We had introduced our children to camping when we were in Yorkshire and as they grew older we became more ambitious as to where we went. Of course my favourite is France, because I speak the language and love the French way of life.

We went from a large ridge tent to a frame tent, and for a short while to a caravan, and then to four successive motor caravans, we have ended up with a Citroen D15 Romahome, which is small, economical and cruises at any legal speed.

ROOTES MAESTROS
"In their own words."

Now that the children are grown up and do their own thing, we enjoy our little van and have done some extensive trips in it, such as three trips to the interior of Northern Spain and several to the Pyrenees. We had previously been right down the Yugoslav Adriatic coast. Also down the Italian coast as far as Salerno, and to the Dolomites, Switzerland and Belgium.

We love to explore Wales, and keep away from large towns when touring. In August 2001 my wife and I made our 31st camping trip to the Continent. In addition I suppose I must have driven at least half a million miles there as a Competition Manager.

Sadly we are too old to own Boxer dogs which are rather energetic when young, but we have learned to understand cats, which are all different in character and always respond to attention and love, but tend to be a lot more self-willed than dogs.

It was in 1981 that the Beneficiaries of the W.W. Bertrand Trust, which owned the Roy Cove Estate on West Falkland (in which I had an interest) decided to wind up the trust and sell the property to the Falkland Island Co. It was fortunate that the matter was terminated just before the Argentines invaded the islands, and I still have the envelope, which enclosed the letter sending me the final payment, which is dated the day before the Argies arrived. It was another bit of luck, because it was enough to compensate us for the miserable redundancy terms I got from Rootes in 1969/1970.

We are also lucky in another respect, for as parents get older they so often find that their grown up children float off to the ends of the earth, and so one sees them less often. We have three children with families that live within a radius of twenty miles from us, and so we see them and their children quite often.

John Sprinzel and his wife Caryl live in Kaunakaki in the Hawaiian Islands, but he still drives Austin Healey Sprites, by invitation, in places such as New Zealand, and Tasmania and he still sees Willy Cave when he comes over here. I live not far away from Silverstone, I can often go to see some of my old friends at the BRDC clubhouse and I make a point of going to the Vintage Sports Car Club meetings whenever I can.

Tigers at Le Mans: 1964

Because this is meant to be a book of record, which covers all the major motorsport programmes tackled by the Rootes Competitions Department, I must describe the short-lived, one-off, expedition to the Le Mans 24 Hour race, which was made with Tigers in 1964. This was not a happy experience for Rootes, and if only the company could have expunged it from the corporate memory in later years, then they undoubtedly would have done so.

As described in an earlier Chapter, Marcus Chambers's own reminiscences make it clear that the Tiger expedition to Le Mans in 1964 was neither planned, nor carried out, in the way that he would have wanted to do it, if he could have been involved from the very beginning. Indeed, as Marcus has already made clear, and as Graham Rood's splendid book *The Works Tigers* spells out in considerable detail, it was not a successful effort. There was no time to make sure that the cars would be properly tested, they were never likely to be competitive in this highly-prestigious event – the basic problem being that a decision to take part had been strongly influenced by Engineering, and Marketing, with all manner of company political input involved, rather than solely in Competitions.

First steps

As already noted, by 1963 Rootes had a considerable amount of experience at Le Mans, because 1.6litre 'works' Alpines had been campaigned, with honour, in 1961, 1962 and 1963. As has already been detailed in the section on 'works' Alpines, in the first year, the Alpines won the prestigious Index of Thermal Efficiency (a complex calculation of a car's running average, and the fuel it was using, was involved), in the second year the cars were significantly faster, the best of them finishing up 15th, and averaging 93.24mph, while in the third year both the cars had to retire, both with engine failure. The fastest lap time reached at Le Mans by the 1.6litre cars was 5min. 4sec, which meant that they were being lapped by the leading Ferraris at least once in every five laps, which must have been very discouraging.

Even so, to compete at Le Mans with any sort of honour is to catch a disease, for in spite of the length, the noise, the way that French officialdom can be so stifling and – not least – the expense of it all, this can be one of the most glamorous events in the calendar. It was soon after the Alpines had returned from Le Mans in 1963, that Norman Garrad (for it was him, and not Marcus Chambers, who was involved in the conception of the project) began to think of ways in which the still-secret Tiger could be used to spread motor racing 'fairy dust' all over the company's image. This, incidentally, was well before Chrysler took any interest – financial or otherwise – in Rootes, so there were no company-political implication to muddy the waters.

Knowing, as he already did, that the forthcoming Tiger would use a version of Ford's new V8 engine, that Carroll Shelby's AC Cobra race cars were also using the same engines, and also that the 1964 Ford GT40 was to use a derivative of the same power unit, made it easy for Garrad to home in on the idea of making a special racing version

ROOTES MAESTROS
"In their own words."

of the new car. The fact that Carroll Shelby's California-based organisation had also been involved in the genesis of the Tiger road car all made this pipe-dream more attractive.

Before the end of 1963 (and already making this a perilously tight programme), Norman Garrad had talked to his boss, Timothy Rootes, board discussions had also taken place, Engineering (particularly development chief Peter Wilson) had added their opinions about performance, styling, and engineering, and it was decided that Tigers – or, rather cars based on Tigers – should be entered at Le Mans in 1964. The 'go' decision was apparently not made until the very end of 1963, and major decisions about the engineering of the car were not taken until January 1964, the 'interrregnum' when Norman Garrad was just moving on, and Marcus Chambers had not yet joined the company.

Who did what, and when?

Bear in mind, right away, that only six months then elapsed between the 'why don't we…?' decision, and the start of one of the world's most highly-publicised, high-profile motor races. In hindsight, this was far too short a time scale for a company like Rootes, which had only limited experience of the Le Mans race: even for a vastly more experienced concern, it would have been politicians call a 'courageous' move to take. Even the mighty Ford-USA, whose Ford GT programme was going ahead at the same time, would allow 12 months with the same event in mind, and would have an experienced motor racing boss like John Wyer in command – and they would also fail at the first two attempts.

Indeed, and without slinging any mud at this stage, I should really point out several basic problems:

** Ford V8 engine experience in long-duration/endurance events was still very limited

** For marketing reasons, styling, as opposed to aerodynamic considerations, was dominant when it came to shaping the body.

** Once again, for marketing reasons, the standard road car's platform, inner structure, front and rear suspensions were all to be retained, though they were by no means ideal for motor racing purposes.

The most important decision of all, however, was – who should build the cars? Rootes Competitions, after all, lacked the experience (and the space at Humber Road), Engineering (which was still at Humber Road, just a few hundred yards away, at this time) was also short of space, and there was little money, or time, to rectify this problem.

The cars, therefore, would have to be built – if not finally prepared – outside the company, and this is where Rootes struck a major problem – they had never done this sort of deal before. All previous race and rally cars had been made ready in the 'works' Competition Department.

Because Lotus was tied up with Ford, and Cooper with BMC, the choice of Lister (not only independent, but with great sports car motor racing credentials) was obvious.

Once Lister was on board, they made it clear that they would prefer to engineer a complete new tubular chassis frame, which could then be clothed in what we would not call a 'silhouette' body style. Brian Lister's initial recommendation was that there should be a light tubular space frame chassis, to be clothed in an aluminium shell wholly produced by Williams and Pritchard, because this could result in a much lighter car than standard, and one which might still handle acceptably at Le Mans. These cars, after all, were to race at Le

Tigers at Le Mans: 1964

Mans as prototypes, so they would not have to comply with any homologation requirements.

Rootes, though, would have none of it. The car, they decided, could have a different external shape, but would have to based on the pressed steel body/chassis monocoque of the Alpine/Tiger two-seater. It would be heavier, of course, but it would be 'all their own', a fact which could be advertised if the cars should hopefully perform with honour.

Shaping the car was almost equally as controversial a project, for if the cars had been sent to Le Mans with nothing more than modified versions of the hard-top style which had served the Alpines so well in 1962 and 1963, their aerodynamic drag would have been far too high, and their top speed would have been quite uncompetitive.

Because the Le Mans circuit was then dominated by the four-mile Mulsanne Straight (in modern times that straight has been broken up by two chicanes), the top speed of any car which competed there was of vital importance. Here, for instance, is what some of the cars achieved in 1963, and would achieve in 1964:

Car	(Year)	Engine size (cc)	Top speed (mph)
Ferrari 250P	(1963)	2,953	174
Ford GT	(1964)	4,727	191
Sunbeam Alpine	(1963)	1,592	123
MG MGB	(1963)	1,798	140
Triumph Spitfire	(1964)	1,147	137

and, as we later learned:

Sunbeam Tiger	(1964)	4,260	162

The lessons to be learned from this little chart (and, to be fair, Rootes did not realise just how fast the 4.7litre Fords would be until they encountered them at the Test Day trials in April 1964) was that with a body shell/style based on that of the standard car, the Le Mans Tigers would be way off the pace.

In a very short time, much work was done in attempting to produce a wind-cheating body. The artistic shape was mainly to the credit of Ron Wisdom of the Rootes styling department, who was working within a very constricting brief. While being instructed to keep the front end close to that of a production car, he was able to re-shape the passenger cabin, by re-raking the windscreen pillars (they leaned back much more than normal), by crafting a fastback hard top and – eventually – by adding a small transverse rear spoiler to balance the aerodynamic loading.

Much work was done in the wind tunnel at the MIRA Proving Ground, just a few miles away from the main Rootes factory, the result being that the race car was predicted to be aerodynamically stable to high race speeds, and that if the promised engine power of 260bhp was achieved, then a top speed of 170mph might be possible. As we now know, in race trim the Tigers proved to be capable of 162mph (this figure being the official one, clocked by the organisers' speed trap on the Mulsanne Straight itself).

Because Rootes still had absolutely no knowledge of the way to race-tune the 4.2litre Ford V8 engine which would power the Tiger, they elected to 'buy in' expertise from Carroll Shelby, whose race team was not only producing powerful engines for use in its own Cobra race cars, but was also advising Ford-USA on many such matters. Shelby was therefore contracted to provide race engines, with a target bhp of 275 from

Above: The prototype Sunbeam Tiger Le Mans pictured on its first outing at Mallory Park, after collection from Listers in Cambridge, April 1964. Keith Ballisat, standing by the car, was also Competitions Manager for Shell.

Below: An overhead view of the Le Mans Tiger, 7734 KV. Note that the car was still badged as an Alpine, the picture pre-dating the release of the Tiger.

Tigers at Le Mans: 1964

4.2litres – and their recommendation, to use enlarged engines of 4,727cc (as would be used in the Ford GTs, and in the Cobras) was rejected by Rootes on the grounds that it was the 4,260cc engine which would be used in the road cars, and that any publicity would be enhanced if the 'as used in the road car' gambit could be employed.

For all those reasons, Brian Lister was speedily contracted to build three cars – where the very first car would be used for testing, development, and to prove out the design, the second and third cars to be used in the race itself. Number plate collectors will want to know that they were:

'Mule'	7734 KV
Competition No. 8	(Driven by Claude Dubois/Keith Ballisat) ADU 179B
Competition No. 9	(Driven by Peter Procter/Jimmy Blumer) ADU 180B

The choice of drivers was interesting, for only two of them had previously raced or rallied a 'works' Sunbeam car.

Peter Procter, of course, was probably the most accomplished of the quartet, was a race and rally driver of great repute, who had been one of the few who could get more than the capability of the Sunbeam Rapier out of that ageing chassis. Like Procter, Jimmy Blumer was north-of-England based, and had built up a great record in club and national racing, including (most recently) success in the first wave of Ford Cortina GTs to hit the tracks in the UK.

Claude Dubois was a Belgian-based entrepreneur who became a well-respected race driver, and had already competed at Le Mans (for Triumph) before joining Rootes for this race. Keith Ballisat, although with a European-sounding name, was British-based, and was not only a young and still-improving racing driver at this time, but also worked in the Motorsport/marketing of Shell, so as this oil company had a close relationship with Rootes, his appointment as the fourth driver was logical.

Unhappily this programme appears to have been ill-starred right from the start, without enough time to do the engineering, not enough time to do all the testing needed to turn 'good idea' into 'oven ready race car', and not enough time to carry out race-long endurance testing beforehand. Even so, the project took on a momentum all of its own, and even though all of Marcus Chambers's wide experience told him that it was sensible to cancel the entry, there were compelling Public Relations reasons why this would make no sense.

Other sources have suggested that a great deal of naivete was involved, but the author simply rejects this, not only because of the proven track records of the main characters involved – Chambers, Wilson, Lister, Shelby and Procter for instance – but because the team also enjoyed behind-the-scenes assistance and advice from Mike Parkes, who was not only an accomplished racing driver, but who had been a Rootes employee much responsible for the birth of the Hillman Imp.

Mike, more than any other individual, pointed out just how short of straight line performance the Tigers were going to be, for as he was by then an important employee of Ferrari, he had realised that the 250P generation of racing sports cars could reach more than 190mph when it was clear that the Tigers would struggle to beat 160mph.

Note only that, but as Marcus has pointed out, once Mike Parkes had driven the 'Mule' at the test weekend: '...he was polite, but

ROOTES MAESTROS
"In their own words."

inferred that we had a lot more to do before we could become even slightly competitive. We were no longer in the Alpine class, something that the Rootes management failed to grasp even when the race was over....'

Then, and even later, there were still some Rootes enthusiasts who suggested that to compare a Tiger with a race-winning Ferrari was to compare apples with pears, but this was to hide their heads in the sand. Whether Rootes liked it or not, they were proposing to run 4.2litre prototype engined cars at Le Mans where, by definition, they would have to compete head-on against rival prototypes with engines which might be even larger.

That 30mph short-fall in straight-line performance was going to be a huge drawback. A quick back-of-the-envelope calculation suggested that the Le Mans Tiger might lose out up to 30 seconds every lap *on the Mulsanne Straight alone*, this being backed up by the difference in lap times which later became apparent – 3min. 49.5seconds by the 3litre Ferrari which won the race, and 4min. 26.4 sec which Mike Parkes had achieved in a Tiger at the Le Mans test days – an actual difference of 36.9 seconds. Averaged out over the entire motor race, this meant that the leading Ferraris would (and did) lap the Tigers every seven or eight laps, which must have been extremely discouraging for everyone at Rootes.

In the previous Chapter, Marcus Chambers has already noted, in detail, the problems which were encountered in the first half of 1964, not merely in making the Le Mans Tigers competitive (which, unhappily, they demonstrably were not), but in getting two cars to the start line. He has already detailed the traumas, and the way that his team

Lined up in front of their pits before the start of the 1964 Le Mans 24 Hour race. Number 9 (ADU 180B) is the Procter/Blumer car and number 8 (ADU 179B) is the Ballisat/Dubois car.

Tigers at Le Mans: 1964

buckled down so valiantly to turning a no-hoper into something more competitive.

The very first car (the 'Mule') did not run until March 1964, and was the only car which could be taken to Le Mans for the test/practice weekend in mid-April, (was originally entered as a 'Sunbeam Thunderbolt') while the two race cars were not finished off, at Listers of Cambridge and Williams & Pritchard (who supplied the special coachwork) until the week before they had to be shipped over to France. The fourth and last engine which Shelby had built and race tuned did not arrive until 12 May – just five weeks before the race itself.

On race-weekend, the best which could be said of the two Tigers was that they sailed through rigorous pre-race scrutineering with few dramas (this was Le Mans, after all, where officials seemed to delight in making difficulties) and they looked immaculate. They were, at least, a very smart representation of the way that a 'works' Rootes competition car could look.

The fact that ADU 179B ran its engine bearings after only one-and-a-half laps of pre-race practice (that was less than ten minutes – and meant that the mechanics had to tackle an overnight engine change – and they only had one spare engine!), and that ADU 180B was seen to be suffering from low engine oil pressure even when newly fitted and run, made everyone suspicious of the quality of the Shelby-supplied engines, for which 275bhp was claimed.

Knowing in their hearts that although the cars were as fast as they could ever have been made in the desperately short time available, the cars set out at 4.00PM on race-day itself, with the sole objective of reaching the finish. The cars' handling, at least, was adequate for this fast and relatively billiard-table-smooth circuit, and when the engines had been persuaded to run properly in pre-race testing the cars were achieving up to 165mph in a straight line, so all that now remained was to hope for the best.

It was in vain. After one hour the two cars were running 24th and 26th, after two hours they were 24th and 27th, but after just three

Keith Ballisat in the Tiger he shared with Claude Dubois at Le Mans in 1964. The car retired with engine failure after completing only 37 laps.

Above: The Peter Procter/Jimmy Blumer car, 1964 Le Mans 24 Hour race. The car retired after 118 laps after a major engine blow-up in front of the pits.

Below: Jimmy Blumer in the Tiger. The effect of the blow-up was to jam the steering mechanism and force Peter Procter to bring the car to rest by running it against the pit counter.

Above: The Keith Ballisat/Claude Dubois Tiger entering the Tertre Rouge corner at the beginning of the Mulsanne Straight at Le Mans, 1964. The car retired with engine failure after completing only 37 laps.

Below: Keith Ballisat turning through Mulsanne corner at Le Mans in 1964.

ROOTES MAESTROS
"In their own words."

hours the engine of the Dubois/Ballisat car (No 8) let go with a bang, due to a broken piston, which consumed everything inside the power unit, and saw the stricken car parked on the side of the track in a cloud of oil smoke.

The second Tiger (No. 9) then carried on, picking up places gradually, so that after six hours it was in 21st place, and after nine hours (after midnight, that is!) it was up to 18th, before Peter Procter, who was driving at the time, was approaching the pits at more than 160mph when the engine crankshaft shattered, locking up everything, and eventually pitching the Tiger into the pit counter, and out of the race.

At that moment, it seemed, the entire Le Mans project came to an abrupt end, for Rootes never again attempted to race cars at Le Mans, and had no further use for the three cars. We now know that 7734KV (the 'Mule') and ADU 179B (which had expired after three hours), were soon sold off, while ADU 180B was retained for a while, and lent to Bernard Unett, who was not only an accomplished young racing driver, but was also a junior development engineer in Engineering, and therefore in the care of Peter Wilson.

We also know that Bernard eventually made a great success out of this car, re-developing the rear suspension layout, making myriad other changes, and from mid 1965 somehow 'acquiring' a larger 289CID/ 4,727cc type of Ford-USA V8 engine. Used at British national level, Bernard and ADU 180B went on to win 11 races, and to take nine second places in the 1965 *Autosport* Championship – which was a quite remarkable turn-round from the shambles which had been the 1964 Le Mans race.

This episode in Rootes' motorsport history is not one remembered with great pride by anyone, though one should emphasise that Marcus Chambers and all his team at Humber Road did the absolute most that they could, with such limited resources. As fellow-author, and Tiger authority Graham Rood, has commented:

'The Le Mans episode had not been a particular success, but, like all competition, within this "failure" a lot had been learned – the main lesson being that time is needed to be able to produce a good competition car from a standard production vehicle. Adequate finance is also a pre-requisite – but time, unfortunately, cannot be purchased. Rootes had the technical ability, the engineering experience, and the access to the requisite driving skills but …. the available time was just too short.'

Fortunately, there was more time, and that 'little bit of luck' which Marcus so aptly mentions, for the Tiger rally programme to be more of a success.

Tigers in rallying: 1964-1966

Although every detail of the 'works' Tigers' rally programme has already been lovingly detailed and published in Graham Rood's magnificent book *The Works Tigers*, (as published in 2007 by Mercian Manuals) we should certainly not curtail coverage in this all-encompassing book about cars conceived, developed, and campaigned by the 'Rootes Maestros'. It goes without saying that this Chapter would have been infinitely more difficult to compile if Graham had not generously given permission for us to comb his researches for coverage in this book.

This Graham (Graham Robson, author, that is....) would like to go on record with his opinion that the 'works' Sunbeam Tiger was always one of the great might-have-beens of European rallying, for all manner of 'ifs' can be applied to its short career, which was certainly blighted by inter-company politics:

** If Chrysler had not taken a stake in Rootes at exactly the wrong time, the Ford-engined Tiger production car might have had a longer, and even more illustrious career, with much more support regarding engine and transmission development from Ford-USA..

** If Rootes could have given more attention to the Tiger's motorsport programme, the competition cars might have been even more competitive.

** If Rootes had been allowed to carry on with the 'works' Tiger rally programme for – say – two more seasons – it would certainly have outpaced the Austin-Healey 3000, and might have become an outright winner on several tarmac events. It is agreed, however, that it could never have been made competitive on gravel-surfaced special stages rallies.

** If the same amount of motorsport development attention could have gone into the Tiger project, as eventually went into the Imp programme, the rally cars might have become faster and more reliable than they actually were.

The fact is that the engineering team, led by Des O'Dell, was certainly capable of getting more out of a very promising package, the drivers (led by Peter Harper) were able to put in winning performances, and the cars as abandoned to their fate in mid-1966 were not nearly at the peak of their capabilities.

As already explained in the previous Chapter, the Tiger road-car programme came together at high speed in 1963 and 1964, and the decision to enter cars in the Le Mans 24 Hour race was taken at top management level even before Marcus Chambers joined the company. Marcus discovered that so much work was needed, by all his team, to turn the 'good idea' of a Le Mans entry into anything approaching a credible effort, that there was quite literally, no time to start work on rally cars until the summer of 1964.

As Marcus Chambers has already made clear in his biographical note, he arrived at Humber Road in February 1964, the production car was launched at the New York Motor Show in April 1964, and the first car for assessment as a rally car was not

ROOTES MAESTROS
"In their own words."

available at Humber Road until July of the same year, so time was always terrifyingly short.

Homologation for use in motorsport originally came in July 1964, this homologation document being up-dated and expanded in 1965, and again in 1966. As with every seriously-conceived and campaigned rally car of which the author has knowledge, homologation (on the basis of the number of cars actually constructed, as opposed to the number *claimed* to have been constructed), was premature by some weeks, but as every other rival British manufacturer – BMC (i.e. Mini-Cooper and Austin-Healey), Ford and Triumph for instance - were all up to the same tricks, no-one ever complained about this.

In fairness, by the time a 'works' Tiger first started a rally – the San Martino di Castrozza, in Italy, in September 1964 – enough production cars already existed to make homologation justified, but the team's actual rally development programme had barely begun. Between then, and June 1966 (the Gulf London Rally, the last occasion when a 'works' Tiger appeared, albeit unofficially), a total of seven 'works' Tigers started 14 events, and were backed up by two more cars used for practice, testing and as 'chase' cars only..

As far as Tiger enthusiasts were concerned, the best result was the Outright win in the 1965 French Alpine (which was annulled by a last-minute, post-event, scrutineering disqualification), but the most officially valiant performances were outright victory in the 1965 Police Rally, third overall in the 1966 Tulip, and a magnificent fourth in the snow-swept 1965 Monte. Although Marcus's biographical note suggests that when the Tigers were officially retired, it was 'time for a new effort', the fact is that the Tiger was still nowhere near the peak of its performance when that time came.

It did not help, of course, that by this time the most demanding, and most prestigious, of rallies were becoming rougher and more physically damaging than ever before, which mean that a successful rally car not only needed to be very fast, to handle and to brake well, but it also had to be physically very strong. Marcus Chambers already knew what a hard-time was meted out to the 'Big Healey', Triumph was discovering all the same unpalatable truths, and now he had to come to terms with the same battering being inflicted on the Tigers.

As did his opposition, he found that it was one thing to build competitive cars, but it was quite another to build cars which would not be banged to pieces by awful 'road' surfaces, or which struggled to gain traction on loose surfaces. Right from the start, therefore, it was plain that the Tiger could be a winner on tarmac events, and those which relied on pace over hard-surfaced special stages, but that it would always struggle on loose surfaces (like the RAC and the Scottish), or on snow-and-ice (like Monte Carlo).

First cars

Immediately after the Le Mans 24 Hour race of 1964, Humber Road took delivery of five very early production Tigers, all with left-hand-steering, which had been built at the Jensen factory in West Bromwich in June 1964. Records indicate that these were, indeed, extremely early-build cars, carrying Chassis numbers 9470011 to 9470015 inclusive. It was (and remained) Marcus's intention to use four of those cars for rallying, and to keep one of them (which, superstitiously, carried Chassis number….13, by the way) for practice/testing only.

As we now know, the very first car to start a rally was ADU 311B (which carried Chassis Number 11), this being one of five

Tigers in rallying: 1964-1966

ADU 311B was the very first 'works' Tiger, and was completed in 1964. Magnificently restored, and well-loved, it survives to this day.

cars on which work had started simultaneously at the end of July. This incorporated as much knowledge as the team had amassed on an appraisal trip which Marcus describes in his biographical note, as much modification as could be incorporated at the time, and it is also worth noting that this was at the very beginning of Des O'Dell's substantial influence on the cars.

On this appraisal trip, the worrying failures had been the tendency to overheat on hill-climbs in a Mediterranean climate, the failure of the Panhard rod bracket (strangely enough, Ford had a similar problem when developing the original Escort Twin-Cam), and a suspicion that the suspension dampers (not competition type on the appraisal car) might not be up to the job.

One problem that was immediately apparent – and there would be no long-term solution, because this was the way that the production car was marketed, which constrained what could be homologated – was that the Tiger was inflicted with 13in. road wheels. Making the wheels themselves strong enough was never going to be a problem – the Tiger, as we now know, was probably the first British car to use magnesium-alloy Minilites (they were certainly used by 'Tiny' Lewis' car on the San Martino di Castrozza in September 1964) – but acquiring 13in. tyres to cope with an engine which everyone hoped would develop more than 200bhp, was never going to be easy.

For all the usual commercial reasons, Rootes was contracted to Dunlop for its competition tyres, so it was with cap in hand that Marcus, and his deputy Ian Hall, approached the Dunlop Competition department at Castle Bromwich, in

ROOTES MAESTROS
"In their own words."

Birmingham, for supplies. Dunlop, to be fair, was an extremely competent special-tyre manufacturer, but was in a quandary. As Marcus so well knew, the Healey 3000s which he had so diligently developed 'in a previous life', at BMC, were still using 15in. rims and so were the Triumph TR4s. Ford (about to use Goodyear tyres, in any case) used 13in. rims, but their cars were not nearly as powerful.

As far as Rootes and the Tiger was concerned, the compulsory use of 13in. wheels on rally cars was going to be a 'suck-it-and-see' exercise for some time to come. Fortunately, the first few events in the programme were all to be in temperate conditions (Castrozza or Geneva), cold (RAC) or wintry (Monte Carlo, so tyre overheating was not likely to be a problem.

Getting started

Way back in 1963-1964, when the Tiger competition programme was first being shaped - pre-Marcus Chambers, as it were – the thought was that if the prototype cars performed well at Le Mans, then production cars might also perform with honour on the Tour de France.

This proposal, however, was soon knocked on the head, for several inter-related reasons. Not only was there great gloom after the cars had not performed well at Le Mans, but there was continuing concern about the idea of having to use 13in. racing tyres on an event where there would be hour-long speed tests on several noted French race circuits, not least at Le Mans, Monza and Rheims, where long straights would lead to very high speeds. Rootes, having already campaigned Rapiers (successfully) in the Tour de France, knew all about those challenges. Even though one of Rootes' faithful sponsors, Shell, were also much involved in the Tour de France, this did not ease Rootes's own financial constraints.

Accordingly, the Tour de France was firmly deleted from the schedule, and in its place, just weeks later, Chambers decided to enter just one car in a minor event in Italy to get some experience, followed by a full team effort in the Geneva Rally, which was a full-blown European Championship event. On the first rally, it was thought, Rootes could continue to learn all about the Tiger as a rally car where there would be little British media interest (and if the car developed embarrassing problems, who would ever know?), while the Geneva was one of those popular and compact events in the Swiss and French Alps where power on speed hill climbs and good handling on selective sections in France, would be important. Traction, or the lack of it, was not likely to be an issue.

Accordingly, for the Tiger's debut in late September, a single entry was made in the San Martino di Castrozza Rally (this was a small resort town situated in the Italian Dolomites), which would provide a good test on appropriately demanding roads. Not only this, but as Ian Hall later commented: 'Even better, this Dolomites rally finished a week or two before the Geneva, so we could recce that on the way home....'

There was time only to prepare a single new Tiger for this event, the car chosen being ADU 311B. This car, and its identity, incidentally, became a very hard-working member of the 'works fleet. Not only did it compete in (or practice for) nine events in less than two years, but it also featured in the last two 'works' outings of all – Acropolis and Gulf London in 1966.

Working to the homologation papers which had just been approved for this new model, the rally car had been prepared very hurriedly (and there had been no chance for pre-event practice or reconnaissance), and

Tigers in rallying: 1964-1966

although it did not yet have the most powerful 4.2litre Ford-USA V8 engine which would finally become available, its 'chassis' was as up-to-the-mark as was possible. Magnesium Minilite wheels were featured (not only were they lighter than standard, but had wider rims – 5.5 inches instead of 4.5 inches), while front and rear bumpers and the decorative details inside the front grille aperture were all removed (the current homologation regulations – which would be changed for 1966 – all authorised this). Not only that, but following the appraisal which had been made in the trip to the French Alps in July, cooling vents were let into the front wings, above and behind the wheel arch cut outs. As already found on the 'works' Healeys and Triumph TR4s, this was a successful and effective way of channelling as much hot air out of the engine bay as was possible.

The only untested item fitted, at the very last minute, was the extra-large 87.6 litre/ 19.75 gallon fuel tank, though a correctly calibrated fuel gauge could not be finalised in time: this, as became apparent, was crucial to what happened on the event.

By any standards, this was to be a low-key start to what Rootes hoped would be a glittering career for the Tiger, as they were providing no service support on the event. Once the car left the UK, it was on its own, and would see no Competitions Department mechanics again until it returned to Geneva weeks later.

One way to increase the fuel range of a thirsty rally Tiger is to fit a very large extra fuel tank. Even so, there was still space for the spare wheel – though a second spare was often carried on the outside of the boot lid.

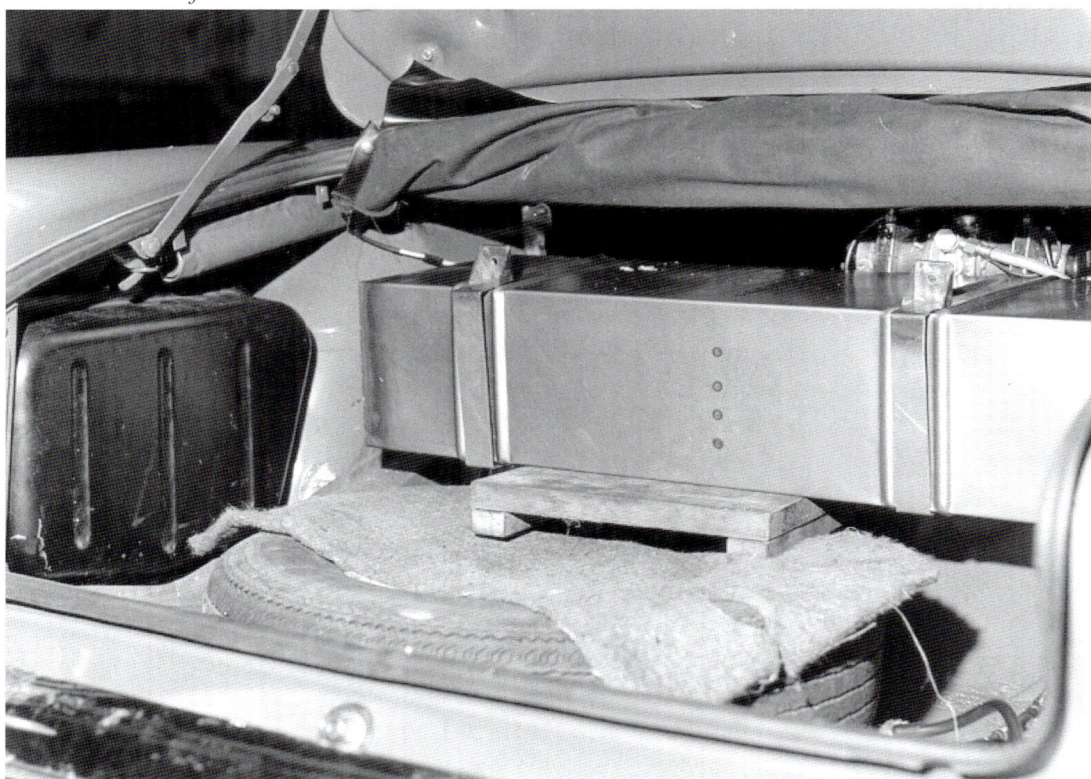

ROOTES MAESTROS
"In their own words."

This shot of the Tiger's engine bay showed how neatly the big 4.2litre Ford-USA V8 engine fitted into a space originally arranged to accept a Rootes four-cylinder engine. On the rally cars, engine bay overheating was always a potential problem.

With this in mind, most cannily, Marcus Chambers therefore asked 'Tiny' Lewis to drive the car in the San Martino di Castrozza Rally, not because he was necessarily the fastest of all the team pilots, but because he was certainly the most resourceful on-event 'fixer'/mender/driving mechanic in the whole outfit. For this event, too, Ian Hall acted not only as the manager of the effort, but acted as co-driver too – something which apparently kept him extremely busy throughout.

The fact that the fuel gauge calibration was soon found to be faulty (Lewis and Hall tried to work out what the reading actually meant in terms of fuel contents....) didn't help, and in fact the car ran out of fuel, on an autobahn, near the Austrian border on the way to the start!

On the event itself, the still-fresh Tiger gave all the local Italian heroes the fright of their lives (some of them, apparently, had not yet heard of the Tiger, so assumed that this was a merely a super-fast and rather rumbly Alpine Series IV!) but the inevitable happened – the car ran out of fuel in mid stage, with the gauge indicating that there was fuel on board....and that was that.

To its credit, though, once properly fuelled (and after its retirement from the rally in Italy), Lewis and Hall drove across to Switzerland and France, as planned, carried out a recce for the forthcoming Geneva Rally, then returned to Coventry to see three other Tigers being readied for that event. For the time being, ADU 311B then went into retirement – being used for

Tigers in rallying: 1964-1966

pre-Monte Carlo practice, before it started the Tulip Rally, seven months later.

Geneva – an encouraging start

After a summer in which Lady Luck always seemed to be against Rootes, a team success in the Geneva Rally came as an enormous relief. Not only did Marcus Chambers get all his team cars to the finish, but they also won their capacity class, and impressed everyone with their potential.

Here was an event which set almost exactly the perfect challenge for the Tiger, as a newly-homologated rally car. By starting and finishing in Geneva, at the western tip of Switzerland, the 2,000 km/1,250 miles route was very much a 'French Alpine in miniature'. It set the same exhilarating mixture of speed hill climbs, tight road sections, and mountain passes (often *exactly* the same as some of the popular Alpine Rally sections), in a more compact format, and in more temperate weather conditions.

With both Peter Harper and Peter Procter temporarily out of the team (both had recently competed, for Ford-USA, in Mustangs in the ten-day Tour de France), Marcus made up his three-car Tiger team of two established members, and one new arrival. 'Tiny' Lewis and Rosemary Smith were the regulars, while the third car was to driven by Peter Riley.

Not only was Riley a seasoned driver - in recent years he had been a member of the Austin-Healey, and the Ford 'works' teams – but his wife was Pat Moss's one-time co-driver, Ann Wisdom (now Ann Riley, of course). Apart from his driving experience, Peter also brought with him much recent knowledge about the capability of the Austin-Healey 3000, and could therefore be expected to know if Tiger development was moving in the proper direction.

One matter over which Peter could have no influence – though he, like his team-mates, was all too aware of it – was that the rally Tigers were quite heavy. Although Ian Hall (who prepared the Homologation Forms which the RAC, and then the international FIA, approved) somehow managed to insert an unladen weight of 980kg/2,161lb, which was quite ludicrously well under whatever could be achieved – and what the cars, in fact, weighed. Independent figures (technical analyses in Autocar, for example) put the real unladen weight at 1,202kg/2,644lb, and the fully-equipped rally cars usually weighed more than this.

The fact that the stated weight was much less than the real weight was not at all unique in rallying at this time - once again, Rootes was only doing what its rivals had been doing for some time, and it meant that all manner of weight-saving measures could be taken without much chance of the minimum homologated weight being approached. Safety roll cages were not yet fitted to rally cars at this point in history (this would, undoubtedly, have bought a substantial weight penalty as well as making the cars inherently safer), and there had not been time, or inclination, to have light alloy panels for passenger doors, or the bonnet, pressed, which would have been authorised by the FIA Appendix J regulations of this period.

All three cars which started the Geneva Rally – AHP 294B, AHP 295B and ADU 312B – were brand new (and, because of a delay in sourcing some features not designed until the results of the San Martino di Castrozza were known) and little tested before the event. Was it to Rootes' relief that BMC did not enter a 'works' Austin Healey 3000 for this particular event, where it would, perforce, have been in the same class and category?

At this stage, please note, the engines were still only lightly tuned. Even though Des

Peter Riley (right) and Robin Turvey drove AHP 295B into second place in its class, in the 1964 Geneva Rally.

O'Dell, who had mountains of Ford V8 experience from his previous work on the Ford GT40s, had not yet had time to recommend much modification work. Not that this worried Marcus Chambers too much at that point, as the Tigers probably had as much power, and certainly they had more torque, as any other car in the event except the 4.7litre Ford Falcon of Henri Greder, which was expected to set all the running.

To get to the start in Geneva, the three rally cars and their service support vehicles, were air-lifted from Coventry airport to Calais by one of British Air Ferries' ugly but capacious car ferry aircraft, after which Marcus Chambers treated the run down through France as a shakedown exercise for his new machines.

In this, he was wise, for Peter Riley's car started misfiring (the problem, quickly identified and solved, was traced to a faulty engine electrical distributor), while Lewis' car suffered from prematurely burnt out clutch linings, for which there was no obvious reason. That meant that the hard-working – no doubt over-worked, in fact – mechanics were faced with an overnight strip down on all three cars, to fit and adjust new clutches on all the cars.

As ever, on this event, a performance handicap system was applied – one which soon proved to be favouring smaller engined cars – so Chambers judged that his 4.2litre Tigers had little chance of winning the event, though he was hopeful of a good result in the GT category.

And so it proved, even though the special-bodied Triumph Spitfires were quite astonishingly fast in their class, and Greder's amazingly powerful Ford Falcon was even more impressive than one of its sisters had been on the Monte Carlo Rally in the early part of the year. With a number of familiar French Alpine and Tulip Rally sections included – the St Jean Circuit, the Col du Rousset, Mont Ventoux and Mont Revard among them – the team was usually in familiar territory. Fortunately the Tigers cars continued to be reliable, and one bonus which arch-mechanic 'Tiny' Lewis discovered was a tendency for a rubber cooling hose in the radiator circuitry to

Tigers in rallying: 1964-1966

Dressed for dinner, not to go rallying, this was the Rootes 'works' team and their three Sunbeam Tigers after taking 1-2-3 in class in the 1964 Geneva Rally. Left to right: Peter Riley, Robin Turvey, Marcus Chambers, Rosemary Smith, Margaret Mackenzie, 'Tiny' Lewis and Barry Hughes.

collapse at high engine speeds, for the water flow to be disrupted, and for overheating then to ensue. The solution (to insert a metal coil inside the hose) solved the problem – one of the very first 'find-it-and-fix it' problems in what was already becoming an intensive rally programme.

Although fresh, and quite unexpected, snow proved to be a problem in gaining traction on the climb of the Col de la Colombiere, this was eventually surmounted, and all the Tigers (which were becoming increasingly more competitive as the event progressed) survived to reach the finish in the centre of Geneva. As expected, the handicapping system hit hard at the 4.2litre engined Tigers, which may explain why a 'works' Triumph Spitfire (with 1.15 litres) was slower on most of the timed sections, but still finished well ahead of the Tigers in the results !

And the result itself? First, second and third in the class, but a near miss in the Manufacturers' team prize category. Fast though he and his Tiger actually was, 'Tiny' Lewis could only finish 11th overall on handicap. 37 of the 72 starters reached the finish – and Rootes were quietly pleased with the outcome of this, their first serious outing with a new car. However, it was fascinating to see what Peter Riley had to say in his post-rally report (to Marcus Chambers) on the car. Quoting a running fuel economy of no better than 6mpg on stages, and no more than 10mpg overall, he also suggested that the actual developed power

231

ROOTES MAESTROS
"In their own words."

'does not feel anything near the quoted 200+ bhp'. However, after replying to many detail questions about the car's engineering, Riley summarised that:

'This car, with development, is quite capable of winning outright. It has all the basic specification required, and I am sure will prove Rootes' most successful rally car ever.'

However:

'A great deal more power is required, and I am sure advice can be obtained from the American exponents. The braking must be improved with four discs. The steering should be more responsive.'

All in all, this was an encouraging start to the car's career – and, in fact, Marcus Chambers and Des O'Dell were looking forward to making major changes to the Tiger's specification in the coming months.

RAC Rally – a pointless diversion

I choose my next few sentences after a great deal of thought. Looking back, the entry of a single Tiger – not even officially under the 'works' umbrella – for the 1964 RAC Rally was really an expensive and rather pointless expedition, as the drivers chosen, and the event itself, were not suited to each other. Even so, the fact that the Reverend Rupert Jones was to drive the car, was a good talking point at the time, and the National press made much of the occasion.

Although everyone in the Rootes 'works' team – from Marcus Chambers down to the team of mechanics – had huge experience of the RAC Rally, for this event, which now included a long and impressive list of high-speed special stages in the route, had seen great performances by the 'works' Rapiers in recent years. There was only so much, and only so many hours, which Rootes could allocate during the winter of 1964/1965, and for every perfectly justified marketing reason, the company decided to concentrate on the forthcoming Monte Carlo Rally instead.

The RAC Rally deal, therefore, was worked out between Marcus Chambers, and the Rev. Rupert Jones. Although Rupert was a seasoned competitor – he had acted as a co-driver in several BMC 'works' entries under Chambers and his successor, Stuart Turner (some as tough as the Liege-Rome-Liege Marathon) – he was not a front-line rally driver. In any case, as a practicing Church of England priest, with a parish in Lancashire, close to many of his rallying chums, he could only spare time for the occasional rally appearance.

On this occasion, Rupert chose John Clegg as his co-driver. John was another man local to Vitafoam, was already a rallying stalwart in that infamous and anarchic rallying club of Ecurie Cod Fillet and, incidentally, would later go on to have a busy career in local government.

The deal was that Rootes would provide a completely-prepared left-hand-drive Tiger, while Vitafoam (a motor industry supplier whose HQ was close to where Rupert Jones had his living, and who had sponsored him in the past) would look after the entry – and, by implication, the expense of competition.

Rootes would not provide any finance, but the Tiger would be the best which could possibly be made available – and would have to be returned to the factory afterwards. In fairness, I should point out that the Rootes team would be out on the RAC Rally in numbers, for they would be supporting the official 'works' team of 875cc engined Imps.

Having learned a lot from the team entry in the Geneva Rally, Humber Road put everything they knew into the preparation of the single car for the Vitafoam entry. There was no question of fobbing off the private enterprise team with a battered test car, so instead the fifth of the new 'works'

Tigers in rallying: 1964-1966

rally cars which had originally been built in June 1964 was chosen instead. This was registered AHP 483B, and carried the very early Chassis number of B9470035.

Compared with the Geneva cars, this machine had a slightly more powerful 4.2litre engine – the latest units to be delivered from Ford-USA in Detroit were rated at between 211bhp and 217bhp – which put it on a par with the 'works' Austin-Healey 3000s in a straight line, though it was still years adrift in terms of rally experience and loose-surface handling.

The rest of the preparation was as expected, though there were differences from the Geneva cars – there now being an engine oil cooler mounted up-front, the bonnet being slightly (though not subtly) propped up at the back to allow hot air out of the engine bay, though side vents were not carved out of the front wings.

Minilite wheels, incidentally, were not fitted (perhaps Chambers had suggested that the team would have to pay for each of these quite fragile items which were damaged by the rough tracks….?), the standard pressed-steel wheels being fitted instead. It was a measure of how low-tech. rallying could still be at that point in history, that the Vitafoam team made sure to buy a broom handle to keep in the Tiger at all times, which they could use to ram up the exhaust system to try to clear any blockages which may occur due to impact damage on rough roads!

As already noted, by the mid-1960s the RAC Rally of the period could not only be exhausting, but could also be extremely damaging to the cars. In 1964, it would start from London, go by way of Wales to Scotland, take in a night halt at Perth in Scotland, then return by way of the forests of North Yorkshire, and a sprint on the Snetterton race circuit in Norfolk, before once again finishing in London. This was not the sort of event on which any Tiger could be expected to excel.

Rupert Jones, a realist as well as an enthusiast, could only hope to go fast on tarmac stages, and to keep plodding on in the forests, which was precisely what he set out to do. Steady in the stages, he nevertheless unleashed the Tiger on the fog-bound Oulton Park sprint, was balanced by an 'off' in a Lake District stage, and a halt to sort out an engine distributor malfunction hours after that.

Later the entire front bumper came adrift, but the Tiger excelled itself on the final Snetterton stage before the crew made it to the finish in London. But was it all worth it? They finished in a lowly 45th place – but Rupert Jones claims that without the problems they would actually have ended up about twelfth overall.

And did this prove anything – anything at all? Probably it proved that the Tiger was never going to be competitive on a loose-surfaced rally – and that a great deal more development work would be needed in 1965.

1965 – The Big Push

The 'works' team at Humber Road now had just two months, including the Christmas break (however short it might be….) to prepare for the 1965 Monte Carlo Rally. Company policy dictated that a strong push should be made on all fronts, to present a lot of favourable publicity to the world of motoring, so to try to keep their elders and betters happy, Marcus Chambers was persuaded to enter three 998cc Imps (their fortunes being described in the next section) and two Tigers, with the added complication that a practice car should then be loaned to the one-time Monte winner Maurice Gatsonides to use, though he was not expected to be a major contender.

ROOTES MAESTROS
"In their own words."

Peter Harper (centre) and Ian Hall, with RAC Scrutineer Cecil Mitchell, before the start of the 1965 Monte Carlo Rally, when they finished fourth overall.

Since the team first had to prepare two practice cars (and the same imperative applied to the Imps, too) the pressure on the team at Humber Road can be imagined. As it happens, therefore, ADU 311B (the ex-San Martino Rally car) was made ready for Peter Harper to use on recce, while AHP 294B ('Tiny' Lewis' class-winning car in Geneva) was prepared for Andrew Cowan to practice. Then, and only then, the build of the actual rally cars could begin.

The Monte Carlo Rally of 1965 has gone down in history as one of the most demanding and sensational ever to be held in the history of that famous event. Hit by a monstrous blizzard (after some years of rather mild Montes, this came as a great shock....) the result was that the vast majority of the field was forced out, either because they ran out of time, got stuck in impossible snow drifting conditions, or could simply not see through the falling snow to keep going at any pace.

For this Monte, which was always likely to present an uncertain challenge, Marcus Chambers elected to have them start from London, instead of one of the other eight points spread all over Europe. ADU 312B, which had been driven by Rosemary Smith in Geneva, was allocated to Peter Harper, while AHP 295B (ex-Peter Riley from Geneva) was prepared for Andrew Cowan: the two were allocated starting numbers just four minutes apart, which might (but did not,

234

Above: The Harper/Hall Tiger ready to start the 1965 Monte Carlo, from London, with a 'works' Imp to one side of them, and a 'works' Triumph Spitfire at the other.

Below: Peter Harper re-packing the boot of his Sunbeam Tiger, before leaving Humber Road on the way to start the 1965 Monte Carlo Rally.

ROOTES MAESTROS
"In their own words."

as it happens) cause service-point traffic jams at some point.

There had been little time to advance the specification since the Geneva and RAC Rallies and, indeed, much of the development work before this event centred on the number of different tyres (studded or otherwise) which could be carried, and/or 'dumped' at service points along the way, plus every possible thought on the way of stopping the engine from overheating, while making sure that the occupants were still warm, and that ice did not form on the windows and headlamps! With more than 200bhp still available, ample performance was guaranteed if Dunlop's studded tyres could keep the wheels gripping to the road surfaces.

Marcus Chambers' deputy Ian Hall recalls that this was probably one of the most serious pre-event recce sessions that he had ever carried out, that he personally had prepared a complete road book from Chambery to Monte Carlo Rally – and that he also remembers using driver-to-co-driver intercoms for the first time on an event. They were as well-prepared as was possible. Only a much higher budget, and the availability of more mechanics, tyres and support, could have improved matters.

This particular Monte involved a series of long, boring, and exhausting runs from far-

Peter Harper, Ian Hall, and ADU 312B, burbling carefully over packed snow in the final stages of the 1965 Monte Carlo Rally. Eventually they finished an astonishing fourth place overall.

Tigers in rallying: 1964-1966

flung starting points to St Claude, after which the special stage action on the 550 mile/885km route to Monte Carlo would begin. The two Tigers were faced with visiting Dover, Boulogne, Liege, Arnhem, The Hague, Boulogne once again, then a long anti-clockwise circuit of France before turning east at Montauban in south-west France, then south from St Claude, where all nine routes had finally linked up. Because of the blizzard, conditions were dreadful, and only nine London starters (including both the Tigers) made it through.

What followed in the next two days was one of the most remarkable performances ever put up in the Monte Carlo Rally. Although most outsiders considered that the Tiger was a most unsuitable car for use in the Monte Carlo Rally, on the same event being run off in blizzard-like conditions it was thought that the cars would struggle even to stay on the road. The fact that Peter Harper's Tiger eventually finished fourth overall – beaten only by Timo Makinen's phenomenal Mini-Cooper S, by Eugen Bohringer's Porsche 904, and by Pat Moss-Carlsson's Saab 96 Sport – *all* of them with the more suitable engine-over-driving-wheels layout – was difficult to believe at the time, but simply amazing in practice.

The cynics, of course, later commented that they expected no less of Harper, who already had an amazing success record in this event (in Sunbeam Mk IIIs, and Sunbeam Rapiers), but they could also had to accept that for Andrew Cowan to finish second in his class, and finish eleventh overall, in the second tiger, was equally astonishing. Cowan, after all, was still a new boy in the Rootes 'works' team – and this was his very first rally start in a Tiger. Andrew, in fact, would never complete another event in a Tiger, but no-one ever blamed him for such misfortunes.

Five special stages were held between Chambery and the first arrival at Monte Carlo, and a further six stages were scheduled for the reinstated Mountain Circuit which formed the grand finale of this famous event. All but one crew lost time on the road (only Timo Makinen made it through to the finish without being penalised), but Harper's amazing snow-conditions experience kept the Tiger's penalties to a minimum. To quote his co-driver, Ian Hall: 'Peter was at his awesome best, with his remarkable eyesight, and sensitive car control....'

When the 35 survivors reached Monte Carlo, Harper was in fifth place (two of the stable Citroen DSs, driven by Lucien Bianchi and Jacques Neyret were ahead of him), with Cowan a little further back, eleventh. Harper had lost just six minutes on the road sections, and Cowan just 17 minutes. Many people failed to notice that at this point Andrew Cowan's special stage times were 41 seconds ahead of those of rally-veteran Harper.

We now know that even the legendary pre-event organisation for which Marcus Chambers and Ian Hall became known had faltered a little. Studded tyres had needed to be used so early, and so persistently, on the way, that supplies were running down towards the close. Pragmatically, the team decided that priority for new studded covers should go to Harper, while Cowan would have to make do with used covers instead.

The rest of this story was a happy one, especially for Peter Harper. Although both the Citroens wilted on the last night (Bianchi's car crashed, Neyret's car was not fast enough), Pat Moss-Carlsson used her front-wheel-drive Saab's traction so well that she managed to overtake Peter Harper, the result being that the Tiger finished fourth overall. Only 22 cars made it to the finish –

Success is sweet. The two 'works' Tigers lined up in Monte Carlo in January 1965, after the end of the Monte Carlo Rally. Left to right – Robin Turvey, Andrew Cowan, Ian Hall and Peter Harper.

this confirming the severity of this particular Monte Carlo Rally.

All in all, this was an excellent result for Rootes, and the Tigers, which could not possibly have been expected to go any faster. To quote from my fellow historian Graham Rood's comments:

'Thus in only their second major attempt at rallying with the Tiger, Rootes had finished a fine fourth and 11th overall, and captured the first two places in the GT class. The Harper/Hall Tiger also collected the RAC Challenge Trophy for the highest-placed British competitor driving a British car, and the London Starting Control award.'

After all this drama, the team was happy to get back to Humber Road, take a short time to learn the lessons of the Monte (let us never forget that a team of Imps had also taken part in the same event, and that two of them had also made it to the finish), and to prepare for their future. After all, if the still-developing Tiger could finish in fourth place on such a demanding Monte, how much faster might it then be on good, dry, tarmac, in future?

The chance to find out came on the Tulip Rally in April, where the usual 'Dutch' route started in Holland, made determined tracks for the French mountains close to the German border and the Rhine, before turning north again and ending at the Dutch North Sea coastal resort of Noordwijk-aan-Zee.

Once again, company politics required the 'works' effort to be split between Tigers and Imps – the outcome being that 'Tiny' Lewis and Rosemary Smith would drive the 998cc Imps, while the two Tigers were to be driven by Monte-hero Peter Harper, and by Peter Riley. Sensibly, Marcus Chambers rotated his fleet of Tigers, so that neither of the Monte Cars were used on the Tulip – the Tulip entries being ADU 311B (Peter Harper), the car which had started this programme in Italy in September 1964, and AHP 294B (Peter Riley), the car in which 'Tiny' Lewis had won his class in the Geneva Rally in October 1964.

Changes and development, compared with the earlier entries, were still gradual, but Rootes were still clearly worrying about cooling the engine bay, for both these cars

Tigers in rallying: 1964-1966

were equipped with the front wing vents *and* had the rear end of the bonnets very slightly cracked open to encourage through flow. On this event, as on the Monte, the Tigers carried an extra spare wheel, mounted externally on the top of the boot lid.

Even though the Tulip Rally route was nearly 2,000 miles long, the entire competitive sections were compressed into nineteen speed tests, of which six were cancelled before the start,. The thirteen surviving tests totalled 37 miles – so Rootes felt justified in fitting their Minilite wheels with Dunlop racing tyres. Although this looked wise before the outset, it compromised what the cars could achieve when unseasonal snow falls hit the route in the Geneva area.

As the largest-engined cars in the event, the Tigers were allocated Competition Numbers 1 and 2, which meant that they had to trail-blaze the road sections, and also tackle the speed tests first of all – even ahead of the Austin-Healey 3000 of the Morley Twins, which carried No. 4, and was expected to set equally fast stage times as the Tigers.

Having been flagged off from the Hotel Huis ter Duin in Noordwijk, by film star Richard Burton (who was also resident, filming *The Spy Who Came in from the Cold*), the route looked like being a gentle tour of the Vosges mountains, and picturesque French by-ways – until, that is, the snow began to fall. Peter Harper's Tiger had been three seconds faster than the Morleys' Big Healey on the first stage, after which the BMC car fought back, and began to pull out a lead over the Tiger.

Then, when the first cars (which, as explained, meant the Tigers, with every other car behind them) first encountered fresh snow on the Col de la Schlucht, then on the speed hill-climb of the Ballon d'Alsace (the 'Alsation Balloon'….), the rally descended quickly into farce, the problem for a rally car not being going too slowly, but keeping going at all! Some cars simply could not make progress at all, particularly up the Col de la Faucille (north of Geneva).

'The snow made our progress up the Faucille very slow (racing tyres, remember),' Ian Hall recalls, 'with me bouncing on the back bumper and holding on to the extra spare wheel we had bolted to the boot lid…. However, get up the Faucille we did, despite running No.1 in the rally and about 8 to 10 inches of virgin snow. This was due to the limited slip diff., and the sheer Harper genius.'

Soon after this, Harper was forced out of the rally when he ditched the Tiger to avoid a head-on collision with a French camionette, while Peter Riley found that he simply couldn't get any traction for his Tiger on the Faucille and ran out of time….

Hey ho, win some, lose some. As far as Rootes were concerned, the snow-strewn Tulip had been a waste of time for the Tigers though, as I describe in the next Chapter, the 'works' Imps conquered the snow, kept going, and eventually won, outright.

Targa Florio, Scottish and Police Rallies - diversions

Shortly after the Tulip Rally had been completed, the Reverend Rupert Jones, backed as ever by Vitafoam, persuaded Marcus Chambers that the same Tiger which had given them such a hard time in the RAC Rally of 1964 - AHP 483B – should be re-prepared, much-modified, and entered in the Targa Florio race, which ran over a 72km/ 45 mile road circuit in Sicily.

But just how serious could this entry actually be? The lead driver was to be Peter Harper – a great driver, for sure, but one with no previous experience of the Targa Florio, or of the Tiger as a race car – while his

ROOTES MAESTROS
"In their own words."

second/relief driver was to be Rupert Jones himself, who really had no credible rating of any type as a race driver. One got the distinct impression that this was to be a pleasant way to spend a couple weeks away from England, driving a Tiger fast, but it was not likely to produce any awards, or results.

Although the British drivers who started the Targa Florio invariably fell in love with the event, the location, and the ambience surrounding it, they first of all had to come to terms with the problem of getting the race car down to Sicily. Drivers could fly in to Palermo, but not the cars. Vitafoam had to face putting the race car on to their own trailer, towing it all the way across Europe, through France and Italy, to Naples, then shipping it across the Mediterranean to Palermo by ferry!

Much work, all at the Vitafoam team's premises in Lancashire, went into rebuilding AHP 483B for the Targa Florio. Because this car was to be entered as a prototype – when, incidentally, it would have to compete against the best that Ferrari, and Carroll Shelby's AC Cobra teams could provide – all manner of modifications were allowed. Perhaps it was as well that this was not officially a 'works' entry, for the result was a car which looked inelegant, awkward even – and from the very beginning it was clear that it was not likely to be a contender for victory on the Sicilian road circuit.

Vitafoam decided that the engine should be a full race-tune 4,727cc version of the Ford V8 power unit, which therefore included a massive four-barrel (choke) Holley carburettor. So that this could fit comfortably into the engine bay, the bonnet was provided with a very noticeable 'power bulge', and the rear end of that panel was, as usual, propped open to allow hot air to exit without hindrance. It is interesting to note that this car was never equipped with the vents in the front wings – does that mean that they really didn't work all that well? The standard four-speed transmission was retained which, frankly, left the car rather undergeared on long straights – but there were not too many of them, in Sicily! Official figures show that it was 6 minutes 12 seconds slower than the winning Ferrari over a single lap of the ten lap race.

Would the car have been faster without the hardtop? Probably so, but it was retained, as was the rear bumper, though the front bumper was discarded, and the front-end panel work was re-worked. The exhaust pipes, without silencers, fed out on each side of the car, under/behind the doors.

The result was a race outing which was really not to Rootes' credit. As *Motor Sport*'s Denis Jenkinson wrote, in his race report: Harper came bouncing and wallowing through in the ungainly Sunbeam Tiger....' Although the team did its best, there was little reward, with a car utterly un-suited to this event, except that it made it to the finish, being the second (and last) in its prototype capacity class. Even so, because it was more than 15% slower than the car which won that class (that was, incidentally, the winning Ferrari 275P of Vacarella-Bandini), the organisers declined to list it as a finisher.

In the same month, another 'works' Tiger loan – this time to John Gott, who was the Chief Constable of Northamptonshire, and a long-time successful rally driver – was much more successful. Although Gott had dropped out of the top echelon of rallying (he had previously been BMC's 'team captain' at a time when that famous team was run by Marcus Chambers), he was still a great enthusiast, and demonstrably still fast and safe. Accordingly, when he approached Rootes, for the loan of a car in which to compete in the International Police Rally, he was soon indulged.

The car chosen for this loan was AHP 295B, in which Andrew Cowan had finished

Tigers in rallying: 1964-1966

eleventh in the Monte Carlo, and which had then been used as a practice car for the Tulip Rally. Because the Police Rally was due to start and finish in Liege, using various special tests and navigational sections, AHP 295B was ideally-prepared in Tulip Rally/tarmac form.

Although it was a low-key effort (for 'service' support, Marcus Chambers merely provided himself, mechanic Derek Hughes, and a car full of spares), and an event with little International standing, both Rootes and John Gott took it seriously. This was a short, intensive, but compact event held largely within the borders of Belgium. Gott, ably co-driven by Sergeant 'Nich' Nicholson, performed admirably, tidily and effectively – the outcome being that he won the event outright. Although Chief Constable Gott was years past the point in his career where he had to make any cheap points, he always liked to point out that this was the very first outright win for a Tiger in International competition.

Only four weeks after the Tulip Rally had been completed (and at the same time as a car was being readied for John Gott to use in Belgium), Rootes also prepared one single Tiger for Andrew Cowan to drive in the Scottish Rally. Although this entry fell into the 'High Hopes' category, it was thought to be justified, both on the grounds of good publicity and raising the corporate image.

Not only was Andrew Cowan a Scot, a rising star in motorsport with a thriving farm close to Duns, in Berwickshire, but Rootes never forgot the fact that their Imps were also manufactured in Scotland (at Linwood, west of Glasgow), and that Scotland had several national newspapers of its own which had to be cherished. Cowan, incidentally, had already won the Scottish Rally twice, in his own privately-prepared Sunbeam Rapiers, so the Rootes connection was good and strong.

[As ever, I should recall that there was also to be a strong Imp presence in this event, with three 998cc cars to be driven by other members of the 'works' team.]

But, would the Tiger be effective on the rough, often dusty, gravel stages of the Scottish Highlands? So far Rootes had little gravel-stage experience with the Tiger – nor with the much less powerful relative, the Alpine – for the RAC Rally entry of 1964 had been made by a driver who was a 'Good Chap', but not a front-line pilot. Rootes thought that it might just work – especially as an obvious rival, the Austin-Healey 3000, had already come so close, so often, to winning the RAC Rally, which was a similar event though run off in much worse weather conditions.

Cowan's rally car was to be ADU 311B – the example which had competed in Italy way back in September 1964, and which Peter Harper had unfortunately crashed on the Geneva. Little damaged in that shunt (there was more damage to the driver's morale on that occasion), ADU 311B was re-prepared to what might be described as 'standard loose surface' condition.

Andrew Cowan, for his part, was now thoroughly experienced in Scottish forests, which was probably just as well, for this was an event which started from the HQ of the Royal Scottish Automobile Club in Glasgow, took in forestry stages in the south-west of Scotland, then threaded itself up to Grantown-on-Spey, where a further three loops (and three night halts) featured high-speed action close to Aberdeen, close to Inverness, as well as the forests along the steep sides of Loch Ness.

For the Tiger, everything started badly, for after it had been lined up at the start in Blythswood Square in Glasgow and parked overnight, it then refused to start up again (carburettor flooding was suspected), and needed to be rather humiliatingly pushed

ROOTES MAESTROS
"In their own words."

around the square by many willing helpers before the big V8 finally rumbled into life.

This, if Cowan had only realised it, was an omen of what would then follow. First of all, on the opening stages, the Tiger's front suspension began to wilt under the battering (having such a heavy V8 engine sitting above the front cross-member didn't help), the springing and damping 'crashing through many times too often, so that by the time night fell over Argyll the cross-member itself began to sag. Temporary shoring up was carried out, but this was only the beginning.

Hours later the engine oil filter came adrift, hung down to rub against the steering column coupling of this left-hand-drive sports car, and eventually split, shedding all the engine oil and bringing the car to a halt. Even though this could be bodged up, and although Cowan had a small reservoir of oil in the car, this was not enough. The 'works' Tiger ran on a Shell vegetable oil, but Cowan was obliged to beg what he could scrounge – which turned out to mineral oil. Chemists more knowledgeable than Andrew (or this author, let us be quite candid) knew that the two types of oil were incompatible, but in the dead of a June Scottish night this was no help, and the Tiger had to struggle on, if it could.

Team boss Marcus Chambers, however, decided that the internal damage to the engine might be terminal, so the car was therefore retired soon after daylight, in Glen Coe. Murphy's Law, however, was alive and well that week in Scotland, for Ian Hall carried on using the Tiger as a 'chase' car for the rest of the week, without it missing a beat….

The only good Tiger news was that the Scottish Rootes dealer John Melvin kept his privately-prepared Tiger (EGA 65C) going to the end of the event, and won his capacity class.

French Alpine – wuz they robbed?

July 1965 marked the high point *and* the low point in the Tiger's rallying career. On the one hand, Peter Harper performed magnificently, setting many fastest speed test times and, according to the figures, won the French Alpine Rally outright. On the other hand, the scrutineers insisted that the engine was stripped, found it non-standard in some respects – and disqualified it. 'Outright victory' therefore turned into 'Disqualification', and Rootes' morale plummeted.

The pivot of this argument centred around the size of the valves fitted to the cylinder heads of the engine, a unforeseen glitch which will be described later. For the moment, it is time to glory in the way that the Tiger had been turned from an unknown quantity into a potential winner at European Rally Championship level in a matter of months.

For this high-profile (and highly popular) event, Rootes decided to enter not only three 'works' Tigers, but two 'works' Imps as well, backing them up with all the rather slender resources which were available. While it was the Monte Carlo Rally on which the publicists placed most of their efforts, it was the French Alpine which appealed most to the drivers and their team managers. Rootes had often shone in this glamorous event – not only in Sunbeam-Talbots, but in early-type Sunbeam Alpines, and in Rapiers too – so there was a great amount of tradition to be upheld too.

Most of the Tiger 'fleet' seemed to be committed to the event – ADU 311B, ADU 312B and AHP 295B for the rally itself, with three other cars (including a newly-prepared C-Reg. car) backing them up in the weeks leading up to the event. Although carefully re-prepared, all three rally cars had now

Tigers in rallying: 1964-1966

started several earlier events – it being ADU 312B, for instance, which Peter Harper had driven so magnificently in the Monte Carlo Rally.

It is interesting to note that preparation details were still not yet consistent across the 'fleet'. For the Alpine, for instance, ADU 311B did not have the front wing vents, while AHP 294B and ADU 312B did. On the other hand, all three cars now sported hefty forward-facing scoops in the bonnet panels, this being a real innovation for the rally Tigers, where worries about engine overheating in a hot climate were always feared. As ever, a spare wheel was carried on the outside of the car, on the boot lid.

As always with this glamorous and charismatic event, crews who competed and were not prepared to go flat out for the full four days inevitably ran out of time, for the target speeds on road sections were high (higher than in previous years – the increase in target averages seeming to be a regular occurrence….), and the pressure unrelenting. In 1965 the event started from Marseilles, had two over-night halts at Grenoble, and finished in Monte Carlo. Along the way it took in almost every high pass in the Maritime Alps, a number of special stages and speed hill climb sections.

Pre-rally preparation was as painstaking as usual, and the original plan was that the three cars would be driven by Peter Harper, 'Tiny' Lewis and Peter Riley, but at the last minute Riley had to withdraw (his son was very ill, and Peter had to return home). Accordingly, in a re-shuffle which seemed to be accepted with good grace by the organisers, Marcus

AHP 294B was one of the first batch of works Tiger rally cars, making its debut in the 1964 Geneva Rally and continuing in service until the 1966 Tulip Rally where it was used as a recce car. In this picture it is undergoing a test run rather than taking part in one of the several rallies in which it competed.

ROOTES MAESTROS
"In their own words."

Chambers's deputy, Ian Hall, stepped in as a first driver, his co-driver being Don Barrow (a British rallying specialist, who had already co-driven several BMC cars in the last year or so). On this event, incidentally, Peter Harper's co-driver was the very experienced Lancastrian, Mike Hughes.

Talking about this last-minute change, years later, Ian Hall as most refreshingly honest about the limit of his own driving capabilities (though, in fairness, he was an extremely accomplished driver) – if only that he had often sat alongside Peter Harper, admired what the Stevenage maestro could do, and concluded that as a mere mortal he could never match that….

It didn't help, Ian concluded, that the Morley Twins, in their 'works' Austin-Healey 3000 were to start right behind them, and would probably catch them on the first of the long speed tests to the east of Marseilles.

Having started at night from Marseilles, the event then struck deep in to the Alps the following morning. By that time Peter Harper's Tiger was settling into the top handful of competitors, other cars and crews were beginning to fall out (this including Gunther Klass's 'works' Porsche 904 and Bo Ljungfeldt's 'works' Lotus-Cortina), and unhappily Ian Hall's Tiger was damaged when it hit a wall on the way down the north face of the Col d'Allos, and had to withdraw. 'Tiny' Lewis' Tiger had also retired, having suffered a rear brake failure, which caused a localised fire, which was quite enough to render the car undriveable thereafter.

When the cars arrived in Grenoble, Rene Buchet was leading the GT category in his Porsche 904 – a real 'racer for the road', as opposed to a modified road car, with the Morley Twins' Big Healey second, and Harper's Tiger third. Jean-Pierre Hanrioud's 1.3litre Alpine-Renault A110 was in fourth place behind the Tiger.

Now it was a matter of attrition, in a rally where it always seemed to be hot, where the clock was always ticking, and where there was no time to relax. From Grenoble to Grenoble, by way of famous hill-climb sections including Mont Ventoux, the Col de Rousset and the Chamrousse, Peter Harper faced up to a barrage of opposition from three 'works' Porsche 904s, and of course from the 'works' Austin-Healey 3000.

For Peter, the bad news was that he could not keep up with their pace, but the good news was that retirements continued to mount. Suddenly Buchet put his 904 off the road, Bohringer's 904 lost time on a tight road section, and even the Morleys lost three minutes – whereas Harper (and Hanrioud's Alpine-Renault) both scraped in on time.

The last 1,433km (890 mile) sector from Grenoble was even tougher than the earlier part of the event, ending up with a continuous assault on the highest of passes – Restefond, Allos, Cayolle and Allos once again – but Peter Harper grimly kept the Tiger on the road, up to schedule, while J-P.Hanrioud's Alpine-Renault finally fell back with faulty ignition on the high-powered little Renault engine.

Back in Monte Carlo, Peter Harper and the Tiger was provisionally announced as outright winners – they were, incidentally, the only crew in the Grand Touring Category to finish un-penalised on the road sections, and therefore to qualify for a Coupe des Alpes – but then came the drama of scrutineering.

The organisers, perfectly within their rights, demanded that the cylinder heads of the Tiger's engine should be lifted and removed, so that they could be compared with the car's homologation. Rootes, who had – they were convinced – nothing to hide, was happy to do that, but there was consternation when officials announced that

Tigers in rallying: 1964-1966

because the engine was non-standard the car must be disqualified!

As historian Graham Rood has already pointed out: 'On Sunday morning, however, the scrutineers called Des O'Dell and Marcus Chambers to point out to them that the valve sizes on ADU 312B did not comply with the homologation form, and thus the car was to be disqualified and removed from the results. The [diameter of the] valves, in fact, were smaller than those homologated, and which had since been changed on the production car....'

'We wuz robbed....!' might sound justified, especially as the fitment of smaller valves certainly meant that the engine was less powerful than otherwise it might be, but facts, and measurements, could not be disputed. It now seems that the homologation form was prepared with reference to the engines being used by Shelby in 1964 (and in the unsuccessful Le Mans race cars), where the valves fitted to Ford-USA-built engines as supplied to the rally team were significantly smaller. After the event, but obviously too late to affect the outcome, the homologation form was speedily up-dated.

An official statement circulated by Rootes commented that:

'...by the fitting of smaller valves to the Tiger, we certainly did not gain any advantage in performance, and this was only done to bring the rally car in line with that of the current models.'

Writing much later in his book *Works Wonders*, Marcus Chambers went into the whole saga, chapter and verse, but summed up by commenting: 'So we just said, "What the hell", we'd got a lot of publicity by being excluded, and we left it at that....'

One can only hope that at the time he, Peter Harper, and his bosses took it as equally as that?

Somehow, and it was neither stated nor admitted to at the time, the spirit now began to seep out of the Tiger rallying programme. Although the car still demonstrably had much promise (and, let us never forget, the much-improved Tiger II was due to launch at the start of 1967), particularly on sealed surfaces, it still had some way to go to become faster than the Austin-Healey 3000. Not only that (and the author remembers this, having been closely involved in rallying, even then....), but all over the world of rallying, teams were becoming wary of the enormous potential of the still-new Porsche 911 family.

The fact is, therefore, that after the debacle of the French Alpine Rally of July 1965, the only other 'works' Tiger appearance was a single-car entry, for Peter Harper/Don Barrow, in the RAC Rally at the very end of the season. ADU 311B – the car which had unhappily suffered accident damage on the French Alpine Rally – was re-prepared, this time with a shortened version of the novel bonnet scoop, and intending to use steel wheels instead of the more normal Minilites. Steel wheels, it was thought, were not only more robust than Minilites when faced with rough special stages and the occasional rock - but they were also very much cheaper too!

This was not an event which any Tiger-lover at Rootes cares to remember with pleasure. Soon after starting from a hotel close to London Heathrow Airport, the Tiger tackled the first two stages on Salisbury Plain, the first at Milsdon Down, the second at Rolleston Camp – and it was on one of them that the Tiger was obviously jarred on a major jump, saw the engine move upwards and forwards on its mounting, the fan blades to hit the radiator block – and the inevitable happened.

Within minutes the engine had lost all its water and was boiling, and even though the radiator was speedily changed at the next scheduled service point, the damage was done. Within a very short time the engine

ROOTES MAESTROS
"In their own words."

failed, and the car was retired after it had been towed, powerless, into the Time Control at Bristol Airport.

1966 – So near and Yet ….

The fates, it seemed, were against the Tiger. Not only had all manner of unwanted dramas hit the cars in 1965 – snow storms on the Tulip, homologation problems on the French Alpine, and engine failure on the RAC – but now the sport's homologation rules were to change, and would take further potential out of the Tiger's progress.

These changes had been well flagged in advance, and applied to every manufacturer, but they were nonetheless most unpopular within the sport. To keep down costs – this, for sure, is what the governing body, the FIA had in mind – Group 3 cars like the Tiger would no longer be allowed to use light-alloy, or any other sort of non-standard body panels (they would not, in the words of the old regulations, be allowed to alter the material of panels 'licked by the air stream….'), Perspex instead of glass was to be banned, and alternative cylinder heads would no longer be authorised.

In fairness to Rootes, such special fittings had not been applied to the Tigers in 1965 (because the team knew what was to be enforced in 1966, and was not about to spend heavily on short-term improvements), but it also meant that the cars could not be expected to improve as steadily as hoped. Other cars, incidentally, like the Austin-Healey 3000s, the MGBs, and the very special little Triumph Spitfires were all much affected by the changes, and soon fell out of rallying completely.

Early in the year, in any case, there was a second blow for Rootes, in that the Monte Carlo Rally organisers imposed swingeing penalties against *all* Group 3 cars in the event. The Monte organisers, in any case, were perennially addicted to applying handicaps, which were more or less fair to a particularly type of car, year on year, depending on the mood swings (and chauvinistic tendencies) of the officials at the time !

For 1966, the Monte regulations centred on Group 1 (showroom-standard saloons of which 5,000 had been produced and homologated), and Group 3 sports/GT cars like the Tiger were to have their special times ruined by an 18% extra penalty (or 'tax', almost). This meant, in fact, that no Group 3 car stood a chance of winning the event, and any such cars which started would be competing amongst themselves.

This, therefore, was an event where Rootes would have no chance of victory, because the Rallye Imps could not compete either, as they were not Group 1 cars. Almost any effort, and budget, thrown at the 1966 Monte would be wasted – but because the Monte was still such a high-profile event, Marcus Chambers felt obliged to enter Tigers and standard 875cc Hillman Imps. He must have known that it was all going to be in vain.

What he could not have foreseen was the homologation firestorm which would engulf the event, one which centred on what the organisers insisted was the 'illegal' method in which British teams set about using single-filament quartz-halogen headlamp bulbs which 'dipped' on to other lamps. This farrago is explained, analysed, and condemned in the next Chapter, which refers to the Imps.

Two Tigers were prepared to compete in the event. A brand-new car – FRW 667C was made ready for Andrew Cowan – this being one which therefore complied easily with the newly-applied Homologation regulations (and which carried an 'Alpine', rather than a 'Tiger' badge on the front

246

Tigers in rallying: 1964-1966

wings), while AHP 294B (complete with a new body shell?) was prepared for Peter Harper to drive: this car had not been used since 'Tiny' Lewis had had to retire from the French Alpine. Neither car had the bonnet scoops used in 1965, this sort of change no longer being allowed by the homologation regulations.

To complicate things further, Cowan's car was in the new 'works' Midnight Blue (dark blue) livery, while Peter Harper's car retained the Carnival Red colour scheme with which the rallying Tigers had started their careers in 1964.

Even though Rootes staff were feeling somewhat depressed by the Tiger's ill-luck, technical development continued apace. For Monte Carlo, and to meet the newly-imposed regulations, the engines reverted to a single twin-barrel (instead of four-barrel) carburettor, and an appropriate Ford-USA inlet manifold, this resulting in a slight loss of power, the engines now being rated at approximately 200bhp. The front wing vents once used to keep engine bay temperatures in check were no longer in evidence – the latest set of homologation regulations no longer allowed such extra outlets to be fitted.

As ever, the choice of concentration runs – from starting points to Monte Carlo – was always made complex by consideration of the possible weather conditions, and any chance of gaining good publicity from a particular point. No doubt Marcus Chambers would have liked to concentrate his resources, but had to settle for seeing Andrew Cowan start from London, and Peter Harper from Rheims in France. Since those two routes joined up at Liege, in Belgium, this was no big deal.

After only a few hours, however, this didn't matter at all – for Andrew Cowan unfortunately crashed his brand-new Tiger. As he later commented in his book; *Why Finish Last?*:

'We were on a simple road section of the rally when you go stooging around Northern France and were in no great hurry, when, as we crossed a ridge into a corner, the car started to slide towards the verge. There must have been something under the snow at the edge and we hit this with the front cross-member and the next thing we knew the car somersaulted end over end. '

Happily, neither Andrew nor his co-driver Brian Coyle were injured – but the car was most grievously bent. If there was an un-damaged panel on the Tiger after all the crashing and banging had stopped, then it is not obvious from the pictures. 'The best Tiger we ever built' (according to Des O'Dell) was not used again by the works team, its competitive life being approximately six hours, and not a single special stage !

Bad news for Andrew Cowan was, in a way, better news for Peter Harper, who got all the more attention from the 'works' team because of this. After spending more than two days trundling in a lengthy anti-clockwise loop around rural France, Peter Harper/AHP 294B reached Monte Carlo, both enjoyed a night's rest. And both then set out on the long and demanding 900 mile/ 1,450km *Route Commun*, which reached as far north as Chambery, and was to include five special stages.

Not even half way into this section, it all ended in tears, once again, for the Tiger. After hitting a serious hump (which was marked in the team's pace notes) the Tiger suffered a recurrence of its RAC debacle, when the engine lurched forward on its mountings, the fan punctured the radiator, the engine speedily boiled, blew a gasket, and was eliminated. The only consolation – the *only* one – which could be drawn from this farrago was that the 'works' Tigers were not drawn into the 'lighting fiasco' which followed the end of the event – and which is

ROOTES MAESTROS
"In their own words."

described in the Chapter on Imps, for it resulted in the disqualification among others, of Rosemary Smith's Imp.

The team returned to Humber Road in an atmosphere of gloom, because of the double blow which Monte Carlo had dealt to their spirits. Des O'Dell, in particular, was bereft by the engine-into-radiator clash which was a repeat of the RAC Rally occurrence, for he though he had now solved that problem. Even so, although every one in the 'works' team was shattered by the twin loss of the Tigers from the Monte Carlo Rally, what was due to follow – the Tulip and the Acropolis Rallies – was thought to be more promising. Not only was the Tulip to be run without a handicap system of marking for the very first time, but the Acropolis would surely be the sort of rough and tough event for which the structurally solid Tiger might be ideal.

For the Tulip Rally, Rootes entered only one Tiger – but this was a very special car. Registered FRW 668C, and left-hand-drive like the other 'works' Tigers, it was the seventh and last of the true 'works' Tigers built at Humber Road which actually started an event. It would tackle just this one event, and therefore counts as the definitive 'tarmac'-spec Tiger of them all. In many ways identical to the recently-built Monte cars, FRW 668C had a 200bhp engine, a limited-slip diff., a dual-braking system with dual servos (but still with rear-wheel drum brakes) and of course a driver-to-co-driver intercom system so that the pace notes could be called across the car without the co-driver getting hoarse.

Although the Tulip was much more of a 'touring' event than the Alpine (there were only 88km of speed hill-climb tests in a 2,700 km itinerary), it was still difficult enough to require a full reconnaissance, and attention to every detail on the event itself. The story of the event is easily told. From the very start, three British-based 'works' drivers – Peter Harper, Rauno Aaltonen (BMC Mini-Cooper S) and Vic Elford (Ford Lotus-Cortina) – set a series of fastest times, and scrapped for the lead

Peter Harper on the absolute limit during the 1966 Tulip Rally where, even on tarmac, it was easy enough to unstick the rear tyres of a 'works' Tiger. On the Tulip this brand-new car finished third overall.

Tigers in rallying: 1964-1966

among themselves.

Half way through the event, at Morez, near Geneva, the Tiger was lying in third place overall, and was leading the Group 3 category, this being the way that it would stay for the rest of the event. At Morez, the Tiger was just 43.4 seconds behind the leader – and when the cars finally returned to Noordwijk-aan-Zee two days later that gap had increased to just 82 seconds.

Even so, when the team got back to Coventry, it was once again made clear to them, that the Rootes sales and marketing staff wanted to emphasise the Imp programme, not the Tiger. Simply, and brutally, the Imp needed all the publicity it could get, whereas the Tiger, complete with its Ford-USA engine in a company where Chrysler-USA had a large financial stake, was beginning to look like an orphan.

Unable to do more than lobby for a change of mind (which never came) Marcus Chambers had to accept this, though a singleton Tiger entry in the Greek Acropolis Rally went ahead. It is now worth noting that this was the one and only time that a Tiger tackled the Greek event, which was noted as the roughest, toughest (and, usually, the hottest) rally in the calendar. Chassis and general experience came from previous entries with 'works' Rapiers – there were, let us not forget, some similarities between the chassis/platform of the Tiger, and of the Rapier – but this was nevertheless a rallying journey into the unknown for Marcus Chambers, Des O'Dell, and all.

Just one car – ADU 311B – was made ready for Peter Harper to drive in the event. There was some symmetry here, for ADU 311B was the last true 'works' Tiger to start a rally, one should remember that it had also been the very first in 1964. By then it was a very different car (probably with a replacement body shell), for there were no wing vents behind the front wheels, and of course it was to run in Midnight Blue. Ian Hall had been the co-driver on that event, and he would also be the co-driver on this. Interestingly enough, although Rootes had chosen not to use Minilites on the rough RAC Rally of November 1965, they chose to use them on the even rougher Acropolis: to confuse matters even more, photographs also exist of the car running on steel wheels too !

Although the stiffly-sprung/low-ground-clearance Tiger could not hope to compete head-on against Group 2 saloons, the Harper/Hall combination was professional and effective. A broken throttle linkage at an early stage did not help, but at one point the Tiger was up into fifth place overall behind a 'works' Mini-Cooper S, two Lotus-Cortinas and a Lancia Fulvia. In the end, it slipped back to seventh place, but still won its class and the Group 3 category.

Perhaps it was asking too much of this car that it should be brought back from Greece, treated to a general 'wash-and-brush-up', and loaned to Peter Harper for him to compete (as a 'private' entry) in the British Gulf London, where official 'works' entries were not allowed. As described more closely in the Chapter concerning 'works' Imps, the Gulf London was a long, hard, exhausting event which took in a mass of special stages.

In spite of its creaks, rattle and groans, ADU 311B started the Gulf London, looking just like it had finished on the Acropolis, except that was running on steel wheels. As with Andrew Cowan's embarrassment on the 1965 Scottish, on this occasion the Tiger needed a tow to get it started before taking the 'off' from London Heathrow Airport's Excelsior Hotel.

Then it all went wrong on the very first night. First of all the Tiger plunged off the road in Wykeham Forest, which was not far from Sutton Bank, then after being retrieved it then suffered a puncture in Cropton Forest (near Pickering), then lost a wheel

ROOTES MAESTROS
"In their own words."

completely, and had to abandon, with only three wheels still on the machine.

And that really was the end, for shortly afterwards the team of 'works' Tigers was sold off, and the 'works' team began to concentrate on developing rear-engined Imps instead. Although the Tiger was by no means at the end of its development, there was a growing band of opinion which suggested that rallying was pulling away from the Tiger, rather than the other way around. It was after that final Acropolis Rally that Ian Hall concluded:

'It was this rally that convinced me, at least, that the Tiger had had its day. Ove Andersson's little Lancia Fulvia was the pointer. I felt that the factory should be concentrating all of its limited resources on the Imp, which was the car it wanted to sell. Absolutely no part of the Imp or Tiger was common, so the mechanics were really being asked to do too much in my view. This view eventually prevailed….'

Peter Harper and Ian Hall line up under the famous Parthenon, ready to start the Acropolis Rally of 1966. This was the last time that a 'works' Tiger would start a major European rally, and it would finish seventh, and win its class.

'Works' Imps in rallying: 1964-1968

In five short years, the Rootes Competitions Department turned the rear-engined Imp from an under-powered no-hoper into an extremely competent little rally car. The machine which had started life in 1963 as a 39bhp/875cc 'shopping car' eventually evolved into a 1litre rally car with up to 100bhp, and a race car which had even more power than that. Along the way, the many reliability and teething troubles were ironed out, and before long it had become probably the best-handling rear-engined car the sport had ever seen.

The miracle is that this was all achieved against all the odds – not least that the cars had to compete, head on, against BMC's all-conquering Mini-Cooper S types, often in the face of crippling shortages of finance to do a proper development job. Indeed, it would be fair to say that the transformation could not have been achieved at all if engineer Des O'Dell had not been so stubbornly determined to make it so. Before O'Dell arrived at Rootes, progress had been desultory, but afterwards his skills and know-how gradually transformed the Imp's prospects.

If Norman Garrad (briefly), and Marcus Chambers (throughout his five year tenure at Rootes) had been left to their own devices in this period, it is likely that neither of them would have chosen to develop, and campaign, the Imps. However, because there were marketing imperatives which made it essential, they did a great job in a very short time.

Early days

When the Imp was introduced in May 1963, it was barely in series production at Linwood in Scotland. As an all-new car, it had many development problems which still remained to be solved, and as currently available, it was utterly uncompetitive for any type of motorsport. No pre-launch motorsport development or testing had yet been done – and when it *was* done, Humber Road still had no previous experience of cars like this on which to draw.

Right from the start, however, there were three important reasons why this crazy project might just work. Not only was the basic structure strong, but the handling of the car was already quite miraculously agile – and the rear-mounted Coventry-Climax based engine looked as if it might eventually be persuaded to produce lots and lots of power. Although the production car only had an 875cc power unit, this could quite easily be expanded to 998cc (the capacity class limit was 1,000cc), so if the company could be persuaded to put a limited production 1litre car on to the market, it might become competitive.

Even before detailing what was done on the Imp programme, it is important to summarise the turmoil in which the Rootes motorsport existed in 1963. With Norman Garrad due to retire in the foreseeable future (and, as we know, with a great deal of inter-company debate going on as to who might succeed him), there was no single strong man who could make speedy decisions about the future of Motorsport.

Not only that, but the team almost looked to be breaking up at this time, for Peter Harper was receiving overtures from other teams (in fact he would defect, to Ford-USA, for a time in 1964), Paddy Hopkirk had

ROOTES MAESTROS
"In their own words."

already gone off to drive for Stuart Turner at BMC, and Peter Procter was also mulling over offers which he had, to concentrate on single-seater motor racing.

The Sunbeam Rapier (which had been the main backbone of the Rootes effort for some years) was fast becoming obsolete, this being accelerated not merely by its own 'old age', but because in racing and rallying, Ford's new Cortina GTs and Lotus-Cortinas were adding to its agonies. The car which had been so formidable in the 1959 – 1962 period was getting no faster (and no lighter either!), and could not be expected to improve in the near future.

Experience had also shown that the Alpine, with a 'chassis' developed from that of the Rapier, was not going to be a great race or rally car either, not only because competition from Austin-Healey and Porsche was now too fierce (Triumph found the same problems, at the same time), but because the latest events tended to use rough tracks and special stages of a type which did not suit a two-seater sports car.

The new Sunbeam Tiger (effectively a Ford V8-engined, beefed-up, Alpine) looked extremely promising, but was still on the secret list, would not be launched until April 1964, and would not be available until the middle of that year. Although the signs were that the Tiger could be made formidably fast, it looked as if would also suffer from the same shortcomings as the Alpine – namely that it would be fine on tarmac and sealed surfaces, but would not be suitable for special stages with loose surfaces, or on snow and ice.

All of which left Rootes with a dilemma, which they intended to solve by concentrating effort on the Imps in the near future.

1964

As Marcus Chambers has already noted in his autobiographical comment, Rootes already knew that the Imp engine could be enlarged, strengthened, and made a lot more powerful, but all that was for the future. In the first year, therefore, the company would have to stick with its 875cc power unit, and get on with chassis development as rapidly as it could.

For its very first appearance, the 'works' Imp was provided with a twin-carburettor engine, and a four headlamp nose, for 'Tiny' Lewis (an improbably large-statured driver for such a small car!) to drive in the Welsh Rally. Although the car went off at one stage, and the engine lost all its water when a tap in the heater hose circuit broke, 'Tiny' kept it going, steadily. With stage times sometimes verging on the leader board, this impressed the spectators – and in the end he took eighth overall, not beaten by any other car with a similar engine size. However, because Barrie Williams won so convincingly in his BMC Mini-Cooper 1071S, and Roy Fidler took second place in the 1.15litre Triumph Spitfire, this proved conclusively that more power was certainly needed.

The Monte Carlo Rally which followed, however, was a real disappointment. For this event, where most of the post-event publicity centred on the titanic battle between Paddy Hopkirk's Mini-Cooper S and Bo Ljungfeldt's Ford Falcon Sprint, Rootes prepared a standard Imp for 'Tiny' Lewis, a twin-carburettor (Group 3) Imp for Keith Ballisat, and a standard car for BBC *Wheelbase* staffer Michael Frostick (who was partnered by Gerry Burgess).

At this stage in their career, none of the Imps was yet fast enough, even to battle for the lead in its 850cc – 1,000cc capacity

'Works' Imps in rallying: 1964-1968

class, so little was seen of them during the event, and the new rear-engined cars could not exploit their sure-footed traction on ice and snow. The results sheet showed them to be way down the lists – though there was some local consolation in Coventry, where Ernie Hunt/Roger Mac (in a privately-entered car, 3933 KV) took the *Autosport/RAC* Trophy for the best BIRC (British International Rallies Club) finisher from the Glasgow start.

The Imp programme then slipped in to the background for a time, not because of a lack of interest at Humber Road, but because the massive problems connected with the projected Le Mans 24-Hour race entry of two Sunbeam Tigers all had to be solved. This period has already been covered in an earlier section of this book, and was one which the new team manager, Marcus Chambers, would rather not have encountered.

Even so, one of the ex-Monte Imps was re-prepared for 'Tiny' Lewis to drive on the Tulip Rally, where it was hoped that the usual 'class improvement' handicap timing system might work to the little car's advantage. Unhappily, the Imp only got as far as the second test (the first speed hill-climb, actually) at Saint Roche, just south of the Spa F1 circuit. Pushing on, to the very limit, on a soaking wet circuit, 'Tiny' put the car off the road, where it hit a tree, rolled and was comprehensively wrecked, fortunately with little damage to 'Tiny', except to his morale.

All in all, this was not a happy time for Rootes, as the Rapier had definitely now been retired, and future rallying strategy would centre on the use of Imps, and Tigers. Accordingly, two cars were entered for the Scottish Rally in May, which was to combine dusty and rough special stages, high speeds, and fabulous scenery in an event which went on for five days.

Rosemary Smith, getting her first drive in an Imp, was soon forced to retire, but got the car mended, after which she toured round with the mechanics, acting as 'spares on the hoof' for 'Tiny' Lewis' machine, This needed a carburettor change at an early stage too. But there was still little encouragement, for the car was demonstrably off the pace, and was not yet reliable enough.

A bigger and better effort was needed before the end of the season, this eventually coinciding with the RAC Rally of November 1964. By reading the regulations very carefully, Marcus Chambers had concluded that they should run in Group 2 form, a class in which they would have to compete against the 'works' Saabs and Mini-Cooper S types.

Although the Imps were still obliged to run with standard-size 875cc engines (Rallye Imp homologation would follow in 1966), the cars and their chassis had received much attention in the autumn. The 'works' cars took the start – driven, as expected, by 'Tiny' Lewis and Rosemary Smith, the third car being driven by David Pollard, who had only recently joined the team.

Unfortunately, it all went wrong at an early stage, when Lewis rolled his car on the timed descent of the Porlock toll road (which was being used as a special stage), and although 'Tiny' got the car moving again, it was badly damaged. Because he was close to home at the time (he had a garage business near Bristol) he was able to call in, and hastily have much of the body damage patched up! The fact that he went on to hit a 'works' Ford Cortina GT in a Welsh stage didn't help his cause one tiny bit.

Well before half-distance, and before the rally entered Scotland, Rosemary Smith's car suffered a broken throttle cable. Soon after this, Lewis' car shredded a rubber rear drive shaft joint: Unhappily, this was an endemic problem on these cars, but over time a great deal of development work, and

ROOTES MAESTROS
"In their own words."

modification, would pay off. The problem was that every time the team thought they had solved the transmission problem, the engines were persuaded to develop more power, after which universal joints began to break again, and the vicious circle was resumed.

Soon afterwards, David Pollard's car went off the road at Tummel Bridge, and damaged its front suspension. Clearly this was not an event on which the Imps were destined to shine – and all they could gain was a great deal of (bitter) experience for the future. It was often said, of Rosemary Smith, that she always carried three things in her handbag – lipstick, face powder, and a railway timetable. On this occasion, the timetable was definitely justified.

1965

As far as the Imp was concerned, the big push would follow in 1965. Not only were the cars promised to be more reliable than before, but the 998cc Rallye Imp (as it was called) appeared (though it would not be homologated until 1966), and was a good deal faster than the original cars had ever been. In the first season, therefore, the Rallye Imp could not be used as a 'standard' saloon car, but often appeared in Group 3 (Sports car) categories, or even as a 'prototype' wherever there was provision for such machinery.

This explains why the three 998cc Imps prepared for the Monte Carlo Rally of 1965 were Group 3 cars. 'Tiny' Lewis' car was equipped with twin-choke Weber carburettors (almost a racing specification, in fact), while the Rosemary Smith and David Pollard cars had twin Strombergs: although we did not know it, at the time, the Stromberg installation was that which would figure on the Imp Sport production cars, which were still on the secret list, and would stay so until late 1966.

The 1965 Monte goes down in history as one of those blizzard-afflicted events in which many cars were eliminated by accidents, by blockages, by road conditions, or by any and every combination. Although 237 cars started from nine starting points, the carnage really set in after all routes converged on St Claude, north of Geneva – and only 35 cars, in all, reached Monte Carlo, all of them with lateness penalties except Timo Makinen's Mini-Cooper S. Of those 35, only 22 of them finished the last night's Mountain Circuit.

Along with the two 'works' Tigers (already described) the Imps all started from London (the Duke of York's Barracks, in Chelsea) and, amazingly, two of them fought their way through the blizzards to reach Monte Carlo – only nine crews from that city actually making it to the start of the high-speed action after Chambery. 'Tiny' Lewis' car had gone AWOL along the way, but both Rosemary Smith and David Pollard had made it. Not only that, but to the delight of Rootes' publicists, on the five special stages between Chambery and Monte Carlo, Rosemary set total stage times which were 4min. 17 seconds faster than those of David Pollard. Rosemary, for her part, was only 4min. 10sec adrift of Peter Harper in the mighty 'works' Tiger.

Before the start of the last night's stages – six more were yet to come – the Imps lay in 19th (Pollard) and 26th (Rosemary Smith), though the great news for Rosemary was that the only other Ladies' crews ahead of her were Pat Moss-Carlsson (sixth place in a Saab 96) and Lucette Pointet (Citroen DS19 in 16th place). What followed was another gritty, fast, dangerous and, above all, extremely demanding night's rallying in the mountains behind Monte Carlo. Both the Rallye Imps kept going, and stayed on the road, the result being that David Pollard moved up to 15th place, and Rosemary to

254

'Works' Imps in rallying: 1964-1968

22nd. More importantly, although Pat Moss-Carlsson won the Ladies Award, Rosemary finished second in the category (for Mmle. Pointet dropped out) and had clearly enjoyed herself in this nimble little car.

Was this now the turn of the tide as far as the Imp was concerned? It certainly looked like it, especially as Rosemary Smith and 'Tiny' Lewis then turned out on the Circuit of Ireland at Easter time, and put in another fine performance. This was not a holiday weekend, not by any means, as other top entries came from Paddy Hopkirk (Mini-Cooper S), along with Vic Elford, David Seigle-Morris and Brian Melia (all in 'works' Cortina GTs).

As far as the headliners were concerned, the big battle was between Hopkirk and Elford, but Rootes-watchers always observed that both the 'works' Imps put in workmanlike performances. Both the cars were running in the Group 3 category, with twin-carburettor engines and 998cc engines, and though they never got into the fastest stage times (they were also competing in Hopkirk's class, against a full-house 'works' Mini-Cooper 1275S).

After five action-filled days – the rally started from Bangor in Northern Ireland, and finished in Larne, but took in special stages and timed sections all the way down through the Republic, as far south as Cork and Kerry – the two Imps finished eighth and ninth overall, second ('Tiny' Lewis) and third (Rosemary Smith) in their class. Not only that, but no car with a smaller engine finished above them, and Rosemary Smith won the Ladies' Award.

Victory in the Tulip Rally

That, though, was just the beginning, for what followed on the Tulip Rally – Noordwijk-an-Zee to the Geneva region, then back to Noordwijk – astonished the rallying world and, if truth be told, surprised

The Tulips tell their own story! Rosemary Smith (left) and Valerie Domleo have just won the 1965 Tulip Rally outright, in their nimble 998cc Hillman Imp.

ROOTES MAESTROS
"In their own words."

Rootes themselves. Not only did the two 'works' Imps of Rosemary Smith and 'Tiny' Lewis win their capacity class, but they were so far ahead of any other vehicle in that group that the Tulip's 'class-improvement' handicapping system also gifted them the outright victory too.

Was it any wonder that, in later years, Rosemary once told an interviewer:

'I remember testing, testing, testing. You had to be light on the controls to get the best from the Imp. We had maybe 85bhp in the early days and you could not chuck it around: you had to set it up for a corner, get it turned in with the tail out and then go. Under-steer had to be avoided. The Imp was a lovely car to drive, and although we had rear wheels coming off the team cars and the production cars did have reliability problems, it was a sturdy car at heart ….The Imp was an easy car, but you had to be careful on long undulating straights as it would bounce higher and higher and end up standing on its nose….'

This Tulip was an event hi-jacked by snow. Snow in April/May? Yes – in the mountains north and west of Geneva, this being where most of the drama took place. As the author noted in his *Autocar* report at the time: 'Heavy snowfalls near the Ballon d'Alsace, and later in the Geneva area, caused wholesale holdups and blockages ….Many crews abandoned the struggle, and returned to Champagnole (the next time control), and as a result of marshal's verbal instructions at this point, there was an official protest which sought to have the offending loop cancelled. But reason prevailed when it was realised that more than 70 crews had managed to beat the conditions without winter tyres, and indeed 12 of them were un-penalised on the road sections….'

This was where the Imps proved to be so effective, as their weight-over-rear wheels layout gave them traction where other cars were struggling. For Rootes, in fact, this was as blessing, for in a 2,000 road miles event there were only thirteen speed tests, totalling a mere 37 miles/59 kilometres.

As on the Circuit of Ireland, the Imps were in highly-tuned Group 3 condition, running with the still-not-homologated 998cc engine, and with Minilite magnesium wheels: Rosemary's was registered 8305 KV, an identity which instantly de-fined it among all Imp enthusiasts. Incidentally, the team might have had supplies of racing tyres for selected tests. If one of the mechanics had not punctured one while drilling holes in the front bonnet panel to mount the rally plates ….

Even so, the Imps might not have been the fastest cars in their class, but they were certainly the most reliable, and the most professionally driven too. Not only that, but once it became clear that they were still running 'clean' on the roads while their rivals were stuck in ditches, spinning their wheels madly, or simply not able to proceed, an element of tactics could also be considered.

Faced with such a situation on the Tulip, where 'class improvement' entered the equation, 'Tiny' Lewis; had been here before. In 1961, and while driving a Triumph Herald, he had been neck and neck with Geoff Mabbs in another Herald, chose to retire just before the last control, which boosted Mabbs's score significantly, and delivered an unexpected outright victory. On this occasion, a quick bit of computation showed that retirement would not be needed, the outcome being that the two Imps finished first and second in their class *and* first and second in general classification. It was the first Rootes outright rally victory since 1958 (when Peter Harper's Sunbeam Rapier had won the RAC Rally – and once again, it was unexpected snow which had helped to deliver….

By this time, the Rootes 'works' team effort was on a roll, so only five week later, on the

Above: Rosemary Smith and Val Domleo launch their 'works' Imp up yet another hill climb test in the 1965 Tulip Rally, which they won outright.

Below: Immediately after Rosemary Smith and Val Domleo had won the Tulip Rally in 1965, their gallant little Imp, 8305 KV, was rushed back to London, to go on show in Rootes' Devonshire House showrooms in Piccadilly.

ROOTES MAESTROS
"In their own words."

Rosemary Smith (right) and Val Domleo, looking extremely smart as they pose on 8305 KV, in which they had won the 1965 Tulip Rally. This shot was posed in London as the publicity circus began to unwind.

'Works' Imps in rallying: 1964-1968

rough, hot, high-speed Scottish Rally (which was, in truth, much harder work than the Tulip had been for there were to be 52 stages in 1,700 miles), three 998cc Hillman Imps appeared, this time running with steel wheels, as the Minilite alloys were expected to suffer from the appalling surfaces. 'Tiny' Lewis, Rosemary Smith and David Pollard started, two of them finished, both won major awards – and 'Tiny' Lewis actually finished second overall, in an event where there were no timing handicaps.

It was an event full of incident. Timo Makinen's Austin-Healey 3000 was expected to win, but battered its transmission to death on the rocks, Paddy Hopkirk's Mini-Cooper S also wilted, all three of the 'works' Cortinas went off the road, which left only Roger Clark, in his own privately-prepared Ford Cortina GT, to lead everyone home.

Through, and around, all this carnage, two of the Imps kept going, smoothly, neatly-driven and fast (if not sensationally so).

Unfortunately, David Pollard's Imp had to retire after only three stages when his engine flywheel parted company with the engine crankshaft: mechanics can work miracles of repair at the side of the road, but that miracle was not one of them.

By half distance, at Grantown-on-Spey, Lewis' car was already in second place, ahead of all but Roger Clark's Cortina, and he never faltered at all before the end. After four days of rough going, in the heat of an early Scottish summer, 'Tiny' came home, triumphantly, in second place overall, with Rosemary Smith not only finishing fifth overall, but winning the Ladies' Award too.

Then came the French Alpine which, in 1965, was still the high-point of any rally enthusiast's season. As ever, the Alpine took in all the tight road sections, all the high passes, and all the well-known speed hill-climbs in the mountains between the Mediterranean and Switzerland, but in 1965 the time target schedules were higher and

Rallye Imps always 'flew' very well – straight and level, and although they lacked ultimate power, they were extremely quick, especially on loose-surfaced stages.

ROOTES MAESTROS
"In their own words."

more difficult to sustain, than ever before: only one in three cars which started made it to the finish. Marcus Chambers, in fairness, was hoping for Rootes to win the rally outright with a Tiger (and, as we now know, he nearly did so, only to be foiled by a stupid minor dispute over the engine specification of Peter Harper's car

Even though they realised that the Group 3 schedules were quite beyond the capabilities of the 998cc Imps, Rootes entered two Imps – one of them going to team-regular Rosemary Smith, the other being loaned to Margaret MacKenzie and her husband Joe Lowrey.

As expected, the Imps struggled with the schedule - which was nothing of which to be ashamed, as so did almost everyone else – and though the loaned car soon disappeared, Rosemary (and her co-driver Sheila Taylor) kept going, serenely fast, if not sensationally so. After four days, and innumerable up-and-over assaults on Alpine passes, Rosemary's car (EDU 710C) swept back to the finish in Monte Carlo, not only winning the 1.0litre Grand Touring capacity class, and winning the Ladies' Prize (one almost wrote 'as expected'), but finished fifth overall in the entire GT category. This was a magnificent achievement and more, surely, could not have been expected?

By this time an army of Rootes rally enthusiasts were clamouring for the chance to buy replicas of these capable little machines, so they must have been delighted to see a Rootes announcement, in October 1965, that this was now to be possible. Rootes, however, realised that demand would be limited, and that it would have made no economic sense to build these cars, from new, at the dedicated Imp assembly plant at Linwood.

Accordingly, the deal was that customers first of all had to buy their new Imp de Luxe or Super Imp (or even a Singer Chamois, if the mood took them), and then deliver it to the Rootes competitions department for detail modification. Space had been found close to the main competitions department at Humber Road, so that this could be done without interfering with the 'works' team's activities.

In these workshops, the standard 875cc engine would be replaced by a twin-carburettor 998cc power unit (rated conservatively at 65bhp at 6,200rpm), and at the same time servo assistance would be applied to the brakes, suspension settings revisions would be made, and there would be a special fascia with extra instruments. At the time, the Rootes PR department stated that the cost would be £302 (which was half as much as the price of a standard road car) and that initially supplies would be limited to experienced competition drivers ….'

Performance figures quoted were a 95mph top speed (standard car, 80mph), and 0-60mph in 14.8sec (standard car 23.7mph).

Purely by chance, Hartwell provided *Autocar* with a very specially-prepared 'Group 4' version of their own, which took all the Rallye Imp features, and added more of their own. Engine power was quoted, but with a measured 0-60mph time of 11.1sec, it must have been much more than standard. Interestingly enough, Hartwell quoted £25.25 for a set of four Koni competition dampers, £23 for an engine oil cooler, £49.34 for a set of Minilite wheels, £42.25 for a set of five Dunlop SP41 radial ply tyres, and £18.43 for a special hip-hugging Microcell driver's seat.

For the last event of the season – the RAC Rally – Marcus Chambers spent up to the very limit of his budget. Apart from Peter Harper's Sunbeam Tiger, he also entered no fewer than four Rallye Imps – driven by team regulars Rosemary Smith, 'Tiny' Lewis and David Pollard, but also provided a car for Andrew Cowan, of Duns in Scotland.

'Works' Imps in rallying: 1964-1968

Also present in this up-to-1.0litre GT category were four highly-developed front-wheel-drive Saab Sports to be driven by Erik Carlsson, Pat Moss-Carlsson, Ove Andersson and Ake Andersson, so this was going to a hard-fought battle.

Those were the days in which the RAC Rally was a real challenge, for it started and finished in London, took in 57 special stages as far apart as Exmoor and Scotland (near Perth), Central Wales and the Dalby stages in Yorkshire – and took four days (with only one night halt, at Perth) to unfold. From Rootes, a minor but significant innovation was that the Imps, which had previously been red-painted, had been re-liveried in dark blue with a white stripe along the flanks.

Within hours, Rootes could concentrate its servicing efforts on the Imps, for Peter Harper's Tiger had unfortunately holed its radiator, and it was immediately clear that this was going to be a harum-scarum event, where high speeds and (more importantly) snow on the ground, and on the stages) was going to be a factor. Well before the rally arrived at Perth – and after the Welsh (first time round) and Yorkshire stages had been tackled, only half the original number of runners (86 out of 162 starters) were still on the road, the lead had changed several times, and the weather was getting more wintry by the minute.

Not even the sure-footed Imps could treat this as a routine class-gathering exercise, as Andrew Cowan proved when he rolled his car in Dovey, in central Wales, but he kept going with a misfiring engine for a time – a gritty performance which would pay off in the end. Rosemary Smith, looking band-box smart as ever, knew that she was not likely to beat the Saabs, for which the conditions might have been designed, and kept going at her own pace.

As expected, the Rallye Imps could not match the Scandinavian 'superstars' in this extremely wintry event, but kept going, kept going, and kept going – the result being that 'Tiny' Lewis took a very creditable third place in class, behind the Carlssons, Erik and Pat. Not only that, but the works team took the much coveted Manufacturers' Team Prize. For 'Tiny', Rosemary, and team-recruit Andrew Cowan, this was a difficult event to remember with much pride.

All in all, 1965 had been an eventful year for the Imps, for their performance increased as their reliability improved, and before long they were formidable little 1litre cars. If only they had not matured at the same time as the legendary BMC Mini-Cooper Ss, they would already be seen as outstanding little rally cars. Even so, there was even more excitement, and controversy, to follow in the New Year.

In the meantime, Des O'Dell had channelled some of his extrovert attention from improving the Tigers, with their Ford-USA engines (about which he knew everything), to the altogether different Imps, about which, at first, he knew very little. Documents which have survived from that intensely-experienced time at Humber Road in 1965 show that he tested a whole range of Imp/Rallye, Imp/prototype engine and transmission combinations, usually taking performance figures at the MIRA proving grounds near Nuneaton, which was less than 30 minutes easy drive away from the Humber Road factory in the east of Coventry.

The most startling of all these tests was undoubtedly that of the one-off Hartwell car (registered GRH 5), which was well-and-truly stripped out for use in speed events, and not on rallies. This 998cc machine, still running on twin Stromberg carburettors, produced a 0-60mph time of 11.6sec, and a top speed of 102mph. It also tipped the scales at a mere 1,352lb, showing just what potential was locked away in this little car.

ROOTES MAESTROS
"In their own words."

More typical was the testing of 4525 KV in May 1965, which was good for 92.5mph, and 0-60mph in 14.3sec. More important, too, was the fact that this rally car, which was carrying 7.5 gallons of fuel at the time, checked in at 1,638lb. Perhaps even more significant, especially as the rally cars were now demonstrably seen as having excellent handling, was that 1,000lb of that weight was concentrated over the rear wheels – 61 per cent – which on other cars would normally have promoted oversteer. On the Imp it merely seemed to help even the traction of those driven rear wheels even more than expected.

It was immediately after the RAC Rally that the author persuaded Rootes to loan Rosemary Smith's car (EDU 710C) to *Autocar* for a week, not only to confirm the performance figures (which were just slightly down on those quoted above, but this was a car which had just completed an arduous event, after all….) but so that we could all get a general feel for these interesting and successful little cars. It was technical editor Geoffrey Howard who nominally wrote the feature, though he drew heavily on the impressions of all us.

Some of the impressions, and comments, are fascinating, even today:

'…it feels like a lady's car, looks chic and is complete even to the point of carpets and underfelt...a Triplex heated windscreen was fitted on this car.

'Two of those excellent reclining bucket seats from the Sunbeam Tiger are fitted in the front, with big pedal pads from the same stores bin for the clutch and brake,

In four years Rootes built up quite a fleet of fast and nimble Rallye Imps. This particular 1965 car, EDU 710C, was later loaned to Autocar magazine, where the author drove the car for several days, and confirmed a top speed of around 92mph.

'Works' Imps in rallying: 1964-1968

and the standard brake pedal salvaged for the accelerator....

'High on the scuttle in a little cowl is a rev counter with a faint yellow line at 6,900rpm, and the needle behaves as though there is a magnet there to attract it – the aluminium ohc engine loves to run at the peak, smoothly and healthily all the time, given half a chance.

'The gearbox on this car is quite the lightest and sweetest of all the Imps we have driven ....wheels are wide ones from the Chamois with Dunlop SP44 radial Weathermasters, which run quietly and grip surprisingly well on smooth, wet, roads.

'We had one very memorable run back late on a Sunday night.... It was raining so hard that there seemed to be more water in the air than on the road, but "Rosemary Smith" sliced through with wipers flapping frantically at their faster speed, and the iodine vapours seeming to part the spray for miles ahead....

'First through the quiet lanes in Sussex, up and down through that delightful little gearbox, with the rise and fall of the throbbing exhaust playing tunes to us, and the SPs doing just what was asked – a tail flick here to save winding the steering and a full-blooded slide there (who needs a reason?).

'Did I say this was a ladies' car? Well, it does seem that way, but we'll compromise: a ladies car designed for a man's sport.'

Rootes, for sure, was already proud of its little rally cars – and now we could see why.

1966

Except that it would have been good to look forward to using new rally cars with a lot more horsepower than before (and this, as we now know, was never going to happen), the prospects for the new season looked very promising. Marcus Chambers looked forward to placing his Imps in events whenever, or wherever, their 998cc engines would be eligible. Production of Rallye Imps for private owners was now progressing steadily, and it would not be long, he hoped, before Group 2 homologation was achieved.

First of all, however, he was faced with preparing cars for the Monte Carlo in January where, on this occasion, new regulations imposed by the organisers had made it essential to enter standard, or near-standard, cars to stand a chance of success. Only for strictly standard, Group 1 ('showroom' – even the seats had to be non-reclining types), cars would special stage times for the Monte be assessed as normal, while modified cars would have an 18 per cent penalty applied.

Clearly this had been done, after much behind the scenes lobbying by certain French manufacturers, who were thoroughly depressed at being beaten by cars like the 'works' Imps, Tigers and Minis, to placate the French. As the author's own Monte preview stated in January 1966: 'The Sunbeam Tigers now find themselves very competitive in the Grand Touring category, as erstwhile highly-developed specials become ineligible, while the 998cc Hillman Imp, which had such a good 1965 season, is temporarily in the wilderness, and not usable until after the Monte....'

Rootes, in fact, were so depressed at the prospects of battling against such performance-strangling regulations that Marcus Chambers considered withdrawing from the lists, but was over-ruled by his superiors.

Three Imps were prepared for this uneven contest – a Group 1 875cc car for Rosemary Smith/Valerie Domleo, a Group 2 (but still single-carburettor/875cc) car for 'Tiny' Lewis, and another Group 1 car for Peter Bolton/Gordon Shanley, who were allied to the BBC *Sportsview* programme.

263

Because of the draconian rules laid down by the Monte Carlo Rally organisers in 1966, most of the 'works' Imps were entered as near-standard Group 1 (875cc) cars. This was the Rosemary Smith car starting from London. Notice the headlamp/driving lamp layout, which was to cause so much controversy when the British contingent reached Monte Carlo.

The Group 1 Imp looked very standard indeed, and it was clear that if the co-driver was to get any rest at all on the long run in, then he would have to burrow down into the back seat. Only two extra driving lamps were allowed, wider Singer Chamois wheels were used, and Ferodo VG95/1 brake linings had been standardised.

The Group 2 car, though a little bit more specialised (the engine produced 46bhp, and Sunbeam Tiger front seats had been fitted) had the newly-developed 10.5 gallon fuel tank up front, and was of course carrying a full display of extra driving lamps.

The usual Monte format included a multitude of starting points, but no common route until everyone had reached Monte Carlo for the first time. After this, they faced six special stages on the long *Route Commun,* and a further six stages on the tight and concentrated Mountain Circuit on the final night.

The lighting fiasco

What followed when the cars reached Monte Carlo is a story which has been told so often by Mini-Cooper fans that it is easy to suspect that no other cars, or drivers, were involved. After dominating the event, the 'works' Mini-Coopers, we are repeatedly told, were disqualified from the 1966 Monte, thus handing an unworthy victory to – guess what? – a 'works' Citroen.

True enough, but there was much more to spell out. The fact is that several British teams, including Rootes, who were using Lucas headlamps, were affected – and Rosemary

Above: As prepared for the 1966 "Monte", even though Rosemary Smith's Group 1 875cc Imp felt pitifully slow, she could still make it dance on the snowy stages. Rosemary was the moral victor in the Coupe des Dames contest – until the organisers waded in with their spurious disqualification.

Below: It doesn't always snow on the Monte Carlo Rally – sometimes the roads are just wet, slippery, and thoroughly depressing. Rosemary and Val Domleo on their way to what they thought would be a Coupe des Dames victory in the 1967 event.

ROOTES MAESTROS
"In their own words."

Smith was deprived of victory in the Coupe des Dames category, which she had won.

Monte organisers have often been accused of pursuing a vendetta against the Minis – which had already won the Monte twice – and fastened on so-called discrepancies of headlamp operations as a pretext to get them disqualified. True enough, this is what was finally used as the disqualifying excuse – but along the way other 'works' cars were dragged in, and also summarily thrown out.

Lucas was just at the point of making amazingly bright quartz-halogen headlamp bulbs available, but at the time these were as expensive as gold dust, were available only in tiny quantities to 'works' teams, and could only then be supplied as single-filament items. When original-type QH headlamps were therefore 'dipped', this had to be done by arranging for dipped lighting to come from another pair of lamps.

Any car which only had two headlamps (which meant that other teams such as Triumph and Rover, which had four-headlamp noises, were free from controversy), had to arrange for its extra driving lamps also to act as dipped headlamp beams, for this was also a year in which the organisers insisted that standard cars should only have two extra driving lamps. In Rosemary Smith's case, her Imp (FRW 306C) had seven inch Lucas driving lamps, high mounted, closely positioned inboard of the headlamps themselves.

But was this 'legal' as far as the various road traffic acts, and in particular the Monte Carlo Rally organisers, were concerned? As Stuart Turner has already told us in his best-selling autobiography *Twice Lucky*, he and several rivals/colleagues were uneasy about the implications of the regulations and :

'Even before the event we – and that included Henry Taylor of Ford too – were sufficiently worried about the implications of a Group 1 event, and about the nuances of the latest regulations, that we had flown to Paris to check up on things, so we must have picked up the vibes at an early stage.

'But – and maybe I'm being naïve – until it actually happened I was never really convinced that someone was out to get us…..'

But they were……

In his earlier book *Works Wonders*, Marcus Chambers analysed the regulations, the permissible layout of lights, and all the implications for Rosemary at some length. The fact is that when the provisional results were originally posted, Rosemary was named as the winner of the Coupe des Dames, but that was before the scrutineers got to work on the Mini-Coopers. As is now a matter of record, all the actual stripping, all the detailed inspection of lighting systems, and all the aggravation, surrounded the Mini-Coopers, while Roger Clark's 'works' Lotus-Cortina and the Group 1 875cc Imp stood to one side, to await a verdict.

As a result, and as we now know, the British cars which had been wired up so that their headlamps dipped on to other auxiliary lamps were disqualified on the grounds that Appendix J did not allow this (in other words, Appendix J did not specifically say that it *was* allowed….).

Unhappily, this was the only year in which the redoubtable Ms. Smith won the Ladies' Award – only to have it snatched away from her….

If it is possible to re call what happened on an event which was so comprehensively spoilt by the obtuse organisers, we should now recall that Rosemary's Imp (and that of Peter Bolton) started from London, while 'Tiny' Lewis set out from Rheims. Along the way to Monte Carlo, Lewis' and Bolton's cars both suffered from repeated throttle cable breakages (both of these cars, of course, were running with single carburettor

266

'Works' Imps in rallying: 1964-1968

engines, not with the usual and well-proven twin-Stromberg layouts).

By the end of the event, Rosemary's battle for the Ladies category was over, and won – so she thought at the time – but the two men were nowhere near the head of their classes. Immediately afterwards, Rosemary thought she had won, and so did Rootes' advertising people, but it was not to last, and the stupid, mindless, vindictive disqualifications duly followed.

Rootes duly came home with nothing to show for an extremely good performance in the rally itself. Management, fortunately, realised that the works team could not be blamed for the fiasco (nor were they, for the other major British teams – BMC and Ford – both suffered too), and they realised, more than ever before, that a French soldier named Nicolas Chauvin, a great patriot who was not about to give credit to anyone who was not one of his own nationals, had a lot to answer for.

Like BMC and Ford, Rootes concluded that the only way to shrug off such a shambles was to put it behind them, and start again. There was plenty of opportunity to do that. As we now know, company politics was beginning to weigh against the big V8-engined Tiger (which had a Ford-USA engine, but whose parent company was now effectively controlled by Chrysler), so the time was ripe to concentrate on the Rallye Imps.

Fighting back

With several important events now on the agenda, Humber Road spent the next several weeks building new cars, preparing old ones – and generally getting involved in the Le Mans Tiger project, which meant that 'works' Imps did not re-appear until Easter time, when Rosemary Smith started her 'local' event, the Circuit of Ireland.

As ever, this was a full weekend event, with many special stages, and with important competition coming from 'works' Ford Lotus-Cortina, BMC Minis, and Roy Fidler's 'works' Triumph 2000. Starting from Ballymena in the north of Ireland, and meandering all the way down to Killarney, the event finally ended in Larne.

By this time the Rootes competitions department had also started building the occasional 'Jimp', for loan to deserving cases, and one of these cars (FHP 549C) appeared in the young Colin Malkin's hands. What was a 'Jimp'? It was a semi-detached Rallye Imp, which was controlled by the team's workshop manager Jim Ashworth – 'works' but not works, up-to-date spec., but not serviced on events by the factory – in other words, a car for the 'apprentices' whom Marcus Chambers and his bosses wanted to assess.

In 1966, Colin Malkin was still very much 'the newcomer' as far as Rootes was concerned. FHP 549C was one of Jim Ashworth's well-known 'Jimps' – which were loaned out to deserving cases, but without financial support.

ROOTES MAESTROS
"In their own words."

On an event where several 'works' cars destroyed themselves in accidents, or broke down under the constant strain of high-speed tarmac special stages, Rosemary and Colin both kept going, though neither car could quite keep up with the big-horsepower machinery up front. In the end, it was almost 'situation normal' for Rosemary, who won yet another Ladies' prize, while to the surprise of many (but not to the co-drivers – including the author) who had already been with him), Colin Malkin finished tenth overall in his 'Jimp', led only by 'works' cars, and those with much more horsepower.

Next, with only a few days rest for Humber Road's mechanics and management team, it was time to tackle the Tulip Rally. Peter Harper's magnificent run in the Tiger has already been detailed (he finished third, beaten on handicap only by Rauno Aaltonen's 'works' Mini and Vic Elford's 'works' Lotus-Cortina), but we must not forget the way that 'Tiny' Lewis coped with his under-powered Rallye Imp.

The Tulip ran to its usual format – a start and finish on the North Sea coast of Holland, but long road sections leading to speed hill climbs and special sections in the German and French mountains. Theoretically the hill-climbs were not announced before hand, but it was amazing how many crews seem to have practiced the appropriate pieces of road and made pace note accordingly! Unhappily, too, the usual Tulip 'handicapping' system persisted, and on this occasion, 'Tiny' could not hope to match his performance of 1965 (when, of course, he had finished second overall). A 1litre class win, therefore, was all which could be hoped for – and the burly Bristolian duly delivered.

Only a week later, on the other side of the world, Rosemary Smith was in action in the Shell 4000 Rally, which seemed to take in most little-used roads in Canada, close to the 49th Parallel, and could have been an almost impossible challenge for the little Imp. Rootes' North American importers, however, were keen to see her in action, and since Rootes' fuel company sponsor was Shell, which was also sponsoring the event itself, the deed was done!

For the factory, this was a single car entry (the car was locally registered, where Rosemary took along a local co-driver, Anne Coombe of Toronto, who had all the skills to deal with a rally where navigation and time keeping was sometimes as important as fast driving. The irrepressible Rosemary, however, just carried on doing which she always did best – which was to be faster in a Hillman than any of the men who regularly tried to match her.

With an event starting from Vancouver (on the Pacific Coast) and ending in Quebec city all of six days and 4,100 miles later, this was a real endurance test. Cynical Americans, not only looking at the Imp, which was small by comparison with the American cars which were taking part, but at Rosemary, who was determined to look as elegant and personable as always, were convinced that she would not even survive the passage of Rockies, but by the time they arrived at the Calgary night halt she was already up into sixth place, and showing considerable pace.

Later, on the run from Sault Ste. Marie to Sudbury, the entire rally got bogged down in deep mud on an unmade section, and although Rosemary might have been able to keep kept going if she had not been baulked by other crews, she was delayed for many frustrating minutes. Eventually she had to resort to almost Safari-style bush-craft, disappeared into the undergrowth, and suddenly re-appeared at the head of the bogged down section.

In the end, she lost no less than 310 points at the control alone, which was certainly enough to drop her, and the valiant Imp, from fourth place, which would have put her

'Works' Imps in rallying: 1964-1968

behind two 'works' Lotus-Cortinas and a well-driven Volvo. The fact that Rosemary eventually finished eighth overall (there were only 26 cars which survived, out of 60 starters), was of no consolation to this very competitive lady….

However, and as they say - when the going gets tough, the tough get going. No sooner had Rosemary finished the Shell 4000 in Quebec than she flew back to Europe, and joined the Rootes team which was about to start their practice for the very demanding Acropolis Rally. Apart from Peter Harper's Tiger, there would be three Imps – for Rosemary Smith, 'Tiny' Lewis and Andrew Cowan.

What more need we say about the Acropolis that has not already been made clear in the Rapier section? Here was Europe's toughest event – not only fast but rough, not only hot but dusty, and – above all – not only demanding but exhausting. To enter a team of Imps in such an event fell into the 'High Hopes' category, but their superb traction was certainly an advantage, while there was more and more confidence in what Des O'Dell's development skills had built in to the little car.

The story is easily told, and summarised by the fact that only 38 of the 105 starters finished the event. Ford, BMC, Volvo, Saab and Lancia all turned out in force, but many of their cars could not survive the battering of the Greek terrain. 'Tiny' Lewis' car had to retire after losing reverse gear (it also disappeared over the edge of the road when being man-handled by its crew!), Andrew Cowan's car wilted with a broken engine distributor drive, which left Rosemary as the sole survivor. Although Ove Andersson's Lancia won the entire Group 3 category, and Peter Harper's Tiger followed him closely home, the remarkable Ms. Smith/Imp combination took third in

In May, the weather in Greece, for the Acropolis Rally, tended to be hot, sweaty and dusty, but Rosemary Smith (right) and Val Domleo both looked band-box smart before starting the 1966 rally. Not only did they take third in the Grand Touring Category, but this was the first-ever Imp to finish the rough and tough Acropolis Rally.

Rosemary Smith's Rallye Imp on its way to taking third in the GT category of the 1966 Acropolis Rally. Two other 'works' Imps failed to make it to the finish of the event.

that category too. Against all the odds, it seemed, an Imp had survived the Acropolis Rally.

Back at home, Rootes finally abandoned the Tiger to its fate, and concentrated on the Imp. Next up was the Scottish Rally (which started just two or three days after the Acropolis had ended) – held, as always hoped, in hot and dry conditions in all the glorious special stages of the Highlands. Three 'works' Imp entries soon turned into just one – for Andrew Cowan's car devoured its own gearbox, while Lewis' car sheared its engine distributor drive, then broke its transmission.

On the other hand, by driving just within her own, and the car's limits Rosemary kept going and finished a very creditable third overall, beaten only by Tony Fall's 'works' Mini-Cooper 1275S and Jerry Larsson's Saab Sport. Although the car had lost reverse gear before the end, Rosemary won her fourth Ladies' award in eight weeks – all in Imps – which was an amazing feat. That Imp, by the way, carried the registration number of 4525 KV, nominally dating back to 1963, but certainly a machine which had been re-shelled at least once in a hard-working 'works'; career.

Rootes, in fact, was keeping 4525 KV extremely busy at this time, for within three weeks of the Scottish, it was out once again, this time competing in the Gulf London Rally as a 'private' entry - for official 'works' cars could not compete in this heavily sponsored event. Rosemary, none-the-less, turned up, nominally without support (and if you believed that, you would believe anything), while Andrew Cowan also appeared in a 'Jimp'.

Here was another tough, fast, and above all arduous event, starting and finishing in London, though with 34 special stages strewn all around Great Britain, and with no

270

Above: Major Bob Tennant-Reid of the RSAC releases Rosemary Smith's re-shelled 4525 KV to compete in the Scottish Rally of 1966....

Below: ....and by driving like this she took third overall, an excellent performance on a fast and rough event.

ROOTES MAESTROS
"In their own words."

official overnight halt at all. Real endurance stuff, on and around British roads!

Peter Harper's Tiger soon took the edge off Rootes' hopes, by crashing in an early stage in Yorkshire, while (as the author's *Autocar* report stated at the time): 'Rosemary Smith had a broken rear damper changed on her Rallye Imp. The Imp was also suffering the normal gearbox troubles and Rosemary, never at her best at this time of day [it was 05.00HR], was threatening to catch the next train back to London. Val Domleo said nothing, but looked philosophical.'

This was truly a marathon of attrition, as car after car fell out with major mechanical problems, and neither Imp looked like winning the event. Andrew Cowan struggled on, with a recalcitrant transmission (no third gear, second having to be held in place), but at least stayed in touch with the larger-engined/more powerful opposition, while Rosemary Smith's car also finished up lacking all but first and top gears: for once she was defeated in the Ladies' contest – by Pat Moss-Carlsson, in a loaned 'works' Saab.

After such a hectic few weeks, the 'works' team deserved a rest, but did not get it, for they now had to settle down and prepare three cars for the French Alpine, which was to be run in early September. As far as the crews were concerned, this was certainly the most popular event of the year – fine weather, fine scenery, simple regulations, and high average speeds needed to keep a clean sheet – but for team mechanics it always put exceptional demands on the cars themselves.

By 1967 Rootes' 'A-Team' had solid, fast, but still under-powered Rallye Imps to enjoy on suitable events. Left to right: Robin Turvey, Peter Harper, Rosemary Smith, Val Domleo, Andrew Cowan and Brian Coyle, ready to start the French Alpine Rally of 1966.

4525 KV was a hard-worked car in 1966. Here it is rushing through the French countryside on the 1966 French Alpine Rally where, unhappily like all the Imps in the event, it retired with major mechanical trouble.

In Rootes case, this year, the news was suddenly all bad – although three Imps were entered – for Peter Harper, Rosemary Smith and Andrew Cowan to drive – none of them finished. Simply and brutally, there was mechanical carnage, with retirements caused by a broken engine distributor, a cracked engine sump (and loss of engine oil) and a broken drive shaft universal joint. Best to write this one off to experience, perhaps – Rootes will forget all about it if you will ….

It was not until November that the team had licked its wounds, and prepared for Britain's own RAC Rally, which was due to start and finish in London, and on this occasion was considerably glamorised by the *Sun* daily newspaper, and by the appearance of F1 race drivers Jim Clark (Ford Lotus-Cortina) and Graham Hill (BMC Mini-Cooper 1275S) in the lists. Rootes, for their part, had a positive fleet of Rallye Imps – for Peter Harper, 'Tiny' Lewis, Andrew Cowan, Rosemary Smith and Jenny Nadin - along with support for several other private entrants in 'Jimps'.

The Imps, in fairness, were not expected to be in contention for outright victory – they could surely not be expected to compete, head-on, against the 'works' Lotus-Cortinas or the BMC Mini-Cooper 1275Ss – but if their transmissions could hold together they were certainly strongly in contention for class success. 147 cars, after all, might have entered – but how many would complete all 67 special stages, and get to the finish?

Although Rosemary Smith was, as ever, set to put in a gritty performance, the other cars struck trouble of one type or another. Peter Harper's car was the first to suffer, with transmission failure on the very first day, while 'Tiny' Lewis charged off the road in Greystoke forest in Cumbria (though he was able to continue). Even so, by the

273

This montage shows Rosemary Smith's Rallye Imp starting out on the 1966 RAC Rally, the crew – Val Domleo was Rosemary's co-driver – and the car hard at work in a Forestry Commission special stage. Rosemary finished fourteenth overall.

'Works' Imps in rallying: 1964-1968

middle of the event, at Aviemore in Scotland, Andrew Cowan was leading his class in the Group 3 category, with 'Tiny' Lewis and Rosemary Smith behind.

Soon after the restart, Andrew Cowan's car broke its transmission (with more than 80bhp from the Rallye Imp's 998cc engines, this was always likely to happen), Colin Malkin's 'Jimp' suffered a broken crown wheel, and on the final morning, in the Dalby stage in Yorkshire, 'Tiny' Lewis' car suffered a drive failure too. The outcome was that, of all the leading Imps, only that of the ever-reliable Rosemary Smith reached the finish, and even she could finish no higher than 14th, in an event with precious few survivors.

Amazingly, it was not quite the end of the season for the hard-pressed Rootes team. No sooner had they all got back to Humber Road after the RAC Rally, than three cars were hastily re-furbished for Peter Harper, Andrew Cowan and David Pollard to drive on the Welsh Rally, which started and finished in Cardiff.

This event almost became a case of 'getting rid of the empties', for David Pollard put his car off the road – backwards – on the first night, which destroyed several important electric features, and on the second morning, not far from Llandrindod Wells, Peter Harper's car broke its transmission. Only Andrew Cowan's car kept going, at full pelt, and in the end of finished a truly remarkable fifth, with no car of less than 1.3litres ahead of him.

Unhappily, it was now clear that the Imp's transmission was always going to be the limiting factor on further developments, and since a re-design would have required new homologation, there seemed to be no credible answer. The transaxles were always prepared as carefully as possible, but the limits, it seemed, had now been achieved.

1967

For the new season, it seemed that Rootes could look forward to working on just one type of car, and to carry on improving it – the Rallye Imp. The Tigers had been sold off, and at the time there was no other project taking shape behind closed doors.

In the New Year, therefore, Marcus Chambers, Ian Hall and Des O'Dell were concentrating on the Monte Carlo Rally. Three Imps – two Rallye, and a Sunbeam Import Sport - were being readied for Peter Harper, Rosemary Smith and Andrew Cowan – which brought forth the usual corny 'Englishman, Irish-girl and Scotsman, jokes.

This year all the headlines were pointing at BMC, whose Mini-Cooper Ss were seeking revenge for their disgraceful disqualification in 1966, but Rootes were quietly confident in the traction of their rear-engined Imps, and the star quality of their drivers. Technically there was really no advance over 1966, but for marketing reasons the 'works' cars were now known as Sunbeams rather than Hillmans, as the twin-carb. Sunbeam Imp Sport had recently been announced. Incidentally, this meant that the Rallye Imp could now carry a slatted engine cover at all times (like the Sunbeam Imp Sport road car), instead of previously, where it was specifically allowed by some event regulations.

Once again, incidentally, the Monte Carlo organisers had made changes to help (they thought) French cars, this time by limiting each rally car to each use only eight tyres on each of the mountain circuits. Clearly this was going to make the entrants of more powerful cars think carefully, but Rootes were relatively happy, as the nimble Imp had never been heavy in its tyre usage. Not that this cut the pre-rally expense to the team, which still had to carry various tyres – road

As a relative newcomer to Rootes, Colin Malkin drove this 'Jimp' in the 1967 Monte Carlo Rally.

and snow, studded or plain - to the service car park in Monte Carlo.

In what was quite a mild-weather Monte (there was snow, at height, on the most mountainous special stages, but not elsewhere), all three Imps finished, but frankly they were overwhelmed by sheer performance of cars like the Porsche 911s, the BMC Mini-Cooper Ss, the Lancia Fulvias and the Renault 8 Gordinis. This is not to make excuses, but merely to emphasise, as in so many other cases, that (as the Americans would say) 'there is no substitute for cubic inches - which, in English-English, means that' there is no substitute for using larger/more powerful engines.

For Rootes, therefore, this was a battle of attrition, and for victory in the 1litre Group 2 class, which Andrew Cowan eventually won, even though he finished way down at 22nd in General Classification.

For once, Rosemary Smith had little luck on this most glamorous of events, for on the Col de Turini special stage she skidded at one point, hit a wall, broke a rear drive shaft and were forced to retire (they had been leading the Coupe des Dames competition at that point).

Back home, at Easter, the factory sent Rosemary out for her customary 'Easter break'. To compete in the five-day Circuit of Ireland, and with little drama she duly brought her Rallye Imp home in seventh overall, plus what we now thought of as 'the usual' Ladies Prize.

The factory then sent two cars to tackle the Tulip Rally – a Rallye Imp for Peter Harper and a Group 2 Imp Sport for Andrew Cowan – but in both cases it was the usual battle, of good-handling-versus-lack-of-power. The miracle, therefore, was that Peter Harper shrugged off the marking system as much as he could, finishing tenth overall in the event, and third in the GT category, beaten only by Vic Elford's victorious Porsche 911S, and David Friswell's Lotus Elan.

Clearly the 'works' team's budget had been cut to ribbons for 1967 (could this have been connected with the fact that Chrysler assumed total financial control of Rootes at the same time?), for although the North American subsidiary helped finance Rosemary Smith's return trip to the

276

'Works' Imps in rallying: 1964-1968

Canadian Shell 4000 Rally (where she won her habitual capacity class and the Ladies' award), there were no 'works' cars on the Acropolis Rally, so the full works team was held back for the Scottish Rally.

Why so much regular emphasis on the Scottish? Not only because the cars were quite competitive on Scottish stages, of course, but because the Imp was manufactured in Scotland (at Linwood, west of Glasgow), so it made a good impression on the local media if the team supported this event so much.

Although Rootes knew that the Imp wasn't going to win, they thought it would be more competitive than usual and – fingers crossed – that the transmission fragility had now been solved. For that reason, they supplied Peter Harper and Andrew Cowan what (according to the registration numbers) were brand new E-Reg. cars, while Rosemary Smith used FRW 308C, which had already had quite a hard life.

From Glasgow to Grantown-on-Spey, by way of several night-halts at Grantown and much sampling of the famous amber fluids for which this corner of Scotland was noted, the Scottish was a rally which saw a number of hot favourites drop out with breakages, but saw the Imps keep going. BMC and Saab were there, in force – and so were the rough, testing and, above all, dusty Scottish special stages.

Right from the start Andrew Cowan drew rapidly away from his team-mates, and impressed those who thought that a Rallye Imp could no longer be improved. Peter Harper was soon eliminated when he crashed his car, a consequence of a loose petrol pump which dripped fuel on to the exhaust system, started a fire and destroyed the throttle linkage.

By the time 69 of the 96 starters reached the first rest halt, at Grantown, many private owners were already cruising to try to finish but, remarkably, Andrew Cowan's Rallye Imp was fourth overall (close behind Roger Clark's Lotus Cortina, a 'works' Saab V4 and a Mini-Cooper S. Rosemary Smith was further back, in eighth place, but looking as immaculate as usual.

In the next day, Andrew Cowan worked his Rallye Imp up to an amazing second overall behind Roger Clark's Lotus-Cortina (there was no handicap factor involved – Andrew was merely going faster than everyone else!), but this was all in vain, for shortly the engine blew up catastrophically, and left him stranded. Rosemary, on the other hand, carried on serenely, train timetable always to hand, pushed her valiant car up to fourth place overall, but showed no sign of having her nominally two-year-old car breaking up under her.

Rootes then ignored the Gulf London Rally, in spite of its growing reputation as the toughest event in the British Isles, just as they ignored other mid-summer rallies, for all their attention was now focussed on the French Alpine, which was due to take place in September.

Having struggled to keep up to schedule in the 1966 event, seasoned drivers and co-drivers were astonished when they saw the target times being imposed in the 1967 route, for even though road conditions were likely to be perfect, this looked like being (to quote journalist John Davenport): 'the most savage Coupes des Alpes for years'. When the author reported on the event in *Autocar* he also commented that: Brave drivers had blanched, and team managers winced when they studied the layout of this new-style Alpine Rally…. the event was turned into a true road race in the best traditions.

79 cars would start, many of them from prestigious factories, but only 15 would finish, and until the very last day it looked as if the complete Rootes team would make it to the end. On this occasion, RAC

ROOTES MAESTROS
"In their own words."

Champion Roy Fidler (who had previously used Triumph cars) joined Andrew Cowan and Rosemary Smith in the line-up.

Marseilles to Menton (near Monte Carlo), via night-halts at l'Alpe d'Huez, set a fearsome challenge to every crew, the weather was hot, and the mountains were just as high and demanding as ever. After the first day, no Rallye Imp appeared in the top ten – it was asking a lot for it even to snap at the heels of the massed ranks of Porsches and Alpine-Renaults, after all – but all three cars were still running. Then, at the end of the second day, this (according to my *Autocar* report) is what happened:

'Though Rootes were well-placed, with Roy Fidler 12th in his Rallye Imp, Andrew Cowan's car was in dire transmission trouble with the gearbox casing split by a big rock. With the team prize at stake, this had to be changed. In a wet gravel service park, in heavy rain and complete darkness, the heroic Rootes mechanics set about removing the complete engine/gearbox power pack. After mighty efforts involving eight men, with toil, sweat and certainly blood, the new box was installed and the car rebuilt in 45 minutes! At the same time, all team cars were re-tyred and re-braked for the next day's stages....'

The third and last sector was a 29 hour marathon which included all the usual fierce Alpine Rally hills – but although Rootes were all set to take the team prize, their efforts were finally dashed when Roy Fidler's car blew a cylinder head gasket. First there was a water leak, which the crew could replenish, then there was misfiring, and finally the cylinder head gasket failed completely. The car would go no further.

To look down the list of the cars which completed the event is to see drivers who were all heroes. Andrew Cowan and Rosemary Smith finished ninth and tenth overall, neither car being beaten by any rival with an engine of less than 1,300cc. It had been a phenomenal, if fruitless, performance.

All eyes then turned to our own RAC Rally, where Rootes was hoping for an exceptional performance. By a distance, this would be the most formidable event which Rootes would tackle in 1967, for the route was due to link London with Blackpool, the Keilder forests, Wales, and back to London, covering no fewer than 69 special stages.

Not only was the little Rallye Imp well-suited to performing well in British forestry stages, but this time Marcus Chambers and Ian Hall had prepared a car (JVC 123E) for Andrew Cowan which was lighter, more specialised and faster than ever before: Rosemary Smith's car was running to its usual Group 3 specification.

Having read the regulations very carefully, Rootes had chosen to run Andrew in the Group 6 category, which allowed a great deal more freedom than Group 3. In fact, since the Fraser Imps had been raced in ever-improving Group 5 trim, throughout the season, Rootes already knew what they could and how they could idealise the car.

The basis was as before – a 998cc engine figured, of course, but in a higher state of tune, with Weber carburettors and 94bhp – and the same rather fragile transmission had to be used, but the body had been considerably lightened, Perspex instead of side 'glass' was chosen, and there were extra cooling channels channelling cold air towards the hard-worked engine.

It all looked very promising, and even though Andrew was given a competition number as low as No. 46, there were high hopes. Scrutineering was straightforward enough, and there were high hopes – until at the last moment the Man from the Ministry arrived. On the very evening before the start, the rally was abruptly cancelled!

'Works' Imps in rallying: 1964-1968

This was all due to a massive outbreak of foot-and-mouth disease, which was already afflicting tens of thousands of square miles of land which housed cloven-hoofed animals, in the days leading up to the start. Even as the rally guides were being published, it became clear that it was going to be impossible to use much of the original route. To quote a publication which went to press just three days before the start:

'The epidemic of foot-and-mouth disease has necessitated a complete revision of route: all the special stages that fall in Wales and the Lake District, including Oulton Park, have been scrubbed....the rally will go to a new stage at Savernake Forest near Marlborough, before going via Oxford to Silverstone and Mallory....'

In the next few days it got worse, so that co-drivers trying to plot the route and arrange their service schedules (the author was one of them), were dropping with fatigue and frustration. The climax came on the Friday evening, at the Excelsior Hotel at London airport, where at an emotionally charged press conference, the decision was taken to cancel everything.

24 hours later, too, Britain also announced the devaluation of the pound, which left every overseas team manager facing a considerable financial loss before his team could even go home!

The fact that the organisers hastily arranged a televised special stage 'spectacular' on the already-scheduled Camberley special stage, did little to mollify competitors, team managers or sponsors, especially as all over Britain, rallying off the public highway was now to banned for some considerable time.....

1968

With rallying now in such disarray, and with Chrysler taking a more and more parsimonious grip on every aspect of Rootes' finances, the 'works' team didn't see much to be cheerful about in 1968. Even so, as Marcus Chambers commented in his autobiography *Works Wonders*:

'From the end of 1967, one could say that serious works competition in Imps started to decline....In spite of these problems, we managed to get both Rosemary Smith and Andrew Cowan signed up as contracted drivers with a retainer, and we managed not only to stay in business the following year, but also to get ourselves a budget and make a considerable name for ourselves in doing so ....'

As Marcus has pointed out, the Rallye Imp, no question, was now at its current development peak, and as everyone seemed to know that Ford was about to launch a new 'homologation special' (this was the Escort Twin-Cam, which would be homologated in March 1968), prospects looked no brighter than before.

We now know, of course, was that technically it was certainly possible to make Imps much faster and more robust (Colin Malkin, of course, had already proved that point, with his exciting progress in winning the *Motoring News* rally championship), but there was a world of difference in doing this for one or two cars, and in the considerable numbers which would be required to gain homologation for such modifications. 1,140cc engines? Of course, but no fewer than 500 such engines, in 500 cars, would have had to be built before homologation could follow. The same went for different transmissions, and for bodywork modifications.

In 1968, however, the problem was that Rootes soon became committed to competing in the first London-Sydney Marathon, which meant that much of the budget had to be allocated to the testing, reconnaissance and actually carrying out of

ROOTES MAESTROS
"In their own words."

that event. As Marcus Chambers has already pointed out in his autobiographical note, this meant that the original programme for rallying Imps, and Rosemary Smith's contract, both had to be abandoned.

According to Marcus, he had originally intended entering at least two Imps in the Monte Carlo, Tulip, Acropolis, French Alpine and British RAC events, but as we now know, after the Monte all these had to be abandoned. In their place, cars could only be entered at home, in the Circuit of Ireland and Scottish instead. For all Rootes (particularly Imp) enthusiasts, this was a big blow – and one which was mirrored by other 'works' teams in Europe.

Although Andrew Cowan was retained on contract until 1969, poor Rosemary Smith, entering her seventh season with the Rootes 'works' team, had to be cast adrift (finally at least) – but happily she soon gained a Ford 'works' drive in London-Sydney, and later with other teams on other events, which did her already glittering reputation much good.

Before the London-Sydney event was officially announced, and before the trauma over budgets erupted, Rootes were able to enter two Imps in the Monte Carlo Rally – a conventional Group 3/998cc Rallye Imp for Rosemary Smith, and a Group 2/875cc Sunbeam Imp Sport (JHP 100E) for Andrew Cowan – which meant that there was a chance that two separate awards could be lifted: in the event, two awards *were* gained, so the strategy worked.

This was one of those 'mild-weathered' Montes, where the concentration runs to the Mediterranean held few hazards, and high performance over the special stages was everything. Both Imps arrived in Monte Carlo in fine fettle, though Rosemary Smith's Rallye Imp had given everyone a fright by bursting an oil pipe along the way, but happily got it fixed in time.

Although the Imps were not likely to be battling for the lead – 'works' Porsches battled with 'works' Alpine-Renaults, and even the previously victorious Mini-Cooper S types were out-paced – they were reliable, neat to watch, and well-respected on the stages. Nothing, however, could attract attention after spectators had watched the titanic struggle between Vic Elford's Porsche and Gerard Larrousse's Alpine-Renault, so in a way Andrew Cowan finished a lonely 22nd overall, but won his capacity class, while Rosemary Smith finished second in the Ladies' contest behind Pat Moss-Carlsson's 'works' Lancia Fulvia HF.

Then, with the decision to take a Hillman Hunter on the London-Sydney Marathon made, and the budget diverted, the Imp project went virtually into suspended animation – except that, in the British *Motoring News* road rally championship, Colin Malkin began to astonish the spectators with his immense talents.

Then, over the Easter weekend, Rosemary Smith (out of contract perhaps, but still in an Imp, and still determined to show how rapid she still was) put up a remarkable performance in the five-day Circuit of Ireland. For obvious reasons, the headline writers – particularly if they were Irish – spent all their time comparing Roger Clark's Ford Escort Twin-Cam with Paddy Hopkirk's BMC Mini-Cooper S, and quite missed the fact that the imperturbable Ms. Smith was making her way to third place overall – in a 998cc Imp!

That, of course, was the good news, but Andrew Cowan's lightweight 'racer', on the other hand, was eliminated just four minutes into the very first special stage, when he hit a non-competing car, and blocked the road. 'My Circuit of Ireland,' Cowan later wrote, 'was short-lived, as I was collected by a drunken driver shortly after the start, and the accident put me out of the rally….'

Above: Two of the Group 6 'works' rally cars – both crumpled – receive attention on the Scottish Rally of 1968. Colin Malkin's car, on the left of the picture, finished third overall, while Andrew Cowan's battered example just made it to the end after a comprehensive roll.

Below: Colin Malkin's Group 6 Rallye Imp on its way to third place in the 1968 Scottish Rally – a truly stirring performance in hot, dusty, conditions.

One Imp down, and one to go, was not an encouraging prospect, but Rosemary was not about to give in, and kept on, going faster and fast, for their entire weekend.

Normally this would be a busy time of the year for Rootes, but with the Tulip and the Acropolis now off the agenda, there was time to spend time, and to spare, in getting not one, but three very special Imps ready for the Scottish Rally, to be driven by Andrew Cowan, Rosemary Smith and Colin Malkin. Except for the cars which the Alan Fraser

The backdrop is the Craiglynne Hotel in Grantown-on-Spey, which means that this happy team of drivers, mechanics and trade representatives are enjoying the sunshine of the Scottish Rally.

team was now racing in the British Saloon Car Championship, these Group 6 cars were the fastest and most effective Imps so far produced.

Not only did all three cars have 94bhp engines with twin dual-choke Weber carburettors, but they also had glass-fibre instead of steel closing panels, Perspex windows instead of glass, front *and* rear cooling radiators, and front wheel disc brakes on two cars, with Rosemary Smith continuing to rely on servo-boosted drums. Scoops were moulded into the body sides, to duct air to the transmissions and rear engine bay, while the rear seats had been removed completely. Two of the cars were brand new, while Colin Malkin used the car which Andrew Cowan had damaged on the Circuit of Ireland.

Although this was still a five-day event, on this occasion the Scottish was tougher than before, for crews only had one full night's rest in bed. Hot, dusty, and carried out at high-speed, as usual, it was expected to be a benefit for Roger Clark's Escort Twin-Cam, but although Clark duly did win, the performance of the Imps was once again astonishing. Time and again, one of the Imps would be setting times in the top five, and as the stages unfolded, all three cars kept on going, as fast, as nimble and as impressive as ever.

Andrew Cowan ruined his car's rear suspension at one point, and lost time, but found time to have the repair done, then a drive shaft doughnut disintegrated, then he rolled the car – and after that he just kept going with the team prize in mind: as he later reported, the shell was twisted, so much so that left hand bends were fine, but right-handers were a distinct adventure!

Colin Malkin, in his first official works drive, was always quick, and usually spectacular, while Rosemary Smith was as neat, and as consistent as usual. Malkin was running second overall for some hours towards the end, until a front-wheel puncture cost him a lot of time. Even so, third overall (Malkin) and fifth overall (Rosemary Smith) was still an amazing performance.

Just one more Imp performance would be recorded in 1968, in the Gulf London where,

By the end of the 1960s, Colin Malkin was the absolute master of the Rallye Imp, and no-one could get it as far sideways, so often, as he could. JVC 123E was probably the fiercest of all the Imps ever prepared at Humber Road.

in theory there were no 'works' cars – just cars which happened to have been loaned out to unemployed 'works' drivers. This particular event was possibly the toughest ever held in the UK, with up to four days, virtually non-stop, from Manchester to Manchester (but via a three hour 'rest' halt in Manchester at half distance. All this, and more than seventy special stages, made it an event to be remembered, if only for the exhaustion suffered by most crews.

Rootes hastily re-fettled the car in which Colin Malkin had taken third in the Scottish, and loaned it out to Andrew Cowan, who used all his well-known stamina to keep it going. Although never running at the absolute front of the field, he was always in contention (even when the pace was being set by Porsche 911s and Escort Twin-Cams….), and in the second half of the event he was regularly setting 'top six' times. At the end of the event, this car (which had completed by the Scottish and the Gulf London within three weeks of each other) was looking dog-eared, but still finished strongly – seventh overall.

1969

After the famous Hunter had won the London – Sydney Marathon, the team was briefly feted at home, and overseas, but by the spring of 1969 the department had un-officially gone into suspended animation and- theoretically at least – the 'works' career of Imps was over.

The official announcement that the company was to withdraw from Motorsport for the time being, did not come until the very end of May 1969. Even though the company spokesmen made cooing noises about the famous victories of the past, reminding everyone that Peter Harper had used Imps to great effect in the recent ITV 'World of Sport' rally-cross championship, and that Colin Malkin had won everything open to him in British events in 1968. it was a bitter blow to every Imp enthusiast.

Amazingly, there was just time for one telling act of defiance. Even though the axe was about to fall, Des O'Dell had made sure that one of the very last 'works' Imps – in fact it was JDU 48E – was already 'in the

ROOTES MAESTROS
"In their own words."

care' of Andrew Cowan, and after somehow managing to ship a freshly-prepared 998cc engine up to Andrew's house in Scotland, and making sure that a mechanic just happened to be 'on holiday' in that part of the world, Andrew appeared on the Scottish Rally in June, where he was hoping to match Roger Clark's speed in the latest 'works' Escort.

As ever, the Scottish was long, tough, scenic, and a real high-speed special stage challenge, centred on Aviemore, and with 39 special stages: right from the start the Imp was competitive. Clark's Escort soon retired with broken front suspension, Cowan's Imp broke a drive shaft, but by the time the event reached Aviemore from Glasgow, the amazing little Imp was in third place.

On the following day Cowan thrust his way up to second place, suffered more dramas with a gearbox which was about to fail completely, and 'just happened' to have a spare box which could be fitted to keep him going. Even then his troubles were not over, for on the final day his car suffered from a damaged sump shield which impinged on the gearchange linkage, making reverse gear unavailable, and there was a broken steering arm on the Culbin special stage.

In the end, a relieved Cowan finished second overall, behind Simo Lampinen's 'works' Saab V4, and that brought the story of the 'works' Imps' career to an end.

Imps into battle

For the next two years there didn't seem to be much point in going motor racing, as Rootes had no new models with which to compete. Then, in 1965, the much more promising 998cc-engined Rallye Imp came along, and at almost the same time the BRSCC decided to run future Saloon Car Championships for Group 5 cars.

Group 5? Let's just say that this was an Appendix C category which insisted that the car's body shell and basic architecture should be retained, but it then allowed more or less complete freedom to engineers with bright ideas and deep pockets. Introduced in Britain after every *non*-Ford manufacturer complained about the way the Essex company had speedily come to dominate the sport, it allowed every other team to get back on terms - if it could afford it.

For companies like Rootes, which had a potentially promising car, with a fine if under-developed engine, this change of rules was a real windfall of good luck. The Imp, after all, had been developed around a small overhead-valve Coventry-Climax engine, and though it had been substantially de-tuned for mass-production, the bare bones of a race-worthy engine were all there.

The Rootes team, now under Marcus Chambers' management, were soon persuaded, but wisely decided to farm out its racing efforts, and contracted its Kent-based dealer, Alan Fraser, to do the job. Fraser's own privately-prepared Imps had already won several club races in 1965, and his team certainly had the expertise.

Complete with their St Andrew's cross livery on the roof (Alan Fraser was a Scot, and liked people to know it!), the two brand-new, much-lowered and lightened Imps certainly looked the part in 1966. Originally the 998cc engines produced 55bhp in standard form, but 95bhp when race-prepared, but by mid-season Coventry-Climax had produced special cylinder head castings (they knew all about the engine's potential, after all) and peak power soared to 111bhp at 8,400rpm.

Engineer Leslie Sherley-Price made a nimble little road car into a really good-handling race car by re-setting the suspensions, lowering the front roll-centre, fitting a front anti-roll bar, and using wide-rim Minilite wheels. Amazingly for such a

'Works' Imps in rallying: 1964-1968

tail-heavy machine with swing-axle front suspension, neither the road car nor the competition cars ever had any handling deficiencies.

Although the cars were usually driven up to and over their natural limits by heroes such as Bernard Unett (still a Rootes development engineer), Ray Calcutt and Nick Brittan (I wonder whatever happened to him?), season-long experience showed that the 'works' Imps could not quite match the pace of the 'works' Anglias, which had even more power from their Cosworth-inspired overhead-valve engines. But how they tried!

Nick Brittan won his class just once - at Brands Hatch in August - while he and his team mates also notched up five seconds and six thirds in class. However, as *Autosport*'s Paddy McNally wrote in his Seasonal Survey:

'The surprise of the year was just how fast the Hillman Imps were made to go. From being complete nonenties, they steadily improved...and half-way through the season they had really started to buzz. The Climax-designed engine had been worked on for several years with little success, but suddenly the answers were found.....If it had not been for the speed of the Broadspeed Anglias, which really were uncatchable, the Imps would have done much better....'

In 1967 that is precisely what happened. During the winter, fuel injection engines had been tested, front wheel disc brakes were fitted, 13in. rear wheels had seven inch rims, a limited-slip differential added to the already excellent traction and handling, while a Jack Knight five-speed gearbox cluster had been added. As I discovered when I drove the car at Silverstone, this was a race car, no more and no less.

With 115bhp on tap - the little overhead-cam engine peaked at an exhilirating 9,000rpm - this was a real racing engine, such that when I tried the car I was told to start from the line by using 8,000rpm and slip the clutch ! For 1967 Bernard Unett and Tony Lanfranchi drove the cars, with Ray Calcutt backing up on occasion, and this time the cars were right on the pace with the Anglias, which were reputed to produce 130bhp, but didn't handle quite as well. This was the season in which John Rhodes's 1.3litre Minis caught most attention because of the way they generated so much tyre smoke, but only just behind them it was the titanic battles between the Fraser Imps and the Broadspeed Anglias which offered the closest battles.

At the end of the year Unett was placed second to Fitzpatrick's Anglia in the Championship, with Lanfranchi close behind them, but the competition was always much closer than the results suggest. Time after time the Imps and the Anglias would swap places during the race, and there was rarely more than a second or two between the cars at the finish.

Unett won at several of the high-profile 'flagship meetings' - such as the Silverstone 'Martini' event in May, and most notably at the British GP meeting, when his Imp lapped in 1min 53sec (compare *that* with Peter Harper's Rapier times of only a few years earlier).

By this time, though, Chrysler owned Rootes, and (just as British Leyland would also decide a year later) decided that if they could not guarantee victory they did not really want to spend any money, so the Fraser Imp programme was abandoned for 1968. Almost all of Rootes' budget was spent on the London-Sydney Marathon, where Andrew Cowan's Hillman Hunter won - and reaped very little publicity in the process.

Although there were no Anglias to battle against in 1968 (Ralph Broad was running 1.3litre Escorts instead), this was the year

ROOTES MAESTROS
"In their own words."

when Fraser's old cars, suitably updated, had to fight on their own, with limited resources. Appearing only four times, and faced with the almost impossible task of beating fuel-injected 1.0litre 'works' Mini-Cooper Ss. Tony Lanfranchi and Ray Calcutt tried their best, winning classes at Brands Hatch on three of those occasions. Lanfranchi's reward was third in his class.

That, it seemed, was that, for there was absolutely no Rootes presence in the 1969 series, and the Fraser team had withdrawn. Suddenly, though, for 1970, privateer Bill McGovern spotted an opportunity. He, though no other Imp runner, spotted that there was an aching void in the 1.0litre category, and moved swiftly to fill it.

Because the British Championship was run on class basis (which meant that an outstanding 'class' car could win the series, even if it never finished in the top ten), and because British Leyland had completely withdrawn support from saloon car racing, McGovern built a new Rallye Imp, which he badged as a Sunbeam, and proceeded to dominate his class.

In 1970 and yet again in 1971 he had a reliable machine which rarely let him down, he rarely let the car down, and the result was that the Championship Trophy was his. McGovern and a tiny team twice achieved what the factory, for all its commitment, had never even approached. Because they were all in fiercely-contested classes of their own, none of the high-flying Mustangs, Camaros and Escort RS1600s could do anything about this.

Although this could have been very good news for Rootes, which was in the process of being re-named Chrysler United Kingdom Limited, the company did absolutely nothing to promote McGovern's success. Personally, I recall attending a lunch at the technical centre at Whitley, Coventry in 1971, where McGovern had been invited to celebrate his success. He was from one planet, and except for Peter Wilson the Rootes engineers who were obsessed with Avengers and Chrysler 180s were from another, and neither could even understand the other side.

Postscript

At Rootes there was only one other man who *did* understand and he - the new Competition Manager, Des O'Dell, was powerless, for he had no money to spare.

O'Dell, though, was a very stubborn character, who eventually found a way to get back into motor racing. Somehow, in the mid-1970s, he liberated enough of Chrysler's money, backed it with support from Shell and Dunlop, and found a way of entering Bernard Unett in surprisingly fleet Hillman Hunter GLSs, and later in Chrysler Avenger GTs. At a time when the British Saloon Car Championship had slipped back into a rather depressing 'Group 1' format, this brought new faces and new models to the podium again. But these were not exciting cars, or exciting times - Rootes's greatest days on the track had already gone.

'Works' Imps in rallying: 1964-1968

'Works Imps' – list of cars used (1964 to 1968)

Car (Registration No.)	Most important result
4525KV	
4526KV	2nd Overall, 1965 Scottish Rally
7742KV	2nd Overall, 1965 Tulip Rally
8305KV	1st Overall, 1965 Tulip Rally
ADU 635B	
AKV 368C	
EDU 710C (previously 7674VC)	5th Overall, 1965 Scottish Rally Class win, Alpine Rally 1965
EVC 227C	
EVC 922C	
EWK 573C	
EWK 836C	
FRW 303C	
FRW 304C	
FRW 305C	8th Overall, Ladies Award, 1966 Shell 4000 Rally (Canada)
FRW 306C	Coupe des Dames (then disqualified), 1966 Monte Carlo Rally
FRW 308C	4th Overall, 1967 Scottish Rally
FRW 948C	

ROOTES MAESTROS
"In their own words."

FRW 949C

GKV 799D

JDU 46E — 3rd GT Category, 1967 Tulip Rally

JDU 48E — 2nd Overall, 1969 Scottish Rally

JRW 700E

JRW 701E — 2nd, Coupe des Dames, 1968 Monte Carlo Rally

JRW 702E

JVC 123E — 3rd, RAC Rally TV special stage, 1967 RAC

Note: Some of the identities/cars listed were used for practice or testing, and did not take the start in any competitions.

And by the way: Imps in the British Touring Car Championship

Ironically, the Imp's greatest success in the British Saloon Car Championship did not come until Chrysler had mothballed the Humber Road premises. Although Alan Fraser's 'works'-backed cars had been worthy 'class' cars in the mid-1960s, it was George Bevan's privately-run example which won the Championship, outright, in 1970, 1971 and 1972.

It all depended, you see, on who was writing the regulations at the time – and *that*, make no mistake, was heavily influenced by which of the British manufacturers was shouting the loudest. There were two Championship upheavals at this time – one when Group 5 cars were admitted from 1966, the other being when Group 2 rules were applied from 1970.

Time for a very short history lesson. The British Saloon Car Championship was first held in 1958, took time to settle down, before Group 2 (as in International rallying) was applied from 1961. Although 'works' Sunbeam Rapiers performed with honour at first, like everyone else they were eventually overwhelmed by the Ford Lotus-Cortinas, which were motorsport's very first 'homologation specials'.

So that more manufacturers might be attracted to the sport, to compete on level terms, Group 5 regulations were introduced for 1966, and would be in use for the next four seasons. Group 5, effectively, mean that any four-seater saloon would be able to race in highly-modified condition, just as long as the standard body shell, standard engine cylinder block, and standard gearbox casing was retained.

For Rootes, this was a miracle, and very encouraging. In Group 2, the Rapiers had been quite uncompetitive with the very specialised Lotus-Cortinas, nor would matters improve under Group 5. With Imps, though, it was going to be a different story.

Whereas the single-carburettor Imps (only 39bhp as standard!), could not match the BMC Mini-Cooper and Mini-Cooper S types (which were also 'homologation specials'), under Group 5, the cars could be Rallye Imps, the rear-mounted engines could run up to the 1litre class limit, and be race-tuned at least up to 'Coventry Climax' levels. Quite suddenly, up to 100-bhp might be available, and even against the new-fangled Broadspeed Ford Anglias (which would also be joining in the 1litre class, this would make them class-competitive.

Although Marcus Chambers was not about to run true 'works' race cars of his own (Humber Road was busy enough with Tiger rally cars and with 'works' Imp rally cars in 1966), he was immediately directed to give support to Rootes dealer Alan Fraser's team instead. And how did Fraser get so much support? Maybe it was because he was based in Kent, and maybe it was because there were still links with the Rootes organisation through its Commer/Karrier operations in that British county. Who knows...?

Getting started

Because there hadn't seemed to much point in going motor racing in recent years, Rootes had no readily-developed and competitive models with which to compete. This all

As prepared for the British Saloon Car Championship in 1966 and 1967, Alan Fraser's Imps were liveried in white and blue, with the Scottish Saltire on the roof.

changed when the Rallye Imp came along, and Group 5 was adopted.

For manufacturers like Rootes, who had a potentially promising car, with a fine if under-developed engine and chassis, this change of rules was a real windfall of good luck. The Imp, after all, had been developed around a small overhead-camshaft Coventry-Climax engine, and though this had been substantially de-tuned for mass-production, the bare bones of a race-worthy engine were all there.

The Rootes team, were soon convinced that they had been right to be told to support Alan Fraser to go motor racing on their behalf. Fraser, after all, was a real petrol-head of his own, had gone racing and rallying on his own, with a modicum of success, and his privately-prepared Imps had already won several club races in 1965. His still-young team certainly had the expertise.

The new team made an impact almost at once, not merely because they produced cars which were astonishingly competitive, but because they always looked, and sounded, magnificent. Complete with their St Andrew's cross Saltire livery on the roof of otherwise blue and white cars (Alan Fraser was a Scot, and liked people to know it!), the brand-new, much-lowered and lightened Imps certainly looked the part in 1966.

Originally their 998cc engines had originally produced 55bhp in standard form (for the Rallye Imp was a genuine, off-the-shelf special-edition model from Rootes at the time), they immediately had 95bhp when race-prepared, but by mid-season Coventry-Climax had been persuaded to produce special cylinder head castings (they knew all about the engine's potential, after all, having been involved with this power unit, from the mid-1950s), and peak power soared to 111bhp at 8,400rpm. Any engine, after all, which had originally been designed by a Coventry-Climax team led by Walter Hassan, and which included Harry Mundy as its chief designer, must surely stand a chance?

And by the way:
Imps in the British Touring Car Championship

In passing, and just to emphasise that most people eventually know most other people in the world of motorsport, I should note that Ford's long-time engine homologation guru, John Griffiths, was involved in the Imp project at this time. After starting work, in Lancashire, as an apprentice in the railway electrification industry, then moving to work on a float glass project at Pilkingtons:

'One day I saw an advert in, I think it was, *Autocar*, from ERA in Dunstable, I joined them as a junior fuel injection engineer. I knew very little about fuel injection at the time! After that I moved on from ERA to develop the engines of the Alan Fraser racing Imps. I'd met Brian Lovell in 1965 at ERA, he knew the Alan Fraser team in Sevenoaks, who were developing the Imp engine for racing, and we moved down there in 1965. We made those 998cc Imps very fast – just as fast as Ralph Broad's Broadspeed "works" Anglia 105Es....'

Fraser's chief engineer, Leslie Sherley-Price, then made a nimble little road car into a really good-handling race car by re-setting the suspensions, lowering the front roll-centre, fitting a front anti-roll bar, and using wide-rim Minilite wheels. Amazingly for such a tail-heavy machine with swing-axle front suspension, neither the road car nor the competition cars ever showed any handling deficiencies.

Although the cars were usually driven up to and over their natural limits by heroes such as Bernard Unett (who was already a Rootes development engineer, and would later become British Touring Car Champion three times, in 1974, 1976 and 1977, each time in Chrysler Avenger GTs prepared by Des O'Dell's team at Humber Road), Ray Calcutt (whose 'day job' had been as a policeman) and Nick Brittan (who would later become a entrepreneur in the devising, and running, of transcontinental historic car rallies), season-long experience showed that the 'works' Imps were quick, but could not consistently match the pace of the 'works' Broadspeed Anglia 105Es, which produced even more power from their Cosworth-inspired 1litre overhead-valve engines, and whose star driver was John Fitzpatrick. But how they tried!

While Nick Brittan won his class just once - at Brands Hatch in August - he and his team

On one unforgettable occasion, at Silverstone, at the end of 1966, the author sampled one of the Fraser Imps (left), a 'works' Rallye Imp rally car (right), and a Broadspeed Ford Anglia. At this moment Ian Hall is driving the Fraser car, and author Robson is actually in the passenger seat of the Anglia.

ROOTES MAESTROS
"In their own words."

mates also notched up five seconds and six thirds in class. However, as *Autosport*'s Paddy McNally wrote in his Seasonal Survey at the end of the 1966 season:

'The surprise of the year was just how fast the Hillman Imps were made to go. From being complete nonenties, they steadily improved...and half-way through the season they had really started to buzz. The Climax-designed engine had been worked on for several years with little success, but suddenly the answers were found.....If it had not been for the speed of the Broadspeed Anglias, which really were uncatchable, the Imps would have done much better....'

Perhaps McNally was over-egging the pudding, for the reason that the Imp engines had enjoyed so little success in earlier years was that the regulations had obliged them to run with a single carburettor, and at a mere 875cc. Rootes knew, and Alan Fraser knew, that an unrestricted 1litre engine, with such an efficient head, with light overhead camshaft valve gear, and a great deal of racing experience locked away inside, should do the trick.

In 1967, in only their second year of Group 5 racing, that is precisely what happened. During the winter, fuel injection engines had been tested, front wheel disc brakes were fitted, 13in. rear wheels were given seven inch rims to provide even more grip, a limited-slip differential added to the already excellent traction and handling, while a Jack Knight five-speed gearbox cluster (which fitted into the existing casing, as the regulations said it should) had been added. As I discovered when I later drove one of the team cars at Silverstone, this was now a dedicated little race car, no more and no less.

With 115bhp on tap - the little overhead-cam engine was now peaked at an exhilarating 9,000rpm - this was a real racing engine, so highly tuned that when I tried the car, I was firmly told to start from the line by using no less than 8,000rpm and to slip

Bernard Unett at the wheel of one of the ultra-fast, 115bhp, 1litre Rallye Imps which raced so successfully in British Saloon Car events in the late 1960s.

And by the way: Imps in the British Touring Car Championship

the clutch – but not for long ! For 1967 Bernard Unett and Tony Lanfranchi drove the regular team cars, with Ray Calcutt backing up on occasion, and this time the cars were right on the pace with the Anglias, even though they were now reputed to produce 130bhp, but didn't seem to handle quite as well. This, of course, was the season in which John Rhodes's 1.3litre Mini-Cooper S caught most of the crowd's attention because of the way it generated so much tyre smoke from the front wheels of its Dunlop racing tyres, but only just behind him there was usually a titanic battle developing between the blue Fraser Imps and the maroon Broadspeed Anglias, which always offered the closest battles.

At the end of the season, Bernard Unett was placed second to Fitzpatrick's Anglia in the 1-litre Championship Class, with Lanfranchi close behind them, but the competition was always even closer than the results suggest. Time after time the Imps and the Anglias would swap places during the race (certainly they would swap paintwork too), and there was rarely more than a second or two between the cars at the finish of an event.

Unett won at several of the high-profile 'flagship meetings' - such as the Silverstone 'Martini' event in May, and most notably at the Silverstone British GP meeting, when his Imp lapped in 1min 53sec (compare *that* with Peter Harper's Rapier times of only a few years earlier – saloon car races had come on a long way in a short period).

By this time, though, Chrysler had taken majority financial control of Rootes, and (just as British Leyland would also decide a year later) decided that if they could not guarantee victory in motorsport, they did not really want to spend any money, so the Fraser Imp programme was immediately abandoned for 1968. As we now know, almost all of Rootes' budget was spent on the London-Sydney Marathon, where Andrew Cowan's Hillman Hunter won – yet that was an victory from which Rootes reaped very little publicity in the process.

Although there were no Anglias to battle against in 1968 (Ralph Broad had moved up one, and was running new-type 1.3litre Escorts instead), this therefore was the year when Fraser's old cars, suitably updated, had to fight on their own, with strictly limited resources. Although they appeared only four times, and were faced with the almost impossible task of beating fuel-injected 1.0litre 'works' Mini-Cooper Ss, Tony Lanfranchi and Ray Calcutt tried their expert best, winning classes at Brands Hatch on three of those occasions. Though he deserved more, Lanfranchi's reward was third in his class.

That, it seemed, was that, for there was to be absolutely no Rootes presence in the 1969 BTCC series. Among other rule changes was one which banned the use of alternative, non-homologated, cylinder heads, so the Coventry-Climax 'specials' could not longer find a home in the tail of the Fraser Imps. The Sevenoaks-based team therefore withdrew from the 1litre class, which was dominated by Alec Poole in the Equipe Arden Mini-Cooper 970S.

Then, for 1970, the RAC moved the goalposts yet again, dumping the Group 5 category which had been popular, and so successful, in favour of the Group 2 category once again. Not that this could benefit the Imps all that much, as Chrysler UK had now put the Competitions Department into suspended animation, and Des O'Dell was struggling to keep a slimmed-down 'Special Tuning' operation afloat.

Suddenly, though, for 1970, privateer George Bevan (his driver being Bill McGovern) spotted an opportunity. He, though no other Imp runner, saw that there was no longer to be a Mini-Cooper S presence, nor was there a 1litre Ford Escort,

Bill McGovern's immaculate Rallye Imp won the British Saloon Car Championship three times in succession – 1970, 1971 and 1972.

so he spotted that an aching void had once again developed in the 1litre category. Bevan, whose privately-prepared Imps had already been successful at club level, moved swiftly to fill it.

Because the British Championship was still to be run on a class basis (which meant that an outstanding 'class' car could win the entire Championship, even if it never managed to finish in the top ten). Because he could see the opportunity, and because British Leyland had completely withdrawn their support from saloon car racing (the expense of preparing for the London – Mexico World Cup Rally was sucking up all their funds!), Bevan decided to build up a new race car, built around the bare bones of a 1966 Hillman Imp, which he soon upgraded to Rallye Imp status (which is what hundreds, if not thousands, of private owners had done before him), badged it as a Sunbeam, and proceeded to dominate his class.

Fortunately, too, Bevan struck up a fine relationship with Des O'Dell, who was able to support the programme – more with pieces than with money. As O'Dell later admitted:

'After the first year's [Special Tuning] trading we had a surplus of £28,000, so I was able to contemplate some sponsorship. I arranged a meeting with George Bevan, who agreed to contest the British Touring Car Championship with help from my department.'

Many years later, it became clear that Chrysler had probably committed more than £10,000 in hard cash. It also became clear that Bevan had sometimes found it very difficult to stay on terms with Des O'Dell:

'….It was not a marriage made in heaven, more a marriage of convenience '(Author Martyn Morgan Jones comments). It was often fraught, especially during the early years … it was simply a clash of personalities. Both men were hard-working, highly capable, motivated and self-sufficient.'

And by the way: Imps in the British Touring Car Championship

As we now know from the history of this car, so graphically told in Martyn Morgan Jones' book *The British Saloon Car Championship – Bevan and McGovern Imp*, the Bevan car was not only faster, but handled even better, than the Fraser Imps had ever been, while Bill McGovern did everything that could be expected of him.

George Bevan always insisted that he was a 'kitchen utensil manufacturer' who just happened to go motor racing as a hobby, rather than the other way round. His car – there was only one machine, by the way, which was used for all three Championship-winning seasons - had a 998cc engine which produced just 110bhp, aided at first by a Piper camshaft (not the same profile as that previously used by Fraser's cars, though a Fraser cam was adopted in 1971) and a pair of Weber DCOE twin-choke carburettors, all allied to a Jack Knight four-speed gearbox cluster and limited-slip differential.

Drum brakes were fitted for early races in 1970, but once Des O'Dell had managed to get front-wheel discs homologated, these were used instead. Bevan later measured the performance, the car clocking 0 - 60mph in just seven seconds and (with suitable gearing) it had a 136mph top speed. Not bad for a family run-about!

In 1970, 1971 and yet again in 1972 he had a reliable machine which rarely let him down, he rarely let the car down, and the result was that the Championship Trophy was his. McGovern and a tiny team three times achieved what the factory-backed cars, for all their commitment, had never even approached. Because they were all in fiercely-contested classes of their own, none of the high-flying Mustangs, Camaros and Escort RS1600s could do anything about this.

Not that the RAC's Championship marking system made it easy for Bevan. In 1970 and 1971, McGovern won by just four points (72 against 68 in 1970, 80 against 76 in 1971) whereas he stretched that Championship-winning margin to eight points in 1972.

In 1970 McGovern won his class eight times in eleven races, in 1971 he won ten out of the twelve rounds, and in 1972 he won all ten rounds which were run in the series that year. Invariably his car was fastest in its class, but could not always finish, sometimes because it was barged off the track.

Publicity-wise, although this could have been very good news for Chrysler United Kingdom Limited, which was the company which had taken over from anything previously including the 'Rootes' name in its title, the company did little to promote McGovern's on-going and repeated successes, except to run one or two self-congratulatory display adverts.

ROOTES MAESTROS
"In their own words."

London-Sydney Marathon: The Hunter victory of 1968

Although victory in the original London-Sydney Marathon probably counts as the most famous success ever claimed by the Rootes Competitions Department, it was not only un-expected, but outside the mainstream of what Marcus Chambers's team was trying to achieve at the time.

Every Rootes enthusiast knows, I am sure, that a Hillman Hunter won this event outright – but how many realise that this was the very first rally in which a Works Hunter had taken part? How many people, therefore, realise that before 1968 no-one in motorsport, not even Des O'Dell, knew anything about the strengths and weaknesses of the Hunter's structure, nor of its suspension? How many, for that matter, realise just how much testing, development – and original heartache – went into the refinement of a rally car which would win the world's most prestigious event.

Why don't we....?

When it was originally announced, London to Sydney sounded like the answer to a question that no-one had yet bothered to ask. 'Works' teams like Rootes were already busy enough, thank you very much, their budgets were already spoken for, and drivers used to driving flat-out for four or at the most five days did not warm to the idea of taking 24 days to reach the other side of world.

It all began, they say, at a lunch in the *Daily Express* building, towards the end of 1967. Britain's economy was in a mess, the pound has just been de-valued, and the 'I'm Backing Britain' (of working extra hours without pay….) campaign had just started up. Looking to gain a great deal of favourable publicity, the Proprietor of the *Daily Express*, Sir Max Aitken, got together with two of his business associates, Jocelyn Stevens and Tommy Sopwith, to create a motoring event which the *Express* could sponsor, and which, by suitable editorial drum-beating, might help raise the country's spirit.

Why not, they said, organise a trans-continental motor rally from London to Sydney in Australia? Such an event, it was thought, might act as a showcase for British engineering and British enterprise, and might just help boost export sales in the countries through which it would pass. None of the individuals involved on that day – except for Tommy Sopwith, who was not only a businessman, but had been a successful saloon car race driver in recent years – knew anything about motor sport, but in his family-bred buccaneering way, Sir Max Aitken was certain that expertise could be gathered. It soon came, in the shape of Dean Delamont of the RAC, and Sopwith's friend (and sometime racing rival) Jack Sears.

Having the good idea was one thing, and finding a co-sponsor in Australia (Sir Frank Packer's *Daily Telegraph* of Sydney) was another. Setting a route through the Balkans and the Middle East was a major problem (but at least the various countries were not actually fighting with each other at this time), but the truly important hurdle which had to be cleared was in attracting the right sort of entry.

Although the event was launched, rather modestly, in Monte Carlo immediately after

ROOTES MAESTROS
"In their own words."

the rally of January 1968, it got a rather cool welcome at first. This is what the author wrote in *Autocar*'s The Sport pages on 1 February 1968:

'In last Friday's *Daily Express* you will perhaps have seen the announcement of the £10,000 London-Sydney Marathon, which is being sponsored by the *Express*, co-organised by the *Express* and the RAC, and approved of by the Society of Motor Manufacturers and Traders. First prize for this 'greatest ever car race', as claimed by its sponsors, is to be £10,000, and it is due to start on 23 November, two days after the finish of the RAC Rally of Great Britain (15-21 November).

To put your minds at rest, any of you may recall the banning of town-to-town races soon after the turn of the century, and the £500 fine imposed by the RAC themselves - when two well-known drivers went from Cape Town to Cairo, and the manufacturer of their car advertised the run as a 'record' – this is *not* a race. The route will cover 10,000 miles, there will be no scheduled rest halts between the start in London, and Bombay, when the P & O ship *Chusan* will take the surviving cars to Fremantle for the 3,000 mile final stretch across Australia to Sydney. The finish will be around 17 December. It will be a straight test of crew endurance and reliability – with, of course, a tight time schedule – and will entail high speeds.

One cannot help feeling that to start the Marathon two days after the RAC Rally finishes is bound to affect the entries for one or other event – and is seems a great pity that the RAC Rally should suffer. There is, apparently, a hope that the Marathon may be put off a day – but it is all inextricably tied up with the sailing time from Bombay of the good ship *Chusan*, whose timetable is like that of a railway.

'Returning from the Monte Carlo Rally, colleague Graham Robson says that he has talked at length with Jack Sears and Stuart Turner of the London-Sydney Marathon organising committee. There is certainly no question of this being a race, and in view of the endurance nature of the event, they are not expecting many works rally drivers to be interested. Clearly this event clashes directly with training for the 1969 Monte Carlo Rally and we think that team drivers would rather concentrate on the Monte. The London to Istanbul sections (through Western Europe) will be at respectable average speeds and the main competitive sections will be from Istanbul to Bombay, and from Fremantle to Sydney.'

Such opinions were rife for weeks- not only in the media, but also within the motorsport industry. Then, gradually but persistently, publicists from major car companies like Ford, BMC/British Leyland, Rootes, Citroen and Holden of Australia began to realise that this could become one of the biggest, longest-running, motorsport stories of the decade, if not of all time. Members of the organising committee, such as Jack Sears, lobbied each manufacturer very successfully, sometimes by telling an individual that his rivals had already decided to enter – then telling rivals the same thing!

As Marcus Chambers had already confirmed, it took time to get approval (especially as, in Rootes/Chrysler terms, 'new money' would be involved), and his case was certainly strengthened by the fact that Rootes' new Technical Director, Cyril Weighell, had accompanied him on the 1968 Monte Carlo Rally. Weighell not only saw Rootes return a very competent result, but was also presented with a London-Sydney Marathon launch leaflet at the end of the event.

Although January to November sounded like an eon in motorsport terms, Rootes had

London-Sydney Marathon: The Hunter victory of 1968

no illusions about the problem. Apart from the financial/budget problem, there was a real conundrum to be solved – what car should be used? The regulations for the event, in any case, were so flexible that almost any sort of machine could be eligible. In North American terms, this was therefore a 'Run what you brung....' type of event.

Driver Andrew Cowan later explained that:

'Des O'Dell, who was to become Team Manager part way through the preparations for this event, wanted to have me run a Group 6 Hillman Imp, as he felt we should go for broke, and probably collect the prize at Bombay for the fastest car to that point. The car he had in mind had been prepared for the 1967 RAC Rally of Great Britain and was the most powerful Imp we had produced. This was Des's baby and he thought it would be the car to use, but the more we thought about the event, the more we realised we needed a bigger car if only to carry more spare parts and wheels. It was then that we plumped for the Hillman Hunter and the original idea was that Brian Coyle and I would run in it alone as is was not until later that we realised we would have to run three-up.'

More than 10,000 road miles linked London with Sydney, by way of Bombay, Perth and a journey across the Indian Ocean, in November/December 1968. Except at Bombay and on the boat, there were no official rest halts on this monumental event.

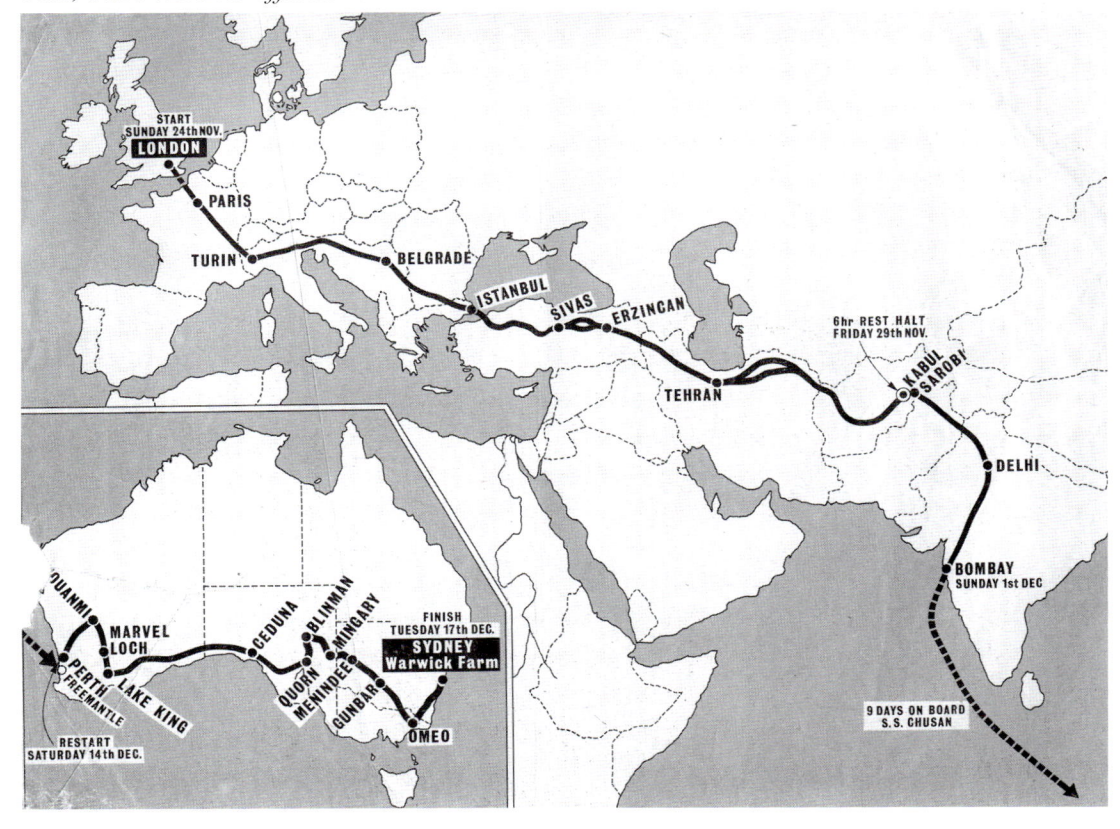

ROOTES MAESTROS
"In their own words."

Choosing a Hunter was one thing, but finalising the specification, testing it, and proving it out, was going to be a major undertaking:

'I know at one stage we thought it would be a good idea to fit a Chrysler Valiant V8 engine in a Hunter, as smooth V8 power seemed to be called for, but this was obviously a bit of a pipe-dream as even if it *was* feasible we hadn't even had the Hunter in normal form on a rally, far less one developed to this stage. At the same time a V8 Hunter was not the type of Hunter we sold by any stretch of the imagination, so that idea was scrapped almost as soon as we had thought of it....'

Des O'Dell therefore started preparing a more sensible derivative of the Hunter. Once again, Andrew Cowan tells the story:

'Up in the corner of the competition department at that time was the wreckage of the one and only Hillman Hunter we had prepared for rallying. Again, we had thought about entering a Hunter in the RAC Rally the previous year and one car was actually prepared for the [French] Alpine for private entrant Harry Skelton and my Scottish friend Gerry Birrell to drive. This car, however, was withdrawn on the start line of that event, and whilst Gerry was driving it, as a support car to the Imps, something went wrong, and he crashed on the Col de Galibier....

'We had two initial problems. First, we hadn't rallied a Hunter, and didn't know what might break on the rough stuff we were going to meet, and secondly we had to have our spare parts sent off weeks in advance of the event and would rely on bits in the far corners of the world....'

And so it all began. Much of the testing (the car was GVC 432D) produced its own unique results, but Cowan makes much of the fact that O'Dell kept looking at the experience Ford had already gained with its

Left to right – Des O'Dell, Andrew Cowan and Colin Malkin, with GVC 432D, the Hunter test car, on yet another development day at the Chobham test track in Surrey.

Des O'Dell was convinced that he had to test a Hunter to absolute destruction, and put it through heat, dust, water and awful road conditions, before beginning to prepare the Marathon cars. GVC 432D was the long-suffering test car which spent much of its time being abused in the summer of 1968.

Cortina GT and Lotus-Cortina rally cars (and was now doing with the first of the Escort Twin-Cams). The Hunter, after all, had a very similar monocoque body shell, MacPherson strut front suspension and simple leaf-spring rear suspension – no-one at Rootes ever denied that the original Cortina had been the 'template' for the new Hunter when it was being engineered in 1964 – 1966 – so much of what had been done to improve the Fords (all of which was in the public domain) could be done to improve the Hunters too.

The story of the work which went in to producing the finalised specification could, no doubt, fill a book all of its own. From the spring of 1968, when serious development work began on the project, all improvement on the existing Imps was suspended, and except for the entries so successfully made in the Scottish and Gulf London Rallies, there was little evidence of these little cars inside Humber Road.

First it was necessary to start testing with the repaired 1967 Hunter – the well-known rough-road course at the military testing facility at Bagshot was used repeatedly, as indeed it was by other 'works' teams of the period – and original results, carried out before the Scottish Rally, were encouraging. As first conceived, the 'Marathon' Hunter featured a seriously strengthened body shell and suspension components, a de-tuned Rapier H120 type of engine, a Tiger-type Salisbury 4HA rear axle, and provision for carrying all manner of extra kit, including monstrous extra-fuel-capacity (36 gallon) petrol tanks, and the ability to transport extra spare wheels on the roof of the shell: calculations, by the way, showed that four extra wheels would add up to 160lb.....

Before long another car (new for this task, but carrying a 1966 registration plate – so what is new about the cloning of rally cars?) was made ready for Andrew Cowan and Brian Coyle to make a reconnaissance run over the proposed route from London to Bombay. While they were away, Colin Malkin was brought in to get on with more and more testing (Des O'Dell was adamant, and he was right, that there was no substitute for rough road mileage, which would

ROOTES MAESTROS
"In their own words."

eventually break *something*, after which he could analyse the failure, and rectify the problem). When the testing progressed to high-speed work at MIRA, company employee and well-respected British race driver Bernard Unett was also drafted in, and was amazed how stable the rally car had actually become.

More and more testing found more and more stress problems, which resulted in the body shell being progressively stiffened up, glass being replaced by Perspex, steel panels by aluminium, and a stiffening cage inside the cabin. Half shafts broke, and were reinforced, sump guards were progressively developed (the definitive item was made by TechDel, and was a magnesium casting, coated by a skin of sheet steel), while the major disappointment was that the alloy wheels proposed by Dunlop did not stand up to the job, and had to be abandoned. Marcus Chambers has already pointed out, that choosing Minilites as an alternative was easy enough, but that gaining financial approval to buy a stock was difficult!

Another big, long-running, argument was about the overdrive gearbox. Overdrive, for sure, was going to be used (Rootes had used these Laycock-derived items on 'works' rally cars since the original Alpines of 1953), but neither Laycock nor the transmission specialist inside Rootes' Engineering department wanted it to be applicable to second gear and below. However, as Andrew Cowan later commented:

'Des O'Dell realised that never once had an overdrive let anyone down. It had stopped working, it is true, but this still left the car with all its normal gears, and we argued for having the overdrive was so long as it worked and its value was there even though it didn't last the whole event. As it transpired, overdrive was fitted to all four gears, and

Andrew Cowan posed inside a Rootes factory, in the RAF entry's Hunter. Next stop London, scrutineering and the start of the Marathon.

London-Sydney Marathon: The Hunter victory of 1968

we never had a moment's bother with it the entire way ….'

Not that the choice of 1,725cc engine was going to overstress the overdrive transmission too much. The following are official figures : whereas the standard Hunter produced only 72bhp (and the contemporary Sunbeam Rapier 79bhp), the still-secret Holbay version of the engine which was intended for use in the Sunbeam Rapier H120 produced 93bhp, so it was decided to settle for a slightly-detuned version of the Holbay power unit.

By September 1968, even Des O'Dell had agreed that it was too late to make further modifications to the Marathon build specification, so the team then settled down to building the cars themselves. By this time, for sure, Marcus Chambers realised that he would certainly over-spend his budget, but reasoned that if he won no-one would really care, yet if he lost he would probably be out of a job anyway.

This was the programme cover of the 1968 Marathon, in which the leading cars did not even feature.

Both the cars which started the event from the Crystal Palace motor racing circuit in south-east London, therefore, were the very best which the Rootes 'works' team could build, and were the combination of a great deal of testing, development, proving and (let us be honest about this, a bit of fingers-crossed work too). Both cars were in corporate blue, with white stripes along the flanks, matt black anti-dazzle bonnet panels, full width 'roo' bars across the nose (lined with mesh), and with spare wheels mounted on the roof. There were no fewer than six extra driving lamps facing forwards – one on the roof, one at waist level just ahead of the windscreen, and four on the nose (two of them hidden behind the mesh of the 'roo' bar – which meant that the electrical system alternator and heavy-duty battery would have a tough time.

Having survived all the conventional panics – this time there were not only late deliveries of components to cope with, but a factory strike which actually stopped all work being done on the cars for eight days. Even so, and as Marcus Chambers has already noted: 'by a miracle both cars were ready by 22 November'.

Whereas Ford supported six 'works' Lotus-Cortinas, and BMC four BMC 1800 'Super Land Crabs', Rootes could only afford to build two 'Marathon' Hunters. They were:

No. 45 LHP 676F   Flt.Lt. David Carrington/Sqdr. Leader Tony King/ Flt.Lt. J.H.Jones

No. 75 MKV 15G   Andrew Cowan/ Brian Coyle/Colin Malkin

Still unhappy that he had to release other one-time star drivers because of his financial

303

Was the Hunter's 'works' crew so pre-occupied before the start at Crystal Palace in south London, that it could not find time to make friends with the newly-crowned Miss World, Penelope Plummer of Australia? Don't you believe it....

constraints, Marcus Chambers must have been quietly pleased to see that both Rosemary Smith and Peter Harper were to compete in Lotus-Cortinas which carried factory support.

Andrew Cowan's route survey had many benefits, and would certainly contribute to the success which followed – most notably that he and Brian Coyle convinced themselves that a third crew member – Colin Malkin, who had just won the British Rally Championship in his 'works'-loaned Rallye Imp – should join them. Although Marcus Chambers and Des O'Dell both grumbled about costs, complications, and about the way that a third crew member had to be accommodated in a four-seater saloon, Andrew got his way, and lined up at Crystal Palace as confident as he could possibly be.

When Andrew Cowan came to write *Why Finish Last?*, he summed up this period succinctly and perfectly:

'By now we had lived with the car for about six months and everyone was getting keyed up for the start. Behind the scenes the last minute preparations had been made, and these included two sets of orders for their entire team detailing every single move they would make....'

The European sections – easy for some....

Although Rootes money-men had grumbled about the cost of the team's practice and testing sessions, it certainly paid off in the end. The story of Andrew Cowan's route survey adventures could fill a book (of course there *was* a book – *Why Finish Last?* – which he wrote after the famous victory), but one major conclusion which he reached was that with the exception of two particular sections – one in Turkey, the other in Afghanistan – it should be possible for a determined crew to complete the entire nine-day route to Bombay without losing any time. In fact, in the whole of that time, there were just 220 miles of flat-out motoring – nearly three hours of it in Turkey and an hour of it in Afghanistan.

304

London-Sydney Marathon: The Hunter victory of 1968

If the placing of service crews, and the supply of replacement parts, was properly organised in advance, it should also be possible to keep the car fit and well. Indeed, if there was enough time in hand at Bombay, before the car had to be loaded on board the *Chusan*, then something approaching a complete re-build should be possible.

More important, it was not going to be as tiring as was originally thought. Andrew was gratified by the amount of sleep he actually got in the first nine days. When his major rival, Roger Clark, came to write his own autobiography (*Sideways to Victory*) in the 1970s, he commented:

'It wasn't the flat-out endurance test some people had prophesied, and though there wasn't an official night stop between London and Bombay we certainly didn't go short of sleep. I reckon that by the time we rolled in to Bombay, I had had more good sleep than I normally get, and most of it in beds too. We slept on the cross-channel boat, in beds in Turin, Belgrade (about 11 hours), Istanbul and Sivas, and all of this was before we had been given a single hard-working competitive section….'

Andrew's strategy for rest in the car, while it was moving, was:

'In general terms, Colin was in the back of the car most of the time, whilst Brian sat in the passenger seat for 90% of the rally. Colin had the worst trip of the three of us. When he was driving and I was in the back, it was usually a section when we could easily do it easily on time, but when he was in the back trying to sleep, I was driving my heart out on one that was tight for time, and he was being bounced around….'

Historians are still grateful to Britain's *Autosport* magazine, which published a complete 'score-card' of the rally – all the way, control by control, of the route from London to Sydney – so it is still possible to analyse what happened, when, and to whom. Just as Andrew Cowan had forecast, unless they struck mechanical problems, virtually no competitor – serious or dilettante – lost time on any road section before reaching Sivas, which was a city in the very centre of Turkey, more than twelve hours beyond the main control in Istanbul.

Although the first car of 100 entrants (of which 98 actually started) – Bill Bengry's Ford Cortina GT – left Crystal Palace at 2.00PM on Sunday, 24 November, the *Daily Express* was determined to squeeze every ounce of publicity out of its investment before the cars left England and started the long trek through Europe, to the Middle East, Afghanistan, and India. This explains why all cars were first obliged to drive back into the very centre of London, and to cross Westminster Bridge (with Big Ben and the Houses of Parliament in the background to provide a suitable photo-opportunity, before making for Dover, and catching a ferry to Calais.

Even at Crystal Palace, Rootes nerves were still jangling, not only because team-recruit Colin Malkin needed a special mechanic's escort to stop him wandering nervously off, and getting lost in the crowd, but because, by the lucky of the draw (and it had been no more and no less than that) the 'works' Hunter did not leave until one-hour-and-a-quarter after the first car had left.

Although this did not worry Andrew Cowan at first – later in the event, he would pull up rapidly towards the head of the field as other crews lost time – he felt remote from some rivals, such as Roger Clark (No. 48), Paddy Hopkirk (No. 51) and Rauno Aaltonen (No. 61).

Even by then, other team's stars begin to hit trouble. Ford effectively lost two Lotus-

ROOTES MAESTROS
"In their own words."

Cortinas before the Iron Curtain was breached, for Peter Harper's car suffered a failed water pump, which led to the engine boiling and a head gasket failing, while Bengt Soderstrom's car suffered a broken engine cam follower.

Turkey and onwards ….

Then came the re-start from Sivas, where Andrew was faced with the first time in which he would have to drive flat-out – flat-out, that is, for three hours – for Erzincan, knowing that he would certainly lose time (as would, he assumed) all his rivals. The distance along the shorter (mud-afflicted) route was 175 miles, and the target time was 2hr 45 minutes, but no-one really expected to meet that. Not even rally-favourite Roger Clark, in the Lotus-Cortina, was expecting to be unpenalised.

Having practiced this section more than once, and having discovered that there was free choice of routes, he had to make a decision as to which way to go – the northern route, which was further but with more predictable surfaces, or the southern loop, which was shorter but might be mud-bound if the rains had been too heavy.

Luckily (and it *was* lucky, make no mistake), Andrew chose to go north, and although he had to cope with other traffic, made it to Erzincan only 21 minutes late. Andrew later confirmed that he overtook no fewer than 31 rally cars on that section alone - and that some made it more difficult than others! Amazingly, Andrew was already up among the leaders, with a car which, though totally reliable up to this point, he thought to be too heavy and too under-powered to win the event.

At that point, therefore, at the Erzincan control, the leader board looked like this:

Position	Car (Crew)	Penalty
1st	Ford Lotus-Cortina (Roger Clark/Ove Andersson)	6 minutes
2nd	Ford Taunus 20MRS (Gilbert Staepelaere/Simo Lampinen)	14 minutes
3rd	Citroen DS21 (Lucien Bianchi/Jean-Claude Ogier)	16 minutes
4th=	Ford Taunus 20MRS (Dieter Glemser/Martin Braungart)	17 minutes
4th=	BMC 1800 (Paddy Hopkirk/Tony Nash/Alec Poole)	17 minutes
4th=	BMC 1800 (Rauno Aaltonen/Henry Liddon/Paul Easter)	17 minutes

Then three other cars and:

10th	Hillman Hunter (Andrew Cowan/Brian Coyle/Colin Malkin)	21 minutes

In the meantime the RAF crew, led by Flt. Lt. David Carrington, were still in contention, but had lost 38 minutes at the Erzincan control.

The 45 hours of motoring which followed – to Teheran (the capital of Iran), and then on to Kabul (the capital of Afghanistan) – was frankly boring after this exciting little

Service en route for the Marathon winning Hunter, and its 'RAF crew' team mate. Andrew Cowan made sure that he had so much time in hand at controls such as Belgrade, Teheran, and Bombay that the car could virtually be rebuilt while the crew took some sleep.

interlude, but at least the crew ensured that the Hunter had a lot of time in hand to take service, almost a complete rebuild – and enjoy some hours in beds - at the Iran National factory in Teheran (Hillman Hunters, badged as Peykans, were being assembled in Iran), before clocking in at the Teheran control.

The long drag to Kabul – 23hr 33 minutes was scheduled, but many crews were up to ten hours early in reaching the Afghan capital – was non-competitive (at least, this is what the organisers intended), yet the fact is that more than half the entry lost time, and slipped even further out of contention, while quite a number did not make it that far at all. It was on this sector that another of the 'works' Fords, that of Rosemary Smith, struck trouble, when her engine blew a piston. Tony Fall's 'works' BMC 1800 broke its steering linkage, and Terry Hunter's well-fancied Porsche 911 broke its engine. Not only that, but Dieter Glemser's German Ford engine broke its camshaft drive, while Rauno Aaltonen's BMC 1800 broke its front suspension.

For Rootes, however, the biggest problem encountered was that the RAF entry had suffered a big accident when it plunged into a big hole in the un-made road, which badly damaged its front suspension. Although repairs were eventually made, with the help of Iran National technicians, this cost them three hours, and put then right out of contention.

Then came the second of the 'impossible' sections, the sprint up and over the Lataban Pass from Kabul to Sarobi. Set at a target time of only one hour, it was always going to be quite impossible, even though the Afghan authorities had taken some of the sting out of the challenge for having the loose surfaces re-graded just a day or so before the arrival of the Marathon.

Like all the top entrants, Andrew Cowan realised that although the Marathon could not be won over this section, it could certainly be lost, and swears that he could

The Hunter's most fearsome rivals in the London-Sydney Marathon included the Ford Lotus-Cortinas, and a team of five BMC 1800s. This 1800 was being driven by Tony Fall – but he could never achieve the same times as the rugged Hunter.

have been several minutes faster if he had not been so cautious in driving through the hanging dust. As it was, everyone – every single car in the Marathon – lost time on this one section. Roger Clark's Lotus-Cortina lost just five minutes, as did Paddy Hopkirk (BMC 18000 and Lucien Bianchi (Citroen DS21), but without taking a single unnecessary risk, the valiant Hunter lost just six minutes, and consolidated its place.

Once again, however, the RAF car was in trouble, this time when it lost a rear wheel (the story is that a spacer behind the rear hub was faulty), the brake back plate, drums and shoes had all been mashed up in the resulting carnage, so a further 4 hours 15 minutes, which meant that it was now completely out of the running, and was – as the football tabloid press would now say these days – merely 'driving for pride', down in 53rd place.

All that now remained was the long, drawn-out, trek eastwards into India, to go through the nation's capital of Delhi, then to fight one's way through ever increasing traffic (people, cars, trucks and buses and animals) to reach Bombay. With 40 hours 46 minutes allowed for this, every fit crew/car combination was guaranteed safe arrival at Bombay, where the general classification was:

Position	Car (Crew)	Penalty
1st	Ford Lotus-Cortina (Roger Clark/ Ove Andersson)	11 minutes

The Hunter charges up and over the Lataban Pass in Afghanistan, losing just six minutes on the target schedule – before arriving in Bombay in sixth place overall.

2nd	Ford Taunus 20MRS (G.Staepelaere/ S.Lampinen)	20 minutes
3rd	Citroen DS21 (L.Bianchi/ J-C. Ogier)	21 minutes
4th	(P.Hopkirk/A.Nash/ A.Poole)	22 minutes
5th	BMC 1800 (R.Aaltonen/H.Liddon/ P.Easter)	24 minutes
6th	Hillman Hunter (A.Cowan/B.Coyle/ C.Malkin)	27 minutes

Like most of the 'works' teams, Cowan found that he had more than six hours in hand before having to check in at the Bombay control, so Des O'Dell's mechanics were able to carry out a very thorough service/repair/rebuild operation. Within minutes, it seemed, major items like the complete rear axle, the dampers, the struts and the cylinder head (because fuel supplies were known to be of a higher octane, more predictable in quality, in Australia, a low-compression head was being exchanged for a higher compression example), and a new windscreen was also fitted.

After that, as Andrew later wrote:

'Next day the car was steam cleaned before being loaded on the *Chusan* for the trip, and I now had to sit down and think about Australia …. When the results came out, we were pleased to see we were in sixth place overall, so this meant only five cars would run ahead of us in Australia….'

Sydney or bust….

After the drama, the dust, the speeds, and the exhaustion of the first half of the Marathon, an enforced rest on board the P

309

ROOTES MAESTROS
"In their own words."

& O ship *Chusan* was a complete contrast. This graceful old ship, which was already 18 years old (it would finally be retired in 1973, incidentally), was on its regular scheduled voyage, this time the difference being that 72 rally cars, their crews, and a number of team bosses and media crews were all on board. The cars were securely locked away below decks, and there was no chance of working on them while the ship was at sea.

At first glance, an eight day cruise over the hot Indian Ocean, to Freemantle, the port close to Perth, might sound like paradise – and for the first 24 hours it probably was – but for a really dedicated rally driver it was inevitable that boredom would soon set in. With nothing to do except eat, sleep, drink and sunbathe (and to all that again the following day, and the day after that....) most of the drivers ended up wishing for something fresh to do.

Some, like Andrew, quietly worried at what lay ahead, for the route across Australia looked as if it would be much more demanding that the London – Bombay had turned out to be. Would the Hunter stay in one piece? Would there be enough service (apart from Marcus Chambers and Des O'Dell, only three dedicated Humber Road mechanics would be in Australia)? Had Brian Coyle's recce been thorough enough?

Some found solace in little ways – such as throwing each other into the ship's pool with their clothes on – whereas the organisers worked up a bit of publicity by having Roger Clark 'drive' the ship for a short period, and making pretty patterns with the wake of the propellers.

This was the point at which the Australian crews (who, frankly, had been humiliated by the pace of the Europeans in the first half of the event) started spreading tall stories about the horrors of what was to come. Harry Firth, Ian Vaughan and Bruce Hodgson (all of them in 'works' Ford-Australia Ford Falcon GTs) were the worst offenders, each and all of them forecasting that the Europeans would be blown away by what they were about to experience in the 67 hour/ 3,000 mile dash across their continent, and that the Australian 'experts' would leave them well behind.

This was, of course, a classic wind-up, made that much less believable by the obvious exaggerations involved, but since Brian Coyle (though not Andrew) had recently carried out a full pre-event route survey in Australia, he merely sat back, absorbed what the Australians were saying, then re-briefed Andrew and Colin with a more accurate estimate of conditions and prospects when they were alone.

This might all have been a routine voyage for P & O (even though the captain ordered that the pool be emptied at one point when the high jinks became too high !), but it was ultimately very boring for rally drivers. When cornered by a media crew on arrival at Fremantle, perhaps unwisely Paddy Hopkirk was asked for his impressions of the trip. Paddy, quick as a flash, commented that:

'It's the best advert I can think of for flying....'

When the event re-started from Perth on the evening of 14 December, everyone in the Rootes team was raring to go once again. The car felt as good as new, the crew was well rested, and Andrew realised how much the next three days would matter:

'I have never driven a car so hard for so long as I did that Hunter in the Australian sections. We knew we had to gain every second we could get, and I drove flat out from start to finish, grabbing whatever time I could for meals....throughout the whole

London-Sydney Marathon: The Hunter victory of 1968

Australian section we were never overtaken save on the Nullabor Plain [that is in the west of Australia] where the Ford Falcons were cruising at 110mph, and we were running at a modest 85mph.'

This was a near to a flat-out motor race as road conditions, and the Australian police, would allow, with the distance between some controls up to seven hours, but with many others below two hours, and one of them (close to the end) down to a mere 42 minutes. As far as the drivers were concerned, however, the lull came before the storm. After they were flagged off from Perth (by Gough Whitlam, who later became a controversial Prime minister in Australia) the first section was a seven year stretch to Youanmi (where the Hunter had a full hour in hand), followed by a four hour stretch to Marvel Loch, where only 21 cars escaped without penalty, two hours to Lake King (Roger Clark cleaned this, the Hunter dropped five minutes, taking fifth place from Paddy Hopkirk's BMC 1800), then a seemingly endless 14hr 52 minute drive across the Nullabor Plain (all day, in the heat of a southern Australia spring) to Ceduna, and a further 6hr 18minute drag to Quorn.

This, though, is where the event suddenly threw itself into turmoil, for it was its way to Quorn that Roger Clark's Lotus-Cortina broke a valve and damaged a piston. Even though the Ford mechanics cannibalised Eric Jackson's sister car to repair that of Clark (by a complete head change), he was nevertheless 14 minutes late at Quorn, and dropped to third place. The Staepelaere/Lampinen Ford Taunus now led the event....

What followed could not even have been forecast by lovers of tall stories. Not even a top Hollywood writer could have scripted what was to follow. Fourteen tight road sections totalling 33 hours – all of them on public roads in the populated south-east corner of Australia – brought the event to a climax. The lead would change hands several times, crashes and breakdowns proliferated, and the Hunter would not finally take the lead until the very last competitive section.

Although Clark's Lotus-Cortina regained second place at Brachina, and Cowan's Hunter moved up to fourth, the leader board looked stable, with Lucien Bianchi's Citroen still out in front then, north of Murrindal (close to Melbourne) the Lotus-Cortina suddenly broke its rear axle, lost nearly 100 minutes in getting it changed, and falling out of contention. Suddenly the Hunter was third, though only 12 minutes behind the Citroen.

Shortly, the Staepelaere/Lampinen Taunus 20MRS crashed and broke a steering tie-rod, losing nearly three hours in getting it repaired – and the Hunter found itself in second place! Then, the most dramatic events occurred on the last tight (two hour) from Hindmarsh Station to Nowra. Bianchi's Citroen was a secure eleven minutes ahead of the Hunter until, to quote Quentin Spurring's report in *Autosport*:

'As the cars came down from the mountains towards Nowra, and a quiet Sunday afternoon drive towards Sydney [Bianchi]... handed the driving over to Ogier so that he could snatch a bit of sleep before the inevitable pomp and ceremony of the finish. Then it happened: with Ogier powerless to do anything about it, two youths in a Mini collided with the Citroen, and pushed it off the road. Bianchi was trapped inside the wrecked car for 20 minutes while help – summoned by Paddy Hopkirk, who had to drive back along the road to warn a group of spectators about the accident – came in the form of some cutting equipment....'

ROOTES MAESTROS
"In their own words."

Paddy might have been penalised by this good Samaritan act, but was not, and by the time Andrew Cowan came on the scene, the rescue operation was already under way: happily, Lucien Bianchi would make a full recovery.

The Hillman Hunter, and its intrepid crew of Andrew Cowan, Brian Coyle and Colin Malkin, therefore, had pulled off a quite unexpected victory in the world's most highly publicised transcontinental rally. At the finish, in front of a 10,000 crowd at the Warwick Farm race track near Sydney, car and crew all looked grubby and exhausted, though this was quite excusable.

Andrew Cowan's own reminiscences of this famous win, and what happened afterwards, now follow in the next section.

Victory cures all ills, even exhaustion, for a time at least. Left to right – Andrew Cowan, Brian Coyle and Colin Malkin seated on the roof of their Hunter, enjoying the champagne.

312

London-Sydney Marathon: The Hunter victory of 1968

Above: This was the souvenir signed photograph of the victorious Hunter charging through standing water on the Marathon.

Below: Interest in the Hunter's Marathon victory was immense, as this shot from Sydney confirms. This must, of course, have been at least one day after the finish, for the crew are looking extremely neat in their laundered shirts!

ROOTES MAESTROS
"In their own words."

Andrew Cowan's memories of the London-Sydney Marathon

Twenty-five years after Andrew Cowan won the London-Sydney Marathon of 1968, he was looking forward to the 'Retrospective' event which would follow in 1993. In this interview, taped at the time and never previously published, Andrew and his co-driver Colin Malkin recalled that great occasion:

'We never thought we could win London - Sydney from the front, but we always knew that we had the strongest car. Before the start, I don't think we ever thought we could win, but we always hoped we could finish in the first three. There was always the feeling that the other guys would make a mistake, and I might win.'

'I was a wee bit worried by the number of cars which actually got to Bombay. We hadn't expected that. But we were sixth overall at that point, and that was magic. With the Australian horror sections still to come, we didn't think we could go wrong.'

'I'm sure other people, rather than me, could have won in the Hunter, but then I had nothing to prove - unlike Roger Clark and his Lotus Cortina, who was expected to lead after the first difficult section.'

Even today, Andrew Cowan shakes his head at the frugal way that Rootes tackled the event:

'We had no service at all from Teheran to Bombay, none at all. Not many Rootes enthusiasts know that. The three mechanics we had for the event, they flew on from Teheran to Bombay, and took the lids off the boxes of parts. We knew we would have no more than 40 minutes for service there. In fact, we made up for lost time there, changing the cylinder head which we'd used for the poor petrol in the Middle East, ready for the better fuel in Australia. We changed the front struts, fitted a new rear axle, a new gearbox and overdrive - we nearly had a new car.'

Colin Malkin, who was sitting in on this conversation, then reminded Andrew that:

'There was also the story of the cylinder head washers which fell down into the sump during the change. There was no time to get them out. They were still there at the finish!'

In the early planning period, Andrew thought he would go two up, with his regular co-driver Brian Coyle alongside him ('We were used to doing three or four days on rallies, non stop, like the Liege, in those days'), but as the enormity of the event sank in, it was decided to take Colin Malkin as reserve driver/third crew member. Colin, at the time, was the young star who was driving Rallye Imps in British events, but although Andrew and Colin had tested together this was the very first time they had shared a rally car.

'I'm still happy that we went three up,' Andrew says. 'That was another detail. I think that Lucien Bianchi and Jean-Claude Ogier had their Citroen accident on the last day because Bianchi was asleep, Ogier met that Mini on the crest of a brow, driving a left hand drive car, and went the wrong way by instinct. He was very tired.

'The problem with going three up was that this meant carrying even more weight, and

315

ROOTES MAESTROS
"In their own words."

the car was already heavy. Don't forget that we had three spare wheels and tyres bolted to the roof - incidentally we never had a puncture, the whole rally! But we weren't too worried about weight by then, we were covering all eventualities. Even then, we were all exhausted.

'Incidentally, there was one point in Australia where Colin was in the back seat, and began to feel the heat, and went to sleep. When I tried to wake him up, he was unconscious, I couldn't waken him because he'd been driving when I was asleep, and not getting any rest when I was going hard.

'From our view it wasn't worth the risk and Colin doesn't think that a two up car could possibly have won it.'

Roger Clark incidentally, who was two up in the 'works' Lotus Cortina with Ove Andersson, doesn't agree. Having led for much of the event, two unavoidable problems then dropped them back to tenth place, but neither was due to the crew being exhausted.

Was there a game plan, made in advance, as to who would drive, and where?:

'The plan was that I would only drive the competitive sections, and Colin would drive everywhere else. Brian was not scheduled to drive at all, he was in the passenger seat all the time.

'That is what happened, more or less, though on the road sections down to Turkey we drove turn and turn about. The plan, though, was to ensure that I was one hundred per cent fresh for the stages.'

'Even in Australia, where much of the route was difficult, there were sections where Colin could drive and I was able to sleep.

'But I remember, on the road from Delhi to Bombay, that we stopped at a level crossing, I was driving, and I was falling to sleep. I remember the car was very quiet, then Brian suddenly woke up, and said "Hey, get going, the crossing's open again....". Yes, we were very tired by then, we'd been in a car for all that time. Apart from the stop in Teheran, where we actually went to bed, at the rest halt in Kabul, we'd been on the move the whole time.

'On really long sections,' Colin Malkin broke in, 'the others would go to sleep, and put a small post card into the card holder on the dashboard, which faced the driver and was lit by a small aircraft light. Brian had prepared these cards beforehand: one card could cover 500km or 600km!'

Was it a happy crew? Sure it was - the fact that Colin Malkin still works for Andrew, at Ralliart, today, must prove something:

'The main row we had was near the end', Andrew laughs, 'about a day away from Sydney. Colin was absolutely unconscious in the back of the car, and I couldn't even drag him out of the back seat to drive a section. In the end he was just conscious enough to throw his arms around, and make a few remarks....'

Before the event started, did Andrew try to get into training, go to keep fit classes, or go jogging?:

'No, I didn't, but I was very fit in those days. I was a very active farmer, still working a seven day week. In any case, in those days rally drivers never thought about jogging, or going to bed early instead they used to take wakey wakey pills to keep going. It was quite legal then....

'There was a lot of excitement ahead of the event, the adrenalin had started to flow months before we started, so I was never frightened of the eight days and nights on the way to India.

Andrew Cowan's memories of the London-Sydney Marathon

'On the other hand, we did go carefully into the whole question of dieting. The RAF, who later put a crew in the other Hunter, helped us with this. We were all concerned about the food, and very concerned about getting ill.

'We were really quite worried, so we found out where to go, to be taught. We found out where the military were trained in survival, and we were really after their food packs. They gave us a course on health, hygiene and nutrition. I'm not aware of the other 'works' teams even doing this. It was only after this that the RAF came back and asked Rootes if it would prepare a car for them to take on the Marathon.'

Working alongside Rootes' own doctors, a foolproof set of inoculations was provided, and because the team was warned that water supplies would always be suspect east of Turkey, they and the service crews were given water purifying kits. As Andrew wrote in his book:

'Part of our spare parts packages, which we flew out to various places, was a dustbin. What the crew would do as soon as they reached their service point would be to fill the dustbin up with water, put a set amount of powder into it, and then wait 20 minutes before taking a test cupful. Into this you would drop a tablet and if the water turned red you had to add more powder until it became a neutral colour....'

But there was more invaluable advice:

'What particularly amazed us was to be reminded how many times your hand touches your mouth during the day - and this is how you transmit germs, and how you get all the digestion trouble. I'd have to tie my hands behind my back to stop me touching my mouth but this was just part of what we were told.'

The RAF provided rations Andrew and Brian Coyle completed a recce from London to Bombay, using a primus stove and cooking up the rations provided. Andrew remembers much of this as very tasty, but Colin Malkin, on the other hand, didn't enjoy that sort of food at all:

'I didn't trust any of it. I ate the oatmeal biscuits, and the cheese,' Colin quipped, 'but that was all. Oh yes, plus bread that we bought in Paris - I ate that until it was a week old, but nothing else. There was one meal we ate in Teheran, which was cooked in the garage dealership.'

Because the Hunter was not nearly as fast as the Ford Lotus Cortinas, the Porsche 911s or reputedly the Australian Falcon GTs, there was really no such thing as setting out to drive tactically:

'We drove flat out, all the time. We just drove it as fast as it would go, all the time. It handled very well, even three up and on the gravel type roads. The Turkish stages suited us very well. We thought we'd be miles behind the others, but it worked well. We were very fast downhill.

'On this and other Marathons, I was never in a position where I had the fastest car, so I couldn't be expected to win. Whether this affected my attitude to London - Sydney or not, I'm not sure. Because the whole of the Australian route was so tight there really wasn't a problem we just had to go flat out, all the time.'

Even though money was very tight, the team prepared as carefully as possible:

'I surveyed the whole of the London Bombay route beforehand, just once. Colin and I then flew out to Ankara, and hired a Volkswagen, to recce the Sivas to Erzincan

ROOTES MAESTROS
"In their own words."

section again. We'd heard there was a short cut, a choice of route, and the organisers later admitted that one route was 80km shorter, but this included a valley with a river which was known to overflow its banks and flood the road.

'The other road was more mountainous, and longer, so we simply couldn't decide what to do, we would be tackling this stage in November, don't forget. On the event I actually made the decision about 100 yards before the junction that mattered, it was up to me to decide. The reason I changed my mind, *not* to take the short cut, was that there was a puddle in the road! That's where we could have blown it all....'

'When we drove the VW back to the airport from the mountains, we were very tight for time, we got two punctures, so we hid the car in the airport car park. Incidentally,' Colin reminded us all, 'we'd arranged for a telegram to come from a Turkish man, a forester who lived in the middle of the stage, to see if the short cut was clear. But he couldn't get through to us from Sivas. Later we found that Jim Porter, working for Ford, was stuck down there, and couldn't get back!'

Even when the Marathon reached Australia, neither driver had ever set foot in that country before. Brian Coyle had carried out a recce, but neither Andrew nor Colin had driven there at all. They had to rely totally on Brian's route notes, made at low speeds in a standard car borrowed from Chrysler Australia. Even so:

'The threat from the Australian crews never materialised, because the cars and their crews were simply not fast enough. We had a lot of trouble with the Australians in the first half of the event. Trying to pass them on the special stages was difficult. They took it very easy in Turkey, sauntering around

As Marcus Chambers wrote so vividly in his autobiography – after the Hunter won the London-Sydney Marathon of 1968, he simply didn't care who would have to up the tab for flying the car back to the UK – but BOAC (later British Airways) did the transporting job.

Home Again! The Marathon winners – left to right, Andrew Cowan, Brian Coyle and Colin Malkin – complete with the magnificent trophy, return to London in time for Christmas 1968.

thinking that they would catch us all in Australia. They were fast up the straights but not on the twisty sections. In Australia they never got near us; I don't think they appreciated the professionalism of the European crews, I don't think they realised our pace.'

After the finish, and after the Hunter had won the event, were Rootes under-prepared for the triumph?:

'Absolutely. The only person who got anything organised in Australia was Jenny Nadin, who was working for Rootes Public Relations. She got the publicity going. Yet I didn't feel let down. All I'd wanted to do was to win the event, and I'd done that.

'When we got back to Heathrow, there was a super reception. Gilbert Hunt was there, so was television. Piccadilly was closed down so that the car could be photographed.

'Rootes actually set up a special company so that Colin, Brian and I could endorse products and become millionaires overnight. Well, I never believed in that, but all the bosses believed it. We made very little out of that. The event prize was £10,000, of which I think we got £2,000 each, £2,000 then went to Des O'Dell, and £2,000 went to the mechanics guess who decided on that sort of split up? Des, of course! 'Rootes, well, they gave us a Sunbeam Rapier H120 each [Colin Malkin, then in the motor trade, sold his on very shortly afterwards!], but no money. I received an extended contract, but there was nothing for the others.

'We had parties and dinners all over the place, including a reception at Linwood where the Hunter bodies were being made at the time. There really wasn't much financial gain for this win, and we certainly

A great story, needing no words! Not only did the Rootes team celebrate the London-Sydney Marathon victory, but important team members were invited to a prestigious reception in honour of the Commonwealth Heads of Government in the weeks which followed.

In honour of the Commonwealth Heads of Government

The Prime Minister and Mrs Harold Wilson

request the honour of the company of

Mr. Colin Malkin

at a Reception at Lancaster House, St. James's on Thursday, 9th January, 1969, at 10.00 p.m.

Dinner Jacket or National Dress

Cars to approach Lancaster House by way of Cleveland Row

Please reply to: The Secretary, Government Hospitality, 72, Whitehall, S.W.1

Andrew Cowan's memories of the London-Sydney Marathon

To meet the Teams participating in the London/Sydney Marathon Motor Rally, 1968.

The High Commissioner for Australia and the Agents General for New South Wales, Victoria, Queensland, South Australia and Western Australia have pleasure in inviting

Mr. C. Malkin

for drinks in the Main Hall, Australia House on Friday 22nd November, 1968.

R.S.V.P.
Reception Office,
Australia House.

5 p.m. - 7 p.m.

ROOTES MAESTROS
"In their own words."

didn't have a fee for driving in it. My annual contract, I think, was about £2,000 - £3,000 for the season.

'After Christmas, I was asked to go on a Round the World promotional tour, to Frankfurt, Istanbul, Iran, Bombay, Bangkok, Singapore, Australia, New Zealand, then Manila in the Phillipines – which was where I got a call direct from John Rowe at the factory, to tell me that the competitions department had been closed!'

A real case of Thank You and Goodbye! Having done the Scottish Rally in an Imp, therefore, Andrew then moved to British Leyland, ready to drive a Triumph 2.5PI on the Daily Mirror World Cup Rally of 1970. At least, as a working farmer, his livelihood had not been killed off but it was no way to thank a winning driver for a magnificent achievement.

Colin retained his links with Rootes/Chrysler for a time, but like most people he found it difficult to get on with Des O'Dell:

'I got sacked regularly, about every month, but he usually hired me again.' Later Colin drove Lancias in British events, a 'works' Escort in the 1970 World Cup Rally, but returned to Chrysler to drive Avengers in the 1970s.'

Andrew himself moved on considerably after he won the London Sydney Marathon in 1968. Twenty five years later, at 56 years of age, and as a director of Ralliart UK, he was running Mitsubishi's World Championship rally team. The man who drove a 100bhp Hillman Hunter to victory in 1968 was controlling a team of Group A four wheel drive Lancers, whose turbocharged engines produced well in excess of 300bhp. For the rest of the 1990s he ran that team, eventually providing cars for Tommi Makinen to win four consecutive World Rally Championship titles.

- and, as he confirmed at the time (1993) of this interview:

Twenty five years after he won the original London-Sydney Marathon, Andrew Cowan is trying to repeat the trick. Not only will he

Forty years on, photographed in 2008, the Hillman Hunter which Andrew Cowan drove to win the 1968 London-Sydney Marathon looks as good as new.

Andrew Cowan's memories of the London-Sydney Marathon

be using the same car, rebuilt for the occasion, but co-driver Colin Malkin will once again be in the car throughout.

'It was Nick Brittan's idea,' Andrew says.' He called me, asked me if I was interested in going again, but where was the car?

'Well, even though I didn't have a clue about my Mitsubishi commitments for Spring 1993 at the time, I was interested, and I knew exactly where the car was - it was in store at my farm in Scotland!'

'I'm delighted to be doing the event, because I take my hat off to Nick Brittan for having the idea, and for pushing it through. I've been very impressed with what he's done so far.'

Fortunately for Andrew, Colin Malkin, and Ralliart, there will be no clash of interests between modern rallying and the London-Sydney Marathon of 1993. The Tour de Corse clashes with the Marathon, but Mitsubishi never planned to enter this event, which is a specialised all tarmac, all pace notes occasion.

Happily too, the Royal Scottish Automobile Club, which has now owned the car for more than 20 years, agreed to lend it for renovation, so that Andrew could drive it once again, and it was to be the first car to leave the start line at Chelsea Harbour in April 1993. The canny Scots, however, insisted that after the event, the car must then be re-restored and handed back to them, in original condition.

'To be honest, I haven't done much driving in the car since it was restored,' Andrew commented. But during this interview, he abandoned all pre Monte Carlo Mitsubishi business for a time, jumped into the old car, and disappeared into the Warwickshire lanes.

By that time the restored car was looking a lot smarter than when it had finished the Marathon in 1968:

'We got the wrinkles in the roof in Australia, when Colin was driving. It's an amazing story. Because we couldn't afford to send a car to Australia to do a proper recce. Brian Coyle went across there, got a Chrysler rep. to drive him in a road car, and they covered the route, quite slowly, just to make route notes.

'Well in advance, there had been stories about "the pothole". After Youanmi, after Lake King, the route struck off east [towards Sydney]. Soon after leaving Lake King there was a hole in the road ....we had read of Gunnar Palm (of Ford) breaking the steering on a recce car, and having to reverse for 40 miles to get help, Henry Liddon of BMC had hit the same hole too.

'It was totally unsighted you couldn't see it in advance, and it was on a totally straight section where everyone was doing at least 80 - 90mph. Brian Coyle hit the same hole, when with the Chrysler rep., but he was only doing about 20 mph.

'On the event, Colin was driving, and was doing about 90mph. I was just getting down in the back seat, Brian was saying: "Remember the hole,", Colin was ready for it when Wallop! I was up against the roof, then when the car came down I realised it was out of control!

'I remember coming down shouting: "Keep your foot in it, Colin, keep your foot in it!", and Colin swore back: 'What the **** do you think I'm doing?". I could hear the trees crashing around us, and the bushes going over the roof...'

Colin Malkin, sitting in on this discussion, then chimed in:

'We were just a few seconds wrong. The same second that Brian called it, I hit the hole. The side of the road had big ditches. Well, it went into one ditch, came out, dived across into the other ditch, I just couldn't hold it...'

Andrew, however, thinks that if the team hadn't done so much testing at Bagshot, so much jumping in a heavy laden condition, then they would have been out of the Marathon, then and there:

323

ROOTES MAESTROS
"In their own words."

'I was trying to pick myself up from the floor in the back, it was a horrific accident. There were two great big dents in the roof above the pillars....

'That was the only big incident we had in the event.'

In 1993 the driving regime was all set to be very different from that of 1968. With a three man crew, Brian Coyle rarely left his front passenger seat, Colin Malkin sat in the rear seat when Andrew was driving the flat out sections, swopping with Colin whenever needed. However, as Colin still remembered:

'I didn't get a lot of sleep. When I was driving, Andrew was in the back, snoring his head off, but when he came to drive quickly I was in the back, and there was no chance of any rest.'

For 1993, which was to be a totally different event with lots of night halts, Andrew chose a two man crew. Colin Malkin, who accompanied Andrew on his other great Marathon victory drives (London-Sydney in 1977 and Round South America in 1978), was working for Ralliart at Rugby, and was an obvious choice for the co-driver's job in 1993.

'Although I was originally a driver,' Colin said, 'I now enjoy co-driving. Andrew and I went all the way round South America, in the Mercedes, on pace notes, and I enjoyed it.'

In 1993 Andrew was to do most of the driving:

'Colin's a better navigator than I am, so where the navigation is tricky I'll drive.

Thank goodness for all the night halts. For old men like Colin and myself that's the only way we can do it now! We know we can't rev it to 6,000rpm in every gear, every day, but we'll be driving at a pace where we don't think we'll break anything. We know we're not going to get any service at least half of the entry is going to go off the road, or blow up their cars. We don't think we are going to get lost, because the navigation is pretty basic.'

Brian Coyle co-drove with Andrew, in a Triumph 2.5 PI, in the 1970 World Cup Rally, and also spent some time co-driving for Colin Malkin in Rallye Imps, but then gradually drifted away from the sport:

'In fact I've completely lost touch with Brian,' Andrew regrets. 'I haven't spoken to him for years. He was once married to my sister, but they divorced, and we gradually drifted apart.'

Friends Re-united! Andrew Cowan (left) and Peter Procter met up again at the Silverstone Classic event of July 2008. Both still drive fast and enthusiastically, and both love to reminisce of their time in Rootes cars.

What followed? Chrysler, Talbot and Des O'Dell

Although this book tells the story of the Rootes Competition Department under two Maestros – Norman Garrad and Marcus Chambers – it has not attempted to cover that activities of what became, successively, the Chrysler, Talbot, Peugeot-Talbot then Peugeot-UK operations. Until he retired in 1992, after 27 years with Rootes/Chrysler/Peugeot-Talbot, all those operations were successively (and successfully) managed by Des O'Dell, who had of course joined Marcus Chambers at Humber Road in 1964.

As already made clear in Marcus Chambers's narrative, within months of the famous victory achieved on the London-Sydney Marathon, the Rootes Competitions Department was put into suspended animation. Marcus himself was moved to the Engineering Department where, under Development chief Peter Wilson, he became Proving Grounds Manager, charged with finding a suitable site for the company to develop new testing facility.

[It is not generally known that Rootes already had a test site, at Wellesbourne airfield (a few miles south of Warwick) – though this was too small, and with too restricted prospects, to be available for expansion. Marcus's strong recommendation, by the way, was that Rootes/Chrysler should acquire the lease of the ex-USAF base at Bruntingthorpe, near Leicester, but this was never taken up]

When Marcus Chambers was moved sideways from Humber Road, and out of Competitions, his colleague Des O'Dell was immediately made up to become Manager, and would stay in that job until the early 1990s. Over the years in which he was at Rootes – Chrysler, Talbot, or Peugeot – call it what you will - O'Dell gained (and cherished) a reputation as a very straight-talking, sometimes abrasive, but above all knowledgeable and effective engineer and manager. As Des himself once commented, in later life:

'Some people think I am a pain, while others think I'm wonderful. I don't know how I'd prefer to be remembered, but I think I managed to get a bit done….

Born at Cardington, in Bedfordshire, in 1927, Des originally wished that he could become a fighter or bomber pilot in the RAF, but instead completed his compulsory National Service in REME (the Royal Electrical and Mechanical Engineers) in the late 1940s. Returning home, he first opened a small garage business, then joined Aston Martin (who were at Feltham in Middlesex), to work as an experimental development engineer.

One thing led to another. Within Aston Martin he first became known as an excellent fitter/fixer (and, almost by definition, wheeler-dealer), not only under John Wyer, but eventually as the leader of the Production Quality department of Aston Martin at Newport Pagnell. When Wyer moved out, to head up the new Ford GT40 design/build operation in Slough, he soon enticed O'Dell to join him, where from 1963 he became one of the key players who built the cars and oversaw their development.

It was not until Rootes had embarked on their ill-fated mission to race Sunbeam Tigers in the Le Mans 24 Hour race, that O'Dell first became connected with the company. Separately, but at about the same

325

ROOTES MAESTROS
"In their own words."

time, it seems, both Marcus Chambers and Peter Wilson approached John Wyer, seeking someone to help them get a grip on the Ford V8 engines, and on chassis development in general, the result being that Des joined Rootes in November 1964.

From then on, with Marcus Chambers as the Manager, Ian Hall as what we would now call the 'Co-ordinator', and O'Dell as *de facto* 'Rally Engineer', the Humber Road operation became gradually more purposeful, and more professional. As already recounted, much of the work which went into making the Imps reliable, faster and stronger, was to O'Dell's credit, and virtually all the work done on the Hillman Hunter for the London-Sydney Marathon was to his credit too.

What happened after London-Sydney was at once gratifying and poignant. And Des himself said:

'After the London-Sydney Marathon, I had lots of offers of jobs. Gilbert Hunt, our managing director, doubled my salary on the spot, and asked me if we would like to enter the Safari Rally, adding that building the cars for homologation would be no problem. Peter Wilson was a fantastic ally. He made me up to Team Manager and told people in Rootes who was responsible for the L to S Marathon win because, despite all the publicity, many people didn't know. There was talk of a great expansion in the Comps Department, and my office was redecorated. Two months later, we all got the sack....'

Although there is a tiny element of legend and exaggeration in that remark (Peter Wilson was never Des's boss, nor did he have the power to make such promotions – but there is no doubt that he had great influence in motorsport matters), for no 'Safari Hunter' could possibly have been urged through the Rootes/Chrysler planning system in less than two years, but the general drift is accurate.

After a terrific tussle – first, Comps was to be closed down, then the total staff was to be reduced to four, and eventually the workforce settled at eight people – Des was allowed to carry on, running what was effectively a Chrysler Special Tuning operation, looking after cars like the Rallye Imp and (from 1970/1971) the Hillman Avenger. The same old and very basically-equipped workshops in Humber Road, were retained.

Any profit which could be made from selling goods and services could be used to run the operation – and eventually it became possible for the Department to offer sponsorship to operations like George Bevan with the Imp which won the British Saloon Car Championship, and eventually to finance an in-house return to saloon car racing.

Along the way, Special Tuning developed the Hunter GLS, and eventually the Avenger GT, into class-competitive race cars, push-rod Avengers became competitive in rallying, and the Avenger Tiger (with a highly-tuned 1.6litre engine) was a successful limited-edition machine. The Avenger-BRM on the other hand (which had a 1.6litre engine featuring a 16-valve, twin-overhead-camshaft cylinder head designed by BRM – this, originally, having been a Rootes Engineering project, to match the Ford Escort RS1600) was a failure, even in British rallies, for it was not powerful enough. Except in British events, there was no 'works' team activity at this time, though several cars were supplied to other teams and individuals – a young Henri Toivonen, for instance, became known in a Finnish-maintained Chrysler Sunbeam before he became famous in Britain, in the 'works' Talbot team, and in other 'works' teams

Still with big ambitions, however, in 1978 Des set out to build 'a better Escort' (as he always called it....), by mating the Chrysler

What followed? Chrysler, Talbot and Des O'Dell

Sunbeam hatchback (which had a shortened Avenger platform) with a 2.2litre 16-valve Lotus engine. Backed, as ever, by Peter Wilson, Des O'Dell persuaded Chrysler to put this car into production as the Chrysler Sunbeam-Lotus, but by the time it went on sale in mid-1979 Chrysler had sold out all its European operations to Peugeot of France, and this new car was speedily re-badged Talbot Sunbeam-Lotus, for 'Talbot' was a trade mark which Peugeot had acquired as part of the historic Rootes heritage

This was a success: it was on sale from 1979 to 1981, and was produced jointly by Lotus in Norfolk, and Peugeot-Talbot at Linwood, 2,308 of these 150bhp models were produced, and Des's perseverance and persuasive advocacy saw the 'works' team revived, and back on the world stage by 1980. Henri Toivonen, in fact, would win the RAC Rally outright in 1980, defeating a fleet of Ford Escorts, while with help from Peugeot in France, the team then went on to win the World Rally Championship for Manufacturers in 1981.

After this, Peugeot (under Jean Todt) set out to design the new four-wheel-drive 205 Turbo 16 rally car (just 200 such machines would be produced in France), with Des working in France, as a consultant, for up to two years while the car was engineered. In the meantime, Humber Road continued in its 'Special Tuning' activities, and eventually built up a whole series of well-respected British one-make Championships for Peugeot 205s and other related models.

It was in such one-make Championships, where the rewards (sporting and financial) were generous for successful drivers, that new 'young lions' like Richard Burns, Colin McRae and Jonny Milner all found fame, and Des was proud of that. When his 65th birthday loomed up in 1992, Des reluctantly retired, after 27 years service, when he had battled against all the odds to keep what some of us still call the 'Rootes Group' motorsport operation in business. He enjoyed only seven years of retirement in Warwickshire, and died in 1999.

His successor was Mick Linford, who produced cars as exciting as the British Touring Car Championship Peugeot 406s – but the operation was finally closed down in the early 2000s when Peugeot concentrated its efforts in France.

ROOTES MAESTROS
"In their own words."

Competition Highlights: Motorsport success 1948-1972

There isn't enough space for us to list each and every entry, in every race, rally or record attempt. Here, though, are the highlights, and most successful performances, of a fascinating period. In all but events specially marked, these were by 'works' cars.

Year	Event	Car	Rootes drivers	Result
1948	French Alpine	Sunbeam-Talbot 90	George Murray-Frame	1st in 2litre Class
1949	Monte Carlo Rally	Sunbeam-Talbot 80	George Hartwell, Nick Haines, Peter Monkhouse	Team Prize, Best Non-French cars
	Circuit of Ireland	Sunbeam-Talbot 90	John Cutts	1st in Class
	French Alpine	Sunbeam-Talbot 90 Sunbeam-Talbot 80	George Hartwell George Murray-Frame	5th Overall, 1st in Class
			George Hartwell, George Murray-Frame Norman Garrad, A.G.Douglas Clease	Best Non-French team
1950	Monte Carlo Rally	Humber Super Snipe	Maurice Gatsonides	2nd Overall
	French Alpine	Sunbeam-Talbot 90	George Murray-Frame	Class win and 6th overall
		Sunbeam-Talbot 90	Norman Garrad	2nd in Class
			George Murray-Frame George Hartwell Norman Garrad	Team Award
1951	RAC Rally	Sunbeam-Talbot 90	George Hartwell	2nd overall, 2nd in class
	French Alpine	Sunbeam-Talbot 90	John Cutts	3rd in Class

329

ROOTES MAESTROS
"In their own words."

1952	Monte Carlo Rally	Sunbeam-Talbot 90	Stirling Moss	2nd Overall
	French Alpine	Sunbeam-Talbot 90 Sunbeam-Talbot 90 Sunbeam-Talbot 90	Stirling Moss George Murray-Frame Mike Hawthorn (All won Coupes des Alpes for unpenalised runs. They also won the Manufacturers' Team Prize. Murray-Frame won his class.)	
	MCC National Rally	Sunbeam-Talbot 90	Sheila Van Damm	Ladies' Award
	15 Countries in 90 hours	Humber Super Snipe	Stirling Moss, Leslie Johnson, John Cutts, David Humphrey	Success!
1953	Monte Carlo Rally	Sunbeam-Talbot 90	Sheila Van Damm (Leslie Johnson) (Godfrey Imhof) (Stirling Moss)	2nd in Class (Winners of Manufacturers' Team Prize)
	Record runs at Jabbeke and Montlhery	Sunbeam Alpine	Stirling Moss Sheila Van Damm Leslie Johnson	120mph at Jabbeke 111mph for 1 hour at Montlhery
	RAC Rally	Sunbeam-Talbot 90	Ronnie Adams George Hartwell Sheila Van Damm	2nd overall, Class win 3rd in Class Ladies' award
	French Alpine	Sunbeam Alpine Sunbeam Alpine	Leslie Johnson Sheila Van Damm	Class win Ladies' Award
	Lisbon Rally	Sunbeam-Talbot 90 Sunbeam-Talbot 90	Godfrey Imhof Sheila Van Damm	1st in Class, 4th Overall 2nd in Class, 2nd Ladies' award
1954	Monte Carlo Rally	Sunbeam-Talbot 90	Stirling Moss Leslie Johnson Sheila Van Damm	Winners of Manufacturers' Team Prize

Competition Highlights: Motorsport success 1948-1972

	RAC Rally	Sunbeam-Talbot 90	Peter Harper	4th overall, 2nd in class
	Tulip	Sunbeam-Talbot 90	Sheila Van Damm	Ladies Award, 2nd in Class
	Austrian Alpine	Sunbeam-Talbot 90	Sheila Van Damm	1st in Class Ladies' Award
	French Alpine	Sunbeam Alpine	Stirling Moss	3rd in Class (+ Gold Cup for three consecutive unpenalised runs)
			Sheila van Damm	Ladies' Award
	Viking (Norway)	Sunbeam-Talbot 90	Sheila Van Damm	2nd in Class Ladies Award
	Geneva Rally	Sunbeam-Talbot 90	Sheila Van Damm	Ladies' Award
1955	Monte Carlo Rally	Sunbeam Mk III Sunbeam Mk III	Per Malling ** Sheila Van Damm	1st Overall Ladies' Award
			(Per Malling) (Peter Harper) (Sheila Van Damm)	(Team Prize for best three cars of one make)

(** Private entry)

	RAC Rally	Sunbeam Mk III	Sheila Van Damm	2nd in Class Ladies' Prize
	Tulip Rally	Sunbeam Mk III	Peter Harper	2nd in Class
	Viking (Norway)	Sunbeam Mk III	Sheila Van Damm	3rd Overall 3rd in Class
1956	Monte Carlo Rally	Sunbeam Mk III	Peter Harper (Peter Harper) (Sheila Van Damm) (Jimmy Ray)	3rd Overall (Team Prize for best three cars of one make)

ROOTES MAESTROS
"In their own words."

	RAC Rally	Sunbeam Mk III	Peter Harper	2nd in Class
	Mille Miglia	Sunbeam Rapier	Peter Harper/ Sheila Van Damm	1st in Class
	Tulip Rally	Sunbeam Rapier	John Melvin **	1st in Class

(** Private entry)

1957	Mille Miglia	Sunbeam Rapier	Peter Harper/ Jack Reece	2nd in Class
	Tulip Rally	Sunbeam Rapier	Jimmy Ray	1st in Class, 7th Overall
1958	Monte Carlo Rally	Sunbeam Rapier	Peter Harper	1st in Class, 5th Overall
	RAC Rally	Sunbeam Rapier	Peter Harper	1st Overall, 1st in Class
		Sunbeam Rapier	Mary Handley-Page	2in in Ladies Category
	Circuit of Ireland	Sunbeam Rapier	J.E.Dowling **	Class win
	Tulip Rally	Sunbeam Rapier	(Peter Harper, Jimmy Ray, Mary Handley-Page)	(Manufacturers' Team Prize)
	Scottish Rally	Sunbeam Rapier Sunbeam Rapier	R.Crawford ** Alan Fraser **	1st in Class 1st in Class
	French Alpine	Sunbeam Rapier	Peter Harper	1st in Class, 6th overall
		Sunbeam Alpine	Tommy Sopwith	2nd in Class

(** Private entry)

1959	Monte Carlo Rally	Sunbeam Rapier	Ronnie Adams	5th Overall
	Alpine	Sunbeam Rapier	Paddy Hopkirk	3rd Overall, 1st in Class
		Sunbeam Rapier	Peter Jopp	2nd in Class

Competition Highlights: Motorsport success 1948-1972

		Sunbeam Rapier	Ivor Bueb	3rd in Class
	Liege-Rome-Liege	Sunbeam Rapier	Jimmy Ray	1st in Class
	RAC Rally	Sunbeam Rapier Sunbeam Alpine	E.Malkin ** Alan Fraser **	5th Overall 3rd in Class

(** Private entry)

1960	Monte Carlo Rally	Sunbeam Rapier	Peter Harper	4th Overall, 1st in Class
		Sunbeam Rapier Sunbeam Alpine	Werner Lier ** Backlund **	2nd in Class Class win
	Circuit of Ireland	Sunbeam Rapier	J.Piele	Class win
	Tulip Rally	Sunbeam Rapier	Jimmy Ray	2nd in Class
	Acropolis Rally	Sunbeam Rapier	Peter Harper	1st in Class, 3rd Overall
	French Alpine	Sunbeam Rapier Sunbeam Rapier Sunbeam Rapier Sunbeam Alpine	Peter Harper Paddy Hopkirk Peter Jopp Mary Handley-Page	1st in Class 2nd in Class 3rd in Class 3rd in Class
	Silverstone Touring Car Race	Sunbeam Rapier	Paddy Hopkirk	Class win
	Brands Hatch Touring Car Race	Sunbeam Rapier	Peter Harper	Class win
	International Compact Car Race, Riverside, California	Sunbeam Rapier	Peter Harper**	1st in Class, 3rd Overall

(** Private entry)

333

ROOTES MAESTROS
"In their own words."

1961	Carrera Cuidad de Mexico	Sunbeam Rapier	Ricardo Rodriguez Pedro Rodriguez	1st Overall 2nd Overall
	Premio Constucion en La Cuidad de Puebla	Sunbeam Rapier	Ricardo Rodriguez	1st Overall
	SCCA 12-Hour Race, Marboro, USA	Sunbeam Rapier	Dick Nash/Gene Hobbs **	3rd Overall
	Monte Carlo Rally	Sunbeam Alpine	Backlund **	Class Win
	Sebring 12 Hour Race	Sunbeam Alpine	Peter Harper/ Peter Procter	3rd in Class
	East African Safari	Sunbeam Rapier	Valumbia **	1st in Class
	Circuit of Ireland	Sunbeam Rapier	Paddy Hopkirk	1st Overall
	International Trophy Saloon Car Race	Sunbeam Rapier	Peter Harper	1st in Class
	Acropolis Rally	Sunbeam Rapier Sunbeam Rapier	Peter Harper Keith Ballisat	5th Overall, 2nd in Class 6th Overall, 3rd in Class Manufacturers' Team Prize
	Scottish Rally	Sunbeam Alpine Sunbeam Rapier	John Melvin ** D.Hall **	Outright win 1st in Class
	Le Mans 24 Hour Race	Sunbeam Alpine	Peter Harper/ Peter Procter	Winner, Index of Thermal Efficiency

334

Competition Highlights: Motorsport success 1948-1972

	French Alpine	Sunbeam Rapier	Paddy Hopkirk	3rd Overall, 1st in Class
		Sunbeam Rapier	Peter Harper	5th Overall, 2nd in Class
		Sunbeam Rapier	Keith Ballisat	7th Overall, 3rd in Class Manufacturers' Team Prize
		Sunbeam Alpine	Mary Handley-Page	2nd Ladies Award, 3rd in Class
	British Empire Trophy saloon Car Race	Sunbeam Rapier	Peter Harper	1st in Class
	Riverside 3-Hr Race	Sunbeam Alpine	Stirling Moss/ Jack Brabham	1st in Class, 3rd Overall
	RAC Rally	Sunbeam Rapier	Peter Harper	3rd Overall, 1st in Class
		Sunbeam Rapier	Paddy Hopkirk	4th Overall
		Sunbeam Rapier	Peter Procter	Manufacturers' Team Prize
		Humber Super Snipe	Raymond Baxter **	Class Win
	(** Private entry)			
1962	Monte Carlo Rally	Sunbeam Rapier	Paddy Hopkirk	3rd Overall
		Sunbeam Rapier	Peter Procter	4th Overall
		Sunbeam Rapier	Peter Harper	Manufacturers' Team Prize
	Sebring 12-Hour Race	Sunbeam Alpine	Peter Harper/ Peter Procter	3rd in Class
	Circuit of Ireland	Sunbeam Rapier	Paddy Hopklirk	1st Overall
	Touring Car Race, Silverstone	Sunbeam Rapier	Peter Harper	1st in Class

335

ROOTES MAESTROS
"In their own words."

	Event	Car	Driver	Result
	Touring Car Race, Belgian GP	Sunbeam Rapier	Lucien Bianchi	1st Overall
	Acropolis Rally	Sunbeam Rapier	Steven Zannos **	1st in Class
	BARC Race Meeting, Crystal Palace	Sunbeam Rapier	Peter Harper	4th Overall
	Scottish Rally	Sunbeam Rapier	Andrew Cowan **	1st Overall
	Aintree Touring Car Race	Sunbeam Rapier	Peter Harper	1st in Class
	Molyslip Touring Car race	Sunbeam Rapier	Peter Jopp	1st in Class
	Oulton Park Touring Car Race	Sunbeam Rapierr	Peter Harper	1st in Class
	Tour de France	Sunbeam Rapier	Keith Ballisat/ 'Tiny' Lewis	1st in Class
			Peter Harper/ Peter Procter	2nd in Class
			Rosemary Smith/ Rosemary Seers	3rd in Class, Ladies' Prize
	6-Hour Saloon Car Race, Brands Hatch	Sunbeam Rapier	Peter Harper/ Peter Procter	4th overall and 1st in Class
			Peter Jopp/ Peter Pilsworth	2nd in Class
	RAC Rally	Sunbeam Rapier	'Tiny' Lewis	1st in Class
		Sunbeam Rapier	David Pollard	2nd in Class

(** Private entry)

| 1963 | Monte Carlo Rally | Sunbeam Rapier | Peter Harper | 1st in Class |

336

Competition Highlights: Motorsport success 1948-1972

	Event	Car	Driver	Result
	Tour de France	Sunbeam Alpine	Rosemary Smith	6th Overall GT, 3rd in Class, Ladies' Award
1964	Welsh Rally	Hillman Imp (875cc)	'Tiny' Lewis	8th Overall
	Circuit of Ireland	Humber Super Snipe	Adrian Boyd	2nd in Class
	Geneva Rally	Sunbeam Tiger	'Tiny' Lewis	Class win
		Sunbeam Tiger	Peter Riley	2nd in Class
		Sunbeam Tiger	Rosemary Smith	3rd in Class
1965	Monte Carlo Rally	Sunbeam Tiger	Peter Harper	4th Overall/Class win
		Sunbeam Tiger	Andrew Cowan	2nd in Class
		Hillman Imp (875cc)	Rosemary Smith	2nd, Ladies' Award
	Circuit of Ireland	Hillman Imp	'Tiny' Lewis	8th Overall/2nd in Class
		Hillman Imp	Rosemary Smith	3rd in Class Ladies' Award
	Tulip Rally	Hillman Imp	Rosemary Smith	1st Overall
		Hillman Imp	'Tiny' Lewis	2nd Overall
	International Police Rally	Sunbeam Tiger	John Gott	1st Overall
	Targa Florio	Sunbeam Tiger	Peter Harper	2nd in Class
	Scottish Rally	Hillman Imp	'Tiny' Lewis	2nd Overall, Class win
		Hillman Imp	Rosemary Smith	5th Overall, Ladies' Award
		Sunbeam Tiger	John Melvin **	Class win
	French Alpine	Sunbeam Tiger	Peter Harper	Disqualified, from 1st Overall
		Hillman Imp	Rosemary Smith	Class Win Ladies' Award 5th in Category

337

ROOTES MAESTROS
"In their own words."

	RAC Rally	Hillman Imp	'Tiny' Lewis	3rd in Class
		Hillman Imp	Rosemary Smith	Manufacturers'
		Hillman Imp	Andrew Cowan	Team Prize.
1966	Monte Carlo Rally	Hillman Imp (875cc)	Rosemary Smith	Ladies Award (then disqualified)
		Hillman Imp	Patrick Lier **	Class win
		Hillman Imp	'Tiny' Lewis	Class Win
	Circuit of Ireland	Rallye Imp	Rosemary Smith	Ladies' Prize
		Rallye Imp	Colin Malkin **	Class win
	Tulip Rally	Sunbeam Tiger	Peter Harper	3rd overall, Category win
		Rallye Imp	'Tiny' Lewis	Class win
	Shell 4000 Rally (Canada)	Rallye Imp	Rosemary Smith	8th overall, 1st in Class, Ladies' award
	Acropolis Rally	Sunbeam Tiger	Peter Harper	Class win, Category win
		Rallye Imp	Rosemary Smith	3rd in Category, 1st in Class, Ladies' award
	Scottish Rally	Rallye Imp	Rosemary Smith	3rd overall, Ladies' Award
	Gulf London	Rallye Imp	Andrew Cowan**	5th Overall, Class win
	Welsh Rally	Rallye Imp	Andrew Cowan	1st in Class, 5th Overall
		Rallye Imp	Colin Malkin **	2nd in Class
	(** Private entry)			
1967	Monte Carlo Rally	Sunbeam Imp	Andrew Cowan	1st in Class Sport Category
		Rallye Imp	Peter Harper	2nd in Class
		Rallye Imp	Patrick Lier **	1st in Class
	Circuit of Ireland	Rallye Imp	Rosemary Smith	1st in Class, Ladies' Award

Competition Highlights: Motorsport success 1948-1972

	Event	Car	Driver	Result
	Tulip Rally	Rallye Imp	Peter Harper	2nd in Class, 3rd GT Category
	Shell 4000 (Canada)	Rallye Imp	Rosemary Smith	1st in Class, Ladies' Award
	Scottish Rally	Rallye Imp	Rosemary Smith	4th Overall, 1st in Class, Ladies' Award
	French Alpine	Rallye Imp	Andrew Cowan	2nd in Class
		Rallye Imp	Rosemary Smith	3rd in Class, Ladies Award
	RAC Rally	Rallye Imp	Andrew Cowan	3rd Overall, TV special stage

(** Private entry)

1968	Monte Carlo Rally	Rallye Imp	Rosemary Smith	2nd Coupe des Dames
		Sunbeam Imp Sport	Andrew Cowan	1st Class
	Circuit of Ireland	Rallye Imp	Rosemary Smith	3rd Overall, Ladies' Prize
	Scottish Rally	Rallye Imp	Colin Malkin	3rd Overall
			Rosemary Smith	5th Overall, Ladies' Prize
			Andrew Cowan	Team Award
	Gulf London Rally	Rallye Imp	Andrew Cowan	7th Overall
	London-Sydney Marathon	Hillman Hunter	Andrew Cowan/Brian Coyle/Colin Malkin	1st Overall
1969	Scottish Rally	Rallye Imp	Andrew Cowan **	2nd Overall

(** Private entry)

ROOTES MAESTROS
"In their own words."

Competition ROOTES Department

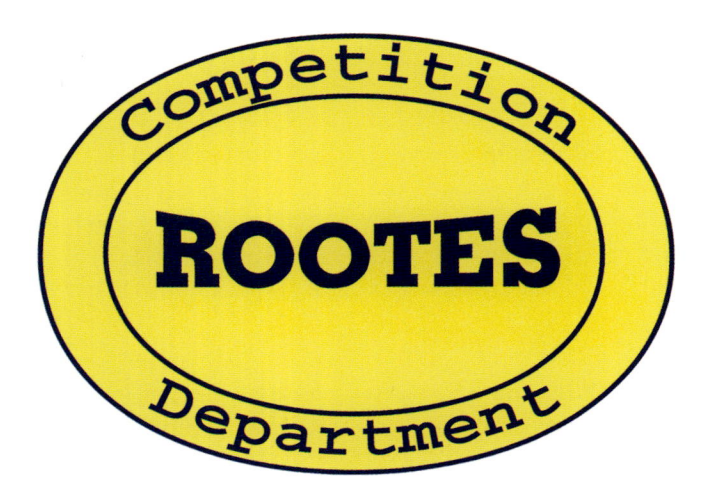

These pictures are the last ever to be seen of a very small, but illustrious organization. Shortly after these photographs were taken, the whole site was levelled to be re-developed, July 2008.

The first view a visitor would see of the entrance and front office/reception of the old Competition Department.

Competition Department images 2008

Above and below views show front and side entrance of the department.

Above: The first view you would see on entering the workshops via the large side doors.

Below: Looking through to the second shop, Alan the caretaker who kindly let us into the department for these photographs to be taken, stands in the centre of the doorway.

Competition Department images 2008

Above: View showing the first shop with Jim Ashworth's and later Des O'Dell's corner office on the right.

Below: View of the third shop where the cars were mainly stored when not in use.

ROOTES MAESTROS
"In their own words."

Left: This view shows the access and entrance to Norman Garrad's elevated offices.

Below: View from the balcony Norman Garrad, Marcus Chambers and Des O'Dell would see of the activities in both first and second shops.

Who - What - Where - When?

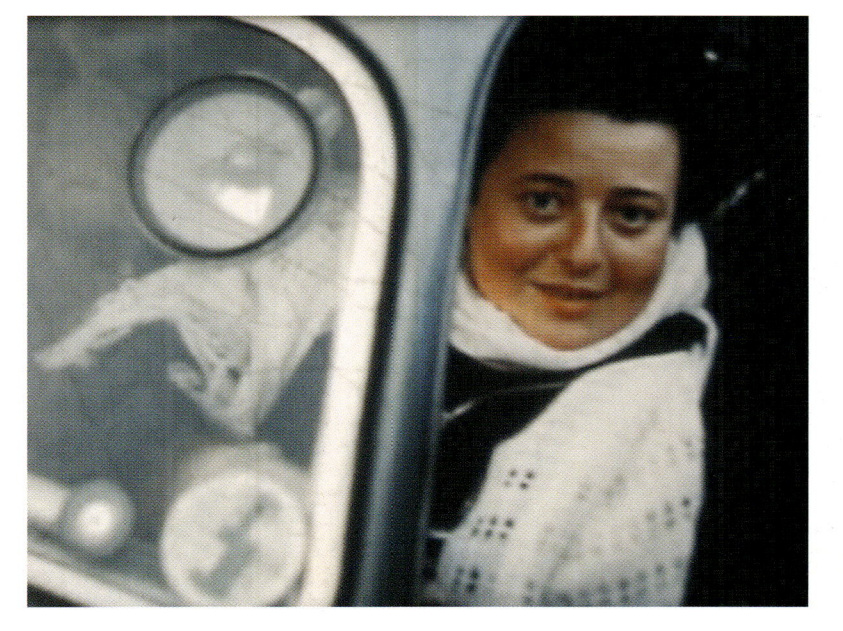

ROOTES MAESTROS
"In their own words."

346

Who - What - Where - When?

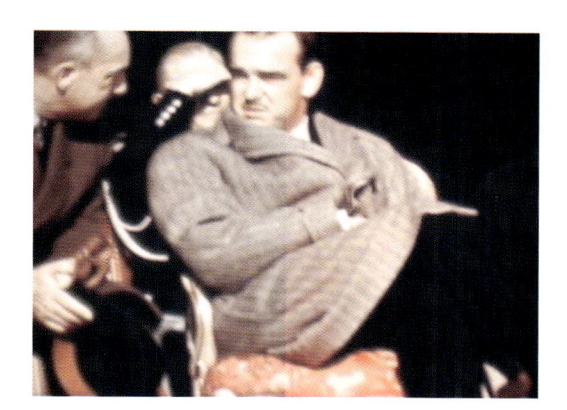

ROOTES MAESTROS
"In their own words."

Who - What - Where - When?

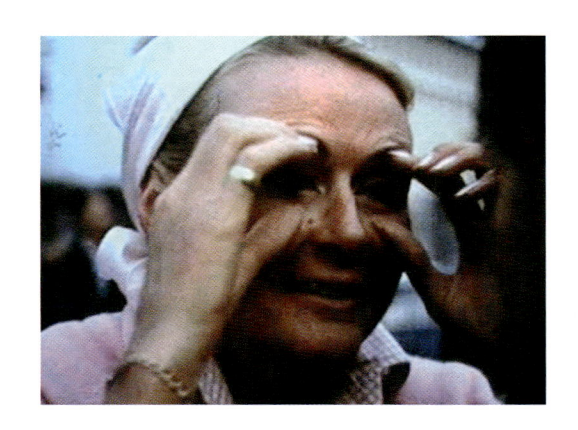

ROOTES MAESTROS
"In their own words."